GRE® Exam Math Workbook

Seventh Edition

Other Kaplan Titles on Graduate School Admissions

Kaplan Get Into Graduate School
Kaplan GRE Exam Comprehensive Program
Kaplan GRE Exam Premier Program
Kaplan GRE Exam Subject Test: Biology
Kaplan GRE Exam Subject Test: Psychology
Kaplan GRE Exam Verbal Workbook
Kaplan GRE Exam Vocabulary in a Box
Kaplan GRE Exam Vocabulary Prep

GRE® EXAM
Math Workbook
Seventh Edition

KAPLAN

PUBLISHING

New York

Published by Kaplan Publishing, a division of Kaplan, Inc.
1 Liberty Plaza, 24th Floor
New York, NY 10006

Printed in the United States of America

August 2008
10 9 8 7 6 5

ISBN-13: 978-1-4195-5221-2

Kaplan Publishing books are available at special quantity discounts to use for sales promotions, employee premiums, or educational purposes. Please email our Special Sales Department to order or for more information at kaplanpublishing@kaplan.com, or write to Kaplan Publishing, 1 Liberty Plaza, 24th Floor, New York, NY 10006.

TABLE OF CONTENTS

kaptest.com/publishing

The material in this book is up-to-date at the time of publication. However, the Educational Testing Service may have instituted changes in the tests or test registration process after this book was published. Be sure to carefully read the materials you receive when you register for the test.

If there are any important late-breaking developments—or changes or corrections to the Kaplan test preparation materials in this book—we will post that information online at **kaptest.com/publishing.** Check to see if there is any information posted there regarding this book.

kaplansurveys.com/books

What did you think of this book? We'd love to hear your comments and suggestions. We invite you to fill out our online survey form at **kaplansurveys.com/books.** Your feedback is extremely helpful as we continue to develop high-quality resources to meet your needs.

Updates to the GRE

Instead of one major overhaul as originally planned, ETS will introduce revisions to the GRE gradually, beginning with two new question types—one math, one verbal—that were introduced into the computer-based GRE in November 2007. On Test Day, you may see just one sample of the new math question type, just one sample of the new verbal question type, OR you won't see either question at all. *For the time being, these new question types do not count toward your score.* As of this printing, ETS has not announced a timeline for when these new types will count toward your score.

NEW QUANTITATIVE QUESTION TYPE—NUMERIC ENTRY

Essentially, the Numeric Entry question type does not provide any answer choices at all. None. Zip. Zero! You have to do the math, work out your answer and type it in the box provided. The most important thing to keep in mind here is to read through the question very carefully; make sure you know exactly what's being asked of you. Then check your work just as carefully. Here's a sample Numeric Entry question and answer explanation.

> **The health club charges $35 per month plus $2.50 for each aerobic class attended. How many aerobic classes were attended for the month if the total monthly charge was $52.50?**

[   ]

Click on the answer box, and then type in a number.
Use backspace to erase.

Answer: 7
Translate the situation into an algebraic equation, and then solve for the unknown variable. We are asked to find the number of classes attended; assign the variable x to represent the number of aerobics classes attended. The monthly fee is $35, plus $2.50 for every class attended, or 2.5 times x (the number of classes).

So the equation is $35 + 2.5x = 52.50$, where x equals the number of aerobic classes attended. Subtract 35 from both sides of the equation: $2.5x = 17.5$. Divide both sides by 2.5, and $x = 7$.

STAY ON TOP OF THE LATEST DEVELOPMENTS

As ETS makes further announcements, you can depend on Kaplan to provide you with the most accurate, up-to-the-minute information. You can get updates by visiting us at Kaptest.com/NEWGRE.

Good Luck!

How To Use This Book

Kaplan has prepared students to take standardized tests for more than 50 years. Our team of researchers know more about preparation for the GRE than anyone else, and you'll find their accumulated knowledge and experience throughout this book. The GRE is a standardized test, and so, every test covers the same content in roughly the same way. This is good news for you; it means that the best way to prepare is to focus on the sort of questions you are likely to see on Test Day. The main focus of this book is on strategic reviews, exercises, and practice tests with explanations that will help you brush up on any math skills you may have forgotten. If possible, work through this book a little at a time over the course of several weeks. There is a lot of math to absorb, and it's hard to do it all at once.

STEP 1: THE BASICS

In Part One of this book, "Getting Started," we'll provide you with background information on the quantitative section of the test, what it covers, and how it's organized.

STEP 2: MATH CONTENT REVIEW

Once you have the big picture, focus on the content. Part Two of this book, "Math Content Review," gives you a complete tour of the math that you will see on Test Day. The material in the math content review is divided into particular subjects. Each subject begins with a review, followed by practice questions organized by level of difficulty. This structure makes it easy for you to pinpoint the math concepts you need to review and quickly get your skills up to speed.

We suggest that you quickly skim the content review that introduces a section and then try the exercise. If you find difficult, go back to the content review before moving on. If you do well on the exercise, try the basic problem set that follows it. Once you feel that you have a good grasp on the basics of this subject, try the intermediate and advanced problem sets. Answers and explanations for the practice problems appear at the end of the chapter. Read the explanations to all the questions—even those you got right. Often the explanations will contain strategies that show you how you could have gotten to the answer more quickly and efficiently.

STEP 3: BECOME FAMILIAR WITH GRE QUESTION TYPES

The GRE contains three main question types: Quantitative Comparisons, Word Problems, and Data Interpretation. Part Three of this book covers these types with strategies and sample questions. Your focus here should be to familiarize yourself with the question types so you won't be trying to figure out how to approach them on Test Day.

Now you're ready to begin preparing for the math section of the GRE. Good luck!

PART ONE

Getting Started

Chapter 1
Introduction to GRE Math

If you're considering applying to graduate school, then you've already seen all the math you need for the GRE—in junior high. The only problem is, you may not have seen it lately. When was the last time you had to add a bunch of fractions without a calculator? The math that appears on the GRE is almost identical to the math tested on the SAT or ACT. You don't need to know trigonometry. You don't need to know calculus.

No matter how much your memories of junior high algebra classes have dimmed, don't panic. The GRE tests a limited number of core math concepts in predictable ways. Certain topics come up in every test, and, chances are, these topics will be expressed in much the same way; even some of the words and phrases appearing in the questions are predictable. Since the test is so formulaic, we can show you the math you're bound to encounter. Practice on test-like questions, such as those in the following chapters, will prepare you for the questions you will see on the actual test.

Here is a checklist of core math concepts you'll need to know for the GRE. These concepts are vital, not only because they are tested directly on every GRE, but also because you need to know how to perform these simpler operations in order to perform more complicated tasks. For instance, you won't be able to find the volume of a cylinder if you can't find the area of a circle. We know the math operations on the following list are pretty basic, but make sure you know how to do them.

GRE MATH BASICS

Add, subtract, multiply and divide fractions. (Chapter 2)

Convert fractions to decimals, and vice versa. (Chapter 2)

Add, subtract, multiply, and divide signed numbers. (Chapter 2)

Plug numbers into algebraic expressions. (Chapter 3)

Solve a simple algebraic equation. (Chapter 3)

Find a percent using the percent formula. (Chapter 2)

Find an average. (Chapter 2)

Find the areas of rectangles, triangles, and circles. (Chapter 5)

HOW MATH IS SCORED ON THE GRE

The GRE will give you a scaled quantitative score from 200 to 800. (The average score is 575.) This score reflects your performance on the math portion of the GRE compared to all other GRE test takers.

UNDERSTANDING THE QUANTITATIVE SECTION

In the Quantitative section, you'll have 45 minutes to complete 28 questions, which consist of three question types: Quantitative Comparisons, Word Problems, and Data Interpretation.

The chart below shows how many questions you can expect of each question type, as well as the amount of time you should spend per question on each question type, very roughly speaking.

	Quantitative Comparison	**Word Problems**	**Data Interpretation**
Number of Questions	about 14	about 10	about 4
Time per Question	45 to 60 seconds	1.5 to 2 minutes	2 to 3 minutes

Overview of the Quantitative Section Question Types

As someone famous once said, "Know thine enemy." You need to know firsthand the way this section of the test is put together if you want to take it apart.

Word Problems

In the Quantitative section on the GRE, you will have to solve problems that test a variety of mathematical concepts. Word Problems typically deal with core math concepts: percentages, simultaneous equations, symbolism, special triangles, multiple and oddball figures, combinations and permutations, standard deviation, mean, median, mode, range, and probability.

You can expect about 10 Word Problems. As with other question types, the more questions you get right, the harder the questions you will see.

Strategies, and sample questions can be found in chapter 5.

Quantitative Comparisons

On Quantitative Comparisons, or QCs, as we like to call them, instead of solving for a particular value, your job is to compare two quantities. At first, these questions tend to throw test-takers because of their unique format. But once you become used to them, they should actually take less time to solve than other math question types.

Doing well on QCs begins with understanding what makes them different from other math questions. The difficulty of the QCs will depend on how well you are doing in the section. In each question, you'll see two mathematical expressions. One is in Column A, the other in Column B. Your job is to compare them. Some questions include additional information about one or both quantities. This information is centered, and is essential to making the comparison.

Strategies and sample questions for QCs can be found in chapter 6.

Data Interpretation

Data Interpretation questions are statistics-oriented. You will likely be presented with a set of tables, charts, or graphs, which are followed by three to five questions.

Strategies and sample questions can be found in chapter 7.

BACKDOOR STRATEGIES

Sometimes applying common sense or backdoor strategies will get you to the correct answer more quickly and easily. The key is to be open to creative approaches. Often this involves taking advantage of the question format. These three methods are extremely useful when you don't see—or would rather not use—the textbook approach to solving a question.

Picking Numbers

Picking numbers is a handy strategy for "abstract" problems—ones using variables either expressed or implied—rather than numbers. An expressed variable appears in the question ("Jane had *x* apples and 3 oranges . . ."). Questions with implied variables describe a problem using just numbers, but the only way to solve the problem is by setting up an equation that uses variables.

Problems that lend themselves to the picking numbers strategy involve simple math, but the variables make the problem complex. They include those where both the question *and* the answer choices have variables, expressed or implied; where the problem tests a number property you don't recall; or where the problem and the answer choices deal with percents or fractions.

Step 1. Pick Simple Numbers

These will stand in for the variables.

Step 2. Try Them Out

Try out all the answer choices using the numbers you picked, eliminating those that gave you a different result.

Step 3. Try Different Values

If more than one answer choice works, use different values and start again.

Backsolving

Some math problems don't have variables that let you substitute picked numbers, or they require an unusually complex equation to find the answer. In cases like these, try backsolving: Simply plug the given answer choices back into the question until you find the one that works. Unfortunately, there are no hard-and-fast rules that identify a picking numbers question from a backsolving problem. You have to rely on two things: The experience you gain from answering practice questions, and your instinct. Combining these two skills will point you to the fastest solution for answering a problem. If you do this using the system outlined below, it shouldn't take long.

Step 1. Estimate Whether the Answer Will Be Small or Large

Eyeball the question and predict whether the answer will be small or large. Your estimate needn't (and shouldn't) be precise; it just has to reflect your "feel" for the relative size of the answer.

Step 2. Start with B or D

For small-quantity answers, start backsolving with answer choice B; for large-quantity answers, start with D. By starting with B or D, you have a 40% chance of getting the correct answer in a single try because GRE answers are listed in order of ascending size. For example, if you start with B, you have these three possibilities: B is right, A is right (because B is too big), or B is too small.

Step 3. Test the Choice That You Did *Not* Start With

If B is too small or D is too large, you'll have three choices left. In either case, testing the middle remaining choice immediately reveals the correct answer.

Elimination

How quickly can you solve this problem?

> Jenny has 228 more marbles than Jack. If Bob gave each of them 133 marbles, she will have twice as many marbles as Jack. How many marbles does Jenny have?
>
> ◯ 95
>
> ◯ 190
>
> ◯ 228
>
> ◯ 323
>
> ◯ 456

If you know a bit about number properties, you can solve it without doing any calculations. If Jenny and Jack each had 133 more marbles (an odd number), Jenny would have twice as many (an even number) as Jack. Since an even number minus an odd number is an odd number, Jenny must have an odd number of marbles. That allows us to eliminate B, C, and E. Since Jenny has 228 more marbles than Jack, you to eliminate A as well. Therefore, the correct answer *has* to be (D) and you didn't have to do any math to get it!

Elimination works on fewer problems than either picking numbers or backsolving. Where you can apply it, it's very fast. When you can't, the other two methods and even the straightforward math are good fallback strategies. You should use elimination if:

- the gap between the answer choices is wide and the problem is easy to estimate, or
- you recognize the number property the test-maker is really testing.

Number properties—the inherent relationships between numbers (odd/even, percent/whole, prime/composite)—are what allow you to eliminate in correct answers in number-property problems without doing the math.

For full examples of how these strategies work, pick up a copy of Kaplan's *GRE Exam Premier Program* or *GRE Exam Comprehensive Program*.

MATH CONTENT ON THE GRE

Arithmetic—About a third of all questions.

Algebra—About a sixth of all questions.

Geometry—About a third of all questions.

Graphs—About a sixth of all questions.

About a quarter of all questions are presented in the form of word problems.

COMPUTER ADAPTIVE TESTING (CAT)

The GRE CAT is a little different from the paper-and-pencil tests you have probably seen in the past.

You choose answers on the GRE CAT by pointing and clicking with a mouse. You won't use the keyboard in the math portion of the test. Each test is preceded by a short tutorial that will show you exactly how to use the mouse to indicate your answer and move through the test.

How a CAT Finds Your Score

These computer-based tests "adapt" to your performance. This means the questions get harder or easier depending on whether you answer them correctly or not. Your score is not directly determined by how many questions you get right, but by how hard the questions you get right are.

When you start a section the computer:
- Assumes you have an average score.
- Gives you a medium–difficulty question.

If you answer a question correctly:

- Your score goes up.
- You are given a harder question.

If you answer a question incorrectly:

- Your score goes down.
- You are given an easier question.

After a while you will reach a level where most of the questions will seem difficult to you. At this point you will get roughly as many questions right as you get wrong. This is your scoring level. The computer uses your scoring level in calculating your scaled score.

Another consequence of the test's adaptive nature is that for the bulk of the test you will be getting questions at the limit of your ability. While every question is equally important to your final score, harder questions generate higher scores and easier questions lower scores. You want to answer as many hard questions as possible. This is a reason to concentrate your energies on the early questions. Get these right and you are into the harder questions, where the points are. The sooner you start to see harder questions, the higher your final score is likely to be.

There are a few other consequences of the adaptive nature of the test that you should consider.

- There is no preset order of difficulty; the difficulty level of the questions you're getting is dependent on how well you have done on the preceding questions. The harder the questions are, the better you are doing. So, if you seem to be getting only hard questions, don't panic: It's a good sign!

- Once you leave a question, you cannot return to it. That's it. Kiss it good-bye. This is why you should never rush on the CAT. Make sure that you have indicated the right answer before you confirm it and move on. The CAT rewards meticulous test takers.

- In a CAT you must answer a question to move on to the next one. There's no skipping around. If you can't get an answer, you will have to guess in order to move on. Consequently, intelligent guessing can make the difference between a mediocre and a great score. Guess intelligently and strategically—eliminate any answer choices that you can determine are wrong and guess among those remaining. The explanations to the questions in this book will demonstrate techniques for eliminating answer choices strategically.

- One final, important point. There is a penalty for unanswered questions on the CAT. Every question you leave unanswered will decrease your score by a greater amount than a question that you answered incorrectly! This means that you should answer all the questions on the test, even if you have to guess randomly to finish a section.

PART TWO

Math Content Review

Chapter 2
Arithmetic

Most of the problems you will see on the GRE involve arithmetic to some extent. Among the most important topics are number properties, ratios, and percents. You should know most of the basic definitions, such as what an integer is, what even numbers are, etcetera.

Not only do arithmetic topics covered in this unit themselves appear on the GRE, but they are also essential for understanding some of the more advanced concepts that will be covered later. For instance, many of the rules covering arithmetic operations, such as the commutative law, will be important when we discuss variables and algebraic expressions. In addition, the concepts we cover here will be needed for word problems.

NUMBER OPERATIONS

Number Types

The number tree is a visual representation of the different types of numbers and their relationships.

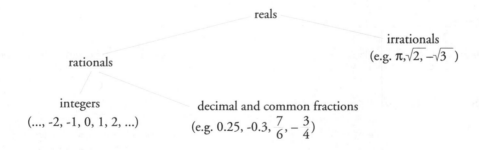

Real Numbers: All numbers on the number line; all the numbers on the GRE are real.

Rational Numbers: All numbers that can be expressed as the ratio of two integers (all integers and fractions).

Irrational Numbers: All real numbers that are not rational, both positive and negative (e.g., π, $-\sqrt{3}$).

Integers: All numbers with no fractional or decimal parts: multiples of 1.

Order of Operations

PEMDAS = Please Excuse My Dear Aunt Sally—This mnemonic will help you remember the order of operations.

P = Parentheses
E = Exponents
M = Multiplication
D = Division $\Big\}$ in order from left to right
A = Addition
S = Subtraction $\Big\}$ in order from left to right

Example: $30 - 5 \cdot 4 + (7 - 3)^2 \div 8$

First perform any operations within **Parentheses**. (If the expression has parentheses within parentheses, work from the innermost out.)	$30 - 5 \cdot 4 + 4^2 \div 8$
Next, raise to any powers indicated by **Exponents**.	$30 - 5 \cdot 4 + 16 \div 8$
Then do all **Multiplication** and **Division** in order from left to right.	$30 - 20 + 2$
Last, do all **Addition** and **Subtraction** in order from left to right.	$10 + 2$ 12

Laws of Operations

Commutative law: Addition and multiplication are both **commutative**; it doesn't matter **in what order** the operation is performed.

Example: $5 + 8 = 8 + 5;\ 2 \times 6 = 6 \times 2$

Division and subtraction are **not** commutative.

Example: $3 - 2 \neq 2 - 3;\ 6 \div 2 \neq 2 \div 6$

Associative law: Addition and multiplication are also **associative**; the terms can be **regrouped** without changing the result.

Example: $(a + b) + c = a + (b + c)$ $(a \times b) \times c = a \times (b \times c)$

$(3 + 5) + 8 = 3 + (5 + 8)$ $(4 \times 5) \times 6 = 4 \times (5 \times 6)$
$8 + 8 = 3 + 13$ $20 \times 6 = 4 \times 30$
$16 = 16$ $120 = 120$

Distributive law: The **distributive law** of multiplication allows us to "distribute" a factor among the terms being added or subtracted. In general, $a(b + c) = ab + ac$.

Example: $4(3 + 7) = 4 \times 3 + 4 \times 7$
$4 \times 10 = 12 + 28$
$40 = 40$

Division can be distributed in a similar way.

Example: $\dfrac{3 + 5}{2} = \dfrac{3}{2} + \dfrac{5}{2}$

$\dfrac{8}{2} = 1\dfrac{1}{2} + 2\dfrac{1}{2}$

$4 = 4$

Don't get carried away, though. When the sum or difference is in the **denominator**, no distribution is possible.

Example: $\dfrac{9}{4 + 5}$ is NOT equal to $\dfrac{9}{4} + \dfrac{9}{5}$.

Fractions

$\dfrac{4}{5}$ ⟵ numerator
⟵ fraction bar (means "divided by")
⟵ denominator

Equivalent fractions: The value of a number is unchanged if you multiply the number by 1. In a fraction, multiplying the numerator and denominator by the same nonzero number is the same as multiplying the fraction by 1; the fraction is unchanged. Similarly, dividing the top and bottom by the same nonzero number leaves the fraction unchanged.

Example: $\dfrac{1}{2} = \dfrac{1 \times 2}{2 \times 2} = \dfrac{2}{4}$

$\dfrac{5}{10} = \dfrac{5 \div 5}{10 \div 5} = \dfrac{1}{2}$

Canceling and reducing: Generally speaking, when you work with fractions on the GRE you'll need to put them in **lowest terms**. That means that the numerator and the denominator are not divisible by any common integer greater than 1. For example, the fraction $\dfrac{1}{2}$ is in lowest terms, but the fraction $\dfrac{3}{6}$ is not, since 3 and 6 are both divisible by 3. The method we use to take such a fraction and put it in lowest terms is called **reducing.** That simply means to divide out any common multiples from both the numerator and denominator. This process is also commonly called **canceling.**

Example: Reduce $\dfrac{15}{35}$ to lowest terms.

First, determine the largest common factor of the numerator and denominator. Then, divide the top and bottom by that number to reduce.

$\dfrac{15}{35} = \dfrac{3 \times 5}{7 \times 5} = \dfrac{3 \times 5 \div 5}{7 \times 5 \div 5} = \dfrac{3}{7}$

Addition and subtraction: We can't add or subtract two fractions directly unless they have the same denominator. Therefore, before adding, we must find a common denominator. A common denominator is just a **common multiple** of the denominators of the fractions. The **least common denominator** is the **least common multiple** (the smallest positive number that is a multiple of all the terms).

Example: $\frac{3}{5} + \frac{2}{3} - \frac{1}{2}$. Denominators are 5, 3, 2. $LCM = 5 \times 3 \times 2 = 30 = LCD$

Multiply numerator and denominator of each fraction by the value that raises each denominator to the LCD.

$$\left(\frac{3}{5} \times \frac{6}{6}\right) + \left(\frac{2}{3} \times \frac{10}{10}\right) - \left(\frac{1}{2} \times \frac{15}{15}\right)$$

$$= \frac{18}{30} + \frac{20}{30} - \frac{15}{30}$$

Combine the numerators by adding or subtracting and keep the LCD as the denominator.

$$= \frac{18 + 20 - 15}{30} = \frac{23}{30}$$

Multiplication:

Example: $\frac{10}{9} \times \frac{3}{4} \times \frac{8}{15}$

First, reduce (cancel) diagonally and vertically.

$$\frac{{}^{2}\cancel{10}}{{}_{3}\cancel{9}} \times \frac{{}^{1}\cancel{3}}{{}_{1}\cancel{4}} \times \frac{\cancel{8}^{2}}{\cancel{15}_{3}}$$

Then multiply numerators together and denominators together.

$$\frac{2 \times 1 \times 2}{3 \times 1 \times 3} = \frac{4}{9}$$

Division: Dividing is the same as multiplying by the **reciprocal** of the divisor. To get the reciprocal of a fraction, just invert it by interchanging the numerator and the denominator. For example, the reciprocal of the fraction $\frac{3}{7}$ is $\frac{7}{3}$.

Example: $\frac{4}{3} \div \frac{4}{9}$

To divide, invert the second term (the divisor), and then multiply as above.

$$\frac{4}{3} \div \frac{4}{9} = \frac{4}{3} \times \frac{9}{4} = \frac{{}^{1}\cancel{4}}{{}_{1}\cancel{3}} \times \frac{\cancel{9}^{3}}{\cancel{4}_{1}} = \frac{1 \times 3}{1 \times 1} = 3$$

Complex fractions: A complex fraction is a fraction that contains one or more fractions in its numerator or denominator. There are two ways to simplify complex fractions.

Method I: Use the distributive law. Find the least common multiple of all the denominators, and multiply all the terms in the top and bottom of the complex fraction by the LCM. This will eliminate all the denominators, greatly simplifying the calculation.

Example:

$$\frac{\frac{7}{9} - \frac{1}{6}}{\frac{1}{3} + \frac{1}{2}} = \frac{18 \cdot \left(\frac{7}{9} - \frac{1}{6}\right)}{18 \cdot \left(\frac{1}{3} + \frac{1}{2}\right)}$$

LCM of all the denominators is 18.

$$= \frac{\frac{^2\cancel{18}}{1} \cdot \frac{7}{\cancel{9}_1} - \frac{^3\cancel{18}}{1} \cdot \frac{1}{\cancel{6}_1}}{\frac{^6\cancel{18}}{1} \cdot \frac{1}{\cancel{3}_1} + \frac{^9\cancel{18}}{1} \cdot \frac{1}{\cancel{2}_1}}$$

$$= \frac{2 \cdot 7 - 3 \cdot 1}{6 \cdot 1 + 9 \cdot 1}$$

$$= \frac{14 - 3}{6 + 9} = \frac{11}{15}$$

Method II: Treat the numerator and denominator separately. Combine the terms in each to get a single fraction on top and a single fraction on bottom. We are left with the division of two fractions, which we perform by multiplying the top fraction by the reciprocal of the bottom one. This method is preferable when it is difficult to get an LCM for all the denominators.

Example:

$$\frac{\frac{7}{9} - \frac{1}{6}}{\frac{1}{3} + \frac{1}{2}} = \frac{\frac{14}{18} - \frac{3}{18}}{\frac{2}{6} + \frac{3}{6}} = \frac{\frac{11}{18}}{\frac{5}{6}} = \frac{11}{18} \div \frac{5}{6} = \frac{11}{{}_3\cancel{18}} \times \frac{\cancel{6}^1}{5} = \frac{11}{15}$$

Example:

$$\frac{\frac{5}{11} - \frac{5}{22}}{\frac{7}{16} + \frac{3}{8}} = \frac{\frac{10}{22} - \frac{5}{22}}{\frac{7}{16} + \frac{6}{16}} = \frac{\frac{5}{22}}{\frac{13}{16}} = \frac{5}{{}_{11}\cancel{22}} \times \frac{\cancel{16}^8}{13} = \frac{40}{143}$$

Comparing positive fractions: If the numerators are the same, the fraction with the smaller denominator will have the larger value, since the numerator is divided into a smaller number of parts.

Example: $\frac{4}{5} > \frac{4}{7}$ i.e.:

 >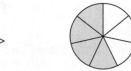

If the denominators are the same, the fraction with the larger numerator will have the larger value.

Example: $\frac{5}{8} > \frac{3}{8}$ i.e.:

 >

If neither the numerators nor the denominators are the same, express all of the fractions in terms of some common denominator. The fraction with the largest numerator will be the largest.

Example: Compare $\dfrac{11}{15}$ and $\dfrac{13}{20}$.

$$\dfrac{11}{15} = \dfrac{11 \times 20}{15 \times 20}$$
$$= \dfrac{220}{15 \times 20}$$

$$\dfrac{13}{20} = \dfrac{13 \times 15}{20 \times 15}$$
$$= \dfrac{195}{20 \times 15}$$

Since $220 > 195$, $\dfrac{11}{15} > \dfrac{13}{20}$.

Notice that it is not necessary to calculate the denominators. A shorter version of this method is to multiply the numerator of the left fraction by the denominator of the right fraction and vice versa (cross-multiply). Then compare the products obtained this way. If the left product is greater, then the left fraction was greater to start with.

Example: Compare $\dfrac{5}{7}$ and $\dfrac{9}{11}$.

$$5 \times 11 \,?\, 9 \times 7$$
$$55 < 63 \qquad\qquad \text{so } \dfrac{5}{7} < \dfrac{9}{11}$$

Sometimes it is easier to find a common **numerator**. In this case, the fraction with the **smaller** denominator will be the **larger** fraction.

Example: Compare $\dfrac{22}{19}$ and $\dfrac{11}{9}$.

Multiply $\dfrac{11}{9} \times \dfrac{2}{2}$ to obtain a common numerator of 22.

$$\dfrac{11}{9} = \dfrac{11 \times 2}{9 \times 2} = \dfrac{22}{18}$$

Since $\dfrac{22}{19} < \dfrac{22}{18}$, $\dfrac{22}{19} < \dfrac{11}{9}$.

As before, the comparison can also be made by cross-multiplying.

$$22 \times 9 < 11 \times 19, \text{ so } \dfrac{22}{19} < \dfrac{11}{9}$$

Mixed Numbers: Mixed Numbers are numbers consisting of an integer and a fraction. For example, $3\dfrac{1}{4}, 12\dfrac{2}{5},$ and $5\dfrac{7}{8}$ are all mixed numbers. Fractions whose numerators are greater than their denominators may be converted into mixed numbers, and vice versa.

Example: Convert $\frac{23}{4}$ to a mixed number.

$$\frac{23}{4} = \frac{20}{4} + \frac{3}{4} = 5\frac{3}{4}$$

Example: Convert $2\frac{3}{7}$ to a fraction.

$$2\frac{3}{7} = 2 + \frac{3}{7} = \frac{14}{7} + \frac{3}{7} = \frac{17}{7}$$

Decimal Fractions

Decimal fractions are just another way of expressing common fractions; they can be converted to common fractions with a power of ten in the denominator.

Example: $0.053 = \frac{53}{10^3}$ or $\frac{53}{1,000}$

Each position, or **digit**, in the decimal has a name associated with it. The GRE occasionally contains questions on digits, so you should be familiar with this naming convention:

Comparing decimal fractions: To compare decimals, add zeros to the decimals (after the last digit to the right of the decimal point) until all the decimals have the same number of digits. Since the denominators of all the fractions are the same, the numerators determine the order of values.

Example: Arrange in order from smallest to largest: 0.7, 0.77, 0.07, 0.707 and 0.077.

$$0.7 = 0.700 = \frac{700}{1,000}$$

$$0.77 = 0.770 = \frac{770}{1,000}$$

$$0.07 = 0.070 = \frac{70}{1,000}$$

$$0.707 = 0.707 = \frac{707}{1,000}$$

$$0.077 = 0.077 = \frac{77}{1,000}$$

$70 < 77 < 700 < 707 < 770$; therefore, $0.07 < 0.077 < 0.7 < 0.707 < 0.77$

Addition and subtraction: When adding or subtracting one decimal to or from another, make sure that the decimal points are lined up, one under the other. This will ensure that tenths are added to tenths, hundredths to hundredths, etcetera.

Example: $0.6 + 0.06 + 0.006 =$

$$
\begin{array}{r}
0.6 \\
0.06 \\
+\ 0.006 \\
\hline
0.666
\end{array}
$$

Answer: 0.666

Example: $0.72 - 0.072 =$

$$
\begin{array}{r}
0.72 \\
-\ 0.072 \\
\hline
\end{array}
=
\begin{array}{r}
-\ 0.072 \\
\hline
0.648
\end{array}
$$

Answer: 0.648

Multiplication and division: To multiply two decimals, multiply them as you would integers. The number of decimal places in the product will be the total number of decimal places in the factors that are multiplied together.

Example: $0.675 \times 0.42 =$

$$
\begin{array}{r}
0.675 \\
\times\ 0.42 \\
\hline
1350 \\
2700 \\
\hline
0.28350
\end{array}
$$

(3 decimal places)
+ (2 decimal places)

(5 decimal places)

Answer: 0.2835

When dividing a decimal by another decimal, multiply each by a power of 10 such that the divisor becomes an integer. (This doesn't change the value of the quotient.) Then carry out the division as you would with integers, placing the decimal point in the quotient directly above the decimal point in the dividend.

Example: $0.675 \div 0.25 =$
           $67.5 \div 25 =$

Multiply each decimal by 100 by moving the decimal point two places to the right (since there are two zeros in 100).

$$
\begin{array}{r}
2.7 \\
25 \overline{)\ 67.5} \\
\underline{50\ \ } \\
17\ 5 \\
\underline{17\ 5} \\
0
\end{array}
$$

Answer: 2.7

NUMBER OPERATIONS EXERCISE

Solve the following problems. (Answers are on the following page.)

1. $\dfrac{1}{2} + \dfrac{1}{3} + \dfrac{1}{4} =$

2. $\dfrac{12}{25} + \dfrac{13}{5} =$

3. $\dfrac{6}{21} + \dfrac{7}{3} =$

4. $\dfrac{1}{16} - \dfrac{3}{4} + 1\dfrac{7}{8} =$

5. $4\left(\dfrac{1}{3} + \dfrac{1}{12}\right)$

6. $\dfrac{1}{2}\left(\dfrac{1}{3} + \dfrac{1}{4}\right) =$

7. $\dfrac{1}{24}(36 + 60) =$

8. $0.021 + 0.946 + 1.324 =$

9. $\left(\dfrac{12}{16} - \dfrac{3}{6}\right)^2 =$

10. $1.69 \times 0.002 =$

11. $30.17 \times 1.01 =$

12. $7 + 5 \times \left(\dfrac{1}{4}\right)^2 - 6 \div (2 - 3) =$

13. $4(1.24 - (0.8)^2) + 6 \times \dfrac{1}{3} =$

14. $\dfrac{\dfrac{5}{6} + \dfrac{3}{2} + 2}{\dfrac{1}{3} + \dfrac{4}{9} + 4} =$

15. $\dfrac{0.25 \times (0.1)^2}{0.5 \times 40} =$

(Handwritten work:)

$\dfrac{1}{16} - \dfrac{3}{4} + \dfrac{15}{8}$

$\dfrac{1}{16} - \dfrac{6}{8} + \dfrac{15}{8}$

$\dfrac{1}{16} - \dfrac{21}{8}$

$\dfrac{1}{16} - \dfrac{42}{16}$

$\dfrac{1 - 12 + 30}{16} = \dfrac{-11 + 30}{16} = \dfrac{19}{16}$

ANSWER KEY—NUMBER OPERATIONS EXERCISE

1. $\frac{13}{12}$ or $1\frac{1}{12}$

2. $\frac{77}{25}$ or $3\frac{2}{25}$

3. $\frac{55}{21}$ or $2\frac{13}{21}$

4. $\frac{19}{16}$ or $1\frac{3}{16}$

5. $\frac{5}{3}$ or $1\frac{2}{3}$

6. $\frac{7}{24}$

7. 4

8. 2.291

9. $\frac{1}{16}$

10. 0.00338

11. 30.4717

12. $13\frac{5}{16}$

13. 4.4

14. $\frac{39}{43}$

15. 0.000125

NUMBER OPERATIONS TEST

Solve the following problems and select the best answer from those given. (Answers and explanations are at the end of this chapter.)

1. $3.44 =$

    ◯ $\dfrac{14}{25}$

    ◯ $\dfrac{33}{25}$

    ◯ $3\dfrac{11}{50}$

    ◯ $3\dfrac{11}{25}$

    ◯ $3\dfrac{22}{25}$

2. $6\dfrac{3}{4} - 6.32 =$

    ◯ 0.33

    ◯ 0.39

    ◯ 0.43

    ◯ 0.57

    ◯ 0.68

3. $0.125 + 0.25 + 0.375 + 0.75 =$

    ◯ $1\dfrac{5}{8}$ 1.6

    ◯ $1\dfrac{1}{2}$ 1.5

    ◯ $1\dfrac{3}{8}$

    ◯ $1\dfrac{1}{4}$ 1.25

    ◯ $1\dfrac{1}{8}$ 1.

4. Which of the following is less than $\dfrac{1}{6}$?

    ◯ 0.1667

    ◯ $\dfrac{3}{18}$

    ◯ 0.167

    ◯ 0.1666

    ◯ $\dfrac{8}{47}$

5. $\dfrac{(0.02)(0.0003)}{0.002} =$

    ◯ 0.3

    ◯ 0.03

    ◯ 0.003

    ◯ 0.0003

    ◯ 0.00003

6. $1 + \dfrac{1}{2} + \dfrac{1}{4} + \dfrac{1}{6} + \dfrac{1}{8} =$

    ◯ $\dfrac{25}{24}$

    ◯ $\dfrac{13}{12}$

    ◯ $\dfrac{35}{24}$

    ◯ $\dfrac{47}{24}$

    ◯ $\dfrac{49}{24}$

7. $\dfrac{12}{\frac{1}{4}} =$

   ◯ 48

   ◯ 3

   ◯ $\dfrac{1}{3}$

   ◯ $\dfrac{1}{16}$

   ◯ $\dfrac{1}{48}$

8. Which of the following lists three fractions in ascending order?

   ◯ $\dfrac{9}{26}, \dfrac{1}{4}, \dfrac{3}{10}$

   ◯ $\dfrac{9}{26}, \dfrac{3}{10}, \dfrac{1}{4}$

   ◯ $\dfrac{1}{4}, \dfrac{9}{26}, \dfrac{3}{10}$

   ◯ $\dfrac{1}{4}, \dfrac{3}{10}, \dfrac{9}{26}$

   ◯ $\dfrac{3}{10}, \dfrac{9}{26}, \dfrac{1}{4}$

9. $\dfrac{7}{5} \cdot \left(\dfrac{3}{7} - \dfrac{2}{5}\right) =$

   ◯ $\dfrac{1}{165}$

   ◯ $\dfrac{1}{35}$

   ◯ $\dfrac{1}{25}$

   ◯ $\dfrac{9}{15}$

   ◯ 1

10. Which of the following fractions is closest in value to the decimal 0.40?

    ◯ $\dfrac{1}{3}$

    ◯ $\dfrac{4}{7}$

    ◯ $\dfrac{3}{8}$

    ◯ $\dfrac{5}{9}$

    ◯ $\dfrac{1}{2}$

11. $\dfrac{\frac{1}{6} + \frac{1}{3} + 2}{\frac{3}{4} + \frac{5}{4} + 3} =$

    ◯ $\dfrac{1}{3}$

    ◯ $\dfrac{1}{2}$

    ◯ $\dfrac{5}{8}$

    ◯ $\dfrac{2}{3}$

    ◯ 1

12. For which of the following expressions would the value be greater if 160 were replaced by 120?

    I. $1,000 - 160$

    II. $\dfrac{160}{1 + 160}$

    III. $\dfrac{1}{1 - \dfrac{1}{160}}$

    ○ None

    ○ I only

    ○ III only

    ○ I and II

    ○ I and III

$$\frac{5}{9}, \frac{5}{12}, \frac{23}{48}, \frac{11}{24}, \frac{3}{7}$$

13. What is the positive difference between the largest and smallest of the fractions above?

    ○ $\dfrac{1}{12}$

    ○ $\dfrac{5}{36}$

    ○ $\dfrac{1}{4}$

    ○ $\dfrac{1}{3}$

    ○ $\dfrac{7}{18}$

14. If x, y, and z are all positive and $0.04x = 5y = 2z$, then which of the following is true?

    ○ $x < y < z$

    ○ $x < z < y$

    ○ $y < x < z$

    ○ $y < z < x$

    ○ $z < y < x$

15. $\dfrac{59.376 \times 7.094}{31.492 \times 6.429}$ is approximately equal to which of the following?

    ○ 0.02

    ○ 0.2

    ○ 2

    ○ 20

    ○ 200

NUMBER PROPERTIES

Number Line and Absolute Value

A **number line** is a straight line that extends infinitely in either direction, on which real numbers are represented as points.

As you move to the right on a number line, the values increase.

Conversely, as you move to the left, the values decrease.

Zero separates the positive numbers (to the right of zero) and the negative numbers (to the left of zero) along the number line. Zero is neither positive nor negative.

The **absolute value** of a number is just the number without its sign. It is written as two vertical lines.

> **Example:** $|-3| = |+3| = 3$

The absolute value can be thought of as the number's distance from zero on the number line; for instance, both $+3$ and -3 are 3 units from zero, so their absolute values are both 3.

Properties of −1, 0, 1, and Numbers In Between

Properties of zero: Adding or subtracting zero from a number does not change the number.

> **Example:** $0 + x = x; \quad 2 + 0 = 2; \quad 4 - 0 = 4$

Any number multiplied by zero equals zero.

> **Example:** $z \times 0 = 0; \quad 12 \times 0 = 0$

Division by zero is **undefined**. When given an algebraic expression, be sure that the denominator is not zero. $\frac{0}{0}$ is also undefined.

Properties of 1 and −1: Multiplying or dividing a number by 1 does not change the number.

> **Example:** $x \div 1 = x; \quad 4 \times 1 = 4; \quad -3 \times 1 = -3$

Multiplying or dividing a number by -1 changes the sign.

Example: $y \times (-1) = -y$; $6 \times (-1) = -6$; $-2 \div (-1) = -(-2) = 2$;
$(x - y) \times (-1) = -x + y$

Note: The sum of a number and -1 times that number is equal to zero. Zero times -1 is zero.

Example: $a + (-a) = 0$; $8 + (-8) = 0$; $0 \times (-1) = 0$; $\dfrac{2}{3} \div \left(-\dfrac{2}{3}\right) = -1$

The **reciprocal** of a number is 1 divided by the number. For a fraction, as we've already seen, the reciprocal can be found by just interchanging the denominator and the numerator. The product of a number and its reciprocal is 1. Zero has no reciprocal, since $\dfrac{1}{0}$ is undefined.

Properties of numbers between -1 and 1: The reciprocal of a number between 0 and 1 is greater than the number.

Example: The reciprocal of $\dfrac{2}{3} = \dfrac{1}{\frac{2}{3}} = \dfrac{3}{2} = 1\dfrac{1}{2}$, which is greater than $\dfrac{2}{3}$.

The reciprocal of a number between -1 and 0 is less than the number.

Example: The reciprocal of $-\dfrac{2}{3} = \dfrac{1}{\left(-\frac{2}{3}\right)} = -\dfrac{3}{2} = -1\dfrac{1}{2}$, which is less than $-\dfrac{2}{3}$.

The square of a number between 0 and 1 is less than the number.

Example: $\left(\dfrac{1}{2}\right)^2 = \dfrac{1}{2} \times \dfrac{1}{2} = \dfrac{1}{4}$, which is less than $\dfrac{1}{2}$.

Multiplying any positive number by a fraction between 0 and 1 gives a product smaller than the original number.

Example: $6 \times \dfrac{1}{4} = 1\dfrac{1}{2}$, which is less than 6.

Multiplying any negative number by a fraction between 0 and 1 gives a product greater than the original number.

Example: $-3 \times \dfrac{1}{6} = -\dfrac{1}{2}$, which is greater than -3.

All these properties can best be seen by observation rather than by memorization.

Operations with Signed Numbers

The ability to add and subtract signed numbers is best learned by practice and common sense.

Addition: Like signs: Add the absolute values and keep the same sign.

Example: $(-6) + (-3) = -9$

Unlike signs: Take the difference of the absolute values and keep the sign of the number with the larger absolute value.

Example: $(-7) + (+3) = -4$

Subtraction: Subtraction is the inverse operation of addition; subtracting a number is the same as adding its inverse. Subtraction is often easier if you change to addition, by changing the sign of the number being subtracted. Then use the rules for addition of signed numbers.

Example: $(-5) - (-10) = (-5) + (+10) = +5$

Multiplication and division: The product or the quotient of two numbers with the same sign is positive.

Example: $(-2) \times (-5) = +10; \quad \dfrac{-50}{-5} = +10$

The product or the quotient of two numbers with opposite signs is negative.

Example: $(-2)(+3) = -6; \quad \dfrac{-6}{2} = -3$

Odd and Even

Odd and even apply only to integers. There are no odd or even noninteger numbers. Put simply, even numbers are integers that are divisible by 2, and odd numbers are integers that are not divisible by 2. If an integer's last digit is either 0, 2, 4, 6, or 8, it is even; if its last digit is 1, 3, 5, 7, or 9, it is odd. Odd and even numbers may be negative; 0 is even.

A number needs just a single factor of 2 to be even, so the product of an even number and **any** integer will always be even.

Rules for Odds and Evens:

Odd + Odd = Even	Odd $\times$ Odd = Odd
Even + Even = Even	Even $\times$ Even = Even
Odd + Even = Odd	Odd $\times$ Even = Even

You can easily establish these rules when you need them by picking sample numbers.

Example: $3 + 5 = 8$, so the sum of any two odd numbers is even.

Example: $\frac{4}{2} = 2$, but $\frac{6}{2} = 3$, so the quotient of two even numbers could be odd or even (or a fraction!).

Factors, Primes, and Divisibility

Multiples: An integer that is divisible by another integer is a **multiple** of that integer.

Example: 12 is multiple of 3, since 12 is divisible by 3; $3 \times 4 = 12$.

Remainders: The remainder is what is left over in a division problem. A remainder is always smaller than the number we are dividing by.

Example: 17 divided by 3 is 5, with a remainder of 2.

Factors: The **factors**, or **divisors**, of a number are the positive integers that evenly divide into that number.

Example: 36 has nine factors: 1, 2, 3, 4, 6, 9, 12, 18, and 36.
We can group these factors in pairs:
$1 \times 36 = 2 \times 18 = 3 \times 12 = 4 \times 9 = 6 \times 6$

The **greatest common factor**, or **greatest common divisor**, of a pair of numbers is the largest factor shared by the two numbers.

Divisibility tests: There are several tests to determine whether a number is divisible by 2, 3, 4, 5, 6, and 9.

A number is divisible by 2 if its last digit is divisible by 2.

Example: 138 is divisible by 2 because 8 is divisible by 2.

A number is divisible by 3 if the **sum** of its digits is divisible by 3.

Example: 4,317 is divisible by 3 because $4 + 3 + 1 + 7 = 15$, and 15 is divisible by 3.
239 is **not** divisible by 3 because $2 + 3 + 9 = 14$, and 14 is not divisible by 3.

A number is divisible by 4 if its last two digits are divisible by 4.

Example: 1,748 is divisible by 4 because 48 is divisible by 4.

A number is divisible by 5 if its last digit is 0 or 5.

Example: 2,635 is divisible by 5. 5,052 is **not** divisible by 5.

A number is divisible by 6 if it is divisible by both 2 and 3.

> **Example:**   4,326 is divisible by 6 because it is divisible by 2 (last digit is 6) and by 3
> (4 + 3 + 2 + 6 = 15).

A number is divisible by 9 if the sum of its digits is divisible by 9.

> **Example:**   22,428 is divisible by 9 because 2 + 2 + 4 + 2 + 8 = 18, and 18 is divisible by 9.

Prime number: A **prime** number is an integer greater than 1 that has no factors other than 1 and itself. The number 1 is not considered a prime. The number 2 is the first prime number and the only even prime. (Do you see why? Any other even number has 2 as a factor, and therefore is not prime.) The first ten prime numbers are 2, 3, 5, 7, 11, 13, 17, 19, 23, 29.

Prime factorization: The **prime factorization** of a number is the expression of the number as the product of its prime factors. No matter how you factor a number, its prime factors will always be the same.

> **Example:** $36 = 6 \times 6 = 2 \times 3 \times 2 \times 3$ or $2 \times 2 \times 3 \times 3$ or $2^2 \times 3^2$

> **Example:** $480 = 48 \times 10 = 8 \times 6 \times 2 \times 5$
> $= 2 \times 4 \times 2 \times 3 \times 2 \times 5$
> $= 2 \times 2 \times 2 \times 2 \times 3 \times 2 \times 5$
> $= 2^5 \times 3 \times 5$

The easiest way to determine a number's prime factorization is to figure out a pair of factors of the number, and then determine their factors, continuing the process until you're left with only prime numbers. Those primes will be the prime factorization.

> **Example:**   Find the prime factorization of 1,050.

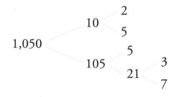

> So the prime factorization of 1,050 is $2 \times 3 \times 5^2 \times 7$.

Consecutive Numbers

A list of numbers is **consecutive** if the numbers either occur at a fixed interval, or exhibit a fixed pattern. All the consecutive numbers you will encounter on the GRE are integers. Consecutive numbers could be in ascending **or** descending order.

> **Example:**   1, 2, 3, 4, 5, 6 . . . is a series of consecutive positive integers.

> **Example:**   −6, −4, −2, 0, 2, 4 . . . is a series of consecutive even numbers.

> **Example:**   5, 7, 11, 13, 17, 19 . . . is a series of consecutive prime numbers.

NUMBER PROPERTIES EXERCISE

Solve the following problems. (Answers are on the following page.)

1. $(-3) \times (4) \times \left(-\frac{1}{6}\right) \times \left(-\frac{1}{12}\right) \times 16 =$

2. $|6 + (-3)| - |-3 + 6| =$

3. $\left|-\left(\frac{1}{4}\right)^2\right| =$

4. Which of the following numbers is divisible by 3: 241, 1,662, 4,915, 3,131?

5. Which of the following numbers is divisible by 4: 126, 324, 442, 598?

6. Which of the following numbers is divisible by 6: 124, 252, 412, 633?

7. What are the first five prime numbers greater than 50?

Find the prime factorization of each of the following:

8. 36

9. 48

10. 162

11. 208

Decide whether each of the following is odd or even. (Don't calculate! Use logic.)

12. $42 \times 21 \times 69$

13. $24 + 32 + 49 + 151$

14. $\left(\frac{90}{45} + \frac{25}{5}\right) \times 4$

15. $(2,610 + 4,987)(6,321 - 4,106)$

ANSWER KEY—NUMBER PROPERTIES EXERCISE

1. $-\dfrac{8}{3}$

2. 0

3. $\dfrac{1}{16}$

4. 1662

5. 324

6. 252

7. 53, 59, 61, 67, 71

8. $2 \times 2 \times 3 \times (3)$

9. $2 \times 2 \times 2 \times 2 \times 3$

10. $2 \times 3 \times 3 \times 3 \times 3$

11. $2 \times 2 \times 2 \times 2 \times 13$

12. Even

13. Even

14. Even

15. Odd

NUMBER PROPERTIES TEST

Solve the following problems and choose the best answer. (Answers and explanations are at the end of the chapter.)

Basic

1. How many odd integers are between $\frac{10}{3}$ and $\frac{62}{3}$?

    ⟋ Nineteen
    ⟋ Eighteen
    ⟋ Ten
    ⟋ Nine
    ⟋ Eight

2. What is the greatest integer that will divide evenly into both 36 and 54?

    ⟋ 6
    ⟋ 9
    ⟋ 12
    ⟋ 18
    ⟋ 27

3. Which of the following is not a factor of 168?

    ⟋ 21
    ⟋ 24
    ⟋ 28
    ⟋ 32
    ⟋ 42

4. Which of the following is a multiple of all three integers 2, 3, and 5?

    ⟋ 525
    ⟋ 560
    ⟋ 615
    ⟋ 620
    ⟋ 660

5. What is the smallest positive integer that is evenly divisible by both 21 and 9?

    ⟋ 189
    ⟋ 126
    ⟋ 63
    ⟋ 42
    ⟋ 21

6. If the sum of three different prime numbers is an even number, what is the smallest of the three?

    ⟋ 2
    ⟋ 3
    ⟋ 5
    ⟋ 7
    ⟋ It cannot be determined from the information given.

7. The integers A, B, and C are consecutive and $A < B < C$. If $A^2 = C$, which of the following could be the value of A?

    I. -1
    II. 0
    III. 2

    ⟋ I only
    ⟋ III only
    ⟋ I and II only
    ⟋ I and III only
    ⟋ I, II, and III

Intermediate

8. If n is an odd number, which of the following must be even?

   ○ $\dfrac{n-1}{2}$

   ○ $\dfrac{n+1}{2}$

   ○ $n^2 + 2n$

   ○ $2n + 2$

   ○ $3n^2 - 2n$

9. What is the smallest integer greater than 1 that leaves a remainder of 1 when divided by any of the integers 6, 8, and 10?

   ○ 21

   ○ 41

   ○ 121

   ○ 241

   ○ 481

10. If the product of two integers is odd, which of the following must be true?

    ○ The sum of the two integers is an odd number.

    ○ The difference between the two integers is an odd number.

    ○ The square of either integer is an odd number.

    ○ The sum of the squares of the two integers is an odd number.

    ○ The difference between the squares of the two integers is an odd number.

11. For how many positive integers x is $\dfrac{130}{x}$ an integer?

    ○ 8

    ○ 7

    ○ 6

    ○ 5

    ○ 3

12. In the repeating decimal $0.097531097531\ldots$, what is the 44th digit to the right of the decimal point?

    ○ 0

    ○ 1

    ○ 3

    ○ 7

    ○ 9

13. What is the greatest integer that will always evenly divide the sum of three consecutive even integers?

    ○ 2

    ○ 3

    ○ 4

    ○ 6

    ○ 12

14. The sum of three consecutive integers is 312. What is the sum of the next three consecutive integers?

    ○ 315

    ○ 321

    ○ 330

    ○ 415

    ○ 424

15. The integer P is greater than 7. If the integer P leaves a remainder of 4 when divided by 9, all of the following must be true EXCEPT

    ○ The number that is 4 less than P is a multiple of 9.

    ○ The number that is 5 more than P is a multiple of 9.

    ○ The number that is 2 more than P is a multiple of 3.

    ○ When divided by 3, P will leave a remainder of 1.

    ○ When divided by 2, P will leave a remainder of 1.

Advanced

16. If the product of two integers is an even number and the sum of the same two integers is an odd number, which of the following must be true?

    ○ The two integers are both odd.
    ○ The two integers are both even.
    ○ One of the two integers is odd and the other is even.
    ○ One of the integers is 1.
    ○ The two integers are consecutive.

17. If both the product and sum of four integers are even, which of the following could be the number of even integers in the group?

    I. 0
    II. 2
    III. 4

    ○ I only
    ○ II only
    ○ III only
    ○ II and III only
    ○ I, II, and III

18. A wire is cut into three equal parts. The resulting segments are then cut into 4, 6 and 8 equal parts respectively. If each of the resulting segments has an integer length, what is the minimum length of the wire?

    ○ 24
    ○ 36
    ○ 48
    ○ 54
    ○ 72

19. How many positive integers less than 60 are equal to the product of a positive multiple of 5 and an even number?

    ○ Four
    ○ Five
    ○ Nine
    ○ Ten
    ○ Eleven

AVERAGES

The average (arithmetic mean) of a group of numbers is defined as the sum of the values divided by the number of values.

$$\text{Average value} = \frac{\text{Sum of values}}{\text{Number of values}}$$

Example: Henry buys three items costing $2.00, $0.75, and $0.25. What is the average price?

$$\text{Average price} = \frac{\text{Sum of prices}}{\text{Number of prices}} = \frac{\text{Total price}}{\text{Total items}} = \frac{\$2.00 + \$0.75 + \$0.25}{3}$$

$$= \frac{\$3.00}{3} = \$1.00$$

On the GRE you might see a reference to the **median**. If a group of numbers is arranged in numerical order the median is the middle value. For instance, the median of the numbers 4, 5, 100, 1, and 6 is 5. The median can be quite different from the average. For instance, in the above example, the average was $1.00, while the median is simply the middle of the three prices given, or $0.75.

If we know the average of a group of numbers, and the number of numbers in the group, we can find the **sum** of the numbers. It's as if all the numbers in the group have the average value.

$$\text{Sum of values} = \text{Average value} \times \text{Number of values}$$

Example: The average daily temperature for the first week in January was 31 degrees. If the average temperature for the first six days was 30 degrees, what was the temperature on the seventh day?

The sum for all 7 days = $31 \times 7 = 217$ degrees.
The sum of the first six days = $30 \times 6 = 180$ degrees.
The temperature on the seventh day = $217 - 180 = 37$ degrees.

For evenly spaced numbers, the average is the middle value. The average of consecutive integers 6, 7, and 8 is 7. The average of 5, 10, 15, and 20 is $12\frac{1}{2}$ (midway between the middle values 10 and 15).

It might be useful to try and think of the average as the "balanced" value. That is, all the numbers below the average are less than the average by an amount that will "balance out" the amount that the numbers above the average are greater than the average. For example, the average of 3, 5 and 10 is 6. 3 is 3 less than 6 and 5 is 1 less than 6. This in total is 4, which is the same as the amount that 10 is greater than 6.

Example: The average of 3, 4, 5, and x is 5. What is the value of x?

Think of each value in terms of its position relative to the average, 5.

  3 is 2 less than the average.
  4 is 1 less than the average.
  5 is at the average.

So these 3 terms together are $1 + 2 + 0$, or 3, **less** than the average. Therefore, x must be 3 **more** than the average, to restore the balance at 5. So x is $3 + 5$ or 8.

Average Rate (Average A per B)

$$\text{Average } A \text{ per } B = \frac{\text{Total } A}{\text{Total } B}$$

Example: John travels 30 miles in 2 hours and then 60 miles in 3 hours. What is his average speed in miles per hour?

$$\text{Average miles per hour} = \frac{\text{Total miles}}{\text{Total hours}}$$

$$= \frac{(30 + 60) \text{ miles}}{(2 + 3) \text{ hours}} = \frac{90 \text{ miles}}{5 \text{ hours}} = 18 \text{ miles/hour}$$

STATISTICS AND PROBABILITY

You'll also have to know some basic statistics and probability for the test. Like mean, mode, median, and range, **standard deviation** describes sets of numbers. It is a measure of how spread out a set of numbers is (how much the numbers deviate from the mean). The greater the spread, the higher the standard deviation. You'll never actually have to calculate the standard deviation on test day, but here's how it's calculated:

- Find the average (arithmetic mean) of the set.
- Find the differences between the mean and each value in the set.
- Square each of the differences.
- Find the average of the squared differences.
- Take the positive square root of the average.

Example: For the 5-day listing that follows, which city had the greater standard deviation in high temperatures?
  High temperatures, in degrees Fahrenheit, in 2 cities over 5 days:

September	1	2	3	4	5
City A	54	61	70	49	56
City B	62	56	60	67	65

Even without calculating them out, you can see that City *A* has the greater spread in temperatures, and therefore the greater standard deviation in high temperatures. If you were to go ahead and calculate the standard deviations following the steps described above, you would find that the standard deviation in high temperatures for City *A* = $\sqrt{\frac{254}{5}} \approx 7.1$, while the same for City *B* = $\sqrt{\frac{74}{5}} \approx 3.8$.

Probability revolves around situations that have a finite number of outcomes.

$$\text{Probability} = \frac{\text{Number of desired outcomes}}{\text{Number of total possible outcomes}}$$

Example: If you have 12 shirts in a drawer and 9 of them are white, the probability of picking a white shirt at random is $\frac{9}{12} = \frac{3}{4}$. The probability can also be expressed as 0.75 or 75%.

Many hard probability questions involve finding the probability of a certain outcome after multiple repetitions of the same experiment or different experiments (a coin being tossed several times, etc.). These questions come in two forms: those in which each individual event must occur a certain way, and those in which individiual events can have different outcomes.

To determine multiple-event probability where each individual event must occur a certain way:

- Figure out the probability for each individual event.
- Multiply the individual probabilities together.

Example: If 2 students are chosen at random from a class with 5 girls and 5 boys, what's the probability that both students chosen will be girls? The probability that the first student chosen will be a girl is $\frac{5}{10} = \frac{1}{2}$, and since there would be 4 girls left out of 9 students, the probability that the second student chosen will be a girl is $\frac{4}{9}$. So the probability that both students chosen will be girls is $\frac{1}{2} \times \frac{4}{9} = \frac{2}{9}$.

To determine multiple-event probability where individual events can have different types of outcomes, find the *total number of possible outcomes*. Do that by determining the number of possible outcomes for each individual event and multiplying these numbers together. Find the *number of desired outcomes* by listing out the possibilities.

Example: If a fair coin is tossed 4 times, what's the probability that at least 3 of the 4 tosses will come up heads?

There are 2 possible outcomes for each toss, so after 4 tosses there are a total of $2 \times 2 \times 2 \times 2 = 16$ possible outcomes. List out all the possibilities where "at least 3 of the 4 tosses" come up heads:

H, H, H, T   H, T, H, H   H, H, H, H
H, H, T, H   T, H, H, H

There's a total of 5 possible desired outcomes. So the probability that at least 3 of the 4 tosses will come up heads is

$$\frac{\text{Number of desired outcomes}}{\text{Number of possible outcomes}} = \frac{5}{16}.$$

AVERAGES EXERCISE

In #1–7, find the average. Answer 8–10 as directed. (Answers are on the following page).

1. 10, 12, 16, 17, 20

2. 0, 3, 6, 9

3. 12, 24, 36, 48, 60

4. −0.01, 0.06, 1.9, 1.8, 2.1

5. −4, −2, 4, 0, 2

6. $\dfrac{1}{2}, \dfrac{1}{3}, \dfrac{1}{6}, \dfrac{1}{12}$

7. 100, 100, 100, 0

8. What is the value of x if the average of 2, 4, 6, and x is 3?

9. What is the value of x if the average of −4, 0, 6, and x is 8?

10. If the average of 8, 3, 12, 11, and x is 0, then $x = ?$

ANSWER KEY—AVERAGES EXERCISE

1. 15
2. $4\frac{1}{2}$
3. 36
4. 1.17
5. 0
6. $\frac{13}{48}$
7. 75
8. 0
9. 30
10. −34

AVERAGES TEST

Solve the following problems and choose the best answer. (Answers and explanations are at the end of this chapter.)

Basic

1. If the average (arithmetic mean) of a and -5 is 10, then $a =$

    ○ 25
    ○ 15
    ○ 5
    ○ -10
    ○ -15

2. What is the average (arithmetic mean) of $\frac{1}{2}$ and $\frac{1}{4}$?

    ○ $\frac{1}{6}$
    ○ $\frac{1}{3}$
    ○ $\frac{3}{8}$
    ○ $\frac{5}{9}$
    ○ $\frac{3}{4}$

3. If the average (arithmetic mean) of 8, 11, 25, and p is 15, then $8 + 11 + 25 + p =$

    ○ 16
    ○ 44
    ○ 56
    ○ 60
    ○ 64

4. The average (arithmetic mean) of 6 consecutive integers is $18\frac{1}{2}$. What is the average of the first 5 of these integers?

    ○ $12\frac{1}{2}$
    ○ 15
    ○ 16
    ○ $17\frac{1}{2}$
    ○ 18

5. A violinist practices one hour a day from Monday through Friday. How many hours must she practice on Saturday in order to have an average (arithmetic mean) of two hours a day for the six-day period?

    ○ 5
    ○ 6
    ○ 7
    ○ 8
    ○ 12

6. The average (arithmetic mean) of six numbers is 6. If 3 is subtracted from each of four of the numbers, what is the new average?

    ○ $1\frac{1}{2}$
    ○ 2
    ○ 3
    ○ 4
    ○ $4\frac{1}{2}$

Intermediate

7. What is the sum of the five consecutive even numbers whose average (arithmetic mean) is 12?

   - ⬭ 30
   - ⬭ 60
   - ⬭ 90
   - ⬭ 120
   - ⬭ 150

8. If the temperature readings at noon for three consecutive days are $+9°$, $-6°$, and $+8°$, what must the reading be at noon on the fourth day for the average (arithmetic mean) noon temperature of all four days to be $+4°$?

   - ⬭ $-11°$
   - ⬭ $-7°$
   - ⬭ $+2°$
   - ⬭ $+4°$
   - ⬭ $+5°$

9. Jerry's average (arithmetic mean) score on the first three of four tests is 85. If Jerry wants to raise his average by 2 points, what score must he earn on the fourth test?

   - ⬭ 87
   - ⬭ 88
   - ⬭ 89
   - ⬭ 91
   - ⬭ 93

10. What is the average (arithmetic mean) of n, $n + 1, n + 2,$ and $n + 3$?

    - ⬭ $n + 1$
    - ⬭ $n + 1\frac{1}{2}$
    - ⬭ $n + 2$
    - ⬭ $n + 2\frac{1}{2}$
    - ⬭ $n + 6$

11. If the average (arithmetic mean) of $x + 2, x + 4,$ and $x + 6$ is 0, then $x =$

    - ⬭ -4
    - ⬭ -3
    - ⬭ -2
    - ⬭ -1
    - ⬭ 0

12. Fifteen movie theaters average 600 customers per theater per day. If six of the theaters close down but the total theater attendance stays the same, what is the average daily attendance per theater among the remaining theaters?

    - ⬭ 500
    - ⬭ 750
    - ⬭ 1,000
    - ⬭ 1,200
    - ⬭ 1,500

Advanced

13. If the average (arithmetic mean) of 18 consecutive odd integers is 534, then the least of these integers is

   ◯ 517
   ◯ 518
   ◯ 519
   ◯ 521
   ◯ 525

Monday	$75.58
Tuesday	$75.63
Wednesday	$75.42
Thursday	$75.52
Friday	

14. The table above shows the closing price of a stock during a week. If the average (arithmetic mean) closing price for the five days was $75.50, what was the closing price on Friday?

   ◯ $75.35
   ◯ $75.40
   ◯ $75.42
   ◯ $75.45
   ◯ $75.48

15. The average (arithmetic mean) of 6 positive numbers is 5. If the average of the least and greatest of these numbers is 7, what is the average of the other four numbers?

   ◯ 3
   ◯ 4
   ◯ 5
   ◯ 6
   ◯ 7

16. If the average (arithmetic mean) of a, b, and 7 is 13, what is the average of $a + 3$, $b - 5$, and 6?

   ◯ 7
   ◯ 9
   ◯ 10
   ◯ 12
   ◯ 16

RATIOS

A ratio is a comparison of two quantities by division.

Ratios may be written either with a fraction bar $\left(\frac{x}{y}\right)$ or with a colon ($x{:}y$) or with English terms (ratio of x to y). We recommend the first way, since ratios can be treated as fractions for the purposes of computation.

Ratios can (and in most cases, should) be reduced to lowest terms just as fractions are reduced.

Example: Joe is 16 years old and Mary is 12.

The ratio of Joe's age to Mary's age is $\frac{16}{12}$. (Read "16 to 12.")

$\frac{16}{12} = \frac{4}{3}$ or 4:3

In a ratio of two numbers, the numerator is often associated with the word *of;* the denominator with the word *to.*

The ratio **of** 3 **to** 4 is $\frac{\text{of } 3}{\text{to } 4} = \frac{3}{4}$.

$$\boxed{\text{Ratio} = \frac{\text{of} \ldots}{\text{to} \ldots}}$$

Example: In a box of doughnuts, 12 are sugar and 18 are chocolate. What is the ratio of sugar doughnuts to chocolate doughnuts?

$$\text{Ratio} = \frac{\text{of sugar}}{\text{to chocolate}} = \frac{12}{18} = \frac{2}{3}$$

We frequently deal with ratios by working with a **proportion**. A proportion is simply an equation in which two ratios are set equal to one another.

Ratios typically deal with "parts" and "wholes." The whole is the entire set; for instance, all the workers in a factory. The part is a certain section of the whole; for instance, the female workers in the factory.

The ratio of a part to a whole is usually called a fraction. "What fraction of the workers are female?" means the same thing as "What is the ratio of the number of female workers to the total number of workers?"

A fraction can represent the ratio of a part to a whole:

$$\frac{\text{Part}}{\text{Whole}} \text{ or Part : Whole.}$$

Example: There are 15 men and 20 women in a class. What fraction of the students are female?

$$\text{Fraction} = \frac{\text{Part}}{\text{Whole}}$$

$$= \frac{\text{\# of female students}}{\text{Total \# of students}}$$

$$= \frac{20}{15 + 20}$$

$$= \frac{^4\cancel{20}}{\cancel{35}_7}$$

$$= \frac{4}{7}$$

This means that $\frac{4}{7}$ of the students are female, or 4 out of every 7 students are female, or the ratio of female students to total students is 4:7.

Part : Part Ratios and Part : Whole Ratios

A ratio can compare either a part to another part or a part to a whole. One type of ratio can readily be converted to the other **if** all the parts together equal the whole and there is no overlap among the parts (that is, if the whole is equal to the sum of its parts).

Example: The ratio of domestic sales to foreign sales of a certain product is $3:5$. What fraction of the total sales are domestic sales? (Note: This is the same as asking for the ratio of the amount of domestic sales to the amount of total sales.)

In this case the whole (total sales) is equal to the sum of the parts (domestic and foreign sales). We **can** convert from a **part : part** ratio to a **part : whole** ratio.

Of every 8 sales of the product, 3 are domestic and 5 are foreign. The ratio of domestic sales to total sales is $\frac{3}{8}$ or $3:8$.

Example: The ratio of domestic to foreign sales of a certain product is $3:5$. What is the ratio of domestic sales to European sales?

Here we cannot convert from a **part : whole** ratio (domestic sales : total sales) to a **part : part** ratio (domestic sales : European sales) because we don't know if there are any other sales besides domestic and European sales. The question doesn't say that the product is sold only domestically and in Europe, so we cannot assume there are no African, Australian, Asian, etc., sales, and so the ratio asked for here cannot be determined.

Ratios with more than two terms: Ratios involving more than two terms are governed by the same principles. These ratios contain more relationships, so they convey more information than two-term ratios. Ratios involving more than two terms are usually ratios of various parts, and it is usually the case that the sum of these parts does equal the whole, which makes it possible to find **part : whole** ratios as well.

Example: Given that the ratio of men to women to children in a room is 4:3:2, what other ratios can be determined?

Quite a few. The **whole** here is the number of people in the room, and since every person is either a man, a woman, or a child, we can determine **part : whole** ratios for each of these parts. Of every nine (4 + 3 + 2) people in the room, 4 are men, 3 are women, and 2 are children. This gives us three **part : whole** ratios:

$$\text{Ratio of men : total people} = 4 : 9 \text{ or } \frac{4}{9}$$

$$\text{Ratio of women : total people} = 3 : 9 = 1 : 3 \text{ or } \frac{1}{3}$$

$$\text{Ratio of children : total people} = 2 : 9 \text{ or } \frac{2}{9}$$

In addition, from any ratio of more than two terms, we can determine various two-term ratios among the parts.

$$\text{Ratio of women : men} = 3 : 4$$

$$\text{Ratio of men : children} = 4 : 2$$

And finally if we were asked to establish a relationship between the number of adults in the room and the number of children, we would find that this would be possible as well. For every 2 children there are 4 men and 3 women, which is 4 + 3 or 7 adults. So:

$$\text{Ratio of children : adults} = 2 : 7, \text{ or}$$

$$\text{Ratio of adults : children} = 7 : 2$$

Naturally, a test question will require you to determine only one or at most two of these ratios, but knowing how much information is contained in a given ratio will help you to determine quickly which questions are solvable and which, if any, are not.

Ratio Versus Actual Number

Ratios are always reduced to simplest form. If a team's ratio of wins to losses is 5 : 3, this does not necessarily mean that the team has won 5 games and lost 3. For instance, if a team has won 30 games and lost 18, the ratio is still 5:3. Unless we know the **actual number** of games played (or the actual number won or lost), we don't know the actual values of the parts in the ratio.

Example: In a classroom of 30 students, the ratio of the boys in the class to students in the class is 2 : 5. How many are boys?

We are given a part to whole ratio (boys : students). This ratio is a fraction. Multiplying this fraction by the actual whole gives the value of the corresponding part. There are 30 students; $\frac{2}{5}$ of them are boys, so the number of boys must be $\frac{2}{5} \times 30$.

$$\frac{2 \text{ boys}}{{}_1\cancel{5} \text{ students}} \times \cancel{30}^6 \text{ students} = 2 \times 6 = 12 \text{ boys}$$

PICKING NUMBERS

Ratio problems that do not contain any actual values, just ratios, are ideal for solving by picking numbers. Just make sure that the numbers you pick are divisible by both the numerator and denominator of the ratio.

Example: A building has $\frac{2}{5}$ of its floors below ground. What is the ratio of the number of floors above ground to the number of floors below ground?

◯ 5:2

◯ 3:2

◯ 4:3

◯ 3:5

◯ 2:5

Pick a value for the total number of floors, one that is divisible by both the numerator and denominator of $\frac{2}{5}$. Let's say 10. Then, since $\frac{2}{5}$ of the floors are below ground, $\frac{2}{5} \times 10$, or 4 floors are below ground. This leaves 6 floors above ground. Therefore, the ratio of the number of floors above ground to the number of floors below ground is 6:4, or 3:2, choice (2).

We'll see more on ratios, and how we can pick numbers to simplify things, in the Word Problems chapter.

Rates

A rate is a ratio that relates two different kinds of quantities. Speed, which is the ratio of distance traveled to time elapsed, is an example of a rate.

When we talk about rates, we usually use the word *per,* as in "miles per hour," "cost per item," etcetera. Since *per* means "for one," or "for each," we express the rates as ratios reduced to a denominator of 1.

Example: John travels 50 miles in two hours. His average rate is

$$\frac{50 \text{ miles}}{2 \text{ hours}} \text{ or 25 miles per hour}$$

Note: We frequently speak in terms of "average rate," since it may be improbable (as in the case of speed) that the rate has been constant over the period in question. See the Average section for more details.

RATIOS EXERCISE

Reduce each of the following ratios to lowest terms. (Answers are on the following page.)

1. $8 : 128$

2. $72 : 20$

3. $14.2 : 71$

4. $6.9 : 2.1$

5. $1.6 : 0.4 : 0.16$

6. $0.75 : 1.85$

7. $81 : \dfrac{1}{3}$

8. $\dfrac{1}{3} : \dfrac{1}{4}$

9. $\dfrac{5}{12} : \dfrac{1}{12}$

10. $\dfrac{3}{16} : \dfrac{5}{8}$

ANSWER KEY—RATIOS EXERCISE

1. 1 : 16
2. 18 : 5
3. 1 : 5
4. 23 : 7
5. 20 : 5 : 2
6. 15 : 37
7. 243 : 1
8. 4 : 3
9. 5 : 1
10. 3 : 10

RATIOS TEST

Solve the following problems and choose the best answer. (Answers and explanations are at the end of the chapter.)

Basic

1. In a certain pet show there are 24 hamsters and 9 cats. What is the ratio of cats to hamsters at this pet show?

   - ⬭ 1 : 4
   - ⬭ 1 : 3
   - ⬭ 3 : 8
   - ⬭ 2 : 3
   - ⬭ 3 : 4

2. If the ratio of boys to girls in a class is 5 : 3, and there are 65 boys, how many girls must there be in the class?

   - ⬭ 13
   - ⬭ 18
   - ⬭ 26
   - ⬭ 36
   - ⬭ 39

3. On a certain street map, $\frac{3}{4}$ inch represents one mile. What distance, in miles, is represented by $1\frac{3}{4}$ inches?

   - ⬭ $1\frac{1}{2}$
   - ⬭ $1\frac{3}{4}$
   - ⬭ $2\frac{1}{3}$
   - ⬭ $2\frac{1}{2}$
   - ⬭ $5\frac{1}{4}$

4. After spending $\frac{5}{12}$ of his salary, a man has $140 left. What is his salary?

   - ⬭ $200
   - ⬭ $240
   - ⬭ $300
   - ⬭ $420
   - ⬭ $583

5. In a local election, votes were cast for Mr. Dyer, Ms. Frau, and Mr. Borak in the ratio of 4 : 3 : 2. If there were no other candidates and none of the 1,800 voters cast more than one vote, how many votes did Ms. Frau receive?

   - ⬭ 200
   - ⬭ 300
   - ⬭ 400
   - ⬭ 600
   - ⬭ 900

6. The ratio of men to women at a party is exactly 3 : 2. If there are a total of 120 people at the party, how many of them are women?

   - ⬭ 36
   - ⬭ 40
   - ⬭ 48
   - ⬭ 72
   - ⬭ 80

7. The weights of two ships are in the ratio of 5 : 9. If together they weigh 5,600 tons, how many tons does the larger ship weigh?

   - ⬭ 2,000
   - ⬭ 2,400
   - ⬭ 3,000
   - ⬭ 3,200
   - ⬭ 3,600

KAPLAN

8. A laboratory has 55 rabbits, some white and the rest brown. Which of the following could be the ratio of white rabbits to brown rabbits in the lab?

- ○ 1 : 3
- ○ 3 : 8
- ○ 5 : 11
- ○ 3 : 4
- ○ 5 : 1

9. The Greenpoint factory produced two-fifths of the Consolidated Brick Company's bricks in 1991. If the Greenpoint factory produced 1,400 tons of bricks in 1991, what was the Consolidated Brick Company's total output that year, in tons?

- ○ 700
- ○ 2,100
- ○ 2,800
- ○ 3,500
- ○ 7,000

10. A ratio of $3\frac{1}{4}$ to $5\frac{1}{4}$ is equivalent to a ratio of

- ○ 3 to 5
- ○ 13 to 21
- ○ 5 to 7
- ○ 7 to 5
- ○ 5 to 3

11. A certain ship floats with $\frac{3}{5}$ of its weight above the water. What is the ratio of the ship's submerged weight to its exposed weight?

- ○ 3 : 8
- ○ 2 : 5
- ○ 3 : 5
- ○ 2 : 3
- ○ 5 : 3

12. One-twentieth of the entrants in a contest won prizes. If 30 prizes were won, and no entrant won more than one prize, how many entrants did NOT win prizes?

- ○ 30
- ○ 300
- ○ 540
- ○ 570
- ○ 600

13. If a kilogram is equal to approximately 2.2 pounds, which of the following is the best approximation of the number of kilograms in one pound?

- ○ $\frac{11}{5}$
- ○ $\frac{5}{8}$
- ○ $\frac{5}{11}$
- ○ $\frac{1}{3}$
- ○ $\frac{1}{5}$

Intermediate

14. A recipe for egg nog calls for 2 eggs for every 3 cups of milk. If there are 4 cups in a quart, how many eggs will be needed to mix with 6 quarts of milk?

    ○ 12
    ○ 16
    ○ 24
    ○ 36
    ○ 48

15. If the ratio of boys to girls in a class is 5 to 3, which of the following could not be the number of students in the class?

    ○ 32 =5
    ○ 36 = 9
    ○ 40 = 4
    ○ 48 = 12
    ○ 56 = 11

16. A student's grade in a course is determined by 4 quizzes and 1 exam. If the exam counts twice as much as each of the quizzes, what fraction of the final grade is determined by the exam?

    ○ $\dfrac{1}{6}$
    ○ $\dfrac{1}{5}$
    ○ $\dfrac{1}{3}$
    ○ $\dfrac{1}{4}$
    ○ $\dfrac{1}{2}$

17. If cement, gravel, and sand are to be mixed in the ratio 3 : 5 : 7 respectively, and 5 tons of cement are available, how many tons of the mixture can be made? (Assume there is enough gravel and sand available to use all the cement.)

    ○ 15
    ○ 20
    ○ 25
    ○ 30
    ○ 75

18. Bob finishes the first half of an exam in two-thirds the time it takes him to finish the second half. If the whole exam takes him an hour, how many minutes does he spend on the first half of the exam?

    ○ 20
    ○ 24
    ○ 27
    ○ 36
    ○ 40

19. In a certain factory with 2,700 workers, one-third of the workers are unskilled. If 600 of the unskilled workers are apprentices, what fraction of the unskilled workers are not apprentices?

    ○ $\dfrac{1}{9}$
    ○ $\dfrac{1}{7}$
    ○ $\dfrac{1}{5}$
    ○ $\dfrac{1}{3}$
    ○ $\dfrac{1}{2}$

Advanced

20. An alloy of tin and copper has 6 pounds of copper for every 2 pounds of tin. If 200 pounds of this alloy are made, how many pounds of tin are required?

    ○ 25
    ○ 50
    ○ 100
    ○ 125
    ○ 150

21. A sporting goods store ordered an equal number of white and yellow tennis balls. The tennis ball company delivered 30 extra white balls, making the ratio of white balls to yellow balls 6 : 5. How many tennis balls did the store originally order?

    ○ 120
    ○ 150
    ○ 180
    ○ 300
    ○ 330

22. If $a = 2b$, $\frac{1}{2}b = c$, and $4c = 3d$, then what is the ratio of d to a ?

    ○ $\frac{1}{3}$
    ○ $\frac{3}{4}$
    ○ 1
    ○ $\frac{4}{3}$
    ○ 3

23. An oculist charges $30.00 for an eye examination, frames, and glass lenses, but $42.00 for an eye examination, frames, and plastic lenses. If the plastic lenses cost four times as much as the glass lenses, how much do the glass lenses cost?

    ○ $2
    ○ $4
    ○ $5
    ○ $6
    ○ $8

24. If $\frac{1}{2}$ of the number of white mice in a certain laboratory is $\frac{1}{8}$ of the total number of mice, and $\frac{1}{3}$ of the number of gray mice is $\frac{1}{9}$ of the total number of mice, then what is the ratio of white mice to gray mice?

    ○ 16 : 27
    ○ 2 : 3
    ○ 3 : 4
    ○ 4 : 5
    ○ 8 : 9

PERCENTS

Percents are one of the most commonly used math relationships. Percents are also a popular topic on the GRE. *Percent* is just another word for *hundredth*. Therefore, 19% (19 percent) means 19 hundredths

$$\text{or } \frac{19}{100}$$

or 0.19

or 19 out of every 100 things

or 19 parts out of a whole of 100 parts.

They're all just different names for the same thing.

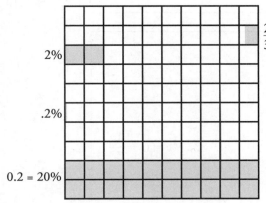

Each box at the left represents 1%. 100 boxes = (100)(1%) = 100% = 1 whole. Note that we have, in increasing order, 0.2%, $\frac{2}{3}$%, 2%, and 20%.

Making and Dropping Percents

To make a percent, multiply by 100%. Since 100% means 100 hundredths or 1, multiplying by 100% will not change the value.

Example: $0.17 = 0.17 \times 100\% = 17.0\% \text{ or } 17\%$

Example: $\frac{1}{4} = \frac{1}{4} \times 100\% = 25\%$

To drop a percent, divide by 100%. Once again, dividing by 100% will not change the value.

Example: $32\% = \frac{32\%}{100\%} = \frac{32}{100} = \frac{8}{25}$

Example: $\frac{1}{2}\% = \frac{\frac{1}{2}\%}{100\%} = \frac{1}{200}$

To change a percent to a decimal, just drop the percent and move the decimal point two places to the left. (This is the same as dividing by 100%.)

Example: $0.8\% = 0.00.8 = 0.008$

Example: $2\dfrac{1}{4}\% = 2.25\% = 0.02.25 = 0.0225$

Common Percent and Fractional Equivalents

$\dfrac{1}{20} = 5\%$	$\dfrac{1}{10} = 10\%$	$\dfrac{1}{8} = 12\dfrac{1}{2}\%$	$\dfrac{1}{6} = 16\dfrac{2}{3}\%$
$\dfrac{1}{5} = 20\%$	$\dfrac{1}{4} = 25\%$	$\dfrac{1}{3} = 33\dfrac{1}{3}\%$	$\dfrac{1}{2} = 50\%$

$10\% = \dfrac{1}{10}$		
$20\% = \dfrac{2}{10} = \dfrac{1}{5}$	$12\dfrac{1}{2}\% = \dfrac{1}{8}$	$16\dfrac{2}{3}\% = \dfrac{1}{6}$
$30\% = \dfrac{3}{10}$	$25\% = \dfrac{2}{8} = \dfrac{1}{4}$	
$40\% = \dfrac{4}{10} = \dfrac{2}{5}$	$37\dfrac{1}{2}\% = \dfrac{3}{8}$	$33\dfrac{1}{3}\% = \dfrac{2}{6} = \dfrac{1}{3}$
$50\% = \dfrac{5}{10} = \dfrac{1}{2}$	$50\% = \dfrac{4}{8} = \dfrac{2}{4} = \dfrac{1}{2}$	$50\% = \dfrac{3}{6} = \dfrac{1}{2}$
$60\% = \dfrac{6}{10} = \dfrac{3}{5}$	$62\dfrac{1}{2}\% = \dfrac{5}{8}$	$66\dfrac{2}{3}\% = \dfrac{4}{6} = \dfrac{2}{3}$
$70\% = \dfrac{7}{10}$	$75\% = \dfrac{6}{8} = \dfrac{3}{4}$	
$80\% = \dfrac{8}{10} = \dfrac{4}{5}$	$87\dfrac{1}{2}\% = \dfrac{7}{8}$	$83\dfrac{1}{3}\% = \dfrac{5}{6}$
$90\% = \dfrac{9}{10}$		
$100\% = \dfrac{10}{10} = 1$		

Being familiar with these equivalents can save you a lot of time on Test Day.

Percent Problems

Most percent problems can be solved by plugging into one formula:

$$\boxed{\text{Percent} \times \text{Whole} = \text{Part}}$$

This formula has 3 variables: percent, whole, and part. In percent problems, generally, the **whole** will be associated with the word *of;* the **part** will be associated with the word *is.* The percent can be represented as the ratio of the part to the whole, or the *is* to the *of.*

Percent problems will usually give you two of the variables and ask for the third. See the examples of the three types of problems below. On the GRE, it is usually easiest to change the percent to a common fraction and work it out from there.

Example: What is 25% of 36?

Here we are given the percent and the whole. To find the part, change the percent to a fraction, then multiply. Use the formula above.

$$\text{Percent} \times \text{Whole} = \text{Part}.$$

Since $25\% = \dfrac{1}{4}$, we are really asking what one-fourth of 36 is.

$$\frac{1}{4} \times 36 = 9.$$

Example: 13 is $33\dfrac{1}{3}\%$ of what number?

Here we are given the percent and the part and asked for the whole.
If Percent $\times$ Whole = Part, then

$$\text{Whole} = \frac{\text{Part}}{\text{Percent}}. \text{ Recall that } 33\frac{1}{3}\% = \frac{1}{3}.$$

$$= \frac{13}{\dfrac{1}{3}}$$

$$= 13 \times \frac{3}{1} = 39$$

We can avoid all this algebra: All we are asked is "13 is one-third of what number?"
13 is one-third of 3×13 or 39.

Example: 18 is what percent of 3?

Here we are given the whole (3) and the part (18) and asked for the percent.
If % $\times$ Whole = Part, then

$$\% = \frac{\text{Part}}{\text{Whole}}$$

Since the part and the whole are both integers, and we're looking for a percent, we're going to have to make our result into a percent by multiplying it by 100%.

$$\% = \frac{18}{3}(100\%) = 6(100\%) = 600\%$$

Note here that we can find the percent as the "is" part divided by the "of" part:

What percent is 18 of 3?

$$\% = \frac{\text{is}}{\text{of}} = \frac{18}{3} = 6 = 600\%$$

Alternative method: The base 3 represents 100%. Since 18 is 6 times as large, the percent equals $6 \times 100\% = 600\%$.

Percent increase and decrease:

$$\% \text{ increase} = \frac{\text{Amount of increase}}{\text{Original whole}}(100\%)$$

$$\% \text{ decrease} = \frac{\text{Amount of decrease}}{\text{Original whole}}(100\%)$$

New Whole = Original whole $\pm$ Amount of change

When dealing with percent increase and percent decrease always be careful to put the amount of increase or decrease over the **original** whole, not the new whole.

Example: If a $120 dress is increased in price by 25 percent, what is the new selling price?
Our original whole here is $120, and the percent increase is 25%. Change 25% to a fraction, $\frac{1}{4}$, and use the formula.

$$\text{Amount of increase} = \% \text{ increase} \times \text{Original whole}$$

$$= 25\% \times \$120$$

$$= \frac{1}{4} \times \$120$$

$$= \$30$$

To find the **new whole** (the new selling price):

New whole = Original whole + Amount of increase

New whole = $120 + $30 = **$150**

Combining percents: On some problems, you'll need to find more than one percent, or a percent of a percent. Be careful. You can't just add percents, unless you're taking the percents of the same whole. Let's look at an example.

Example: The price of an antique is reduced by 20 percent and then this price is reduced by 10 percent. If the antique originally cost $200, what is its final price?

First, we know that the price is reduced by 20%. That's the same thing as saying that the price becomes (100% − 20%), or 80% of what it originally was. 80% of $200 is equal to $\frac{8}{10} \times \$200$, or $160. Then, **this** price is reduced by 10%. 10% × $160 = $16, so the final price of the antique is $160 − $16 = $144.

A common error in this kind of problem is to assume that the final price is simply a 30 percent reduction of the original price. That would mean that the final price is 70 percent of the original, or 70% × $200 = $140. But, as we've just seen, this is NOT correct. Adding or subtracting percents directly only works if those percents are being taken of the same whole. In this example, since we took 20% of the original price, and then 10% of that reduced price, we can't just add the percents together.

More practice with percent word problems can be found in the Word Problems chapter.

PERCENTS EXERCISE

Solve the following problems as directed. (Answers are on the following page.)

Convert to a percent:

1. $0.002 =$

2. $\dfrac{7}{25} =$

3. $1.31 =$

4. $\dfrac{12}{5} =$

5. $\dfrac{1}{400} =$

6. $0.025 =$

7. $\dfrac{1}{80} =$

8. $\dfrac{3}{20} =$

9. $0.675 =$

10. $\dfrac{5}{2} =$

Convert to a fraction:

11. $16\% =$

12. $24\% =$

13. $0.036\% =$

14. $125\% =$

15. $\dfrac{1}{4}\% =$

16. $0.8\% =$

17. $\dfrac{3}{2}\% =$

18. $95\% =$

19. $65\dfrac{1}{2}\% =$

20. $12.6\% =$

Calculate:

21. 50% of $12 =$

22. 75% of $16 =$

23. 150% of $4 =$

24. 24% of $2 =$

25. 10% of $50 =$

ANSWER KEY—PERCENTS EXERCISE

1. 0.2%

2. 28%

3. 131%

4. 240%

5. $\frac{1}{4}\% = 0.25\%$

6. 2.5%

7. 1.25%

8. 15%

9. 67.5%

10. 250%

11. $\frac{4}{25}$

12. $\frac{6}{25}$

13. $\frac{9}{25,000}$

14. $1\frac{1}{4}$ or $\frac{5}{4}$

15. $\frac{1}{400}$

16. $\frac{1}{125}$

17. $\frac{3}{200}$

18. $\frac{19}{20}$

19. $\frac{131}{200}$

20. $\frac{63}{500}$

21. 6

22. 12

23. 6

24. 0.48

25. 5

PERCENT TEST

Solve the following problems and choose the best answer. (Answers and explanations are at the end of this chapter.)

Basic

1. Two hundred percent more than 30 is

    ○ 36
    ○ 60
    ○ 90
    ○ 120
    ○ 360

2. What percent of 1,600 is 2?

    ○ $\frac{1}{8}$%
    ○ 0.8%
    ○ $1\frac{1}{4}$%
    ○ 8%
    ○ $12\frac{1}{2}$%

3. What is 0.25 percent of $\frac{4}{3}$?

    ○ $\frac{1}{3,000}$
    ○ $\frac{1}{300}$
    ○ $\frac{1}{30}$
    ○ $\frac{1}{20}$
    ○ $\frac{1}{3}$

4. What percent of 4 is $\frac{2}{3}$ of 8?

    ○ 25%
    ○ $66\frac{2}{3}$%
    ○ 120%
    ○ $133\frac{1}{3}$%
    ○ 150%

5. Ten percent of 20 percent of 30 is

    ○ 0.3
    ○ 0.6
    ○ 1.5
    ○ 3
    ○ 6

6. If 60 percent of W equals 20 percent of T, what percent is W of T?

    ○ 12%
    ○ $33\frac{1}{3}$%
    ○ 60%
    ○ 120%
    ○ $133\frac{1}{3}$%

7. 36 percent of 18 is 18 percent of what number?

    ○ 9
    ○ 24
    ○ 36
    ○ 40
    ○ 48

8. The price of a newspaper rises from 5 cents to 15 cents. What is the percent increase in price?

   ○ 2%

   ○ 50%

   ○ 150%

   ○ 200%

   ○ 300%

9. Joseph bought a house for $80,000. If he sells it for a profit of 12.5 percent of the original cost, what is the selling price of the house?

   ○ $92,500

   ○ $90,000

   ○ $89,000

   ○ $88,000

   ○ $80,900

10. A closet contains 24 pairs of shoes. If 25 percent of those pairs of shoes are black, how many pairs are NOT black?

    ○ 4

    ○ 6

    ○ 12

    ○ 18

    ○ 20

11. Bob took 20 math tests last year. If he failed six of them, what percent of the math tests did he pass?

    ○ 37.5%

    ○ 60%

    ○ 62.5%

    ○ $66\frac{2}{3}$%

    ○ 70%

12. An item is priced 20 percent more than its wholesale cost. If the wholesale cost was $800, what is the price of the item?

    ○ $900

    ○ $960

    ○ $1,000

    ○ $1,040

    ○ $1,200

13. Over a ten-year period Pat's income rose from $15,000 to $35,000. What was the percent increase in her income?

    ○ $33\frac{1}{3}$%

    ○ 42.8%

    ○ $133\frac{1}{3}$%

    ○ 142.8%

    ○ $233\frac{1}{3}$%

14. Of the 20 people who won prize money, 7 have come forward to claim their winnings. What percent of the people have not yet appeared?

    ○ 20%

    ○ 35%

    ○ 42%

    ○ 65%

    ○ 70%

15. A $100 chair is increased in price by 50 percent. If the chair is then discounted by 50 percent of the new price, at what price will it be offered for sale?

    ○ $150

    ○ $125

    ○ $100

    ○ $75

    ○ $50

Intermediate

16. If 65 percent of x is 195, what is 75 percent of x?

    ○ 215
    ○ 225
    ○ 235
    ○ 250
    ○ 260

17. During October, a store had sales of $30,000. If this was a 20 percent increase over the September sales, what were the September sales?

    ○ $22,500
    ○ $24,000
    ○ $25,000
    ○ $27,000
    ○ $28,000

18. In a state lottery, 40 percent of the money collected goes towards education. If during a certain week 6.4 million dollars were obtained for education, how much money was collected in the lottery during that week, in millions of dollars?

    ○ 25.6
    ○ 16.0
    ○ 8.96
    ○ 8.0
    ○ 2.56

19. A 25-ounce solution is 20 percent alcohol. If 50 ounces of water are added to it, what percent of the new solution is alcohol?

    ○ 5%
    ○ $6\frac{2}{3}$%
    ○ 8%
    ○ 10%
    ○ 20%

20. After getting a 20 percent discount, Jerry paid $100 for a bicycle. How much did the bicycle originally cost?

    ○ $80
    ○ $82
    ○ $116
    ○ $120
    ○ $125

21. A stock decreases in value by 20 percent. By what percent must the stock price increase to reach its former value?

    ○ 15%
    ○ 20%
    ○ 25%
    ○ 30%
    ○ 40%

Advanced

22. The population of a certain town increases by 50 percent every 50 years. If the population in 1950 was 810, in what year was the population 160?

    ◯ 1650
    ◯ 1700
    ◯ 1750
    ◯ 1800
    ◯ 1850

23. Five percent of a certain grass seed is timothy. If the amount of the mixture needed to plant one acre contains 2 pounds of timothy, how many acres can be planted with 240 pounds of the seed mixture?

    ◯ 6
    ◯ 12
    ◯ 20
    ◯ 24
    ◯ 120

24. A brush salesman earns $50 salary each month plus 10 percent commission on the value of his sales. If he earned $200 last month, what was the total value of his sales?

    ◯ $1,000
    ◯ $1,200
    ◯ $1,500
    ◯ $2,000
    ◯ $2,500

25. A man bought 10 crates of oranges for $80 total. If he lost 2 of the crates, at what price would he have to sell each of the remaining crates in order to earn a total profit of 25 percent of the total cost?

    ◯ $10.00
    ◯ $12.50
    ◯ $15.00
    ◯ $100.00
    ◯ $120.00

POWERS AND ROOTS

Rules of Operation with Powers

In the term $3x^2$, 3 is the **coefficient**, x is the **base**, and 2 is the **exponent**. The exponent refers to the number of times the base is multiplied by itself, or how many times the base is a factor. For instance, in 4^3, there are 3 factors of $4:4^3=4 \cdot 4 \cdot 4 = 64$.

A number multiplied by itself twice is called the **square** of that number, e.g., x^2 is x squared.
A number multiplied by itself three times is called the **cube** of that number, e.g., 4^3 is 4 cubed.

To multiply two terms with the same base, keep the base and add the exponents.

Example: $2^2 \cdot 2^3 = (2 \cdot 2)(2 \cdot 2 \cdot 2)$ or $2^2 \cdot 2^3 = 2^{2+3}$

$\qquad\qquad\quad = (2 \cdot 2 \cdot 2 \cdot 2 \cdot 2)$ $= 2^5$

$\qquad\qquad\quad = 2^5$

Example: $x^4 \cdot x^7 = x^{4+7} = x^{11}$

To divide two terms with the same base, keep the base and subtract the exponent of the denominator from the exponent of the numerator.

Example: $4^4 \div 4^2 = \dfrac{4 \cdot 4 \cdot 4 \cdot 4}{4 \cdot 4}$ or $4^4 \div 4^2 = 4^{4-2}$

$\qquad\qquad\quad = \dfrac{4 \cdot 4}{1}$ $= 4^2$

$\qquad\qquad\quad = 4^2$

To raise a power to another power, multiply the exponents.

Example: $(3^2)^4 = (3 \cdot 3)^4$ or $(3^2)^4 = 3^{2\times4}$

$\qquad\qquad\quad = (3 \cdot 3)(3 \cdot 3)(3 \cdot 3)(3 \cdot 3)$ $= 3^8$

$\qquad\qquad\quad = 3^8$

Any nonzero number raised to the zero power is equal to 1. $a^0 = 1$, if $a \neq 0$. 0^0 is undefined.

A negative exponent indicates a reciprocal. To arrive at an equivalent expression, take the reciprocal of the base and change the sign of the exponent.

$$a^{-n} = \frac{1}{a^n} \text{ or } \left(\frac{1}{a}\right)^n$$

Example: $2^{-3} = \left(\dfrac{1}{2}\right)^3 = \dfrac{1}{2^3} = \dfrac{1}{8}$

A fractional exponent indicates a **root**.

$(a)^{\frac{1}{n}} = \sqrt[n]{a}$ (read "the *n*th root of *a*." If no "*n*" is present, the radical sign means a square root.)

Example: $8^{\frac{1}{3}} = \sqrt[3]{8} = 2$

On the GRE you will probably only see the square root. The square root of a nonnegative number *x* is equal to the number which when multiplied by itself gives you *x*. Every positive number has two square roots, one positive and one negative. The positive square root of 25 is 5, since $5^2 = 25$; and the negative square root of 25 is -5, since $(-5)^2 = 25$ also. Other types of roots have appeared on the tests (cube root, or $\sqrt[3]{}$, is an example), but they tend to be extremely rare.

Note: In the expression $3x^2$, only the *x* is being squared, not the 3. In other words, $3x^2 = 3(x^2)$. If we wanted to square the 3 as well, we would write $(3x)^2$. (Remember that in the order of operations we raise to a power **before** we multiply, so in $3x^2$ we square *x* and **then** multiply by 3.)

Rules of Operations with Roots

By convention, the symbol $\sqrt{}$ (radical) means the **positive** square root only.

Example: $\sqrt{9} = +3; \quad -\sqrt{9} = -3$

Even though there are two different numbers whose square is 9 (both 3 and -3), we say that $\sqrt{9}$ is the positive number 3 only.

When it comes to the four basic arithmetic operations, we treat radicals in much the same way we would treat variables.

Addition and Subtraction: Only like radicals can be added to or subtracted from one another.

Example: $2\sqrt{3} + 4\sqrt{2} - \sqrt{2} - 3\sqrt{3} = (4\sqrt{2} - \sqrt{2}) + (2\sqrt{3} - 3\sqrt{3})$ [Note: $\sqrt{2} = 1\sqrt{2}$]

$$= 3\sqrt{2} + (-\sqrt{3})$$
$$= 3\sqrt{2} - \sqrt{3}$$

Multiplication and Division: To multiply or divide one radical by another, multiply or divide the numbers outside the radical signs, then the numbers inside the radical signs.

Example: $(6\sqrt{3}) \times (2\sqrt{5}) = (6 \times 2) \cdot (\sqrt{3} \times \sqrt{5}) = 12\sqrt{3 \times 5} = 12\sqrt{15}$

Example: $12\sqrt{15} \div 2\sqrt{5} = (12 \div 2) \cdot (\sqrt{15} \div \sqrt{5}) = 6\left(\sqrt{\frac{15}{5}}\right) = 6\sqrt{3}$

Example: $\dfrac{4\sqrt{18}}{2\sqrt{6}} = \left(\dfrac{4}{2}\right)\left(\dfrac{\sqrt{18}}{\sqrt{6}}\right) = 2\left(\sqrt{\dfrac{18}{6}}\right) = 2\sqrt{3}$

If the number inside the radical is a multiple of a perfect square, the expression can be simplified by factoring out the perfect square.

> **Example:** $\sqrt{72} = \sqrt{36 \times 2} = \sqrt{36} \times \sqrt{2} = 6\sqrt{2}$

Powers of 10

The exponent of a power of 10 tells us how many zeros the number would contain if written out.

> **Example:** $10^6 = 1,000,000$ (6 zeros) since 10 multiplied by itself six times is equal to 1,000,000.

When multiplying a number by a power of 10, move the decimal point to the right the same number of places as the number of zeros in that power of 10.

> **Example:** $0.029 \times 10^3 = 0.029 \times 1,000 = 0\underset{\text{3 places}}{.029.} = 29$

When dividing by a power of 10, move the decimal point the corresponding number of places to the left. (Note that dividing by 10^4 is the same as multiplying by 10^{-4}.)

> **Example:** $416.03 \times 10^{-4} = 416.03 \div 10^4 = 0\underset{\text{4 places}}{.0416.03} = 0.041603$

Large numbers or small decimal fractions can be expressed more conveniently using scientific notation. Scientific notation means expressing a number as the product of a decimal between 1 and 10, and a power of 10.

> **Example:** $5,600,000 = 5.6 \times 10^6$ (5.6 million)
>
> **Example:** $0.00000079 = 7.9 \times 10^{-7}$
>
> **Example:** $0.00765 \times 10^7 = 7.65 \times 10^4$

POWERS AND ROOTS EXERCISE

Solve the following problems. (Answers are on the following page)

1. $5^4 =$

2. $2^5 =$

3. $4 \cdot 3^3 =$

4. $(4 \cdot 3)^2 =$

5. $(4+3)^2 =$

6. $1.016 \times 10^2 =$

7. $(2^2)^4 =$

8. $(\sqrt{2})(\sqrt{8}) =$

9. $(\sqrt{6})(\sqrt{21}) =$

10. $\dfrac{\sqrt{43}}{\sqrt{2}} =$

11. $(2^5)\left(\dfrac{1}{2^6}\right) =$

12. $\sqrt{5} + \sqrt{125} =$

ANSWER KEY—POWERS AND ROOTS EXERCISE

1. 625

2. 32

3. 108

4. 144

5. 49

6. 101.6

7. $2^8 (=256)$

8. 4

9. $(\sqrt{6})(\sqrt{21}) = (\sqrt{3})(\sqrt{2})(\sqrt{3})(\sqrt{7})$

$\qquad\qquad = (\sqrt{3})(\sqrt{3})(\sqrt{2})(\sqrt{7})$

$\qquad\qquad = 3\sqrt{14}$

10. $\dfrac{\sqrt{48}}{\sqrt{3}} = \sqrt{\dfrac{48}{3}} = \sqrt{16} = 4$

11. $\dfrac{1}{2}$

12. $\sqrt{5} + \sqrt{125} = \sqrt{5} + \sqrt{5 \cdot 25}$

$\qquad\qquad = \sqrt{5} + (\sqrt{5})(\sqrt{25})$

$\qquad\qquad = 1\sqrt{5} + 5\sqrt{5}$

$\qquad\qquad = 6\sqrt{5}$

POWERS AND ROOTS TEST

Solve the following problems and choose the best answer. (Answers are at the end of this chapter.)

Basic

1. $(7-3)^2 =$

   ○ 4
   ○ 9
   ○ 16
   ○ 40
   ○ 49

2. If $a = 3$, then $(3a)^2 - 3a^2 =$

   ○ 0
   ○ 9
   ○ 27
   ○ 54
   ○ 72

3. $2^4 \times 4^3 =$

   ○ 8^{12}
   ○ 8^7
   ○ 6^7
   ○ 2^{10}
   ○ 2^7

4. If $x = 9a^2$ and $a > 0$, then $\sqrt{x} =$

   ○ $-3a$
   ○ $3a$
   ○ $9a$
   ○ $3a^2$
   ○ $81a^4$

5. $\dfrac{4^3 - 4^2}{2^2} =$

   ○ 1
   ○ 2
   ○ 4
   ○ 12
   ○ 16

6. If $3^x = 81$, then $x^3 =$

   ○ 12
   ○ 16
   ○ 64
   ○ 81
   ○ 128

7. If $x = 2$, then $3^x + (x^3)^2 =$

   ○ 18
   ○ 42
   ○ 45
   ○ 70
   ○ 73

KAPLAN

Intermediate

8. Which of the following is NOT equal to 0.0675?

   ⬭ 67.5×10^{-3}

   ⬭ 6.75×10^{-2}

   ⬭ 0.675×10^{-1}

   ⬭ 0.00675×10^{2}

   ⬭ 0.0000675×10^{3}

9. If q is an odd integer greater than 1, what is the value of $(-1)^q + 1$?

   ⬭ -2

   ⬭ -1

   ⬭ 0

   ⬭ 2

   ⬭ It cannot be determined from the information given.

10. If $x > 0$, then $(4^x)(8^x) =$

   ⬭ 2^{9x}

   ⬭ 2^{8x}

   ⬭ 2^{6x}

   ⬭ 2^{5x}

   ⬭ 2^{4x}

11. If $5^n > 10{,}000$ and n is an integer, the smallest possible value of n is

   ⬭ 4

   ⬭ 5

   ⬭ 6

   ⬭ 7

   ⬭ 8

12. What positive number, when squared, is equal to the cube of the positive square root of 16?

   ⬭ 64

   ⬭ 56

   ⬭ 32

   ⬭ 8

   ⬭ 2

Advanced

13. Which of the following is(are) equal to 8^5 ?

    I. $2^5 \cdot 4^5$

    II. 2^{15}

    III. $2^5 \cdot 2^{10}$

    ○ II only

    ○ I and II only

    ○ I and III only

    ○ II and III only

    ○ I, II, and III

14. If $27^n = 9^4$, then $n =$

    ○ $\dfrac{4}{3}$

    ○ 2

    ○ $\dfrac{8}{3}$

    ○ 3

    ○ 8

15. If $xyz \neq 0$, then $\dfrac{x^3 y z^4}{x y^{-2} z^3} =$

    ○ $x^2 y^3 z$

    ○ $x^4 y^{-1} z^7$

    ○ $x^2 y^{-1} z$

    ○ $x^2 y^3 z^2$

    ○ $x^2 y z$

16. If line segments AB and CD have lengths of $10 + \sqrt{7}$ and $5 - \sqrt{7}$ respectively, AB is greater than CD by how much?

    ○ $5 - 2\sqrt{7}$

    ○ $5 + 2\sqrt{7}$

    ○ $15 + 2\sqrt{7}$

    ○ 5

    ○ 15

17. If $x^a \cdot x^b = 1$ and $x \neq \pm 1$, then $a + b =$

    ○ x

    ○ -1

    ○ 0

    ○ 1

    ○ It cannot be determined from the information given.

NUMBER OPERATIONS TEST
ANSWERS AND EXPLANATIONS

1. $3\frac{11}{25}$

We are asked to find the fractional equivalent of 3.44. Since there are two digits to the right of the decimal point, the denominator of the fractional part is 100.

$$3.44 = 3\frac{44}{100} = 3\frac{11}{25}$$

2. **0.43**

The first thing to do in this problem is to put both numbers into the same form. If we convert the $6\frac{3}{4}$ into decimal form, then we can easily subtract, since both numbers would be in decimal form. And, since our answer choices are all in decimal form, we'd need to do no further work. First, let's convert $\frac{3}{4}$ into a fraction with a denominator that is a power of 10 (e.g., 10, 100, 1000, etc.). If we multiply both the numerator and denominator of $\frac{3}{4}$ by 25, then our fraction becomes $\frac{75}{100}$, which is 0.75. So, $6\frac{3}{4}$ is equal to 6.75. Now we can subtract.

$$\begin{array}{r} 6.75 \\ -\ 6.32 \\ \hline 0.43 \end{array}$$

3. $1\frac{1}{2}$

We are asked for the sum of several decimals. Note that all answer choices are in fractional form. Line up the decimal points and add:

$$\begin{array}{r} 0.125 \\ 0.25 \\ 0.375 \\ 0.75 \\ \hline 1.500 = 1.5 = 1\frac{1}{2} \end{array}$$

Or, we could have converted all the decimals to fraction form first. It helps to know these basic conversions by heart.

$$0.125 = \frac{1}{8}, 0.25 = \frac{1}{4}, 0.375 = \frac{3}{8}, 0.75 = \frac{3}{4}.$$

So we add:

$$\frac{1}{8} + \frac{1}{4} + \frac{3}{8} + \frac{3}{4} = \frac{1}{4} + \frac{3}{4} + \frac{1}{8} + \frac{3}{8}$$

$$= 1 + \frac{4}{8}$$

$$= 1\frac{1}{2}$$

4. **0.1666**

We are asked which of the five values is less than $\frac{1}{6}$. Since $\frac{1}{6} = 0.166\overline{6}$ (the bar indicates that the six repeats), $0.1667 > \frac{1}{6}$. No good.

$\frac{3}{18} = \frac{1 \times 3}{6 \times 3} = \frac{1}{6}$. No good.

$0.167 > 0.16\overline{6}$ because the "7" in the third decimal place of 0.167 is greater than the "6" in the third decimal place of 0.16$\overline{6}$. No good.

0.1666 is less than 0.16666. Therefore, it is less than $\frac{1}{6}$, so this is the correct answer.

Just for practice:

$$\frac{1}{6} = \frac{8}{48} \text{ and } \frac{8}{47} > \frac{8}{48} \text{ ; therefore}$$

$$\frac{8}{47} > \frac{1}{6}. \text{ No good.}$$

5. 0.003

Let's start with the numerator. When we multiply decimals, the first step is to simply ignore the decimals and multiply the numbers as if they were whole numbers. The second step is to count the total number of places to the right of the decimal point in both numbers and then move the decimal point this many places to the **left** in our result.

$(0.02) \times (0.0003)$

$2 \times 3 = 6$

0.02   0.0003

2 places + 4 places = 6 places

so $(0.02) \times (0.0003) = 0.000006$

To divide 2 decimals, move the decimal point in both numbers as many places to the right as necessary to make the divisor (the number you're dividing by) a whole number. Then divide:

$$\frac{0.000006}{0.002} = \frac{0.006}{2} = 0.003$$

A better way of doing this is to cancel a factor of 0.002 from numerator and denominator. Since 0.02 is simply 10 times 0.002, we can simply rewrite our problem as 10 times 0.0003. Multiplying a decimal by 10 is the same as moving the decimal point 1 place to the right. So our result is 0.003. This method certainly requires much less calculating, and so it can lead you to be the answer more quickly. Look for ways to avoid extensive calculation.

6. $\dfrac{49}{24}$

There are 2 ways of doing this. One is to estimate the answer and the other is to actually add the fractions. Using the first approach, if the problem had us add $\dfrac{1}{8}$ instead of the $\dfrac{1}{6}$, then our problem would read

$1 + \dfrac{1}{2} + \dfrac{1}{4} + \dfrac{1}{8} + \dfrac{1}{8}$. If you're comfortable using these fractions you might see, with little effort, that this is simply 2. Since $\dfrac{1}{6}$ is actually slightly larger than $\dfrac{1}{8}$, our actual result must be slightly larger than 2. Looking at the answer choices, the only fraction in which the

numerator is more than twice the denom-inator, (in other words, the only value larger than 2) is $\dfrac{49}{24}$. Alternatively, we can simply find a common denominator for the fractions, convert them, and then add them. A quick glance at the answer choices suggests 24 as a common denominator. Converting the fractions we get:

$$\frac{24}{24} + \frac{12}{24} + \frac{6}{24} + \frac{4}{24} + \frac{3}{24} = \frac{49}{24}$$

7. 48

Turn this division problem into multiplication by applying the "invert and multiply" rule:

$$12 \text{ divided by } \frac{1}{4} = 12 \text{ times } \frac{4}{1} = 48$$

8. $\dfrac{1}{4}, \dfrac{3}{10}, \dfrac{9}{26}$

We need to arrange three fractions in ascending order. (Note that the same three fractions appear in each answer choice.)

Method I:

Convert to decimals: $\dfrac{1}{4} = 0.25$

$\dfrac{3}{10} = 0.3$. This is a little less than $\dfrac{1}{3}$, but more than $\dfrac{1}{4}$. $\dfrac{9}{26}$ is harder to express as a decimal, but $\dfrac{9}{26} > \dfrac{9}{27}$, and $\dfrac{9}{27}$ or $\dfrac{1}{3} > \dfrac{3}{10}$. Therefore, $\dfrac{9}{26} > \dfrac{3}{10}$. The correct ascending order is $\dfrac{1}{4}, \dfrac{3}{10}, \dfrac{9}{26}$.

Method II:

If you have trouble comparing fractions directly, try cross-multiplying. Here, we find that $\dfrac{1}{4} < \dfrac{3}{10}$ since $1 \times 10 < 3 \times 4$, and $\dfrac{3}{10} < \dfrac{9}{26}$ since $3 \times 26 < 9 \times 10$ (that is, 78 < 90).

9. $\dfrac{1}{25}$

We could perform the subtraction within the parentheses and then multiply, but it's simpler to use the distributive law.

$$\frac{7}{5} \cdot \left(\frac{3}{7} - \frac{2}{5}\right) = \frac{7}{5} \cdot \frac{3}{7} - \frac{7}{5} \cdot \frac{2}{5}$$

$$= \frac{3}{5} - \frac{14}{25}$$

$$= \frac{3}{5} \cdot \frac{5}{5} - \frac{14}{25}$$

$$= \frac{15}{25} - \frac{14}{25} = \frac{1}{25}$$

10. $\dfrac{3}{8}$

The easiest approach here is to find (quickly) which **two** choices are closest to 0.40—one larger, one smaller, and then find which of **those** is closer. Since $0.4 < \dfrac{1}{2}$, we can eliminate both $\dfrac{5}{9}$ and $\dfrac{4}{7}$—since they are each greater than $\dfrac{1}{2}$, they must be further from 0.4 than $\dfrac{1}{2}$ is.

On the other hand, $\dfrac{3}{8} < 0.4$ (the decimal equivalent of $\dfrac{3}{8}$ is 0.375), and since $\dfrac{1}{3} = \dfrac{3}{9} < \dfrac{3}{8}$, we can eliminate $\dfrac{1}{3}$.

So it comes down to $\dfrac{3}{8}$ or $\dfrac{1}{2}$. Since $\dfrac{3}{8} = 0.375$, it is 0.025 away from 0.4, which is much closer than $\dfrac{1}{2}$ (or 0.5, which is 0.1 away). So $\dfrac{3}{8}$ is the closest.

11. $\dfrac{1}{2}$

Method I:

$$\frac{\dfrac{1}{6} + \dfrac{1}{3} + 2}{\dfrac{3}{4} + \dfrac{5}{4} + 3} = \frac{\dfrac{1}{2} + 2}{\dfrac{8}{4} + 3}$$

$$= \frac{2\dfrac{1}{2}}{5} = \frac{5}{2} \div 5 = \frac{5}{2} \cdot \frac{1}{5} = \frac{1}{2}$$

Method II:

Multiply numerator and denominator by the least common multiple of all the denominators. Here, the LCM is 12:

$$\frac{12\left(\dfrac{1}{6} + \dfrac{1}{3} + 2\right)}{12\left(\dfrac{3}{4} + \dfrac{5}{4} + 3\right)}$$

$$\frac{2 + 4 + 24}{9 + 15 + 36} = \frac{30}{60} = \frac{1}{2}$$

12. I and III

In statement I, if we were to subtract a smaller number from 1,000, then our result will be a larger number. In general, the smaller the number you subtract, the larger the result will be. So, if we substitute 120 for 160 in this expression, our result would be greater. We can eliminate choices that do not include statement I.

Statement II is a little more tricky. Our expression is equivalent to $\dfrac{160}{161}$. If we were to replace each 160 with 120, our result would be $\dfrac{120}{1 + 120}$, which is $\dfrac{120}{121}$. Which is greater? Think of each fraction's distance from 1. Both fractions area tiny bit less than 1. Imagine a number line. $\dfrac{160}{161}$ is $\dfrac{1}{161}$ away from 1, while $\dfrac{120}{121}$ is $\dfrac{1}{121}$ away from 1. Since $\dfrac{1}{161}$ is less than $\dfrac{1}{121}$, that means that $\dfrac{160}{161}$ must be *closer* to 1 than $\dfrac{120}{121}$. And that means $\dfrac{160}{161}$ is a little larger than $\dfrac{120}{121}$. So if we did replace 160 with 120, we would get a smaller result. Eliminate the fourth choice. Statement III is even tougher. We're dividing 1 by a fraction. So we'll have to multiply 1 by the reciprocal of the fraction. In order to get a *larger* reciprocal, we need to start with a *smaller* fraction. So, which is smaller, $1 - \dfrac{1}{160}$ or $1 - \dfrac{1}{120}$? $1 - \dfrac{1}{120}$ is smaller since it is further to the left from 1 on the number line. So by replacing 160 with 120 we get a smaller fraction in the denominator of our expression and, therefore, a *larger* reciprocal. That will give the expression a larger value. So III is part of the correct answer.

13. $\dfrac{5}{36}$

Obviously, we have to start by picking out the largest and smallest fractions. $\dfrac{5}{9} > \dfrac{1}{2}$ and all the others are less than $\dfrac{1}{2}$, so $\dfrac{5}{9}$ is the greatest. The other four are close together,

but it's easy to find a common denominator for

$\dfrac{5}{12}, \dfrac{11}{24}$ and $\dfrac{23}{48}$. Convert everything to 48ths: $\dfrac{5}{12} = \dfrac{20}{48}$

and $\dfrac{11}{24} = \dfrac{22}{48}$, so $\dfrac{5}{12} < \dfrac{11}{24} < \dfrac{23}{48}$. Is $\dfrac{5}{12} < \dfrac{3}{7}$? Using

the cross-multiplication method, $7 \times 5 = 35$, and

$12 \times 3 = 36$, so $\dfrac{5}{12} < \dfrac{3}{7}$.

Now we have to find the difference between $\dfrac{5}{9}$ and $\dfrac{5}{12}$. Let's use the least common denominator, 36.

$$\frac{5}{9} \cdot \frac{4}{4} = \frac{20}{36}, \frac{5}{12} \cdot \frac{3}{3} = \frac{15}{36}$$
$$\frac{20}{36} - \frac{15}{36} = \frac{5}{36}$$

14. $y < z < x$

We're given $0.04x = 5y = 2z$. Let's change the decimal to a fraction and work from there:

$$0.04 = \frac{4}{100} \text{ or } \frac{1}{25}.$$

Therefore, $\dfrac{1}{25}x = 5y = 2z$. Multiply all the terms by 25 to eliminate the fraction in front of x.

$$x = 125y = 50z$$

Since all the terms are positive, we know that it takes more y's than z's to equal one x. Therefore, x is the biggest, followed by z, and y is the smallest.

15. 2

The answer choices are pretty far apart, so we can estimate with impunity.

$\dfrac{59.376 \times 7.094}{31.492 \times 6.429}$ is about $\dfrac{60 \times 7}{30 \times 6}$, or roughly 2.

NUMBER PROPERTIES TEST
ANSWERS AND EXPLANATIONS

1. Eight

Here we're asked for the odd integers between $\frac{10}{3}$ and $\frac{62}{3}$. First let's be clearer about this range. $\frac{10}{3}$ is the same as $3\frac{1}{3}$, and $\frac{62}{3}$ is the same as $20\frac{2}{3}$. So we need to count the odd integers between $3\frac{1}{3}$ and $20\frac{2}{3}$. Well, we can't include 3 since 3 is less than $3\frac{1}{3}$. Similarly, we can't include 21 since it's larger than $20\frac{2}{3}$. So the odd integers in the appropriate range are 5, 7, 9, 11, 13, 15, 17, and 19. That's a total of 8.

2. 18

To answer this question, it is most efficient just to try each answer choice. When asked to choose the "greatest" number that fulfills the given conditions, start with the biggest answer choice. (When asked to choose the "least" number, start with the smallest answer choice.) 27 is indeed a factor of 54—it is exactly half of 54—but it is not among the factors of 36, and so choice (5) is not the correct answer. The next largest choice, 18, divides into 54 exactly three times and into 36 exactly two times, and so this is the correct answer.

3. 32

One way to do this problem is to find the prime factorization of 168:

$$168 = 2 \cdot 84$$
$$= 2 \cdot 2 \cdot 42$$
$$= 2 \cdot 2 \cdot 6 \cdot 7$$
$$= 2 \cdot 2 \cdot 2 \cdot 3 \cdot 7$$

Now we can go through the answer choices. We've already seen that 42 is a factor of 168, and 21 is a factor of 42, so 21 is also a factor of 168. This eliminates choices (1) and (5). Choice (2), 24, is $8 \cdot 3$ or $2 \cdot 2 \cdot 2 \cdot 3$, so it's also a factor of 168. Choice (3), 28, is $4 \cdot 7$ or $2 \cdot 2 \cdot 7$, so 28 is a factor of 168. That leaves only choice

(4). Indeed, 32 has five factors of 2, which is more factors of 2 than 168 has.

4. 660

We know from our divisibility rules that multiples of 2, 3, and 5 all have certain easily recognizable characteristics. All multiples of 5 end with the digits 5 or 0. All multiples of 2 have an even number in the units place. Therefore, any number that is divisible by both 2 and 5 must end with the digit 0. If a number is a multiple of 3, the sum of its digits is a multiple of 3. Of our five choices, we can eliminate (1) and (3) because their last digits are not 0. Now add up the digits in each of the remaining answer choices to see whether they are multiples of 3. For (2), $5 + 6 + 0 = 11$, so 560 is not a multiple of 3. For (4), $6 + 2 + 0 = 8$, so 620 is not a multiple of 3 either. For (5), $6 + 6 + 0 = 12$, so 660 is a multiple of 3. That is the correct answer.

5. 63

In this question, we need to find the smallest integer divisible by both 9 and 21. The fastest method is to start with the smallest answer choice and test each one for divisibility. Choice (5) is clearly divisible by 21, but not by 9. Similarly, choice (4) is just 2×21, but it is not divisible by 9. Choice (3), 63, is divisible by both 21 ($21 \times 3 = 63$) and 9 ($9 \times 7 = 63$). A more mathematical approach is to find the prime factors of 9 and 21, and, by eliminating shared factors, find the **least common multiple**. Breaking each into prime factors:

$$21 = 3 \times 7$$
$$9 = 3 \times 3$$

We can drop one factor of 3 from the 9, since it is already present in the factors of 21. The least common multiple is $3 \times 3 \times 7$, or 63.

6. 2

If the sum of three numbers is even, how many of the three are even? Either all three or exactly one of the three must be even. The sum of three odd numbers can **never** be even, nor can the sum of one odd and two evens. Remember though—we're dealing with three different **prime** numbers. There's only one even prime, 2; all the rest are odd. Therefore, only one of our group can be even, and that must be 2. Since 2 is the smallest prime, it must also be the smallest of the three.

7.   I and III only

Let's try each possibility to see in which case(s) $A^2=C$.

I: If $A = -1$, then $B = 0$ and $C = 1$. $(-1)^2 = 1$. This works.

II: If $A = 0$, then $B = 1$, and $C = 2$. $(0)^2 \neq 2$. No good.

III: If $A = 2$, then $B = 3$, and $C = 4$. $(2)^2 = 4$. This works.

Only I and III satisfy the conditions.

8. $2n + 2$

The simplest approach here is to pick a sample odd value for n, such as 3. If we plug 3 into an expression and get an odd result, then we know that answer choice cannot be right. (We want the one that is even for **any** odd value.)

$$\frac{n - 1}{2} = \frac{3 - 1}{2} = \frac{2}{2} = 1. \text{ Not even.}$$

$$\frac{n + 1}{2} = \frac{3 + 1}{2} = \frac{4}{2} = 2. \text{ Even.}$$

Try another value, such as 1.

$$\frac{1 + 1}{2} = \frac{2}{2} = 1. \text{ So this doesn't \textbf{have} to be even.}$$

$n^2 + 2n = (3)^2 + 2(3) = 9 + 6 = 15$. No. $2n + 2 = 2(3) + 2 = 6 + 2 = 8$. Even. We could try some more values for n here or just use logic: If we double an odd number we get an even result, and if we then add 2, we still have an even number. So this will always be even, and is our answer.

Just for practice:

$3n^2 - 2n = 3(3)^2 - 2(3) = 21$. No.

9.   121

We are asked for the smallest positive integer that leaves a remainder of 1 when divided by 6, 8 or 10. In other words, if we find the smallest integer that is a common multiple of these three numbers, we can add 1 to that number to get our answer. Subtracting 1 from each of our choices gives us 20, 40, 120, 240, and 480. Our best tactic is to work from the smallest up until we get our answer. All are multiples of 10, but 20 is not a multiple of 6 or 8, and 40 is not a multiple of 6; 120 is a multiple of 6 (6×20), 8 (8×15), and 10 (10×12). One more than 120 is 121. Answer choice (3), 121, is thus the smallest number to leave a remainder of 1.

An alternative approach is to find the least common multiple of 6, 8, and 10, and then add 1 to it. Look at their prime factors:

$$6 = 2 \times 3$$
$$8 = 2 \times 2 \times 2$$
$$10 = 2 \times 5$$

So a common multiple must have three factors of 2 (6 and 10 only need one factor, but 8 needs all three), one factor of 3, and one factor of 5.

$$2 \times 2 \times 2 \times 3 \times 5 = 120; 120 + 1 = 121$$

10. The square of either integer is an odd number.

If the product of two integers is odd, then both of the integers must themselves be odd, since just one even factor would make a product even. If we add two odd numbers, we get an even number, and if we subtract an odd number from an odd number, we again get an even number. (For instance, $5 + 3 = 8$; $5 - 3 = 2$.) Choices (1) and (2) are therefore wrong. The square of any odd number is odd (since the square is an odd times an odd), so choice (3) is correct. Since these squares are always odd, if we add them together or subtract one from the other, we get an even number.

11. 8

Since $\dfrac{130}{x}$ will be an integer whenever x evenly divides

into 130, we want to find all the positive integer divisors

(or factors) of 130.

Method I: *Factor pairs*

Let's start by looking for factor pairs. This is easy at first:

$$130 = 1 \cdot 130 = 2 \cdot 65 = 5 \cdot 26 = 10 \cdot 13$$

Are there any more? Do we have to check all the integers from 1 to 130? No. We only have to try integers less than the square root of 130. For any integer x, you can find the smaller integer of its factor pairs by checking the integers up to the square root of x. The square root of 130 is a little less than 12, and it turns out that we've already found all four factor pairs: 1 and 130, 2 and 65, 5 and 26, 10 and 13. There are 8 positive factors of 130.

Method II: *Prime Factoring*

Factor 130 into primes. $130 = 2 \cdot 65 = 2 \cdot 5 \cdot 13$. These three numbers obviously divide 130 evenly, but they are not the only ones. All combinations of these primes will also divide 130 evenly. The combinations are 2, 5, 13, $2 \cdot 5$, $2 \cdot 13$, $5 \cdot 13$, and $2 \cdot 5 \cdot 13$. Don't forget 1—it's also a factor (although **not** a prime). It is not necessary to multiply these products out—we know they are all different. There are a total of 8 factors.

12. 9

First we have to identify the pattern. It consists of the same 6 numerals, 0, 9, 7, 5, 3, and 1, in that order, repeating infinitely. Our job is to identify the 44th digit to the right of the decimal point. Since the patter of 6 numerals will continually repeat, every 6th digit, of the digits to the right of the decimal point, will be the same, namely the numeral 1. So 1 will be the 6th, 12th, 18th, 24th (and so on) digit. Since 44 is just 2 more than 42, which is a multiple of 6, the 44th digit will be the digit 2 places to the right of 1. Well, that's 9.

13. 6

The easiest approach is to work with actual numbers. Let's take 0 and the first two positive even numbers.

(Remember: 0 is even.) Their sum is $0 + 2 + 4 = 6$. Of the answer choices, only (1), (2), and (3) divide evenly into 6. Try another group of three: $2 + 4 + 6 = 12$. Again, 2, 3, and 6 divide evenly into 12. The next group is $4 + 6 + 8 = 18$. By now you should notice that the sums are all multiples of 6. Six will always divide evenly into the sum of 3 consecutive even integers.

14. 321

The hard way to do this problem is to find the exact values of the three consecutive integers, then find the next three, and then add. There's a shorter way, though. Suppose we call the three original integers x, $x + 1$, and $x + 2$. Their sum is 312, so
$x + (x + 1) + (x + 2) = 312$ or $3x + 3 = 312$. The **next** three integers are $x + 3$, $x + 4$, and $x + 5$. What is the value of $(x + 3) + (x + 4) + (x + 5)$? It's $3x + 12$. $3x + 12$ is 9 greater than $3x + 3$. $3x + 3 = 312$, so $3x + 12 = 312 + 9$, or 312.

15. When divided by 2, P will leave a remainder of 1.

We need to find the one choice that isn't **always** true. To find it, let's test each choice. Choice (1) is always true: since $P \div 9$ has a remainder of 4, P is 4 greater than some multiple of 9. And if $P - 4$ is a multiple of 9, then the next multiple of 9 would be $(P - 4) + 9$, or $P + 5$; thus choice (2) is also true. With choice (3), we know that since $P - 4$ is multiple of 9, it is also a multiple of 3. By adding 3s, we know that $(P - 4) + 3$, or $P - 1$, and $(P - 4) + 3 + 3$, or $P + 2$, are also multiples of 3. Choice (3) must be true. And since $P - 1$ is a multiple of 3, when P is divided by 3, it will have a remainder of 1, and choice (4) is always true.

This only leaves choice (5). In simpler terms, choice (5) states that P is always odd. Since multiples of 9 are alternately odd and even (9, 18, 27, 36 . . .), $P - 4$ could either be even or odd, so P also could be either even or odd. Choice (5) is not always true, so it is the correct answer choice.

16. One of the two integers is odd and the other is even.

If two numbers have an even product, at least one of the numbers is even, so we can eliminate choice (1).

If both numbers were even, their sum would be even, but we know the sum of these numbers is odd, so we can eliminate choice (2). If one number is odd and the other is even, their product is even and their sum is odd. Choice (3) gives us what we're looking for. Choices (4) and (5) both can be true, but they're not necessarily true.

17. II and III only

Since these four integers have an even product, at least one of them must be even, so roman numeral I, 0, is impossible. Is it possible for exactly 2 of the 4 to be even? If there are 2 odds and 2 evens, the sum is even, since odd + odd = even and even + even = even. Also, if there's at least 1 even among the integers, the product is even, so roman numeral II **is** possible. Similarly, roman numeral III gives an even product and even sum, so our answer is II and III only.

18. 72

The wire can be divided into three equal parts, each with integral length, so the minimum length must be a multiple of 3. Unfortunately, all of the answer choices are multiples of 3. One of those 3 pieces is cut into 8 pieces, again all with integer lengths, so the length of the wire must be at least 3 · 8 or 24. Another of those three segments is cut into 6 pieces. Now, what does that mean? Each third can be divided into either 6 or 8 segments with integer lengths. In other words, the thirds have an integer length evenly divisible by both 6 and 8. The smallest common multiple of 6 and 8 is 24, so the minimum length of the wire is 3 · 24 or 72.

19. Five

Here we want to determine, basically, how many numbers between 0 and 60 are even multiples of 5. Well, all even multiples of 5 must be multiples of 10. So, the multiples of 10 between 0 and 60 are 10, 20, 30, 40, and 50. That's 5 altogether.

AVERAGES TEST
ANSWERS AND EXPLANATIONS

1. 25

We can plug everything we are given into the standard formula for an average of two numbers and then solve for a. Since we know the average of -5 and a is 10:

$$\frac{\text{Sum of numbers}}{\text{Number of numbers}} = \text{Average of numbers}$$

$$\frac{-5 + a}{2} = 10$$

$$-5 + a = 20 \text{ (multiply both sides by 2)}$$

$$a = 20 + 5 \text{ (add 5 to both sides)}$$

$$a = 25$$

A much faster method is to think in terms of balance: Since -5 is 15 less than the average, a must be 15 **more** than the average, or $10 + 15 = 25$.

2. $\frac{3}{8}$

Our formula's no different just because we are working with fractions: The average is still the sum divided by the number of values.

$$\text{Average} = \frac{\frac{1}{2} + \frac{1}{4}}{2} = \frac{\frac{2}{4} + \frac{1}{4}}{2} = \frac{\frac{3}{4}}{2}$$

$$= \frac{3}{4} \cdot \frac{1}{2} = \frac{3}{8}$$

Notice that the average of $\frac{1}{2}$ and $\frac{1}{4}$ is **not** $\frac{1}{3}$.

3. 60

This problem is easier than it may appear. Here we're told the average of 4 numbers and asked for the sum of these 4 numbers. Well, we can rearrange the average formula so that it reads:

$$\text{Sum} = \text{Number of terms} \times \text{Average.}$$
$$\text{sum} = 4 \times 15$$
$$\text{sum} = 60$$

The whole business of p and the value of 3 of the numbers was unnecessary to solving the problem.

4. 18

The average of evenly spaced numbers is the middle number. The average of 6 such numbers lies halfway between the third and fourth numbers.

Since $18\frac{1}{2}$ is the average, the third number must be 18 and the fourth number 19. The six numbers are

$$16 \quad 17 \quad 18 \quad 19 \quad 20 \quad 21$$

Since the first five numbers are also evenly spaced, their average will be the middle, or third number: 18.

5. 7

To average 2 hours a day over 6 days, the violinist must practice 2×6, or 12 hours. From Monday through Friday, the violinist practices 5 hours, 1 hour each day. To total 12 hours, she must practice $12 - 5$, or 7 hours, on Saturday.

6. 4

If six numbers have an average of 6, their sum is $6 \cdot 6$ or 36. When we subtract 3 from four of the numbers, we subtract $4 \cdot 3$ or 12 from the sum. The new sum is $36 - 12$ or 24, so the new average is $24 \div 6$ or 4.

7. 60

The average of any 5 numbers is $\frac{1}{5}$ of the sum, so if these 5 numbers have an average of 12, their sum is $5 \cdot 12$ or 60. Note that the information about consecutive even numbers is irrelevant to solving the problem. **Any** group of five numbers whose average is 12 will have a sum of 60.

8. $+5°$

If the average temperature over 4 days is $+4°$, the sum of the daily noon temperatures must be $4 \cdot (+4°)$ or $+16°$.

Over the first three days, the sum is $(+9°) + (−6°) + (+8°)$ or $+11°$. On the fourth day, the temperature at noon must be $+5°$ to bring the sum up to $+16°$ and the average, in turn, up to $+4°$.

9. 93

Jerry's average score was 85. His total points for the three tests is the same as if he had scored 85 on each of the tests: $85 + 85 + 85$, or 255. He wants to average 87 over four tests, so his total must be $87 + 87 + 87 + 87 = 348$. The difference between his total score after three tests and the total that he needs after four tests is $348 − 255$ or 93. Jerry needs a 93 to raise his average over the four tests to 87.

Another way of thinking about the problem is to think in terms of "balancing" the average around 87. Imagine Jerry has three scores of 85. Each of the first three is 2 points below the average of 87. So together, the first three tests are a total of 6 points below the average. To balance the average at 87, the score on the fourth test will have to be 6 points more than 87, or 93.

10. $n + 1\frac{1}{2}$

Don't let the n's in the numbers bother you; the arithmetic we perform is the same.

Method I:

Add the terms and divide by the number of terms. Since each term contains n, we can ignore the n and add it back at the end. Without the n's, we get

$$\frac{0 + 1 + 2 + 3}{4} = \frac{6}{4} = 1\frac{1}{2}$$

The average is $n + 1\frac{1}{2}$.

Method II:

These are just evenly spaced numbers (regardless of what n is). Since there are four of them, the average is between the second and third terms: midway between $n + 1$ and $n + 2$, or $n + 1\frac{1}{2}$.

11. −4

The fastest way to solve this problem is to recognize that $x + 2, x + 4$, and $x + 6$ are evenly spaced

numbers, so the average equals the middle value, $x + 4$. We're told that the average of these values is zero, so:

$$x + 4 = 0$$
$$x = −4$$

12. 1,000

The key to this problem is that the total theater attendance stays the same after six theaters close. No matter how many theaters there are:

Total attendance = (Number of theaters) × (Average attendance)

We know that originally there are 15 theaters, and they average 600 customers per day. Plug these values into the formula above to find the total theater attendance:

Total attendance = $(15)(600) = 9,000$

Even after the six theaters close, the total attendance remains the same. Now, though, the number of theaters is only 9:

$$\text{New average attendance} = \frac{\text{Total attendance}}{\text{New number of theaters}}$$
$$= \frac{9,000}{9}$$
$$= 1,000$$

13. 517

The average of a group of evenly spaced numbers is equal to the middle number. Here there is an even number of terms (18), so the average is between the two middle numbers, the 9th and 10th terms. This tells us that the **9th** consecutive odd integer here will be the first odd integer less than 534, which is **533**. Once we have the **9th** term, we can count backward to find the first.

10th	Average		9th	8th	7th
535	534		533	531	529
6th	5th	4th	3rd	2nd	1st
527	525	523	521	519	517

14. $75.35

This is a good opportunity to use the "balance" method. We're told the average closing price for all 5 days: $75.50. We're also given the closing prices for the first 4 days. Using the "balance" method we make the fifth day "balance out" the first 4:

Monday	$75.58	average + $0.08
Tuesday	$75.63	average + $0.13
Wednesday	$75.42	average − $0.08
Thursday	$75.52	average + $0.02
after 4 days		average + $0.15

To make the values "balance out" the fifth day must be (average − $0.15) or $75.35.

15. 4

We can't find individual values for any of these six numbers. However, with the given information we can find the sum of the six numbers, and the sum of just the largest and smallest. Subtracting the sum of the smallest and largest from the sum of all six will leave us with the sum of the four others, from which we can find *their* average.

The sum of all six numbers is (average of all 6 numbers) × (number of values) = 5 × 6, or 30.

The sum of the greatest and smallest can be found in the same way: 2 × average = 2 × 7 = 14. The sum of the other 4 numbers is (the sum of all six) − (the sum of the greatest and smallest) = (30 − 14) = 16.

The sum of the other four numbers is 16. Their average is $\frac{16}{4}$ or 4.

16. 12

The key to doing this problem is to link what we're given to what we need to find. We need to solve for the average of $a + 3$, $b − 5$, and 6. If we could determine their sum, then all we'd need to do is divide this sum by 3 to find their average. Well, we don't know a and b, but we can determine their sum. We are given the average of a, b and 7. Clearly we can figure out the sum of these 3 values by multiplying the average by the number of terms. 13 times 3 = 39. That allows us to determine the sum of a and b. If $a + b + 7 = 39$, then $a + b = 39 − 7$, or 32. Now, remember we're asked for the average of $a + 3$, $b − 5$ and 6. The sum of these expressions can be rewritten as $a + b + 3 − 5 + 6$, or, as $a + b + 4$. If $a + b = 32$, then $a + b + 4 = 32 + 4$, or 36. Therefore, the sum is 36 and the number of terms is 3, so the average is $\frac{36}{3}$, or 12.

RATIOS TEST
ANSWERS AND EXPLANATIONS

1. 3 : 8

We are asked for the ratio of cats to hamsters.

Cats : hamsters $= 9 : 24 = \dfrac{9}{24}$. Reduce the numerator

and denominator by a factor of 3. Thus, $\dfrac{9}{24} = \dfrac{3}{8} = 3 : 8$.

For every 3 cats there are 8 hamsters.

2. 39

Since the ratio of boys to girls is 5 : 3, we know that the number of boys divided by the number of girls must equal five-thirds. And we know that the number of boys equal 65. This is enough information to set up a **proportion**. We know that:

$$\frac{65}{\text{\# of girls}} = \frac{5}{3}$$

In place of "# of girls," let's put "G":

$$\frac{65}{G} = \frac{5}{3}$$

At this point, you might realize that since 65 equals 13 times 5, and the two fractions are equivalent, G must equal 13×3, or 39. Or you can simply cross-multiply $\dfrac{65}{G} = \dfrac{5}{3}$, which gives you:

$$65 \times 3 = 5 \times G$$

Divide by 5: $\quad \dfrac{65 \times 3}{5} = G$

Cancel: $\quad 13 \times 3 = G$

$$G = 39$$

3. $2\dfrac{1}{3}$

In this question, the ratio is implied: for every $\dfrac{3}{4}$ inch of map there is one real mile, so the ratio of inches to the miles they represent is always $\dfrac{3}{4}$ to 1.

Therefore, we can set up the proportion:

$$\frac{\text{\# of inches}}{\text{\# of miles}} = \frac{\frac{3}{4}}{1} = \frac{3}{4}$$

Now $1\dfrac{3}{4}$ inches $= \dfrac{7}{4}$ inches.

Set up a proportion $\dfrac{\frac{7}{4} \text{ inches}}{\text{\# of miles}} = \dfrac{3}{4}$

Cross-multiply: $\quad \dfrac{7}{4} \times 4 = 3 \times \text{\# of miles}$

$$7 = 3 \times \text{\# of miles}$$

$$\frac{7}{3} = \text{\# of miles}$$

or $\qquad\qquad 2\dfrac{1}{3} = \text{\# of miles}$

4. $240

If the man has spent $\dfrac{5}{12}$ of his salary, then he has left $1 - \dfrac{5}{12}$, or $\dfrac{7}{12}$ of his salary. So $140 represents $\dfrac{7}{12}$ of his salary. Set up a proportion, using S to represent his salary:

$$\frac{7}{12} = \frac{140}{S}$$

Cross-multiply: $\quad 7S = 12 \times 140$

$$S = \frac{12 \times 140}{7}$$

$$= 240$$

5. 600

The ratio of parts is 4 : 3 : 2, making a total of 9 parts. Since 9 parts are equal to 1,800 votes, each part represents 1,800 ÷ 9, or 200 votes. Since Ms. Frau represents 3 parts, she received a total of 3 × 200, or 600 votes. (Another way to think about it: Out of every 9 votes, Ms. Frau gets 3, which is $\frac{3}{9}$ or $\frac{1}{3}$ of the total number of votes. $\frac{1}{3}$ of 1,800 is 600.) We could also have solved it algebraically, by setting up a proportion, with F as Ms. Frau's votes

$$\frac{3}{9} = \frac{F}{1,800}$$

$$\frac{3}{9} \times 1,800 = F$$

$$600 = F$$

6. 48

We are given the ratio of men to women at a party, and the total number of people. To find the number of women, we need the ratio of the number of women to the total number of people. If the ratio of men to women is 3 : 2, then for every 5 people, 3 are men and 2 are women. So the ratio of women to total people is 2 : 5. Since 120 people are at the party, $\frac{2}{5} \times 120$, or 48 of them are women.

7. 3,600

We are given a part-to-part ratio and total; we need to convert the ratio to a part-to-whole ratio. If the weights are in the ratio of 5 : 9, then the larger ship represents $\frac{9}{5 + 9}$ or $\frac{9}{14}$ of the total weight. We're told this total weight is 5,600 tons, so the larger ship must weigh

$$\frac{9}{14} \times 5,600 = 9 \times 400 = 3,600 \text{ tons}$$

8. 3 : 8

Before we deal with the laboratory rabbits, think about this. Suppose the ratio of men to women in a room is 2 : 1. The number of women in the room is $\frac{1}{2 + 1}$ or $\frac{1}{3}$ of the total.

Therefore, the total number of people must be a multiple of 3—otherwise we'll end up with fractional people. (Note that this is only true because the ratio was expressed in lowest terms. We could also express a 2 : 1 ratio as 6 : 3, but that doesn't imply that the total must be some multiple of 9. Ratios on the GRE will usually be expressed in lowest terms, so you need not to worry about that too much.)

Returning to our problem, we see that we have 55 rabbits, and presumably want to avoid partial rabbits. The sum of the terms in the ratio must be a factor of 55. There are only four factors of 55 : 1, 5, 11, and 55. The only answer choice that fits this condition is choice (2): the sum of the terms in a 3 : 8 ratio is 11. We can quickly see why the other answer choices wouldn't work. In choice (1), for example, the ratio of white to brown rabbits is 1 : 3. If this were true, the total number of rabbits would be a multiple of 4 (that is, of 1 + 3). Since 55 isn't a multiple of 4, this can't possibly be the ratio we need. Similarly, the ratios in the other wrong choices are impossible.

9. 3,500

If **two**-fifths of Consolidated's output (the bricks produced by the Greenpoint factory) was 1,400 tons, **one**-fifth must have been half as much, or 700 tons. The entire output for 1991 was **five**-fifths or five times as much: 5 × 700 or 3,500 tons.

10. 13 to 21

We are asked which of five ratios is equivalent to the ratio of $3\frac{1}{4}$ to $5\frac{1}{4}$. Since the ratios in the answer choices are expressed in whole numbers, turn this ratio into whole numbers:

$$3\frac{1}{4} : 5\frac{1}{4} = \frac{13}{4} : \frac{21}{4} = \frac{\frac{13}{4}}{\frac{21}{4}} = \frac{13}{4} \times \frac{4}{21}$$

$$= \frac{13}{21} \text{ or } 13 : 21$$

11. 2 : 3

If $\frac{3}{5}$ of the ship is above water, then the rest of the ship,

or $\frac{5}{5} - \frac{3}{5} = \frac{2}{5}$ of the ship must be below water. Then the

ratio of the submerged weight to the exposed weight is

$\frac{2}{5} : \frac{3}{5} = 2 : 3$.

12. 570

If **one**-twentieth of the entrants were prize winners, the number of entrants was **twenty**-twentieths or 20 times the number of prize winners. $20 \times 30 = 600$. This is the **total** number of entrants. All but 30 of these entrants went away empty-handed. $600 - 30 = 570$.

13. $\frac{5}{11}$

Here we can set up a direct proportion:

$$\frac{1 \text{ kilogram}}{2.2 \text{ pounds}} = \frac{x \text{ kilograms}}{1 \text{ pound}}$$

Cross-multiply (the units drop out):

$$1 \times 1 = 2.2(x)$$
$$x = \frac{1}{2.2} = \frac{10}{22} = \frac{5}{11}$$

If you have trouble setting up the proportion, you could use the answer choices to your advantage and take an educated guess. Since 2.2 pounds equals a kilogram, a pound must be a little less than $\frac{1}{2}$ a kilogram. Of the

possible answers, $\frac{11}{5}$ is over 2; $\frac{5}{8}$ is over $\frac{1}{2}$; $\frac{1}{3}$ and $\frac{1}{5}$

seem too small. But $\frac{5}{11}$ is just under $\frac{1}{2}$, and so it should

be the correct answer.

14. 16

Start by putting everything in the same units:

$$6 \text{ quarts} = 6 \text{ quarts} \times \frac{4 \text{ cups}}{1 \text{ quart}} = 24 \text{ cups}$$

Now set up the ratios: the ratio of eggs to milk stays the same, so

$$\frac{2 \text{ eggs}}{3 \text{ cups}} = \frac{x \text{ eggs}}{24 \text{ cups}}$$

Cross-multiply:
$$2 \cdot 24 = 3x$$
$$2 \cdot 8 = x$$
$$x = 16$$

15. 36

The ratio 5 boys to 3 girls tells you that for every 5 boys in the class there must be 3 girls in the class. If there happen to be 5 boys in the class, then there must be 3 girls in the class. If there are 10 boys, then there will be 6 girls; 15 boys means 9 girls, and so on. The total number of students in the class would be 8, 16, or 24 in these three cases. Notice that all these sums are multiples of 8, since the smallest possible total is $5 + 3$ or 8. Any other total must be a multiple of 8. Since 36 is not divisible by 8 (it's the only answer choice that isn't), 36 cannot be the total number of students.

16. $\frac{1}{3}$

The grade is decided by 4 quizzes and 1 exam. Since the exam counts twice as much as each quiz, the exam equals two quizzes, so we can say the grade is decided by the equivalent of 4 quizzes and 2 quizzes, or 6 quizzes. The exam equaled two quizzes, so it represents $\frac{2}{6}$ or $\frac{1}{3}$ of the grade.

17. 25

Since the ratio of cement to gravel to sand is 3 : 5 : 7, for every 3 portions of cement we put in, we get $3 + 5 + 7$ or 15 portions of the mixture. Therefore, the recipe gives us $\frac{15}{3}$ or 5 times as much mixture as cement. We have 5 tons of cement available, so we can make 5×5 or 25 tons of the mixture.

18. 24

The time it takes to complete the entire exam is the sum of the time spent on the first half of the exam and the time spent on the second half. We know the time spent on the first half is $\frac{2}{3}$ of the time spent on the second half. If we let S represent the time spent on the second half, then the total time spent is $\frac{2}{3}S + S$ or $\frac{5}{3}S$. We know this total time is one hour or 60 minutes. So set up a simple equation and solve for S.

$$\frac{5}{3}S = 60$$

$$\frac{3}{5} \cdot \frac{5}{3}S = 60 \cdot \frac{3}{5}$$

$$S = 36$$

So the second half takes 36 minutes. The first half takes $\frac{2}{3}$ of this, or 24 minutes. (You could also find the first half by subtracting 36 minutes from the total time, 60 minutes.)

19. $\frac{1}{3}$

This problem might seem confusing at first, but is not too bad if you work methodically. What we need is the fraction of the unskilled workers that are not apprentices; to find this we need the number of unskilled workers and the number of non-apprentice unskilled workers. There are 2,700 workers total; one-third of them are unskilled, giving us $2{,}700 \times \frac{1}{3} = 900$ unskilled workers. 600 of **them** are apprentices, so the remaining $900 - 600$, or 300 are not apprentices. Then the fraction of unskilled workers that are not apprentices is $\frac{300}{900} = \frac{1}{3}$.

20. 50

Every 8 pounds of the alloy has 6 pounds of copper and 2 pounds of tin. Therefore, $\frac{2}{8}$ or $\frac{1}{4}$ of the alloy is tin. To make 200 pounds of the alloy, we need $\frac{1}{4} \times 200$ or 50 pounds of tin.

21. 300

We can solve this algebraically. Let the number of yellow balls received be x. Then the number of white balls received is 30 more than this, or $x + 30$.

$$\text{So } \frac{\text{\# of white balls}}{\text{\# of yellow balls}} = \frac{6}{5} = \frac{x + 30}{x}$$

Cross-multiply: $6x = 5(x + 30)$

Solve for x: $6x = 5x + 150$

$$x = 150$$

Since the number of white balls ordered equals the number of yellow balls ordered, the total number of balls ordered is $2x$, which is 2×150, or 300.

We could also solve this more intuitively.

The store originally ordered an equal number of white and yellow balls; they ended up with a white to yellow ratio of $6 : 5$. This means for every 5 yellow balls, they got 6 white balls, or they got $\frac{1}{5}$ more white balls than yellow balls. The difference between the number of white balls and the number of yellow balls is just the 30 extra white balls they got. So 30 balls represents $\frac{1}{5}$ of the number of yellow balls. Then the number of yellow balls is 5×30 or 150. Since they ordered the same number of white balls as yellow balls, they also ordered 150 white balls, for a total order of $150 + 150$ or 300 balls.

22. $\frac{1}{3}$

Method I:

We want to eliminate the b's and c's. We start with $a = 2b$. Since $\frac{1}{2}b = c$, we see that $b = 2c$. Then $a = 2(2c) = 4c$. But $4c = 3d$, which means that $a = 3d$. If a is 3 times d, then $\frac{a}{d} = \frac{3}{1}$, or $\frac{d}{a} = \frac{1}{3}$.

Method II:

We're looking for the ratio of d to a, or in other words, the value of the fraction $\frac{d}{a}$. Notice that we can use successive cancellations and write:

$$\frac{d}{a} = \frac{b^1}{a} \times \frac{c^1}{b_1} \times \frac{d}{c_1}$$

Find values for each of the fractions $\frac{b}{a}$, $\frac{c}{b}$, and $\frac{d}{c}$.

$$a = 2b, \text{ so } \frac{b}{a} = \frac{1}{2}$$

$$\frac{1}{2}b = c, \text{ so } \frac{c}{b} = \frac{1}{2}$$

$$4c = 3d, \text{ so } \frac{d}{c} = \frac{4}{3}$$

Now substitute these values into the equation above.

$$\frac{d}{a} = \frac{b}{a} \times \frac{c}{b} \times \frac{d}{c}$$
$$= \frac{1}{2} \times \frac{1}{2} \times \frac{4}{3}$$
$$= \frac{4}{12} = \frac{1}{3}$$

Method III:

And, if all of this algebra confuses you, you can also solve this problem by picking a value for a. Then, by using the relationship given, determine what value d must have and hence the value of $\frac{d}{a}$.

Since terms have coefficients of 2, 3, and 4, it's best to pick a number that's a multiple of 2, 3, and 4. Then we're less likely to have to deal with calculations involving fractions. Say a is 12. Since $a = 2b$, then $b = 6$. Since $\frac{1}{2}b = c$, $c = 3$. Finally, if $4c = 3d$, we get $4 \times 3 = 3d$, or $d = 4$. Then the ratio of d to a is $\frac{4}{12}$, or $\frac{1}{3}$.

23. $4

In each case the examination and the frames are the same; the difference in cost must be due to a difference in the costs of the lenses. Since plastic lenses cost four times as much as glass lenses, the **difference** in cost must be **three** times the cost of the glass lenses.

$$\text{Difference in cost} = \text{Cost of plastic} - \text{Cost of glass}$$
$$s = 4(\text{cost of glass}) - 1(\text{cost of glass})$$
$$= 3(\text{cost of glass})$$

The difference in cost is $42 - 30$, or $12. Since this is 3 times the cost of the glass lenses, the glass lenses must cost $\frac{\$12}{3}$, or $4.

24. 3 : 4

In this question we cannot determine the **number** of white mice or gray mice, but we can still determine their ratio.

Since $\frac{1}{2}$ of the white mice make up $\frac{1}{8}$ of the total mice, the **total** number of white mice must be double $\frac{1}{8}$ of the total number of mice, or $\frac{1}{4}$ of the total number of mice. Algebraically, if $\frac{1}{2} \times W = \frac{1}{8} \times T$, then $W = \frac{1}{4} \times T$. So $\frac{1}{4}$ of the total mice are white. Similarly, since $\frac{1}{3}$ of the number of gray mice is $\frac{1}{9}$ of the total number of mice, $3 \times \frac{1}{9}$ of all the mice, or $\frac{1}{3}$ of all the mice are gray mice. Therefore, the ratio of white mice to gray mice is $\frac{1}{4} : \frac{1}{3}$, which is the same as $\frac{3}{12} : \frac{4}{12}$ or 3:4.

PERCENTS TEST
ANSWERS AND EXPLANATIONS

1. 90

Method I:

We want 200% more than 30; 200% more than 30 is
30 + (200% of 30):

$$30 + 200\%(30) = 30 + 2(30)$$
$$= 30 + 60$$
$$= 90$$

Method II:

200% **more** than a number means 200% plus the
100% that the original number represents. This means
200% + 100%, or 300% **of** the number. 300% means
three times as much, and $3 \times 30 = 90$.

2. $\frac{1}{8}$%

We are asked what percent of 1,600 is 2.

Remember: a percent is a ratio. Compare the part to
the whole:

$$\% = \frac{\text{part}}{\text{whole}} \times 100\%$$
$$= \frac{2}{1,600} \times 100\% = \frac{2}{16}\% = \frac{1}{8}\%$$

Note: $\frac{1}{8}$% means $\frac{1}{8}$ of 1%, or $\frac{1}{800}$.

3. $\frac{1}{300}$

Let's start by converting 0.25% to a fraction (since our
answer choices are expressed as fractions). 0.25 is $\frac{1}{4}$,
but this is 0.25 percent, or $\frac{1}{4}$ of 1%, which is
$\frac{1}{4} \times \frac{1}{100}$, or $\frac{1}{400}$.

$$0.25\% \text{ of } \frac{4}{3} = \left(\frac{1}{400}\right) \times \left(\frac{4}{3}\right)$$
$$= \frac{1}{300}$$

4. $133\frac{1}{3}$%

Translate: **of** means "times," **is** means "equals." $\frac{2}{3}$ of 8
becomes $\frac{2}{3} \times 8$, and let's call the percent we're looking
for p.

$$\frac{2}{3} \times 8 = p \times 4$$
$$\frac{\frac{2}{3} \times 8}{4} = p$$
$$\frac{4}{3} = p$$

We convert $\frac{4}{3}$ to a percent by multiplying by 100%.

$$\frac{4}{3} = \frac{4}{3} \times 100\% = \frac{400}{3}\% = 133\frac{1}{3}\%$$

5. 0.6

We are asked for 10% of 20% of 30. We change our
percents to fractions, then multiply:

$$10\% = \frac{1}{10}; \ 20\% = \frac{1}{5}.$$

So 10% of 20% of 30 becomes

$$\frac{1}{10} \times \frac{1}{5} \times 30 = \frac{3}{5} = 0.6$$

6. $33\frac{1}{3}$%

The question asks us to find W as a percent of T. First,
let's change the percents into fractions:

$$60\% \text{ of } W = 20\% \text{ of } T$$
$$\frac{3}{5}W = \frac{1}{5}T$$

Now solve for W:

$$\frac{5}{3} \cdot \frac{3}{5}W = \frac{5}{3} \cdot \frac{1}{5}T$$

$$W = \frac{1}{3}T$$

$\frac{1}{3}$ is $33\frac{1}{3}$ %, so W is $33\frac{1}{3}$ % of T.

7. 36

This question involves a principle that appears frequently on the GRE: $a\%$ of $b = b\%$ of a. We can show that with this example:

$$36\% \text{ of } 18 = \frac{36}{100} \times 18$$

$$= \frac{18}{100} \times 36$$

$$= 18\% \text{ of } 36$$

So the answer here is 36.

8. 200%

$$\text{Percent increase} = \frac{\text{Amount of increase}}{\text{ORIGINAL whole}} \times 100\%$$

The original whole is the price **before** the increase. The amount of increase is the difference between the increased price and the original price. So the amount of increase is 15¢ − 5¢ = 10¢.

$$\% \text{ increase} = \frac{10¢}{5¢} \times 100\% = 2 \times 100\% = 200\%$$

9. $90,000

Start by converting the percent to a fraction. 12.5 percent is the same as $\frac{1}{8}$. The profit is $\frac{1}{8}$ of $80,000, or $10,000. This gives us a total selling price of $80,000 + $10,000, or $90,000.

10. 18

If 25% of the shoes are black, then 100%−25%, or 75% of the shoes are not black.

$$75\% \text{ of } 24 = \frac{3}{4} \times 24 = 18.$$

11. 70%

We can assume Bob either passed or failed each test; there's no third possibility. This means he passed each test he didn't fail. If he failed 6 tests out of 20, he passed the other 14. Bob passed $\frac{14}{20}$ of the tests. To convert $\frac{14}{20}$ to a percent, multiply numerator and denominator by 5; this will give us a fraction with a denominator of 100. $\frac{14}{20} \times \frac{5}{5} = \frac{70}{100}$ or 70%. (Or realize that since $\frac{1}{20} = 5\%$. $\frac{14}{20}$ must be 14 times as big, or 14 × 5%, or 70%.) Bob passed 70% of his tests.

12. $960

20% is the same as $\frac{1}{5}$, so 20% of 800 = $\frac{1}{5} \cdot 800 = $ 160. The selling price of the item is $800 + $160, or $960.

13. $133\frac{1}{3}$%

The **amount of increase** in Pat's income was $35,000 − $15,000, or $20,000. The formula for percent increase is

$$\frac{\text{Amount of increase}}{\text{Original whole}} \times 100\% = \text{Percent increase}$$

Plugging in the figures for Pat,

$$\frac{\$20,000}{\$15,000} \times 100\% = \frac{4}{3} \times 100\% = 133\frac{1}{3}\%.$$

14. 65%

If 7 of the 20 winners have come forward, the other 13 have not. $\frac{13}{20}$ of the winners have not claimed their prizes

$\frac{13}{20}$ as a percent is $\frac{13}{20} \times 100\% = 13 \times 5\% = 65\%$.

15. $75

Convert percents to fractions: $50\% = \frac{1}{2}$. A 50% increase on $100 is one-half of 100 or $50. So the increased price is $100 + $50, or $150. Now the 50% **decrease** is a decrease from $150, *not* $100. Thus, the amount of decrease from $150 is 50% of $150, or one-half of $150, or $75. Therefore, the final price is $150 − $75, or $75.

16. 225

We first need to find what x is. If 65% of x = 195,

$$\frac{65}{100} \times x = 195$$

$$x = 195 \times \frac{100}{65}$$

$$= 3 \times \frac{100}{1}$$

$$= 300$$

$$75\% \text{ of } 300 = \frac{3}{4} \times 300 = 225.$$

In fact, it's not necessary to calculate the value of x, only the value of 75% x. So we have:

$$x = 195 \times \frac{100}{65}$$

Rather than do the arithmetic now, we can get an expression for 75% of x, and then simplify.

$$75\% \text{ of } x = \frac{3}{4}x$$

$$= \frac{3}{4} \times 195 \times \frac{100}{65}$$

$$= \frac{3}{4\,1} \times \cancel{195}\,3 \times \frac{\cancel{100}\,25}{\cancel{65}\,1}$$

$$= 225$$

17. $25,000

This is a percent increase problem. We need to identify the different items in our equations:

$$\text{New whole} = \text{Original} + \text{Amount of}$$
$$\text{whole} \qquad \text{increase}$$

and

$$\text{Percent increase} = \frac{\text{Amount of increase}}{\text{Original whole}}(100\%)$$

Our new whole is the October sales, the original whole was the September sales. The percent increase, we're told, was 20%. So we can fill in for the first equation:

$$(\text{October}) = (\text{September}) + (\text{Amount of increase})$$

and rewrite the second equation as

$$(\text{Amount of increase}) = (20\%)(\text{September})$$

Putting the equations together we get

$$(\text{October}) = (\text{September}) + (20\%)(\text{September})$$

Now the important thing to realize is that the September sales are equal to 100% of September sales (anything is equal to 100% of itself), so October's sales are actually 100% + 20%, or 120% of the September sales. Therefore,

$$\text{October sales} = (120\%)(\text{September})$$

$$\$30,000 = \frac{6}{5}(\text{September})$$

$$\text{September} = \frac{5}{6} \times \$30,000$$

$$= \$25,000$$

18. 16.0

We're told that 40% of the total equals 6.4 million dollars, and we're asked to find the total. We can write this as an equation:

$$40\% \times w = 6.4$$

$$\frac{4}{10}w = 6.4$$

$$\left(\frac{10}{4}\right)\left(\frac{4}{10}\right)w = \left(\frac{10}{4}\right)(6.4)$$

$$w = \frac{64}{4} = 16$$

We could also have used the answer choices, either multiplying each answer choice by 40% to see which equals 6.4, or realizing that 40% is a little less than $\frac{1}{2}$ and picking the answer choice a bit more than double 6.4, or 12.8. The closest choice is 16.

19. $6\frac{2}{3}$%

We're asked what percent of the new solution is alcohol. The part is the number of ounces of alcohol; the whole is the total number of ounces of the new solution. There were 25 ounces originally. Then 50 ounces were added, so there are 75 ounces of new solution. How many ounces are alcohol? 20% of the original 25-ounce solution was alcohol. 20% is $\frac{1}{5}$, so $\frac{1}{5}$ of 25, or 5 ounces are alcohol. Now we can find the percent of alcohol in the new solution:

$$\% \text{ alcohol} = \frac{\text{alcohol}}{\text{total solution}} \times 100\%$$

$$= \frac{5}{75} \times 100\%$$

$$= \frac{20}{3}\% = 6\frac{2}{3}\%$$

20. $125

The bicycle was discounted by 20%; this means that Jerry paid (100% − 20%) or 80% of the original price. Jerry paid $100, so we have the percent and the part and need to find the whole. Now substitute into the formula:

$$80\% \times \text{Whole} = \$100$$

$$\frac{4}{5} \times \text{Whole} = \$100$$

$$\frac{5}{4}\left(\frac{4}{5} \times \text{Whole}\right) = \$100 \times \frac{5}{4}$$

$$\text{Whole} = \$125$$

The bicycle originally sold for $125.

21. 25%

The key to this problem is that while the value of the stock must decrease and increase by the same **amount**, it doesn't decrease and increase by the same **percent**. When the stock first decreases, that amount of change is part of a larger whole. If the stock were to

increase to its former value, that same amount of change would be a larger percent of a smaller whole. Pick a number for the original value of the stock, $100. (Since it's very easy to take percents of 100, it's usually best to choose 100.) The 20% decrease represents $20, so the stock decreases to a value of $80. Now in order for the stock to reach the value of $100 again, there must be a $20 increase. What percent of $80 is $20? It's $\frac{\$20}{\$80} \times 100\%$, or $\frac{1}{4} \times 100\%$, or 25%.

22. 1750

Since the population increases by 50% every 50 years, the population in 1950 was 150%, or $\frac{3}{2}$ of the 1900 population. This means the 1900 population was $\frac{2}{3}$ of the 1950 population. Similarly, the 1850 population was $\frac{2}{3}$ of the 1900 population, and so on. We can just keep multiplying by $\frac{2}{3}$ until we get to a population of 160.

$$1950: \quad 810 \times \frac{2}{3} = 540 \text{ in } 1900$$

$$1900: \quad 540 \times \frac{2}{3} = 360 \text{ in } 1850$$

$$1850: \quad 360 \times \frac{2}{3} = 240 \text{ in } 1800$$

$$1800: \quad 240 \times \frac{2}{3} = 160 \text{ in } 1750$$

The population was 160 in 1750.

23. 6

5% of the total mixture is timothy (a type of grass) so, to find the **amount** of timothy, we use

$$\% \text{ timothy} \times \text{whole} = \text{amount of timothy.}$$

Thus, the amount of timothy in 240 pounds of mixture is 5% × 240 pounds, or 12 pounds. If 12 pounds of timothy are available and each acre requires 2 pounds, then $\frac{12}{2}$ or 6 acres can be planted.

24. $1,500

The commission earned was $200, less the $50 salary, or $150. This represents 10% of his total sales, or $\frac{1}{10}$ of his total. Since this is $\frac{1}{10}$ of the total, the total must be 10 times as much, or $10 \times \$150 = \$1,500$.

25. $12.50

The man paid $80 for 10 crates of oranges, and then lost 2 crates. That leaves him with 8 crates. We want to find the price per crate that will give him an overall profit of 25%. First, what is 25% or $\frac{1}{4}$ of $80? It's $20. So to make a 25% profit, he must bring in ($80 + $20) or $100 in sales receipts. If he has 8 crates, that means that each crate must sell for $100 ÷ 8, or $12.50.

POWERS AND ROOTS TEST
ANSWERS AND EXPLANATIONS

1. 16

Remember the order of operations. We do what's within the parentheses first, and then square.

$$(7 - 3)^2 = (4)^2 = 16$$

2. 54

Plug in 3 for a. We get

$$(3a)^2 - 3a^2 = [3(3)]^2 - 3(3)^2$$
$$= 9^2 - 3(9)$$
$$= 81 - 27$$
$$= 54$$

3. 2^{10}

To multiply two numbers with the same base, **add** the two exponents. Here, we have two different bases, 2 and 4. We must rewrite one of the numbers such that the bases are the same. Since $4 = 2^2$, we can easily rewrite 4^3 as a power of 2: $4^3 = (2^2)^3$. To raise a power to an exponent, **multiply** the exponents, so $(2^2)^3 = 2^6$.

$$\text{Therefore, } 2^4 \times 4^3 = 2^4 \times 2^6$$
$$= 2^{4+6}$$
$$= 2^{10}$$

4. $3a$

We can find the value of $\sqrt{x}$ by substituting $9a^2$ for x.

$$\sqrt{x} = \sqrt{9a^2}$$
$$= \sqrt{9} \cdot \sqrt{a^2}$$
$$= 3a$$

Note: we could do this only because we know that $a > 0$. The radical sign ($\sqrt{}$) refers to the positive square root of a number.

5. 12

To divide powers with the same base, keep the base and subtract the exponent of the denominator from the exponent of the numerator. First get everything in the same base, since $2^2 = 4 = 4^1$, then:

$$\frac{4^3 - 4^2}{2^2} = \frac{4^3 - 4^2}{4^1}$$
$$= \frac{4^3}{4^1} - \frac{4^2}{4^1}$$
$$= 4^{3-1} - 4^{2-1}$$
$$= 4^2 - 4^1$$
$$= 16 - 4$$
$$= 12$$

Or, since the calculations required aren't too tricky, just simplify following the order of operations.

$$\frac{4^3 - 4^2}{2^2} = \frac{64 - 16}{4} = \frac{48}{4} = 12$$

6. 64

First we need to find the value of x using the equation $3^x = 81$. Then we can find the value of x^3.

We need to express 81 as a power with a base of 3.

$$81 = 9^2 = (3^2)^2 = 3^{2 \times 2} = 3^4$$
$$\text{So } x = 4$$
$$x^3 = 4^3$$
$$= 4 \times 4 \times 4 = 64.$$

7. 73

Substitute 2 for x. Then $3^x + (x^3)^2 = 3^2 + (2^3)^2$
$$= 3^2 + 8^2$$
$$= 9 + 64$$
$$= 73$$

8. 0.00675×10^2

To multiply or divide a number by a power of 10, we move the decimal point to the right or left, respectively, the same number of places as the number of zeros in the power of 10. Multiplying by a negative power of 10 is the same as dividing by a positive power. For instance: $3 \times 10^2 = \dfrac{3}{10^2}$. Keeping this in mind, let's go over the choices one by one. Remember: we are looking for the choice that is NOT equal to 0.0675.

$67.5 \times 10^{-3} = 0.0675$ No good.
$6.75 \times 10^{-2} = 0.0675$ No good.

$0.675 \times 10^{-1} = 0.0675$ No good.

$0.00675 \times 10^2 = 0.675$

$0.675 \neq 0.0675$ This is the correct answer.

9.   0

The product of two negatives is positive, and the product of three negatives is negative. In fact, if we have any odd number of negative terms in a product, the result will be negative; any even number of negative terms gives a positive product. Since q is odd, we have an odd number of factors of -1. The product is -1. Adding 1 to -1, we get 0.

10. 2^{5x}

Remember the rules for operations with exponents. First you have to get both powers in terms of the same base so you can combine the exponents. Note that the answer choices all have base 2. Start by expressing 4 and 8 as powers of 2.

$$(4^x)(8^x) = (2^2)^x \cdot (2^3)^x$$

To raise a power to an exponent, multiply the exponents:

$$(2^2)^x = 2^{2x}$$
$$(2^3)^x = 2^{3x}$$

To multiply powers with the same base, add the exponents:

$$2^{2x} \cdot 2^{3x} = 2^{(2x+3x)}$$
$$= 2^{5x}$$

11.   6

Try approximating to find n. Well, $5^2 = 25$, $5^3 = 125$, so $5^3 > 100$.

Then
$$5^4 > 100 \times 5, \text{ or } 5^4 > 500$$
$$5^5 > 500 \times 5, \text{ or } 5^5 > 2{,}500$$
$$5^6 > 2{,}500 \times 5, \text{ or } 5^6 > 12{,}500$$

5^6 must be greater than 10,000, but 5^5 clearly is a lot less than 10,000. So in order for 5^n to be greater than 10,000, n must be at least 6.

12.   8

We are told that the cube of the positive square root of 16 equals the square of some number. Let's do this slowly, one step at a time.

Step 1:   The positive square root of 16 equals 4.
Step 2:   The cube of 4 is $4 \times 4 \times 4$, or 64.
Step 3:   So we are looking for a positive number whose square is 64, 8 is the answer.

13.   I, II, and III

This question is a good review of the rules for the product of exponential expressions. In order to make the comparison easier, try to transform 8^5 and each of the three options so that they have a common base. Since 2 is the smallest base among the expressions to be compared, let it be our common base. Since $8^5 = (2^3)^5 = 2^{3 \cdot 5} = 2^{15}$, we will look for options equivalent to 2^{15}.

I:
$2^5 \cdot 4^5 = 2^5 \cdot (2^2)^5 = 2^5 \cdot 2^{2 \cdot 5} = 2^5 \cdot 2^{10} = 2^{5+10} = 2^{15}$ OK

II: 2^{15} OK
III: $2^5 \cdot 2^{10} = 2^{5+10} = 2^{15}$ OK

It turns out that all three are equivalent to 2^{15} or 8^5.

14. $\dfrac{8}{3}$

The simplest approach is to express both 9 and 27 as an exponent with a common base. The most convenient base is 3, since $3^2 = 9$ and $3^3 = 27$. Then the equation becomes:

$$27^n = 9^4$$
$$(3^3)^n = (3^2)^4$$
$$3^{3 \times n} = 3^{2 \times 4}$$
$$3^{3n} = 3^8$$

If two terms with the same base are equal, the exponents must be equal.

$$3n = 8$$
$$n = \dfrac{8}{3}$$

15. $x^2 y^3 z$

First let's break up the expression to separate the variables, transforming the fraction into a product of three simpler fractions:

$$\frac{x^3 y z^4}{x y^{-2} z^3} = \left(\frac{x^3}{x}\right)\left(\frac{y}{y^{-2}}\right)\left(\frac{z^4}{z^3}\right)$$

Now carry out each division by keeping the base and subtracting the exponents.

$$\frac{x^3}{x} = x^{3-1} = x^2$$
$$\frac{y}{y^{-2}} = y^{1-(-2)} = y^{1+2} = y^3$$
$$\frac{z^4}{z^3} = z^{4-3} = z^1 = z$$

The answer is the product of these three expressions, or $x^2 y^3 z$.

16. $5 + 2\sqrt{7}$

Subtract the length of CD from the length of AB to find out how much greater AB is than CD.

$$\begin{aligned}
AB - CD &= (10 + \sqrt{7}) - (5 - \sqrt{7}) \\
&= 10 + \sqrt{7} - 5 - (-\sqrt{7}) \\
&= 10 - 5 + \sqrt{7} + \sqrt{7} \\
&= 5 + 2\sqrt{7}
\end{aligned}$$

17. 0

We are told that $x^a \cdot x^b = 1$. Since $x^a \cdot x^b = x^{a+b}$, we know that $x^{a+b} = 1$. If a power is equal to 1, either the base is 1 or -1, or the exponent is zero. Since we are told $x \neq 1$ or -1 here, the exponent must be zero; therefore, $a + b = 0$.

Chapter 3
Algebra

Algebra is the least frequently tested of the major math topics on the GRE—sort of. What we mean is that there won't be that many problems that involve only algebra—maybe 20 percent of your exam. But a lot of the questions on the test will involve algebra to some degree or another. This makes algebra a necessary skill—you have to understand basic equations and how to solve them.

ALGEBRA LEVEL ONE

Terminology

Terms: A **term** is a numerical constant or the product (or quotient) of a numerical constant and one or more variables. Examples of terms are $3x$, $4x^2yz$, and $\frac{2a}{c}$.

Expressions: An **algebraic expression** is a combination of one or more terms. Terms in an expression are separated by either + or − signs. Examples of expressions are $3xy$, $4ab + 5cd$, and $x^2 − 1$.

In the term $3xy$, the numerical constant 3 is called a **coefficient**. In a simple term such as z, 1 is the coefficient. A number without any variables is called a **constant term**. An expression with one term, such as $3xy$, is called a **monomial**; one with two terms, such as $4a + 2d$, is a **binomial**; one with three terms, such as $xy + z − a$, is a **trinomial**. The general name for expressions with more than one term is **polynomial**.

Substitution

Substitution is a method that we employ to evaluate an algebraic expression or to express an algebraic expression in terms of other variables.

Example: Evaluate $3x^2 − 4x$ when $x = 2$.
Replace every x in the expression with 2 and then carry out the designated operations.
Remember to follow the order of operations (PEMDAS).
$3x^2 − 4x = 3(2)^2 − 4(2) = 3 \times 4 − 4 \times 2 = 12 − 8 = 4$

Example: Express $\dfrac{a}{b-a}$ in terms of x and y if $a = 2x$ and $b = 3y$.

Here, we replace every "a" with $2x$ and every "b" with $3y$:

$$\frac{a}{b-a} = \frac{2x}{3y-2x}$$

Symbolism

Symbols such as $+$, $-$, $\times$, and $\div$ should be familiar. However, you may see strange symbols such as Š, ◇, and ♦ on a GRE problem. These symbols may confuse you but the question stem in each of these problems always tells you what a strange symbol does to numbers. This type of problem may seem weird, but it is typically nothing more than an exercise in substitution.

Example: Let $x{*}$ be defined by the equation: $x{*} = \dfrac{x^2}{1 - x^2}$. Evaluate $\left(\dfrac{1}{2}\right)^{*}$.

$$\left(\frac{1}{2}\right)^{*} = \frac{\left(\frac{1}{2}\right)^2}{1 - \left(\frac{1}{2}\right)^2} = \frac{\frac{1}{4}}{1 - \frac{1}{4}} = \frac{\frac{1}{4}}{\frac{3}{4}} = \frac{1}{3}$$

Operations with Polynomials

All of the laws of arithmetic operations, such as the associative, distributive, and commutative laws, are also applicable to polynomials.

Commutative law: $2x + 5y = 5y + 2x$

$5a \times 3b = 3b \times 5a = 15ab$

Associative law: $2x - 3x + 5y + 2y = (2x - 3x) + (5y + 2y) = -x + 7y$

$(-2x)\left(\frac{1}{2}x\right)(3y)(-2y) = (-x^2)(-6y^2) = 6x^2y^2$

Both laws: $2x + 3x^2 - 6x + 4x^2 = 2x - 6x + 3x^2 + 4x^2$ (commutative law)

$\qquad\qquad = (2x - 6x) + (3x^2 + 4x^2)$ (associative law)

$\qquad\qquad = -4x + 7x^2$

Note: This process of simplifying an expression by subtracting or adding together those terms with the same variable component is called **combining like terms**.

Distributive law: $3a(2b - 5c) = (3a \times 2b) - (3a \times 5c) = 6ab - 15ac$

Note: The product of two binomials can be calculated by applying the distributive law twice.

Example: $(x + 5)(x - 2) = x \bullet (x - 2) + 5 \bullet (x - 2)$

$$= x \bullet x - x \bullet 2 + 5 \bullet x - 5 \bullet 2$$

$$= x^2 - 2x + 5x - 10$$

$$= x^2 + 3x - 10$$

A simple mnemonic for this is the word **FOIL.** Using the FOIL method in the above multiplication,

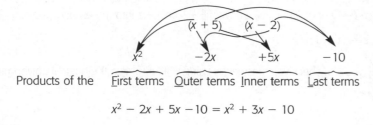

Products of the   First terms   Outer terms   Inner terms   Last terms

$$x^2 - 2x + 5x - 10 = x^2 + 3x - 10$$

Factoring Algebraic Expressions

Factoring a polynomial means expressing it as a product of two or more simpler expressions.

Common monomial factor: When there is a monomial factor common to every term in the polynomial, it can be factored out by using the distributive law.

Example: $2a + 6ac = 2a(1 + 3c)$ (here $2a$ is the greatest common factor of $2a$ and $6ac$).

Difference of two perfect squares: The difference of two squares can be factored into a product:
$a^2 - b^2 = (a - b)(a + b)$.

Example: $9x^2 - 1 = (3x)^2 - (1)^2 = (3x + 1)(3x - 1)$

Polynomials of the form $a^2 + 2ab + b^2$: Any polynomial of this form is equivalent to the square of a binomial. Notice that $(a + b)^2 = a^2 + 2ab + b^2$ (Try FOIL).

Factoring such a polynomial is just reversing this procedure.

Example: $x^2 + 6x + 9 = (x)^2 + 2(x)(3) + (3)^2 = (x + 3)^2$.

Polynomials of the form $a^2 - 2ab + b^2$: Any polynomial of this form is equivalent to the square of a binomial like the previous example. Here, though, the binomial is the difference of two terms: $(a-b)^2 = a^2 - 2ab + b^2$.

Polynomials of the form $x^2 + bx + c$: The polynomials of this form can nearly always be factored into a product of two binomials. The product of the first terms in each binomial must equal the first term of the polynomial. The product of the last terms of the binomials must equal the third term of the polynomial. The sum of the remaining products must equal the second term of the polynomial. Factoring can be thought of as the FOIL method backwards.

Example: $x^2 - 3x + 2$

We can factor this into two binomials, each containing an x term. Start by writing down what we know.

$x^2 - 3x + 2 = (x \quad)(x \quad)$

In each binomial on the right we need to fill in the missing term. The **product** of the two missing terms will be the last term in the polynomial: 2. The **sum** of the two missing terms will be the coefficient of the second term of the polynomial: -3. Try the possible factors of 2 until we get a pair that adds up to -3. There are two possibilities: 1 and 2, or -1 and -2. Since $(-1) + (-2) = -3$, we can fill -1 and -2 into the empty spaces.

Thus, $x^2 - 3x + 2 = (x - 1)(x - 2)$.

Note: Whenever you factor a polynomial, you can check your answer by using FOIL to obtain the original polynomial.

Linear Equations

An **equation** is an algebraic sentence that says that two expressions are equal to each other. The two expressions consist of numbers, variables, and arithmetic operations to be performed on these numbers and variables. To **solve** for some variable we can manipulate the equation until we have isolated that variable on one side of the equal sign, leaving any numbers or other variables on the other side. Of course, we must be careful to manipulate the equation only in accordance with the equality postulate: Whenever we perform an operation on one side of the equation we must perform the same operation on the other side. Otherwise, the two sides of the equation will no longer be equal.

A linear or first-degree equation is an equation in which all the variables are raised to the first power (there are no squares or cubes). In order to solve such an equation, we'll perform operations on both sides of the equation in order to get the variable we're solving for all alone on one side. The operations we can perform without upsetting the balance of the equation are addition and subtraction, and multiplication or division by a number other than 0. Typically, at each step in the process, we'll need to use the reverse of the operation that's being applied to the variable in order to isolate the variable. In the equation $n + 6 = 10$, 6 is being added to n on the left side. To isolate the n, we'll need to perform the reverse operation, that is, to subtract 6 from both sides. That gives us

$n + 6 - 6 = 10 - 6$, or $n = 4$.

Let's look at another example.

Example: If $4x - 7 = 2x + 5$, what is x?

1. Get all the terms with the variable on one side of the equation. Combine the terms.

$$4x - 7 = 2x + 5$$
$$4x - 2x - 7 = 2x - 2x + 5$$
$$2x - 7 = 5$$

2. Get all constant terms on the other side of the equation.

$$2x - 7 + 7 = 5 + 7$$
$$2x = 12$$

3. Isolate the variable by dividing both sides by its coefficient.

$$\frac{2x}{2} = \frac{12}{2}$$
$$x = 6$$

We can easily check our work when solving this kind of equation. The answer we arrive at represents the value of the variable which makes the equation hold true. Therefore, to check that it's correct, we can just substitute this value for the variable in the original equation. If the equation holds true, we've found the correct answer. In the above example, we got a value of 6 for x. Replacing x with 6 in our original equation gives us $4(6) - 7 = 2(6) + 5$, or $17 = 17$. That's clearly true, so our answer is indeed correct.

Equations with fractional coefficients can be a little more tricky. They can be solved using the same approach, although this often leads to rather involved calculations. Instead, they can be transformed into an equivalent equation that does not involve fractional coefficients. Let's see how to solve such a problem.

Example: Solve $\dfrac{x-2}{3} + \dfrac{x-4}{10} = \dfrac{x}{2}$

1. Multiply both sides of the equation by the Lowest Common Denominator (LCD). Here the LCD is 30.

$$30\left(\frac{x-2}{3}\right) + 30\left(\frac{x-4}{10}\right) = 30\left(\frac{x}{2}\right)$$

$$10(x-2) + 3(x-4) = 15(x)$$

2. Clear parentheses using the distributive property, and combine like terms.

$$10x - 20 + 3x - 12 = 15x$$

$$13x - 32 = 15x$$

3. Isolate the variable. Again, combine like terms.

$$-32 = 15x - 13x$$

$$-32 = 2x$$

4. Divide both sides by the coefficient of the variable.

$$x = \frac{-32}{2} = -16$$

ALGEBRA LEVEL ONE EXERCISE

Simplify questions 1–10; factor questions 11–20. (Answers are on the following page.)

1. $2x + 4y + 7x - 6y =$

2. $2x(4y + 3x) =$

3. $x(x^2 + x + 1) - x^2 =$

4. $(y^2 + 1)(x^2 + 1) =$

5. $(2a - b)(2a + b) =$

6. $(4x + y)(x + 4y) - 17xy =$

7. $(x^2 - 1)(x^2 + 1) =$

8. $xyz\left(\dfrac{1}{xy} + \dfrac{x}{zy} + \dfrac{yz}{xyz}\right) =$

9. $\left(\dfrac{zxy}{z}\right)\left(\dfrac{z^2y}{x}\right)\left(\dfrac{z}{y^2}\right) =$

10. $\left(\dfrac{x^4}{y^3}\right)\left(\dfrac{y^2}{x^3}\right)\left(\dfrac{x}{y}\right) =$

11. $x^2 + xy + x =$

12. $y^3 + 2y^2 + y =$

13. $5x^2 - 5 =$

14. $x^4 - x^2 =$

15. $x^2 - 6x + 9 =$

16. $x^2 + 10x + 25 =$

17. $x^2 + x + \dfrac{1}{4} =$

18. $x^2 - 4x + 4 =$

19. $x^2 + 7x + 10 =$

20. $x^2 + 10x + 9 =$

ANSWER KEY—BASIC ALGEBRA EXERCISE

1. $9x - 2y$

2. $8xy + 6x^2$

3. $x^3 + x$

4. $x^2y^2 + x^2 + y^2 + 1$

5. $4a^2 - b^2$

6. $4x^2 + 4y^2$

7. $x^4 - 1$

8. $z + x^2 + yz$

9. z^3

10. $\dfrac{x^2}{y^2}$

11. $x(x + y + 1)$

12. $y(y + 1)^2$

13. $5(x - 1)(x + 1)$

14. $x^2(x - 1)(x + 1)$

15. $(x - 3)^2$

16. $(x + 5)^2$

17. $\left(x + \dfrac{1}{2}\right)^2$ or $\dfrac{(2x + 1)^2}{4}$

18. $(x - 2)^2$

19. $(x + 2)(x + 5)$

20. $(x + 9)(x + 1)$

ALGEBRA LEVEL ONE TEST

Solve the following problems and choose the best answer. (Answers and explanations are at the end of the chapter.)

Basic

1. If $x = -3$, what is the value of the expression $x^2 + 3x + 3$?

    ◯ -21

    ◯ -15

    ◯ -6

    ◯ 3

    ◯ 21

2. If $3x + 1 = x$, then $x =$

    ◯ -2

    ◯ -1

    ◯ $-\dfrac{1}{2}$

    ◯ $\dfrac{1}{3}$

    ◯ $\dfrac{1}{2}$

3. If $0.5959 = 59x$, then $x =$

    ◯ 0.01

    ◯ 0.0101

    ◯ 0.11

    ◯ 0.111

    ◯ 1.01

4. If $5 - 2x = 15$, then $x =$

    ◯ -10

    ◯ -5

    ◯ 1

    ◯ 5

    ◯ 10

5. $5z^2 - 5z + 4 - z(3z - 4) =$

    ◯ $2z^2 - z + 4$

    ◯ $2z^2 - 9z + 4$

    ◯ $5z^2 - 8z + 8$

    ◯ $5z^2 - 8z$

    ◯ $2z^2 - 5z$

6. If $a = -1$ and $b = -2$, what is the value of the expression $2a^2 - 2ab + b^2$?

    ◯ -6

    ◯ -2

    ◯ 0

    ◯ 2

    ◯ 4

7. If $b = -3$, what is the value of the expression $3b^2 - b$?

    ◯ -30

    ◯ -24

    ◯ 0

    ◯ 24

    ◯ 30

8. What is the value of the expression
    $x^2 + xy + y^2$ when $x = -2$ and $y = 2$?

    ◯ -24

    ◯ -4

    ◯ 2

    ◯ 4

    ◯ 6

9. What is the value of a if $ab + ac = 21$ and
    $b + c = 7$?

    ◯ -3

    ◯ -1

    ◯ 0

    ◯ 3

    ◯ 7

10. If $a = 2, b = -1$ and $c = 1$, which of the
    following is (are) true?

    I. $a + b + c = 2$

    II. $2a + bc = 4$

    III. $4a - b + c = 8$

    ◯ I only

    ◯ III only

    ◯ I and II only

    ◯ I and III only

    ◯ I, II, and III

Intermediate

11. If $y \neq z$, then $\dfrac{xy - zx}{z - y} =$

   ◯ x

   ◯ 1

   ◯ 0

   ◯ -1

   ◯ $-x$

12. If $q \times 34 \times 36 \times 38 = 17 \times 18 \times 19$, then $q =$

   ◯ $\dfrac{1}{8}$

   ◯ $\dfrac{1}{6}$

   ◯ $\dfrac{1}{2}$

   ◯ 2

   ◯ 8

13. For all x and y, $(x + 1)(y + 1) - x - y =$

   ◯ $xy - x - y + 1$

   ◯ $xy + 1$

   ◯ $-x - y + 1$

   ◯ $x^2 + y^2 - 1$

   ◯ 1

14. If the product of 4, 5, and q is equal to the product of 5, p, and 2, and $pq \neq 0$, what is the value of the quotient $\dfrac{p}{q}$?

   ◯ $\dfrac{5}{2}$

   ◯ 2

   ◯ $\dfrac{1}{2}$

   ◯ $\dfrac{2}{5}$

   ◯ $\dfrac{1}{10}$

15. If $\dfrac{x + 3}{2} + x + 3 = 3$, then $x =$

   ◯ -3

   ◯ $-\dfrac{3}{2}$

   ◯ -1

   ◯ 0

   ◯ 1

16. Which of the following is equivalent to $3x^2 + 18x + 27$?

   ◯ $3(x^2 + 6x + 3)$

   ◯ $3(x + 3)(x + 6)$

   ◯ $3(x + 3)(x + 3)$

   ◯ $3x(x + 6 + 9)$

   ◯ $3x^2 + x(18 + 27)$

17. In the equation $mx + 5 = y$, m is a constant. If $x = 2$ when $y = 1$, when is the value of x when $y = -1$?

    ○ -1

    ○ 0

    ○ 1

    ○ 2

    ○ 3

18. If $\dfrac{5q + 7}{2} = 8 + q$, then $q =$

    ○ -3

    ○ 0

    ○ 3

    ○ $3\dfrac{1}{4}$

    ○ 9

19. $(a^2 + b)^2 - (a^2 - b)^2 =$

    ○ $-4a^2b$

    ○ 0

    ○ $(2ab)^2$

    ○ $4a^2b$

    ○ b^4

20. If $x = 3$ and $y = 4$, then $\dfrac{xy}{\dfrac{1}{x} + \dfrac{1}{y}} =$

    ○ $\dfrac{7}{12}$

    ○ $\dfrac{12}{7}$

    ○ 12

    ○ $\dfrac{144}{7}$

    ○ 84

Advanced

21. If $abc \neq 0$, then $\dfrac{a^2bc + ab^2c + abc^2}{abc} =$

    ○ $a + b + c$

    ○ $\dfrac{a + b + c}{abc}$

    ○ $a^3b^3c^3$

    ○ $3abc$

    ○ $2abc$

22. The expression $\dfrac{3}{x - 1} - 6$ will equal 0 when x equals which of the following?

    ○ -3

    ○ $-\dfrac{2}{3}$

    ○ $\dfrac{1}{2}$

    ○ $\dfrac{3}{2}$

    ○ 3

23. If $x > 1$ and $\dfrac{a}{b} = 1 - \dfrac{1}{x}$, then $\dfrac{b}{a} =$

    ○ x

    ○ $x - 1$

    ○ $\dfrac{x - 1}{x}$

    ○ $\dfrac{x}{x - 1}$

    ○ $\dfrac{1}{x} - 1$

24. If $m \blacktriangle n$ is defined by the equation $m \blacktriangle n = \dfrac{m^2 - n + 1}{mn}$, for all nonzero m and n, then $3 \blacktriangle 1 =$

    ○ $\dfrac{9}{4}$

    ○ 3

    ○ $\dfrac{11}{3}$

    ○ 6

    ○ 9

25. If $y > 0$ and $3y - 2 = \dfrac{-1}{3y + 2}$, then $y =$

    ○ $\dfrac{1}{3}$

    ○ $\dfrac{\sqrt{3}}{3}$

    ○ 1

    ○ $\sqrt{3}$

    ○ $\sqrt{3} + 1$

26. For all a and b, $a(a - b) + b(a - b) =$

    ○ $a^2 - 2ab + b^2$

    ○ $a^2 - 2ab - b^2$

    ○ $2a^2 + 2ab + b^2$

    ○ $a^2 + 2ab + b^2$

    ○ $a^2 - b^2$

ALGEBRA LEVEL TWO

Inequalities

Inequality symbols:

> \> greater than
>
> \< less than
>
> ≥ greater than or equal to
>
> ≤ less than or equal to

Example: $x > 4$ means all numbers greater than 4.

Example: $x < 0$ means all numbers less than zero (the negative numbers).

Example: $x \geq -2$ means x can be -2 or any number greater than -2.

Example: $x \leq \dfrac{1}{2}$ means x can be $\dfrac{1}{2}$ or any number less than $\dfrac{1}{2}$.

A range of values is often expressed on a number line. Two ranges are shown below.

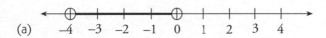

(a) represents the set of all numbers between -4 and 0 **excluding** the endpoints -4 and 0, or $-4 < x < 0$.

(b) represents the set of all numbers greater than -1, up to and **including** 3, or $-1 < x \leq 3$.

Solving Inequalities: We use the same methods as used in solving equations with one exception:

If the inequality is multiplied or divided by a negative number, the direction of the inequality is reversed.

If the inequality $-3x < 2$ is multiplied by -1, the resulting inequality is $3x > -2$.

Example: Solve for x and represent the solution set on a number line: $3 - \dfrac{x}{4} \geq 2$

(1) Multiply both sides by 4. $\qquad\qquad\qquad\qquad 12 - x \geq 8$

(2) Subtract 12 from both sides. $\qquad\qquad\qquad -x \geq -4$

(3) Divide both sides by -1 and change the direction of the sign. $\qquad\qquad\qquad x \leq 4$

KAPLAN)

Note: The solution set to an inequality is not a single value but a range of possible values. Here the values include 4 and all numbers below 4.

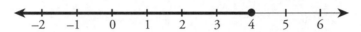

Literal Equations

If a problem involves more than one variable, we cannot find a specific value for a variable; we can only solve for one variable in terms of the others. To do this, try to get the desired variable alone on one side, and all the other variables on the other side.

Example: In the formula $V = \dfrac{PN}{R + NT}$, solve for N in terms of P, R, T, and V.

(1) Clear denominators by **cross-multiplying**.

$$\frac{V}{1} = \frac{PN}{R + NT}$$
$$V(R + NT) = PN$$

(2) Remove parentheses by distributing.

$$VR + VNT = PN$$

(3) Put all terms containing N on one side and all other terms on the other side.

$$VNT - PN = -VR$$

(4) Factor out the common factor N.

$$N(VT - P) = -VR$$

(5) Divide by the coefficient of N to get N alone.

$$N = \frac{-VR}{VT - P}$$

Note: We can reduce the number of negative terms in the answer by multiplying both the numerator and the denominator of the fraction on the right-hand side by -1.

$$N = \frac{VR}{P - VT}$$

Simultaneous Equations

Earlier, we solved one equation for one variable, and were able to find a numerical value for that variable. In the example above we were not able to find a numerical value for N because our equation contained variables other than just N. In general, if you want to find numerical values for all your variables, you will need as many different equations as you have variables. Let's say, for example, that we have one equation with two variables: $x - y = 7$. There are an infinite number of solution sets to this equation: e.g., $x = 8$ and $y = 1$ (since $8 - 1 = 7$), or $x = 9$ and $y = 2$ (since $9 - 2 = 7$), etc. If we are given two **different** equations with two variables, we can combine the equations to obtain a unique solution set. Isolate the variable in one equation, then plug that expression into the other equation.

Example: Find the values of m and n if $m = 4n + 2$ and $3m + 2n = 16$.

(1) We know that $m = 4n + 2$. Substitute $4n + 2$ for m in the second equation.

$$3(4n + 2) + 2n = 16$$
$$12n + 6 + 2n = 16$$

(2) Solve for n.

$$14n = 10$$

$$n = \frac{10}{14} = \frac{5}{7}$$

(3) To find the value of m, substitute $\frac{5}{7}$ for n in the first equation and solve.

$$m = 4n + 2$$

$$m = 4\left(\frac{5}{7}\right) + 2$$

$$m = \frac{20}{7} + \frac{14}{7} = \frac{34}{7}$$

Quadratic Equations

If we set the polynomial $ax^2 + bx + c$ equal to 0, we have a special name for it. We call it a **quadratic equation**. Since it is an equation, we can find the value(s) for x which make the equation work.

Example: $x^2 - 3x + 2 = 0$

To find the solutions, or roots, let's start by doing what we did earlier in this chapter and factoring. Let's factor $x^2 - 3x + 2$. We can factor $x^2 - 3x + 2$ into $(x - 2)(x - 1)$, making our quadratic equation

$$(x - 2)(x - 1) = 0$$

Now, we have a product of two binomials which is equal to 0. When is it that a product of two terms is equal to 0? The only time that happens is when at least one of the terms is 0. If the product of $(x - 2)$ and $(x - 1)$ is equal to 0, that means either the first term equals 0 or the second term equals 0. So to find the roots, we just need to set the two binomials equal to 0. That gives us

$$x - 2 = 0 \text{ or } x - 1 = 0$$

Solving for x, we get $x = 2$ or $x = 1$. As a check, we can plug in 1 and 2 into the equation $x^2 - 3x + 2 = 0$, and we'll see that either value makes the equation work.

Functions

Classic function notation problems may appear on the test. An algebraic expression of only one variable may be defined as a function, f or g, of that variable.

Example: What is the minimum value of the function $f(x) = x^2 - 1$?

In the function $f(x) = x^2 - 1$, if x is 1, then $f(1) = 1^2 - 1 = 0$. In other words, by inputting 1 into the function, the output $f(x) = 0$. Every number inputted has one and only one output (though the reverse is not necessarily true). You're asked here to find the minimum value, that is, the smallest possible value of the function. Minimums are usually found using calculus, but there is no need to use anything that complicated on the GRE.

Any minimum (or maximum) value problem on the test can be solved in one of two simple ways. Either plug the answer choices into the function and find which gives you the lowest value, or use some common sense. In the case of $f(x) \, x^2 - 1$, the function will be at a minimum when x^2 is as small as possible. Since x^2 gets larger the farther x is from 0, x^2 is as small as possible when $x = 0$. Consequently the smallest value of $x^2 - 1$ occurs when $x = 0$. So $f(\emptyset) = \emptyset^2 - 1 = -1$, which is the minimum value of the function.

ADVANCED ALGEBRA EXERCISE

Solve the following problems as directed. (Answers are on the following page.)

Solve each of the following inequalities for x:

1. $3x + 4 > 64$

2. $2x + 1 < 21$

3. $-x + 1 \leq 63 + x$

4. $21x - 42 \leq 14x$

5. $6 > x + 4 > 4$

6. $2x > x + 10 > -x$

Solve each of the following for x in terms of the other variables. (Assume none of the variables equals zero):

7. $abx = c$

8. $a + bx = c + dx$

9. $ax - x = bx + c$

10. $\dfrac{ax}{b + cx} = 1$

Solve each of the following pairs of equations for x and y:

11. $x + y = 2$
    $x - y = 4$

12. $2x + y = 3$
    $2x + 3y = 6$

13. $2x + 3y = 0$
    $-2x + 3y = 6$

14. $21x + 7y = 3$
    $21x + 10y = 3$

15. $x + 2y = 9$
    $2x - 3y = 4$

ANSWER KEY—ALGEBRA LEVEL TWO EXERCISE

1. $x > 20$

2. $x < 10$

3. $x \geq -31$

4. $x \leq 6$

5. $0 < x < 2$

6. $x > 10$

7. $\dfrac{c}{ab}$

8. $\dfrac{c - a}{b - d}$

9. $\dfrac{c}{a - b - 1}$

10. $\dfrac{b}{a - c}$

11. $x = 3, y = -1$

12. $x = \dfrac{3}{4}, y = \dfrac{3}{2}$

13. $x = -\dfrac{3}{2}, y = 1$

14. $x = \dfrac{1}{7}, y = 0$

15. $x = 5, y = 2$

ALGEBRA LEVEL TWO TEST

Solve the following problems and choose the best answer. (Answers and explanations are at the end of this chapter.)

Basic

1. If $3m < 48$ and $2m > 24$, then m could equal which of the following?

   ○ 10

   ○ 12

   ○ 14

   ○ 16

   ○ 18

2. If $a < b$ and $b < c$ which of the following must be true?

   ○ $b + c < 2a$

   ○ $a + b < c$

   ○ $a - b < b - c$

   ○ $a + b < 2c$

   ○ $a + c < 2b$

3. The inequality $3x - 16 > 4x + 12$ is true if and only if which of the following is true?

   ○ $x < -28$

   ○ $x < -7$

   ○ $x > -7$

   ○ $x > -16$

   ○ $x > -28$

4. For all integers m and n, where $m \neq n$, $m \uparrow n = \left| \dfrac{m^2 - n^2}{m - n} \right|$. What is the value of $-2 \uparrow 4$?

   ○ 10

   ○ 8

   ○ 6

   ○ 2

   ○ 0

5. If $a > b > c$, then all of the following could be true EXCEPT

   ○ $b + c < a$

   ○ $2a > b + c$

   ○ $2c > a + b$

   ○ $ab > bc$

   ○ $a + b > 2b + c$

6. If $b \neq -2$ and $\dfrac{a + 3}{b + 2} = \dfrac{3}{5}$, what is b in terms of a?

○ $\dfrac{5}{3}a + 1$

○ $\dfrac{3}{5}a + 3$

○ $\dfrac{5}{3}a + 3$

○ $\dfrac{3}{5}a - 1$

○ $\dfrac{5}{3}a - 3$

7. If $m \neq -1$ and $mn - 3 = 3 - n$, then $n =$

○ 6

○ $\dfrac{6}{m + 1}$

○ $\dfrac{6}{m - 1}$

○ $\dfrac{6}{m + n}$

○ $\dfrac{6}{m - n}$

Intermediate

8. If $d = \dfrac{c - b}{a - b}$, then $b =$

    ○ $\dfrac{c - d}{a - d}$

    ○ $\dfrac{c + d}{a + d}$

    ○ $\dfrac{ca - d}{ca + d}$

    ○ $\dfrac{c - ad}{1 - d}$

    ○ $\dfrac{c + ad}{d - 1}$

9. If $a < b < c < 0$, which of the following quotients is the greatest?

    ○ $\dfrac{a}{b}$

    ○ $\dfrac{b}{c}$

    ○ $\dfrac{c}{a}$

    ○ $\dfrac{a}{c}$

    ○ It cannot be determined from the information given.

10. If $2x + y = -8$ and $-4x + 2y = 16$, what is the value of y?

    ○ -4

    ○ -2

    ○ 0

    ○ 2

    ○ 4

Advanced

11. Which of the following describes all values of x that are solutions to the inequality $|x + 2| > 6$?

    ○ $x > 4$

    ○ $x > 8$

    ○ $x < -8$ or $x > 4$

    ○ $x < 4$ or $x > 8$

    ○ $-8 < x < 4$

12. Let $\boxed{x} = \dfrac{x^2 + 1}{2}$ and $\textcircled{y} = \dfrac{3y}{2}$, for all integers x and y. If $m = \textcircled{2}$, $\boxed{m}$ is equal to which of the following?

    ○ $\dfrac{13}{8}$

    ○ $\dfrac{5}{2}$

    ○ $\dfrac{15}{4}$

    ○ 5

    ○ $\dfrac{37}{2}$

13. If $x^2 - 9 < 0$, which of the following is true?

    ○ $x < -3$

    ○ $x > 3$

    ○ $x > 9$

    ○ $x < -3$ or $x > 3$

    ○ $-3 < x < 3$

14. If $n > 4$, which of the following is equivalent to $\dfrac{n - 4\sqrt{n} + 4}{\sqrt{n} - 2}$?

    ○ $\sqrt{n}$

    ○ $2\sqrt{n}$

    ○ $\sqrt{n} + 2$

    ○ $\sqrt{n} - 2$

    ○ $n + \sqrt{n}$

15. What is the set of all values of x for which $x^2 - 3x - 18 = 0$?

    ○ $\{-6\}$

    ○ $\{-3\}$

    ○ $\{-3, 6\}$

    ○ $\{3, 6\}$

    ○ $\{2, 6\}$

KAPLAN

ALGEBRA LEVEL ONE TEST
ANSWERS AND EXPLANATIONS

1. 3

We want to find the value of the expression when x is -3. Let's plug in -3 for each x and see what we get:

$$x^2 + 3x + 3 = (-3)^2 + 3(-3) + 3$$
$$= 9 + (-9) + 3 = 3$$

2. $-\dfrac{1}{2}$

What we have to do is herd all the x's to one side of the equal sign and all the numerical values to the other side: adding $-x$ to both sides we see that $2x + 1 = 0$. Adding -1 to both sides, we get $2x = -1$. Now we can find out what x must equal by dividing both sides by 2:

$$2x = -1$$
$$\frac{2x}{2} = -\frac{1}{2}$$
$$x = -\frac{1}{2}$$

3. 0.0101

Divide both sides by 59. (Watch your decimal places!)

$$0.5959 = 59x$$
$$\frac{0.5959}{59} = x$$
$$x = 0.0101$$

4. -5

We are given that $5 - 2x = 15$. Solve for x by subtracting 5 from each side of the equation, then dividing each side by -2:

$$5 - 2x = 15$$
$$-2x = 10 \text{ (Subtracting 5 from each side)}$$
$$x = -5 \text{ (Dividing each side by } -2)$$

5. $2z^2 - z + 4$

Before we can carry out any other operations, we have to remove the parentheses (that's what the "P" stands for in PEMDAS). Here we can use the distributive law:

$$z(3z - 4) = z \cdot 3z - z \cdot 4$$
$$= 3z^2 - 4z$$

But this is not all there is to it—we're **subtracting** this whole expression from $5z^2 - 5z + 4$. Since subtraction is the inverse operation of addition, we must change the signs of $3z^2 - 4z$.

$$5z^2 - 5z + 4 - (3z^2 - 4z)$$
$$= 5z^2 - 5z + 4 - 3z^2 + 4z$$

And finally, combining like terms gives us

$$5z^2 - 5z + 4 - 3z^2 + 4z$$
$$= (5z^2 - 3z^2) + (-5z + 4z) + 4$$
$$= 2z^2 - z + 4$$

6. 2

Plug in -1 for each a and -2 for each b:

$$2a^2 - 2ab + b^2 = 2(-1)^2 - 2(-1)(-2) + (-2)^2$$
$$= 2 - 4 + 4$$
$$= 2$$

7. 30

Plug in -3 for b wherever it occurs. Remember to square before multiplying:

$$3b^2 - b = 3(-3)^2 - (-3)$$
$$= 3(9) - (-3)$$
$$= 27 + 3$$
$$= 30$$

8. 4

Here we have two values to substitute for two variables. Plug in -2 for x and 2 for y:

$$x^2 + xy + y^2 = (-2)^2 + (-2)(2) + (2)^2$$
$$= 4 + (-4) + 4$$
$$= 4$$

9. 3

We have to use algebraic factoring to make better use of the first equation. We're given:

$$ab + ac = 21$$
$$a(b + c) = 21$$

We're also told that $b + c = 7$, so substitute 7 for $b + c$ in the first equation:

$$a(b + c) = 21$$
$$a(7) = 21$$

Now solve for a:

$$a = \frac{21}{7} = 3$$

10. I only

Substitute $a = 2$, $b = -1$ and $c = 1$ into the statements.

Statement I: $a + b + c = 2 + (-1) + 1$
$$= 2$$

Statement I is true, so eliminate choice (2).

Statement II: $2a + bc = 2(2) + (-1)(1)$
$$= 4 - 1$$
$$= 3$$

Statement II is false, so eliminate choices (3) and (5).

Statement III: $4a - b + c = 4(2) - (-1) + 1$
$$= 8 + 1 + 1$$
$$= 10$$

Statement III is false and the correct answer is choice (1).

11. $-x$

Whenever you are asked to simplify a fraction involving binomials, your first thought should be: Factor! Since x is in both terms of the numerator, we can factor out x and get

$$xy - zx = x(y - z)$$

Performing this operation on the original fraction, we find that

$$\frac{xy - zx}{z - y} = \frac{x(y - z)}{z - y}$$

Rewriting $(z-y)$ as $-1(y-z)$, we get

$$= \frac{x(y - z)}{-1(y - z)}$$

Now cancel $y-z$ from the top and bottom

$$= \frac{x}{-1} = -x$$

Note: It is important that we are told that $y \neq z$ here; otherwise we could have zero in the denominator, and the expression would be undefined.

KAPLAN

12. $\dfrac{1}{8}$

Don't multiply anything out! If they give you such a bizarre-looking expression, there must be a way to simplify. Notice that each of the numbers on the right side is a factor of a number on the left side. So divide each side of the equation by $34 \times 36 \times 38$ to isolate q:

$$q = \frac{17 \times 18 \times 19}{34 \times 36 \times 38}$$

$$q = \frac{17}{34} \times \frac{18}{36} \times \frac{19}{38}$$

$$q = \frac{1}{2} \times \frac{1}{2} \times \frac{1}{2}$$

$$= \frac{1}{8}$$

13. $xy + 1$

To simplify the expression, first use the FOIL method to multiply the binomials $x + 1$ and $y + 1$, then combine terms.

$$\begin{array}{cccc} F & O & I & L \end{array}$$
$$(x + 1)(y + 1) = xy + x \cdot 1 + y \cdot 1 + 1 \cdot 1$$
$$= xy + x + y + 1$$

So,

$$(x + 1)(y + 1) - x - y$$
$$= xy + x + y +$$
$$1 - x - y$$
$$= xy + 1$$

14. 2

We're told that $4 \times 5 \times q = 5 \times p \times 2$. The number 5 is a common factor so we can cancel it from each side. We are left with $4q = 2p$ or $2q = p$. Dividing both sides by q in order to get the quotient $\dfrac{p}{q}$ on one side, we find $\dfrac{p}{q} = 2$.

15. -1

We start with:

$$\frac{x + 3}{2} + x + 3 = 3$$

Multiply both sides of the equation by 2, to get rid of the 2 in the denominator of the first term.

$$\frac{2(x + 3)}{2} + 2(x + 3) = 2(3)$$
$$(x + 3) + 2(x + 3) = 6$$

Next multiply out the parentheses and combine like terms. Our equation becomes:

$$x + 3 + 2x + 6 = 6$$
$$3x + 9 = 6$$

Now isolate the variable on one side of the equation:

$$3x + 9 - 9 = 6 - 9$$
$$3x = -3$$

Finally divide both sides by the coefficient of the variable.

$$\frac{3x}{3} = \frac{-3}{3}$$
$$x = -1$$

16. $3(x+3)(x+3)$

First factor out the 3 common to all terms:

$$3x^2 + 18x + 27 = 3(x^2 + 6x + 9)$$

This is not the same as any answer choice, so we factor the polynomial.

$x^2 + 6x + 9$ is of the form $a^2 + 2ab + b^2$, with $a = x$ and $b = 3$.

So $x^2 + 6x + 9 = (x + 3)^2$ or $(x + 3)(x + 3)$.

That is $3x^2 + 18x + 27 = 3(x + 3)(x + 3)$.

An alternate method would be to multiply out the answer choices, and see which matches $3x^2 + 18x + 27$.

Choice 1—reject:

$$3(x^2 + 6x + 3) = 3x^2 + 18x + 9$$

Choice 2—reject:

$$3(x + 3)(x + 6) = 3(x^2 + 6x + 3x + 18)$$
$$= 3(x^2 + 9x + 18)$$
$$= 3x^2 + 27x + 3(18)$$

Choice 3—correct:

$$3(x + 3)(x + 3) = 3(x^2 + 3x + 3x + 9)$$
$$= 3(x^2 + 6x + 9)$$
$$= 3x^2 + 18x + 27$$

17. **3**

First, find the value of m by substituting $x = 2$ and $y = 1$ into $mx + 5 = y$, and solving for m.

$$mx + 5 = y$$
$$m(2) + 5 = 1$$
$$2m + 5 - 5 = 1 - 5$$

$$2m = -4$$
$$m = \frac{-4}{2}$$
$$m = -2$$

Since we're told m is a constant, we know that m is -2 regardless of the values of x and y. We can rewrite $mx + 5 = y$ as $-2x + 5 = y$, or $5 - 2x = y$.

Now if $y = -1$, then $5 - 2x = -1$.

Solve for x:
$$5 - 2x - 5 = -1 - 5$$
$$-2x = -6$$
$$x = \frac{-6}{-2}$$
$$x = 3$$

18. **3**

First, get rid of the 2 in the denominator of the left hand side by multiplying both sides by 2.

$$\frac{2(5q + 7)}{2} = 2(8 + q)$$
$$5q + 7 = 16 + 2q$$

Now isolate q on one side.

$$5q + 7 = 16 + 2q$$
$$5q + 7 - 2q = 16 + 2q - 2q$$
$$3q + 7 = 16$$
$$3q + 7 - 7 = 16 - 7$$
$$3q = 9$$
$$\frac{3q}{3} = \frac{9}{3}$$
$$q = 3$$

19. $4a^2 b$

Multiply out each half of the expression using FOIL.

$$(a^2 + b)^2 = (a^2 + b)(a^2 + b)$$
$$= a^4[\textbf{F}] + a^2b[\textbf{O}] + ba^2[\textbf{I}] + b^2[\textbf{L}]$$
$$= a^4 + 2a^2b + b^2$$
$$(a^2 - b)^2 = (a^2 - b)(a^2 - b)$$
$$= a^4[\textbf{F}] + a^2(-b)[\textbf{O}] + (-b)a^2[\textbf{I}]$$
$$+ (-b)^2[\textbf{L}]$$
$$= a^4 - 2a^2b + b^2$$

Now subtract

$$(a^2 + b)^2 - (a^2 - b)^2$$
$$= (a^4 + 2a^2b + b^2)$$
$$- (a^4 - 2a^2b + b^2)$$
$$= a^4 + 2a^2b + b^2 - a^4 + 2a^2b - b^2$$
$$= 2a^2b + 2a^2b$$
$$= 4a^2b$$

20. $\dfrac{144}{7}$

Plug in the given values:

$$\frac{xy}{\dfrac{1}{x} + \dfrac{1}{y}} = \frac{3 \cdot 4}{\dfrac{1}{3} + \dfrac{1}{4}}$$

$$= \frac{12}{\dfrac{4}{12} + \dfrac{3}{12}}$$

$$= \frac{12}{\dfrac{7}{12}}$$

$$= \frac{12}{1} \cdot \frac{12}{7}$$

$$= \frac{144}{7}$$

21. $a + b + c$

In this problem, the expression has three terms in the numerator, and a single term, abc, in the denominator. Since the three terms in the numerator each have abc as a factor, abc can be factored out from both the numerator and the denominator, and the expression can be reduced to a simpler form.

$$\frac{a^2bc + ab^2c + abc^2}{abc}$$

$$= \frac{a(abc) + b(abc) + c(abc)}{abc}$$

$$= \frac{(a + b + c)(abc)}{abc}$$

$$= (a + b + c) \cdot \frac{abc}{abc}$$

$$= a + b + c$$

22. $\dfrac{3}{2}$

We are asked to find x when $\dfrac{3}{x - 1} - 6 = 0$. Clear the denominator by multiplying both sides by $x-1$.

$$\frac{3}{x - 1}(x - 1) - 6(x - 1) = 0(x - 1)$$

$3 - 6(x - 1) = 0$	Remove parentheses.
$3 - 6x + 6 = 0$	Gather like terms.
$9 - 6x = 0$	Isolate the variable.
$9 - 6x + 6x = 0 + 6x$	
$9 = 6x$	
$\dfrac{9}{6} = \dfrac{6x}{6}$	
$\dfrac{3}{2} = x$	

Answer choice 4 is correct. You can check your answer by plugging $\dfrac{3}{2}$ into the original equation:

$$\frac{3}{\dfrac{3}{2} - 1} - 6 = \frac{3}{\dfrac{1}{2}} - 6 = 6 - 6 = 0$$

23. $\dfrac{x}{x-1}$

Since $\dfrac{b}{a}$ is the reciprocal of $\dfrac{a}{b}$, $\dfrac{b}{a}$ must be the

reciprocal of $1-\dfrac{1}{x}$ as well. Combine the terms in

$1-\dfrac{1}{x}$ and then find the reciprocal.

$$\frac{a}{b} = 1 - \frac{1}{x} = \frac{x}{x} - \frac{1}{x} = \frac{x-1}{x}$$

Therefore, $\dfrac{b}{a} = \dfrac{x}{x-1}$.

24. **3**

Here we have a symbolism problem, involving a symbol (▲) that doesn't really exist in mathematics. All you need to do is simply follow the directions given in the definition of this symbol. To find the value of $3 \blacktriangle 1$, simply plug 3 and 1 into the formula given for $m \blacktriangle n$, substituting 3 for m and 1 for n. Then the equation becomes:

$$3 \blacktriangle 1 = \frac{(3)^2 - (1) + 1}{(3)(1)}$$
$$= \frac{9 - 1 + 1}{3}$$
$$= \frac{9}{3}$$
$$= 3$$

25. $\dfrac{\sqrt{3}}{3}$

First clear the fraction by multiplying both sides of the equation by $3y + 2$.

$$(3y + 2)(3y - 2) = \frac{-1}{(3y + 2)} \cdot (3y + 2)$$

$$9y^2 - 6y + 6y - 4 = -1 \qquad \text{Using FOIL.}$$
$$9y^2 - 4 = -1 \qquad \text{Gathering terms.}$$
$$9y^2 - 4 + 4 = -1 + 4 \qquad \text{Isolating the variable.}$$
$$9y^2 = 3$$
$$y^2 = \frac{3}{9}$$
$$y = \sqrt{\frac{3}{9}}$$
$$y = \frac{\sqrt{3}}{\sqrt{9}}$$
$$y = \frac{\sqrt{3}}{3}$$

(Since $y > 0$, y cannot also equal $-\dfrac{\sqrt{3}}{3}$.)

26. $a^2 - b^2$

Here we multiply out the part on each side of the addition sign, then combine like terms. We use the distributive law:

$$a(a - b) + b(a - b) = (a^2 - ab) + (ba - b^2)$$
$$= a^2 - ab + ab - b^2$$
$$= a^2 - b^2$$

Alternatively, we can factor out the common term $(a - b)$, and we're left with a product which is the difference of two perfect squares:

$$a(a - b) + b(a - b) = (a - b)(a + b)$$
$$= a^2 - b^2$$

ALGEBRA LEVEL TWO TEST
ANSWERS AND EXPLANATIONS

1. **14**

If $3m < 48$, then $m < \dfrac{48}{3}$ or $m < 16$. And if $2m > 24$,

then $m > \dfrac{24}{2}$ or $m > 12$. Thus, m has any value

between 12 and 16, or $12 < m < 16$. Choice 3, 14, is
the only answer choice within this range.

2. $a + b < 2c$

We're given two inequalities here: $a < b$ and $b < c$,
which we can combine into one, $a < b < c$. We need
to go through the answer choices to see which **must**
be true.

$b + c < 2a$. Since c is greater than a and b is greater
than a, the sum of b and c must be **greater** than twice
a. For instance, if $a = 1$, $b = 2$, and $c = 3$, then
$b + c = 5$ and $2a = 2$, so $b + c > 2a$. Choice 1 is
never true.

$a + b < c$. This may or may not be true, depending on
the actual values of a, b, and c. If $a = 1$, $b = 2$, and
$c = 4$, then $a + b < c$. However, if $a = 2$, $b = 3$, $c = 4$,
then $a + b > c$. So choice 2 is no good either.

$a - b < b - c$. This choice is easier to evaluate if we
simplify it by adding $(b + c)$ to both sides.
$a - b + (b + c) < b - c + (b + c)$

$c + a < 2b$

As in choice 2, this **can** be true, but can also be false,
depending on the values of a, b, and c. If $a = -1$,
$b = 2$, and $c = 3$, then $c + a < 2b$. But if $a = 1$, $b = 2$,
and $c = 4$, then $c + a > 2b$. Choice 3 is no good.

$a + b < 2c$. We know that $a < c$ and $b < c$. If we add
these inequalities we'll get $a + b < c + c$, or
$a + b < 2c$. This statement is **always** true, so it must be
the correct answer.

At this point on the real exam, you should proceed to
the next problem. Just for discussion, however:
$a + c < 2b$. This is the same inequality as choice 3.
That was no good, so this isn't either.

3. $x < -28$

Solve the inequality for x:

$3x - 16 > 4x + 12$	Subtract $3x$ from each side.
$-16 > x + 12$	Subtract 12 from each side.
$-28 > x$	

or

$x < -28$

4. **2**

A fast way to solve this problem is to notice $(m^2 - n^2)$,
which is the numerator of the fraction in the equation
for $m \uparrow n$, is the difference between two squares.
Remember that this can be factored into the product
of $(m + n)$ and $(m - n)$. So the equation for $m \uparrow n$
can be simplified:

$$m \uparrow n = \left| \frac{m^2 - n^2}{m - n} \right|$$

$$= \left| \frac{(m + n)(m - n)}{m - n} \right| \qquad \text{Factoring the numerator.}$$

$$= |m + n| \qquad \text{Cancelling out } m - n.$$

So, if we substitute -2 for m and 4 for n in the
simplified equation, the arithmetic is much easier, and
we get:

$$-2 \uparrow 4 = |-2 + 4|$$
$$= |2|$$
$$= 2$$

5. $2c > a + b$

For this problem, we must examine each of the answer choices. We are told $a > b > c$, and asked which of the answer choices **cannot** be true. If we can find just one set of values a, b, and c, where $a > b > c$, that satisfies an answer choice, then that answer choice is eliminated.

$b + c < a$. This inequality can be true if a is sufficiently large relative to b and c. For example, if $a = 10$, $b = 3$, and $c = 2$, $a > b > c$ still holds, and $b + c < a$. No good.

$2a > b + c$. This is always true because a is greater than either b or c. So $a + a = 2a$ must be greater than $b + c$. For instance, $2(4) > 3 + 2$.

$2c > a + b$. This inequality can never be true. The sum of two smaller numbers (c's) can never be greater than the sum of two larger numbers (a and b). This is the correct answer.

$ab > bc$. This will be true when the numbers are all positive. Try $a = 4$, $b = 3$, and $c = 2$.

$a + b > 2b + c$. Again this can be true if a is large relative to b and c. Try $a = 10$, $b = 2$, and $c = 1$.

6. $\dfrac{5}{3}a + 3$

First clear the fraction by multiplying both sides by $b + 2$.

$$\frac{a + 3}{b + 2} \cdot (b + 2) = \frac{3}{5} \cdot (b + 2)$$

$$a + 3 = \frac{3b + 6}{5} \qquad \text{Multiply both sides by 5.}$$

$$5(a + 3) = \frac{3b + 6}{5} \cdot 5$$

$$5a + 15 = 3b + 6$$

$$5a + 15 - 6 = 3b + 6 - 6$$

$$5a + 9 = 3b$$

$$\frac{5a + 9}{3} = \frac{3b}{3}$$

$$\frac{5a}{3} + \frac{9}{3} = b$$

$$\frac{5a}{3} + 3 = b$$

7. $\dfrac{6}{m + 1}$

We need to isolate n on one side of the equation, and whatever's left on the other side will be an expression for n in terms of m.

$mn - 3 = 3 - n$ First, get all the n's on one side.

$n + mn - 3 = 3 - n + n$

$mn + n - 3 = 3$

$mn + n = 6$ Then isolate n by factoring and dividing.

$n(m + 1) = 6$

$\dfrac{n(m + 1)}{m + 1} = \dfrac{6}{m + 1}$

$n = \dfrac{6}{m + 1}$

8. $\dfrac{c - ad}{1 - d}$

Solve for b in terms of a, c, and d.

$d = \dfrac{c - b}{a - b}$ Clear the denominator by multiplying both sides by $a - b$.

$d(a - b) = c - b$ Multiply out parentheses.

$da - db = c - b$ Gather all b's on one side.

$b - db = c - da$ Factor out the b's on the left hand side.

$b(1 - d) = c - da$ Divide both sides by $1 - d$ to isolate b.

$b = \dfrac{c - ad}{1 - d}$

9. $\dfrac{a}{c}$

Since the quotient of two negatives is always positive and all the variables are negative, all these quotients are positive. To maximize the value of this quotient we need a numerator with the largest possible absolute value and a denominator with the smallest possible absolute value. This means the "most" negative numerator and the "least" negative denominator.

10. **0**

To solve for y, make the x terms drop out. The first equation involves $2x$, while the second involves $-4x$, so multiply both sides of the first equation by 2.

$$2(2x + y) = 2(-8)$$
$$4x + 2y = -16$$

Adding the corresponding sides of this equation and the second equation together gives us

$$4x + 2y = -16$$
$$+ (-4x + 2y = 16)$$
$$\overline{}$$
$$4x + 2y - 4x + 2y = -16 + 16$$
$$4y = 0$$
$$y = 0$$

11. $x < -8$ or $x > 4$

We can think of the absolute value of a number as the number's distance from zero along the number line. Here, since the absolute value of the expression is greater than 6, it could be either that the expression $x + 2$ is **greater than 6** (more than six units to the right of zero) or that the expression is **less than** -6 (more than six units to the left of zero). Therefore either

$$x + 2 > 6 \qquad \text{or} \qquad x + 2 < -6$$
$$x > 4 \qquad \text{or} \qquad x < -8$$

12. **5**

This is an especially tricky symbolism problem. We're given **two** new symbols, and we need to complete several steps. The trick is figuring out where to start. We are asked to find $\boxed{m}$. In order to do this we must first find the value of m. Since m is equal to $\textcircled{2}$, we can find m by finding the value of $\textcircled{2}$. And we can find $\textcircled{2}$ by substituting 2 for y in the equation given for $\textcircled{y}$. The equation becomes:

$$\textcircled{2} = \frac{3(2)}{2}$$
$$\textcircled{2} = 3$$

Since $m = \textcircled{2}$, then m is equal to 3, and $\boxed{m}$ is just $\boxed{3}$.

We find $\boxed{3}$ by substituting 3 for x in the equation given for $\boxed{x}$:

$$\boxed{3} = \frac{3^2 + 1}{2}$$
$$= \frac{9 + 1}{2}$$
$$= \frac{10}{2}$$
$$= 5$$

So $\boxed{m} = 5$.

13. $-3 < x < 3$

Rearrange $x^2 - 9 < 0$ to get $x^2 < 9$. We're looking for all the values of x that would fit this inequality.

We need to be very careful and consider both positive **and** negative values of x. Remember that $3^2 = 9$ and also that $(-3)^2 = 9$.

We can consider the case that x is positive. If x is positive, and $x^2 < 9$, then we can simply say that $x < 3$. But what if x is negative? x can only take on values whose square is less than 9. In other words, x cannot be less than or equal to -3. (Think of smaller numbers like -4 or -5; their squares are greater than 9.)

So if x is negative, $x > -3$. Since x can also be 0, we can simply write $-3 < x < 3$.

14. $\sqrt{n} - 2$

We must try to get rid of the denominator by factoring it out of the numerator. $n - 4\sqrt{n} + 4$ is a difficult expression to work with. It may be easier if we let $t = \sqrt{n}$. Keep in mind then that $t^2 = (\sqrt{n})(\sqrt{n}) = n$.

Then $\qquad n - 4\sqrt{n} + 4 = t^2 - 4t + 4$

Using FOIL in reverse $\qquad = (t - 2)(t - 2)$

$$= (\sqrt{n} - 2)(\sqrt{n} - 2)$$

So $\qquad \dfrac{n - 4\sqrt{n} + 4}{\sqrt{n} - 2} = \dfrac{(\sqrt{n} - 2)(\sqrt{n} - 2)}{(\sqrt{n} - 2)}$

$$= \sqrt{n} - 2$$

Or pick a number for n and try each answer choice.

15. $\{-3,6\}$

Factor the quadratic

$$x^2 - 3x - 18 = (x + a)(x + b)$$

The product of a and b is $\qquad ab = -18$
The sum of a and b is $\qquad a + b = -3$
Try the factors of -18 that add to -3:
Try $a = 3$ $\;b = -6$ $\qquad 3 \times (-6) = -18$
$$3 + (-6) = -3$$

So $\qquad x^2 - 3x - 18 = (x + 3)(x - 6) = 0$
If this is zero, either $x + 3 = 0$ i.e., $x = -3$
or $x - 6 = 0$ i.e., $x = 6$

The set of values is therefore $\{-3, 6\}$

Chapter 4
Geometry

The geometry tested on the GRE is very basic: lines, triangles, circles. There are only a few fundamental definitions and formulas you need to know. The GRE emphasizes new ways of applying a couple of elementary rules.

DIAGRAMS

Pay a lot of attention to diagrams. There can be a lot of information "hidden" in a diagram. If a diagram of an equilateral triangle gives you the length of one side, for instance, it actually gives the length of all sides. Similarly if you are given the measure of one of the angles formed by the intersection of two lines, you can easily find the measure of all four angles. In fact, many geometry questions specifically test your ability to determine what additional information is implied by the information you are given in the diagram.

The figures on the GRE are **not** drawn to scale unless otherwise stated. The diagrams provide such basic information as what kind of figure you are dealing with (is it a triangle? a quadrilateral?), the order of the points on lines, etc. If a line looks straight in the diagram, you can assume it is straight. But you must be careful when using the diagram to judge relative lengths, angles, sizes, etc., since these may not be drawn accurately. If an angle looks like a right angle, you cannot assume it is one, unless it is marked as such. If one side of a triangle looks longer than another, you cannot assume it is unless some other information tells you that it is. If a figure looks like a square, you don't know it is a square; you only know it is a quadrilateral. This is especially important to bear in mind in the Quantitative Comparison section, where the diagram may lead you to believe that one column is greater, but logic will prove that you need more information.

EYEBALLING DIAGRAMS

If you are stuck and are going to have to guess anyway, try to eliminate answer choices by eyeballing. By *eyeballing*, we mean estimating lengths or measures by comparing to other lengths or measures given in the diagram. If you are given the length of one line, you can use this line to get a rough idea how long another, unmarked line might be. If the size of one angle is marked, use this angle to estimate the size of other angles.

For instance, if you are asked to find the degree measure of an angle, and the answers are widely spaced, you may be able to eliminate some answer choices by deciding if the angle in question is less than or greater than, say, 45°. For this reason you should try to get a feel for what the most commonly encountered angles look like. Angles of 30°, 45°, 60°, 90°, 120° and 180° are the most common, and you will find examples of them in the test and questions which follow.

You can also on occasion use the diagram to your advantage by looking at the question logically. For instance:

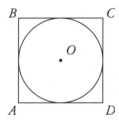

In the figure above, the circle with center O has area 4π. What is the area of square $ABCD$?

○ 4   ○ 2π   ○ 12   ○ 16   ○ 8π

We know from the question stem that we have a square and a circle and we can see from the diagram that the circle is inscribed in the square, that is, touches it on all four sides. Whatever the area of the circle, we can see that the square's area must be bigger; otherwise the circle wouldn't fit inside it. So the right answer must be larger than the area of the circle, that is, larger than 4π. Now we can approximate 4π to a little more than 12. Since the correct answer is larger than 12, it must be either the fourth or fifth choice. (The correct answer is 16.)

This example highlights an important point: π appears very often on geometry problems, so you should have some idea of its value. It is approximately equal to 3.14, but for most purposes you only need remember that it is slightly greater than 3. Two other numbers you should know the approximate values of are $\sqrt{2}$, which is about 1.4, and $\sqrt{3}$, which is about 1.7.

LINES AND ANGLES

A line is a one-dimensional geometrical abstraction—infinitely long with no width. It is not physically possible to **draw** a line; any physical line would have a finite length and some width, no matter how long and thin we tried to make it. Two points determine a straight line; given any two points, there is exactly one straight line that passes through them.

Lines: A **line segment** is a section of a straight line, of finite length with two endpoints. A line segment is named for its endpoints, as in segment AB. The **midpoint** is the point that divides a line segment into two equal parts.

$$\overset{\displaystyle 6}{\underset{\displaystyle A \qquad M \qquad B}{\bullet\!\!-\!\!-\!\!-\!\!\bullet\!\!-\!\!-\!\!-\!\!\bullet}}$$

Example: In the figure above, A and B are the endpoints of the line segment AB and M is the midpoint ($AM = MB$). What is the length of AB?

Since AM is 6, MB is also 6, and so AB is $6 + 6$, or 12.

Two lines are **parallel** if they lie in the same plane and never intersect each other regardless of how far they are extended. If line ℓ_1 is parallel to line ℓ_2, we write $\ell_1 \parallel \ell_2$.

Angles: An **angle** is formed by two lines or line segments intersecting at a point. The point of intersection is called the **vertex** of the angle. Angles are measured in degrees(°).

Angle x, $\angle ABC$, and $\angle B$ all denote the same angle shown in the diagram above.

An **acute angle** is an angle whose degree measure is between 0° and 90°. A **right angle** is an angle whose degree measure is exactly 90°. An **obtuse angle** is an angle whose degree measure is between 90° and 180°. A **straight angle** is an angle whose degree measure is exactly 180° (half of a circle, which contains 360°).

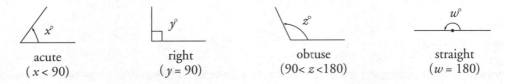

acute
($x < 90$)

right
($y = 90$)

obtuse
($90 < z < 180$)

straight
($w = 180$)

The sum of the measures of the angles on one side of a straight line is 180°.

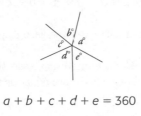

straight
($x + y + z = 180$)

The sum of the measures of the angles around a point is 360°.

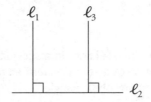

$a + b + c + d + e = 360$

Two lines are **perpendicular** if they intersect at a 90° angle. The shortest distance from a point to a line is the line segment drawn from the point to the line such that it is perpendicular to the line. If line ℓ_1 is perpendicular to line ℓ_2, we write $\ell_1 \perp \ell_2$. If $\ell_1 \perp \ell_2$ and $\ell_2 \perp \ell_3$, then $\ell_1 \parallel \ell_3$:

ℓ_1 ℓ_3

ℓ_2

Two angles are **supplementary** if together they make up a straight angle, i.e., if the sum of their measures is 180°. Two angles are **complementary** if together they make up a right angle, i.e., if the sum of their measures is 90°.

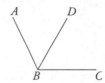

$$c + d = 180 \qquad\qquad a + b = 90$$

A line or line segment **bisects** an angle if it splits the angle into two smaller, equal angles. Line segment BD below bisects $\angle ABC$, and $\angle ABD$ has the same measure as $\angle DBC$. The two smaller angles are each half the size of $\angle ABC$.

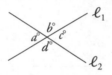

Vertical angles are a pair of opposite angles formed by two intersecting line segments. At the point of intersection, two pairs of vertical angles are formed. Angles a and c below are vertical angles, as are b and d.

The two angles in a pair of vertical angles have the same degree measure. In the diagram above, $a = c$ and $b = d$. In addition, since ℓ_1 and ℓ_2 are straight lines,

$$a + b = c + d = a + d = b + c = 180$$

In other words, each angle is supplementary to each of its two adjacent angles.

If two parallel lines intersect with a third line (called a *transversal*), each of the parallel lines will intersect the third line at the same angle. In the figure below, $a = e$. Since a and e are equal, and $c = a$ and $e = g$ (vertical angles), we know that $a = c = e = g$. Similarly, $b = d = f = h$.

If $\ell_1 \parallel \ell_2$, then,
$a = c = e = g$ and
$b = d = f = h$

In other words, when two parallel lines intersect with a third line, all acute angles formed are equal, all obtuse angles formed are equal, and any acute angle is supplementary to any obtuse angle.

SLOPE

The slope of a line tells you how steeply that line goes up or down. If a line gets higher as you move to the right, it has a positive slope. If it goes down as you move to the right, it has a negative slope.

To find the slope of a line, use the following formula:

$$Slope = \frac{rise}{run} = \frac{change\ in\ y}{change\ in\ x}$$

Rise means the difference between the y-coordinate values of the two points on the line, and *run* means the difference between the x-coordinate values.

Example: What is the slope of the line that contains the points (1, 2) and (4, −5)?

$$Slope = \frac{-5 - 2}{4 - 1} = \frac{-7}{3} = -\frac{7}{3}$$

To determine the slope of a line from an equation, put the equation into the slope-intercept form: $y = mx + b$, where the slope is m.

Example: What is the slope of the equation $3x + 2y = 4$?

$$3x + 2y = 4$$

$$2y = -3x + 4$$

$$y = -\frac{3}{2}x + 2, \text{so } m \text{ is } -\frac{3}{2}$$

LINES AND ANGLES EXERCISE

In #1–6, find the indicated value. (Answers are on the following page.)

1.

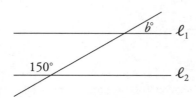

$\ell_1 \parallel \ell_2$
$b = ?$

2.

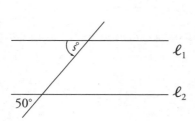

$\ell_1 \parallel \ell_2$
$s = ?$

3.

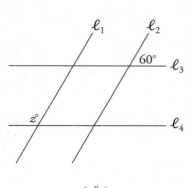

$\ell_1 \parallel \ell_2$
$\ell_3 \parallel \ell_4$
$z = ?$

4.

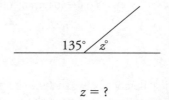

$z = ?$

5.

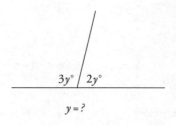

$y = ?$

6.

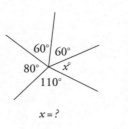

$x = ?$

ANSWER KEY—LINES AND ANGLES EXERCISE

1. 30
2. 50
3. 120
4. 45
5. 36
6. 50

LINES AND ANGLES TEST

Solve the following problems and choose the best answers. (Answers and explanations are at the end of this chapter.)

Basic

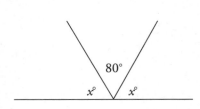

1. In the figure above, what is the value of x?

  ○ 40
  ○ 50
  ○ 60
  ○ 80
  ○ 100

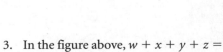

2. In the figure above, what is the measure of $\angle AOE$?

  ○ 35°
  ○ 45°
  ○ 75°
  ○ 105°
  ○ 145°

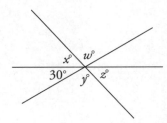

3. In the figure above, $w + x + y + z =$

  ○ 330
  ○ 300
  ○ 270
  ○ 240
  ○ 210

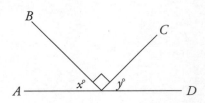

4. In the figure above, what is the value of $x + y$?

  ○ 30
  ○ 60
  ○ 90
  ○ 110
  ○ It cannot be determined from the information given.

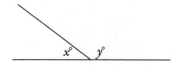

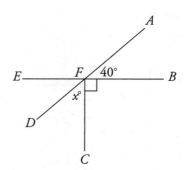

5. In the figure above, if $y = 5x$, then $x =$

    ○ 15
    ○ 30
    ○ 45
    ○ 135
    ○ 150

6. In the figure above, *EB* is perpendicular to *FC*, and *AD* and *EB* intersect at point *F*. What is the value of *x*?

    ○ 30
    ○ 40
    ○ 50
    ○ 60
    ○ 130

Intermediate

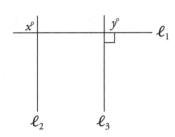

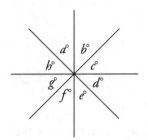

7. In the figure above, if $x = y$, which of the following MUST be true?

   I. $\ell_2 \parallel \ell_3$

   II. $\ell_1 \perp \ell_2$

   III. Any line that intersects ℓ_1 also intersects ℓ_2.

   ○ I only
   ○ II only
   ○ III only
   ○ I and II only
   ○ I, II, and III

9. In the figure above, which of the following MUST equal 180?

   I. $a + b + e + h$

   II. $b + e + g + h$

   III. $a + b + d + g$

   ○ I only
   ○ II only
   ○ I and III only
   ○ II and III only
   ○ I, II, and III

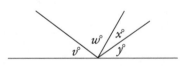

8. In the figure above, $v = 2w$, $w = 2x$, and $x = \dfrac{y}{3}$.

   What is the value of y?

   ○ 18
   ○ 36
   ○ 45
   ○ 54
   ○ 60

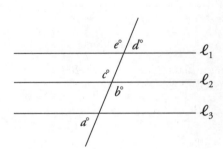

10. In the figure above, ℓ_1 is parallel to ℓ_2 and ℓ_2 is parallel to ℓ_3. What is the value of $a + b + c + d + e$?

    ○ 180
    ○ 270
    ○ 360
    ○ 450
    ○ It cannot be determined from the information given.

Advanced

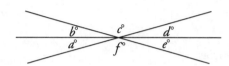

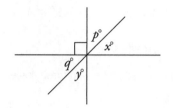

11. Which of the following must be true of the angles marked in the figure above?

    I. $a + b = d + e$

    II. $b + e = c + f$

    III. $a + c + e = b + d + f$

   ◯ I only

   ◯ I and II only

   ◯ I and III only

   ◯ II and III only

   ◯ I, II, and III

13. According to the diagram above, which of the following MUST be true?

    I. $p = x$ and $q = y$

    II. $x + y = 90$

    III. $x = y = 45$

   ◯ I only

   ◯ II only

   ◯ III only

   ◯ I and III only

   ◯ I, II, and III

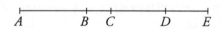

12. In the diagram above, $AD = BE = 6$ and $CD = 3(BC)$. If $AE = 8$, then $BC =$

   ◯ 6

   ◯ 4

   ◯ 3

   ◯ 2

   ◯ 1

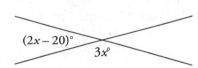

14. In the figure above, $x =$

   ◯ 40

   ◯ 60

   ◯ 80

   ◯ 100

   ◯ 120

TRIANGLES

General Triangles

A **triangle** is a closed figure with three angles and three straight sides.

> ### The sum of the interior angles
> ### of any triangle is 180 degrees.

Each interior angle is supplementary to an adjacent **exterior angle**. The degree measure of an exterior angle is equal to the sum of the measures of the two non-adjacent (remote) interior angles, or 180° minus the measure of the adjacent interior angle.

In the figure below, a, b, and c are interior angles. Therefore $a + b + c = 180$. In addition, d is supplementary to c; therefore $d + c = 180$. So $d + c = a + b + c$, and $d = a + b$. Thus, the exterior angle d is equal to the sum of the two remote interior angles: a and b.

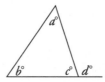

The **altitude** (or height) of a triangle is the perpendicular distance from a vertex to the side opposite the vertex. The altitude can fall inside the triangle, outside the triangle, or on one of the sides.

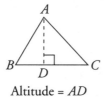
Altitude = AD

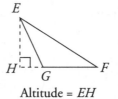
Altitude = EH

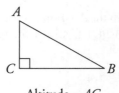
Altitude = AC

Sides and angles: The length of any side of a triangle is less than the sum of the lengths of the other two sides, and greater than the positive difference of the lengths of the other two sides.

$$b + c > a > b - c$$
$$a + b > c > a - b$$
$$a + c > b > a - c$$

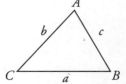

If the lengths of two sides of a triangle are unequal, the **greater angle** lies **opposite the longer side** and vice versa. In the figure above, if $\angle A > \angle B > \angle C$, then $a > b > c$.

Area of a triangle:

Example: In the diagram below, the base has length 4 and the altitude length 3, so we write:

> The area of a triangle is $\frac{1}{2}$ base $\times$ height.

$$A = \frac{1}{2}bh$$

$$= \frac{1}{2} \cdot 4 \cdot 3 = 6$$

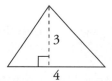

Remember that the height (or altitude) is perpendicular to the base. Therefore, when two sides of a triangle are perpendicular to each other, the area is easy to find. In a right triangle, we call the two sides that form the 90° angle the **legs**. Then the area is one half the product of the legs, or

$$A = \frac{1}{2}bh$$

$$= \frac{1}{2}\ell_1 \times \ell_2$$

Example: In the triangle below, we could treat the hypotenuse as the base, since that is the way the figure is drawn. If we did this, we would need to know the distance from the hypotenuse to the opposite vertex in order to determine the area of the triangle. A more straightforward method is to notice that this is a **right** triangle with legs of lengths 6 and 8, which allows us to use the alternative formula for area:

$$A = \frac{1}{2}\ell_1 \times \ell_2$$

$$= \frac{1}{2} \cdot 6 \cdot 8 = 24$$

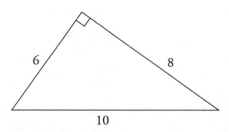

Perimeter of a triangle: The **perimeter** of a triangle is the distance around the triangle. In other words, the perimeter is equal to the sum of the lengths of the sides.

Example: In the triangle below, the sides are of length 5, 6, and 8. Therefore, the perimeter is 5 + 6 + 8, or 19.

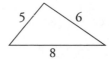

Isosceles triangles: An **isosceles triangle** is a triangle that has two sides of equal length. The two equal sides are called **legs** and the third side is called the **base**.

Since the two legs have the same length, the two angles opposite the legs must have the same measure. In the figure below, $PQ = PR$, and $\angle R = \angle Q$.

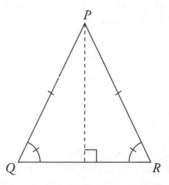

Equilateral triangles: An **equilateral triangle** has three sides of equal length and three 60° angles.

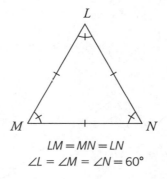

$$LM = MN = LN$$
$$\angle L = \angle M = \angle N = 60°$$

Similar triangles: Triangles are **similar** if they have the same shape—if corresponding angles have the same measure. For instance, any two triangles whose angles measure 30°, 60°, and 90° are similar. In similar triangles, corresponding sides are in the same ratio. Triangles are **congruent** if corresponding angles have the same measure and corresponding sides have the same length.

Example: What is the perimeter of $\triangle DEF$ below?

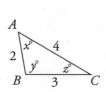
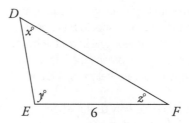

Each triangle has an $x°$ angle, a $y°$ angle, and a $z°$ angle; therefore, they are similar, and corresponding sides are in the same ratio. BC and EF are corresponding sides; each is opposite the $x°$ angle. Since EF is twice the length of BC, **each** side of $\triangle DEF$ will be twice the length of the corresponding side of $\triangle ABC$. Therefore $DE = 2(AB)$ or 4, and $DF = 2(AC)$ or 8. The perimeter of $\triangle DEF$ is $4 + 6 + 8 = 18$.

The ratio of the **areas** of two similar triangles is the **square** of the ratio of corresponding lengths. For instance, in the example above, since each side of $\triangle DEF$ is 2 times the length of the corresponding side of $\triangle ABC$, $\triangle DEF$ must have 2^2 or 4 times the area of $\triangle ABC$.

$$\frac{\text{Area } \triangle DEF}{\text{Area } \triangle ABC} = \left(\frac{DE}{AB}\right)^2 = \left(\frac{2}{1}\right)^2 = 4$$

Right Triangles

A right triangle has one interior angle of 90°. The longest side (which lies opposite the right angle, the largest angle of a right triangle is called the **hypotenuse**. The other two sides are called the **legs**.

Pythagorean Theorem

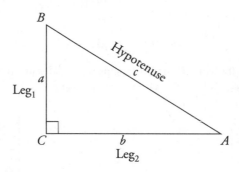

$$(\text{Leg}_1)^2 + (\text{Leg}_2)^2 = (\text{Hypotenuse})^2$$

or

$$a^2 + b^2 = c^2$$

The Pythagorean theorem holds for all right triangles, and states that the square of the hypotenuse is equal to the sum of the squares of the legs.

Some sets of integers happen to satisfy the Pythagorean theorem. These sets of integers are commonly referred to as "Pythagorean triplets." One very common set that you might remember is 3, 4, and 5. Since $3^2 + 4^2 = 5^2$, you can have a right triangle with legs of lengths 3 and 4, and hypotenuse of length 5. This is probably the most common kind of right triangle on the GRE. You should be familiar with the numbers, so that whenever you see a right triangle with legs of 3 and 4, you will immediately know the hypotenuse must have length 5. In addition, any multiple of these lengths makes another Pythagorean triplet; for instance, $6^2 + 8^2 = 10^2$, so 6, 8, and 10 also make a right triangle. One other triplet that appears occasionally is 5, 12, and 13.

The Pythagorean theorem is very useful whenever you're given the lengths of two sides of a right triangle; you can find the length of the third side with the Pythagorean theorem.

Example: What is the length of the hypotenuse of a right triangle with legs of length 9 and 10?

Use the theorem: the square of the length of the hypotenuse equals the sum of the squares of the lengths of the legs. Here the legs are 9 and 10, so we have

$$\text{Hypotenuse}^2 = 9^2 + 10^2$$
$$= 81 + 100$$
$$= 181$$
$$\text{Hypotenuse} = \sqrt{181}$$

Example: What is the length of the hypotenuse of an isosceles right triangle with legs of length 4?

Since we're told the triangle is isosceles, we know two of the sides have the same length. We know the hypotenuse can't be the same length as one of the legs (the hypotenuse must be the longest side), so it must be the two legs that are equal. Therefore, in this example, the two legs have length 4, and we can use the Pythagorean theorem to find the hypotenuse.

$$\text{Hypotenuse}^2 = 4^2 + 4^2$$
$$= 16 + 16$$
$$= 32$$
$$\text{Hypotenuse} = \sqrt{32} = 4\sqrt{2}$$

You can always use the Pythagorean theorem to find the lengths of the sides in a right triangle. There are two special kinds of right triangles, though, that always have the same ratios. They are:

$1 : 1 : \sqrt{2}$

(for isosceles right triangles)

$1 : \sqrt{3} : 2$

(for 30-60-90 triangles)

Fortunately for your peace of mind, these triangles do not appear very frequently on the GRE, and if one does, you can still use the Pythagorean theorem to calculate the length of a side, as we did in the last example.

TRIANGLES EXERCISE

Solve the following questions as directed. (Answers follow the exercise.)

> The sum of the measures of the angles in a triangle is 180°.

In #1–4, find the missing angle:

1.

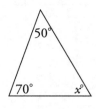

$x = ?$

2.

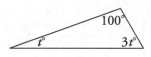

$t = ?$

3.

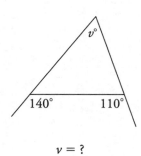

$v = ?$

4.

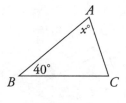

$AB = BC$

$x = ?$

> In a right triangle, $\text{leg}^2 + \text{leg}^2 = \text{hyp}^2$.

In #5–12, find the missing side:

5.

30, 50, b

$b = ?$

6.

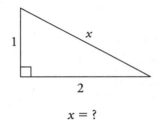

$$x = ?$$

7.

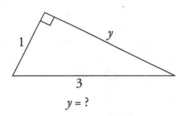

$$y = ?$$

8.

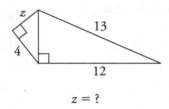

$$z = ?$$

The ratio of the sides in an isosceles right triangle is $1 : 1 : \sqrt{2}$.

9.

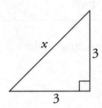

$$x = ?$$

10.

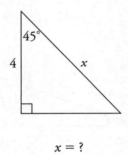

$$x = ?$$

> The ratio of the sides in a 30-60-90 triangle is $1 : \sqrt{3} : 2$.

11.

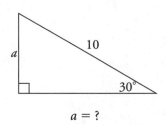

$b = ?$

12.

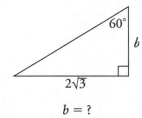

$a = ?$

> The area of a triangle is $\frac{1}{2}$ (base $\times$ height).

In #13–16, find the area of the triangle:

13.

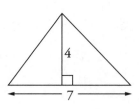

Area = ?

14.

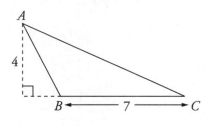

Area = ?

15.

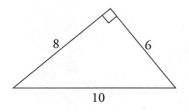

Area = ?

16.

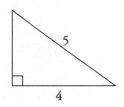

Area = ?

ANSWER KEY—TRIANGLES EXERCISE

1. 60
2. 20
3. 70
4. 70
5. 40
6. $\sqrt{5}$
7. $\sqrt{8}$ or $2\sqrt{2}$
8. 3
9. $\sqrt{18}$ or $3\sqrt{2}$
10. $4\sqrt{2}$
11. 2
12. 5
13. 14
14. 14
15. 24
16. 6

TRIANGLES TEST

Solve the problems below and choose the best answer. (Answers and explanations are at the end of this chapter.)

Basic

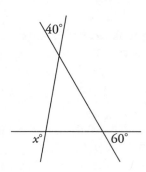

1. In the figure above, $x =$
    ◯ 60
    ◯ 80
    ◯ 85
    ◯ 90
    ◯ 100

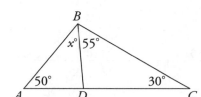

2. In the figure above, what is the value of x?
    ◯ 120
    ◯ 110
    ◯ 90
    ◯ 70
    ◯ 60

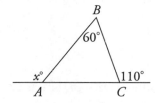

3. In the figure above, $x =$
    ◯ 70
    ◯ 110
    ◯ 130
    ◯ 150
    ◯ 170

4. In $\triangle ABC$ above, $x =$
    ◯ 45
    ◯ 55
    ◯ 60
    ◯ 75
    ◯ 80

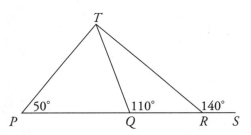

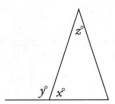

5. In the figure above, if *BD* bisects ∠*ABC*, then the measure of ∠*BDC* is

- ⬭ 50°
- ⬭ 90°
- ⬭ 100°
- ⬭ 110°
- ⬭ 120°

7. In the figure above, $x = 2z$ and $y = 3z$. What is the value of z?

- ⬭ 24
- ⬭ 30
- ⬭ 36
- ⬭ 54
- ⬭ 60

6. In the figure above, what is the measure of ∠*PTR*?

- ⬭ 30°
- ⬭ 50°
- ⬭ 65°
- ⬭ 70°
- ⬭ 90°

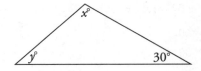

8. In the figure above, what is x in terms of y?

- ⬭ $150 - y$
- ⬭ $150 + y$
- ⬭ $80 + y$
- ⬭ $30 + y$
- ⬭ $30 - y$

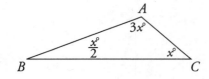

9. In △*ABC* above, *x* =

   ◯ 20

   ◯ 30

   ◯ 40

   ◯ 50

   ◯ 60

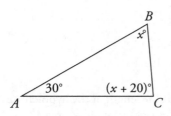

10. In △*ABC* above, *x* =

   ◯ 30

   ◯ 45

   ◯ 60

   ◯ 65

   ◯ 75

11. The angles of a triangle are in the ratio of 2 : 3 : 4. What is the degree measure of the largest angle?

   ◯ 40

   ◯ 80

   ◯ 90

   ◯ 120

   ◯ 150

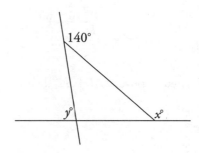

12. In the figure above, *x* + *y* =

   ◯ 40

   ◯ 120

   ◯ 140

   ◯ 180

   ◯ 220

Intermediate

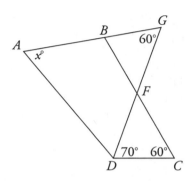

13. In the figure above, if $AD \parallel BC$, then $x =$

   ◯ 20
   ◯ 30
   ◯ 50
   ◯ 60
   ◯ 70

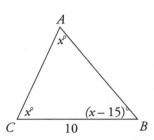

14. In $\triangle ABC$ above, which of the following must be true?

   I. $x > 50$
   II. $AC < 10$
   III. $AB > 10$

   ◯ I only
   ◯ III only
   ◯ I and II only
   ◯ I and III only
   ◯ I, II, and III

15. In the figure above, the area of $\triangle ABC$ is 6. If BC is $\frac{1}{3}$ the length of AB, then $AC =$

   ◯ $\sqrt{2}$
   ◯ 2
   ◯ 4
   ◯ 6
   ◯ $2\sqrt{10}$

16. What is the length of the hypotenuse of an isosceles right triangle of area 32?

   ◯ 4
   ◯ $4\sqrt{2}$
   ◯ 8
   ◯ $8\sqrt{2}$
   ◯ $8\sqrt{3}$

Advanced

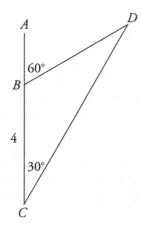

17. In the figure above, if ∠DBA has measure 60°, ∠DCB has measure 30°, and BC = 4, what is the length of BD?

- ○ $\sqrt{2}$
- ○ 4
- ○ $4\sqrt{2}$
- ○ $4\sqrt{3}$
- ○ 8

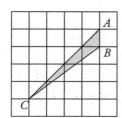

18. The figure consists of 36 squares each with a side of 1. What is the area of $\triangle ABC$?

- ○ 8
- ○ 6
- ○ 4
- ○ 2
- ○ $\dfrac{1}{2}$

19. The lengths of two sides of a right triangle are $\dfrac{d}{3}$ and $\dfrac{d}{4}$, where $d > 0$. If one of these sides is the hypotenuse, what is the length of the third side of the triangle?

- ○ $\dfrac{5d}{12}$
- ○ $\dfrac{d}{\sqrt{7}}$
- ○ $\dfrac{d}{5}$
- ○ $\dfrac{d}{12}$
- ○ $\dfrac{d\sqrt{7}}{12}$

20. What is the length in feet of a ladder 24 feet from the foot of a building that reaches up 18 feet along the wall of the building?

- ○ 26
- ○ 28
- ○ 29
- ○ 30
- ○ 32

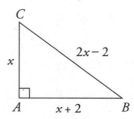

21. In right triangle ABC above, x =

- ○ 6
- ○ 8
- ○ $6\sqrt{2}$
- ○ 10
- ○ 13

POLYGONS

A **polygon** is a closed figure whose sides are straight line segments.
The **perimeter** of a polygon is the sum of the lengths of the sides.
A **vertex** of a polygon is the point where two adjacent sides meet.
A **diagonal** of a polygon is a line segment connecting two nonadjacent vertices.
A **regular polygon** has sides of equal length and interior angles of equal measure.

The number of sides determines the specific name of the polygon. A **triangle** has three sides, a **quadrilateral** has four sides, a **pentagon** has five sides, and a **hexagon** has six sides. Triangles and quadrilaterals are by far the most important polygons on the GRE.

Interior and exterior angles: A polygon can be divided into triangles by drawing diagonals from a given vertex to all other nonadjacent vertices. For instance, the pentagon below can be divided into 3 triangles. Since the sum of the interior angles of each triangle is 180°, the sum of the interior angles of a pentagon is 3 × 180° = 540°.

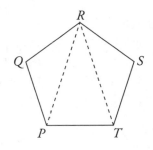

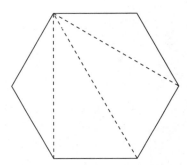

Example: What is the measure of one interior angle of the above regular hexagon?
Find the sum of the interior angles and divide by the number of interior angles, or 6. (Since all angles are equal, each of them is equal to one-sixth of the sum.)
Since we can draw 4 triangles in a 6-sided figure, the sum of the interior angles will be 4 × 180°, or 720°. Therefore, each of the six interior angles has measure $\frac{720}{6}$, or 120 degrees.

QUADRILATERALS

The most important quadrilaterals to know for the GRE are the rectangle and square. Anything could show up on the test, but concentrate on the most important figures and principles. The lesser-known properties can readily be deduced from the way the figure looks, and from your knowledge of geometry.

Quadrilateral: A four sided polygon. The sum of its four interior angles is 360°.

Rectangle: A quadrilateral with four equal angles, each a right angle.

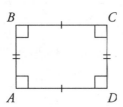

$$AB = CD \qquad AD = CB$$

The opposite sides of a rectangle are equal in length. Also, the diagonals of a rectangle have equal length.

Square: A rectangle with four equal sides.

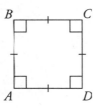

$$AB = BC = CD = DA$$

Areas of quadrilaterals: All formulas are based on common sense, observation, and deductions. Memorizing the formulas will save you time, but *understanding* how the formulas are derived will help you to remember them.

For the case of a rectangle, we multiply the lengths of any two adjacent sides, called the length and width, or:

Area of rectangle = ℓw

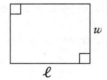

For the case of a square, since length and width are equal, we say:

Area of a square = (side)^2 = s^2

The areas of other figures can usually be found using the methods we'll discuss later in the Multiple Figures section.

QUADRILATERALS EXERCISE

Solve the problems below as directed. (Answers follow the exercise.)

> The sum of the measures of the interior angles of a quadrilateral is 360°.

In #1–6, find the indicated value.

1.

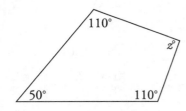

$z = ?$

2.

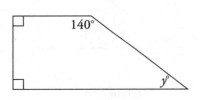

$y = ?$

3.

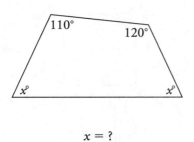

$x = ?$

4.

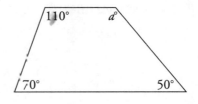

$a = ?$

5.

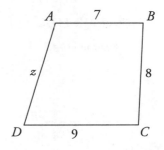

The perimeter of *ABCD* is 34.

$z = ?$

6.

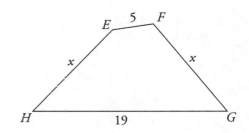

The perimeter of *EFGH* is 48.

$x = ?$

In #7–9, find the perimeter.

7.

Rectangle *ABCD*

Perimeter = ?

8.

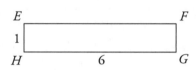

Rectangle *EFGH*

Perimeter = ?

9.

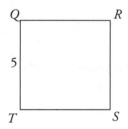

Square *QRST*
Perimeter = ?

Area of rectangle = length × width
Area of square = (side)²

In #10–12, find the area of the quadrilateral.

10.

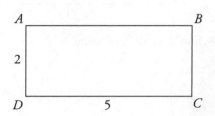

Rectangle *ABCD*

Area = ?

11.

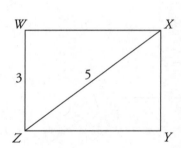

Rectangle *WXYZ*

Area = ?

12.

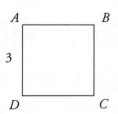

Square *ABCD*

Area = ?

In #13–15, find the indicated diagonal or side.

13.

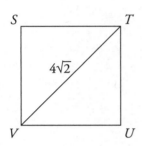

Square *STUV*

ST = ?

14.

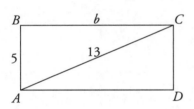

Rectangle *ABCD*

b = ?

15.

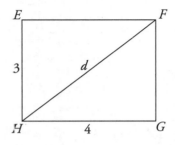

Rectangle *EFGH*

d = ?

ANSWER KEY—QUADRILATERALS EXERCISE

1. 90
2. 40
3. 65
4. 130
5. 10
6. 12
7. 14
8. 14
9. 20
10. 10
11. 12
12. 9
13. 4
14. 12
15. 5

QUADRILATERALS AND OTHER POLYGONS TEST

See the following problems and select the best answer for those given. (Answers are at the end of the chapter)

Basic

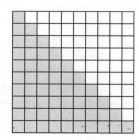

1. If each of the small squares in the figure above has area 1, what is the area of the shaded region?

   ○ 50

   ○ 55

   ○ 59

   ○ 60

   ○ 61

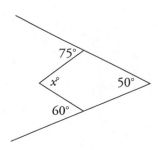

2. In the figure above, x =

   ○ 85

   ○ 90

   ○ 95

   ○ 120

   ○ 140

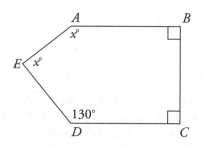

3. In pentagon ABCDE above, x =

   ○ 65

   ○ 75

   ○ 80

   ○ 105

   ○ 115

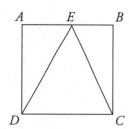

4. What is the ratio of the area of △DEC to the area of square ABCD in the figure above?

   ○ $\frac{1}{4}$

   ○ $\frac{1}{3}$

   ○ $\frac{1}{2}$

   ○ $\frac{2}{1}$

   ○ It cannot be determined from the information given.

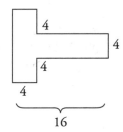

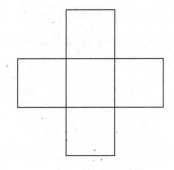

5. The figure above gives the floor dimensions, in meters, of a T-shaped room. If all the sides meet at right angles and 1 meter by 1 meter square tiles cost $2.00 each, how much would it cost to cover the entire room with these tiles?

- ◯ $48.00
- ◯ $72.00
- ◯ $96.00
- ◯ $192.00
- ◯ $198.00

6. The figure above is made up of 5 squares of equal area, with a total area of 20. What is the perimeter of the figure?

- ◯ 20
- ◯ 24
- ◯ 36
- ◯ 48
- ◯ 100

Intermediate

7. If the length of rectangle *A* is one-half the length of rectangle *B*, and the width of rectangle *A* is one-half the width of rectangle *B*, what is the ratio of the area of rectangle *A* to the area of rectangle *B*?

- ⭕ $\dfrac{1}{4}$
- ⭕ $\dfrac{1}{2}$
- ⭕ $\dfrac{1}{1}$
- ⭕ $\dfrac{2}{1}$
- ⭕ $\dfrac{4}{1}$

8. In the figure above, $AD \parallel BC$. What is the perimeter of quadrilateral *ABCD*?

- ⭕ 590
- ⭕ 600
- ⭕ 620
- ⭕ 640
- ⭕ 680

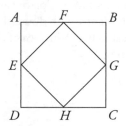

9. The midpoints of the sides of square *ABCD* above are connected to form square *EFGH*. What is the ratio of the area of square *EFGH* to the area of square *ABCD*?

- ⭕ $\dfrac{1}{4}$
- ⭕ $\dfrac{1}{3}$
- ⭕ $\dfrac{1}{2}$
- ⭕ $\dfrac{1}{\sqrt{2}}$
- ⭕ $\dfrac{2}{1}$

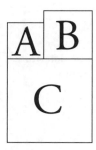

10. In the figure above, *A*, *B*, and *C* are squares. If the area of *A* is 9 and the area of *B* is 16, what is the area of *C*?

- ⭕ 25
- ⭕ 32
- ⭕ 36
- ⭕ 49
- ⭕ 50

11. A frame 2 inches wide is placed around a rectangular picture with dimensions 8 inches by 12 inches. What is the area of the frame, in square inches?

    ○ 44

    ○ 96

    ○ 128

    ○ 144

    ○ 168

12. In quadrilateral $ABCD$, $\angle A + \angle B + \angle C = 2\angle D$. What is the degree measure of $\angle D$?

    ○ 90

    ○ 120

    ○ 135

    ○ 270

    ○ It cannot be determined from the information given.

13. If the area of a rectangle is 12, what is its perimeter?

    ○ 7

    ○ 8

    ○ 14

    ○ 16

    ○ It cannot be determined from the information given.

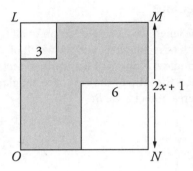

14. In the figure above, square $LMNO$ has a side of length $2x + 1$ and the two smaller squares have sides of lengths 3 and 6. If the area of the shaded region is 76, what is the value of x?

    ○ 5

    ○ 6

    ○ 7

    ○ 11

    ○ 14

Advanced

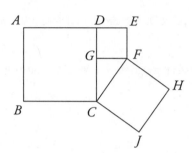

15. In the figure above, square *ABCD* has area 49 and square *DEFG* has area 9. What is the area of square *FCJH*?

○ 25

○ 32

○ 40

○ 48

○ 69

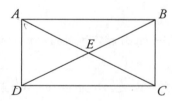

16. In the figure above, *ABCD* is a rectangle. If the area of △*AEB* is 8, what is the area of △*ACD*?

○ 8

○ 12

○ 16

○ 24

○ 32

17. The perimeter of a rectangle is $6w$. If one side as length $\dfrac{w}{2}$, what is the area of the rectangle?

○ $\dfrac{w^2}{4}$

○ $\dfrac{5w^2}{4}$

○ $\dfrac{5w^2}{2}$

○ $\dfrac{11w^2}{4}$

○ $\dfrac{11w^2}{2}$

18. The length of each side of square *A* is increased by 100 percent to make square *B*. If the length of the side of square *B* is increased by 50 percent to make square *C*, by what percent is the area of square *C* greater than the sum of the areas of squares *A* and *B*?

○ 75%

○ 80%

○ 100%

○ 150%

○ 180%

19. A rectangle with integer side lengths has perimeter 10. What is the greatest number of these rectangles that can be cut from a piece of paper with width 24 and length 60?

○ 144

○ 180

○ 240

○ 360

○ 480

CIRCLES

Circle: The set of all points in a plane at the same distance from a certain point. This point is called the **center** of the circle.

A circle is labeled by its center point: circle *O* means the circle with center point *O*. Two circles of different size with the same center are called **concentric**.

Diameter: A line segment that connects two points on the circle and passes through the center of the circle. In circle *O*, *AB* is a diameter.

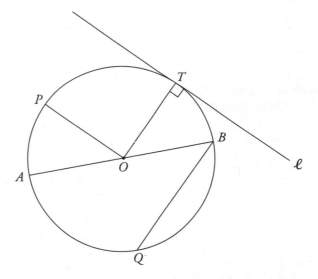

Radius: A line segment from the center of the circle to any point on the circle. The radius of a circle is one-half the length of the diameter. In circle *O*, *OA*, *OB*, *OP*, and *OT* are radii.

Chord: A line segment joining two points on the circle. In circle *O*, *QB* and *AB* are chords. The diameter of the circle is the longest chord of the circle.

Central Angle: An angle formed by two radii. In circle *O*, ∠*AOP*, ∠*POB*, ∠*BOA*, along with others, are central angles.

Tangent: A line that touches only one point on the circumference of the circle. A line drawn tangent to a circle is perpendicular to the radius at the point of tangency. Line ℓ is tangent to circle *O* at point *T*.

Circumference and arc length: The distance around a circle is called the **circumference**. The number π ("pi") is the ratio of a circle's circumference to its diameter. The value of π is 3.1415926 . . . , usually approximated 3.14. For the GRE, it is usually sufficient to remember that π is a little more than 3.

Since π equals the ratio of the circumference to the diameter, a formula for the circumference is

$$C = \pi d$$

or

$$C = 2\pi r$$

An **arc** is a portion of the circumference of a circle. In the figure below, *AB* is an arc of the circle, with the same degree measure as central angle *AOB*. The shorter distance between *A* and *B* along the circle is called the **minor arc**; the longer distance *AXB* is the **major arc**. An arc which is exactly half the circumference of the circle is called a **semicircle** (in other words, half a circle).

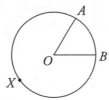

The length of an arc is the same fraction of a circle's circumference as its degree measure is of the degree measure of the circle (360°). For an arc with a central angle measuring *n* degrees,

$$\text{Arc length} = \left(\frac{n}{360}\right)(\text{circumference})$$

$$= \frac{n}{360} \times 2\pi r$$

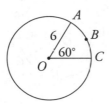

Example: What is the length of arc *ABC* of the circle with center *O* above?

Since $C = 2\pi r$, if the radius is 6, the circumference is $2 \times \pi \times 6 = 12\pi$.

Since $\angle AOC$ measures 60°, the arc is $\frac{60}{360}$, or one-sixth, of the circumference.

Therefore, the length of the arc is one-sixth of 12π, which is $\frac{12\pi}{6}$ or 2π.

Area of a circle: The area of a circle is given by the formula

$$\text{Area} = \pi r^2$$

A **sector** is a portion of the circle, bounded by two radii and an arc. In the circle below with center O, OAB is a sector. To determine the area of a sector of a circle, use the same method we used to find the length of an arc. Determine what fraction of 360° is in the degree measure of the central angle of the sector, and multiply that fraction by the area of the circle. In a sector whose central angle measures n degrees,

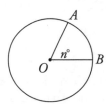

$$\text{Area of sector} = \left(\frac{n}{360}\right) \times (\text{Area of circle})$$

$$= \frac{n}{360} \times \pi r^2$$

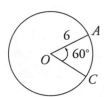

Example: What is the area of sector AOC in the circle with center O above?

Since $\angle AOC$ measures 60°, a 60° "slice" is $\dfrac{60}{360}$, or one-sixth, of the circle. So the sector has area $\dfrac{1}{6} \times \pi r^2 = \dfrac{1}{6} \times 36\pi = 6\pi$.

CIRCLES EXERCISE

Solve the following problems as indicated. (Answers follow the exercise.)

$$\boxed{\text{Circumference} = 2\pi r = \pi d}$$

1. What is the circumference of a circle with the radius 3?

2. What is the circumference of a circle with the diameter 8?

3. What is the circumference of a circle with diameter $\dfrac{3}{4\pi}$?

4. What is the radius of a circle with circumference $\dfrac{7}{2}\pi$?

5. What is the diameter of a circle with circumference $\dfrac{\pi}{2}$?

$$\boxed{\text{Area} = \pi r^2}$$

6. What is the area of a circle with radius 8?

7. What is the area of a circle with diameter 12?

8. What is the area of a circle with radius $\sqrt{2}$?

9. What is the area of a circle with circumference 8π?

10. What is the diameter of a circle with area 49π?

11. What is the circumference of a circle with area 18π?

$$\boxed{\text{Arc length} = \left(\dfrac{h}{360}\right)2\pi r}$$

In #12–15, find the the length of minor arc AB.

12.

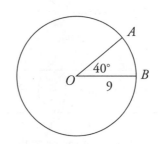

Arc AB = ?

13.

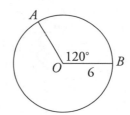

Arc AB = ?

14.

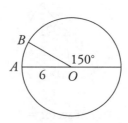

Arc AB = ?

15.

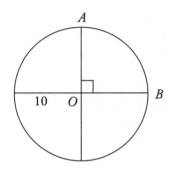

Arc AB = ?

$$\text{Area of sector} = \left(\frac{x}{360}\right)\pi r^2$$

In #16–19, find the area of sector AOB.

16.

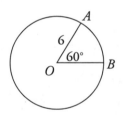

Area of sector = ?

17.

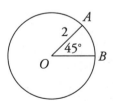

Area of sector = ?

18.

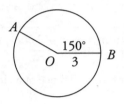

Area of sector = ?

19.

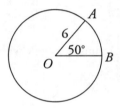

Area of sector = ?

ANSWER KEY—CIRCLES EXERCISE

1. 6π

2. 8π

3. $\dfrac{3}{4}$

4. $\dfrac{7}{4}$

5. $\dfrac{1}{2}$

6. 64π

7. 36π

8. 2π

9. 16π

10. 14

11. $6\pi\sqrt{2}$

12. 2π

13. 4π

14. π

15. 5π

16. 6π

17. $\dfrac{\pi}{2}$

18. $\dfrac{15\pi}{4}$

19. 5π

CIRCLES TEST

Solve the following problems and choose the best answer. (Answers and explanations are at the end of this chapter.)

Basic

1. If the area of a circle is 64π, then the circumference of the circle is

   ○ 8π

   ○ 16π

   ○ 32π

   ○ 64π

   ○ 128π

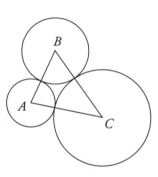

2. If points A, B, and C are the centers of the above circles and the circles have radii of 2, 3, and 4 respectively, what is the perimeter of triangle ABC?

   ○ 9

   ○ 3π

   ○ 12

   ○ 18

   ○ 9π

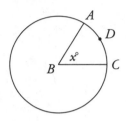

3. In the figure above, the ratio of the circumference of circle B to the length of arc ADC is 8:1. What is the value of x?

   ○ 30

   ○ 45

   ○ 60

   ○ 75

   ○ 90

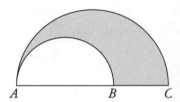

4. The figure above displays two semicircles, one with diameter AB and one with diameter AC. If AB has a length of 4 and AC has a length of 6, what fraction of the larger semicircle does the shaded region represent?

   ○ $\dfrac{1}{3}$

   ○ $\dfrac{4}{9}$

   ○ $\dfrac{1}{2}$

   ○ $\dfrac{5}{9}$

   ○ $\dfrac{2}{3}$

Intermediate

5. A line segment joining two points on the circumference of a circle is one inch from the center of the circle at its closest point. If the circle has a two-inch radius, what is the length of the line?

   ◯ 1

   ◯ $\sqrt{2}$

   ◯ 2

   ◯ $2\sqrt{2}$

   ◯ $2\sqrt{3}$

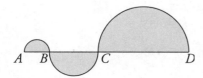

6. Each of the three shaded regions above is a semicircle. If $AB = 4$, $CD = 2BC$, and $BC = 2AB$, then the area of the entire shaded figure is

   ◯ 28π

   ◯ 42π

   ◯ 84π

   ◯ 96π

   ◯ 168π

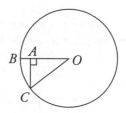

7. In the figure above, if the area of the circle with center O is 100π and CA has a length of 6, what is the length of AB?

   ◯ 2

   ◯ 3

   ◯ 4

   ◯ 5

   ◯ 6

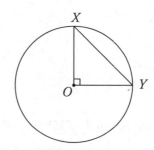

8. In the figure above, O is the center of the circle. If the area of triangle XOY is 25, what is the area of the circle?

   ◯ 25π

   ◯ $25\pi\sqrt{2}$

   ◯ 50π

   ◯ $50\pi\sqrt{3}$

   ◯ 625π

Advanced

9. If the diameter of a circle increases by 50 percent, by what percent will the area of the circle increase?

    ○ 25%

    ○ 50%

    ○ 100%

    ○ 125%

    ○ 225%

10. A lighthouse emits a light which can be seen for 60 miles in all directions. If the intensity of the light is strengthened so that its visibility is increased by 40 miles in all directions, by approximately how many square miles is its region of visibility increased?

    ○ 6,300

    ○ 10,000

    ○ 10,300

    ○ 20,000

    ○ 31,400

11. If an arc with a length of 12π is $\dfrac{3}{4}$ of the circumference of a circle, what is the shortest distance between the endpoints of the arc?

    ○ 4

    ○ $4\sqrt{2}$

    ○ 8

    ○ $8\sqrt{2}$

    ○ 16

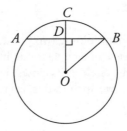

12. In the figure above, O is the center of the circle. If AB has a length of 16 and OB has a length of 10, what is the length of CD?

    ○ 2

    ○ 4

    ○ $2\sqrt{3}$

    ○ $8 - \sqrt{35}$

    ○ $8 - \sqrt{39}$

13. The total area of the four equal circles in the figure above is 36π, and the circles are all tangent to one another. What is the diameter of the small circle?

    ○ $6\sqrt{2}$

    ○ $6 + \sqrt{2}$

    ○ $3\sqrt{2} - 3$

    ○ $6\sqrt{2} - 6$

    ○ $6\sqrt{2} + 6$

MULTIPLE FIGURES

You can expect to see some problems on the GRE that involve several different types of figures. They test your **understanding** of various geometrical concepts and relationships, not just your ability to memorize a few formulas. The hypotenuse of a right triangle may be the side of a neighboring rectangle, or the diameter of a circumscribed circle. Keep looking for the relationships between the different figures until you find one that leads you to the answer.

One common kind of multiple figures question involves irregularly shaped regions formed by two or more overlapping figures, often with one region shaded. When you are asked to find the area of such a region, any or all of the following methods may work:

(1) Break up that shaded area into smaller pieces; find the area of each piece using the proper formula; add those areas together.

(2) Find the area of the whole figure and the area of the **unshaded** region, and subtract the latter from the former.

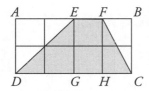

Example: Rectangle *ABCD* above has an area of 72 and is composed of 8 equal squares. Find the area of the shaded region.

For this problem you can use either of the two approaches. First, divide 8 into 72 to get the area of each square, which is 9. Since the area of a square equals its side squared, each side of the small squares must have length 3. Now you have a choice of methods.

(1) You can break up the trapezoid into right triangle *DEG*, rectangle *EFHG*, and right triangle *FHC*.

The area of triangle *DEG* is $\frac{1}{2} \times 6 \times 6$, or 18. The area of rectangle *EFHG* is 3×6, or 18. The area of triangle *FHC* is $\frac{1}{2} \times 6 \times 3$, or 9. The total area is $18 + 18 + 9$, or 45.

(2) The area of the whole rectangle *ABCD* is 72. The area of unshaded triangle *AED* is $\frac{1}{2} \times 6 \times 6$, or 18. The area of unshaded triangle *FBC* is $\frac{1}{2} \times 6 \times 3$, or 9. Therefore, the total unshaded area is $18 + 9 = 27$. The area of the shaded region is the area of the rectangle minus the unshaded area, or $72 - 27 = 45$.

Inscribed and Circumscribed Figures: A polygon is **inscribed** in a circle if all the vertices of the polygon lie on the circle. A polygon is **circumscribed** about a circle if all the sides of the polygon are tangent to the circle.

Square *ABCD* is inscribed in circle *O*.

(We can also say that circle *O* is circumscribed about square *ABCD*.)

Square *PQRS* is circumscribed about circle *O*.

(We can also say that circle *O* is inscribed in square *PQRS*.)

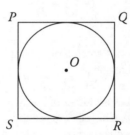

A triangle inscribed in a semicircle such that one side of the triangle coincides with the diameter of the semicircle is a right triangle.

MULTIPLE FIGURES EXERCISE

Solve the following problems as directed. (Answers follow the exercise.)

1.

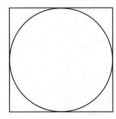

Area of circle = 25π

Perimeter of square = ?

2.

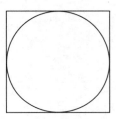

Area of square = 16

Area of circle = ?

3.

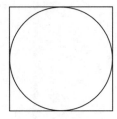

Circumfrence of circle = 6π

Area of square = ?

4.

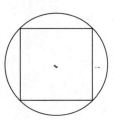

Area of square = 4

Area of circle = ?

ANSWER KEY—MULTIPLE FIGURES EXERCISE

1. 40
2. 4π
3. 36
4. 2π

MULTIPLE FIGURES TEST

Solve the following problems and choose the best answer. (Answers and explanations are at the end of this chapter.)

Basic

1. If a rectangle with a diagonal of 5 inches is inscribed in circle O, what is the circumference of circle O, in inches?

    ◯ 5
    ◯ $\dfrac{5\pi}{2}$
    ◯ 5π
    ◯ 6π
    ◯ 10π

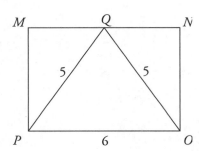

2. In the figure above, triangle PQO is an isosceles triangle with sides of lengths 5, 5, and 6. What is the area of rectangle $MNOP$?

    ◯ 12
    ◯ 18
    ◯ 24
    ◯ 30
    ◯ 36

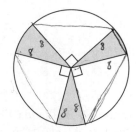

3. In the circle above, three right angles have vertices at the center of the circle. If the radius of the circle is 8, what is the combined area of the shaded regions?

    ◯ 8π
    ◯ 9π
    ◯ 12π
    ◯ 13π
    ◯ 16π

4. If a square of side x and a circle of radius r have equal areas, what is the ratio $\dfrac{x}{r}$?

    ◯ $\dfrac{2}{\pi}$
    ◯ $\sqrt{\pi}$
    ◯ $\dfrac{\pi}{2}$
    ◯ π
    ◯ π^2

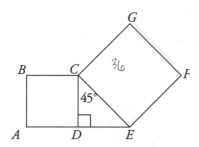

5. In the figure above, *ABCD* and *CEFG* are squares. If the area of *CEFG* is 36, what is the area of *ABCD*?

   ○ 6
   ○ $6\sqrt{2}$
   ○ 9
   ○ 18
   ○ 24

6. A triangle and a circle have equal areas. If the base of the triangle and the diameter of the circle each have length 5, what is the height of the triangle?

   ○ $\dfrac{5}{2}$
   ○ $\dfrac{5}{2}\pi$
   ○ 5π
   ○ 10π
   ○ It cannot be determined from the information given.

Intermediate

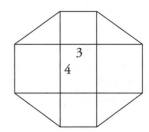

7. The figure above is composed of nine regions: four squares, four triangles, and one rectangle. If the rectangle has length 4 and width 3, what is the perimeter of the entire figure?

   ○ 24

   ○ 28

   ○ 34

   ○ 40

   ○ 44

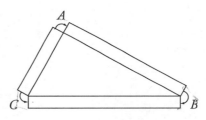

8. Rectangles lie on sides *AB*, *BC*, and *AC* of $\triangle ABC$ above. What is the sum of the measures of the angles marked?

   ○ 90°

   ○ 180°

   ○ 270°

   ○ 360°

   ○ It cannot be determined from the information given.

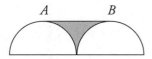

9. The two semicircles above both have radii of 7. If *AB* is tangent to the semicircles as shown, what is the shaded area, to the nearest integer?

   ○ 21

   ○ 42

   ○ 49

   ○ 54

   ○ 77

10. In the figure above, if *EFGH* is a square and the arcs are all quarter-circles of length π, what is the perimeter of *EFGH*?

   ○ 1

   ○ 2

   ○ 4

   ○ 8

   ○ 16

KAPLAN

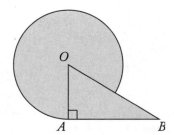

11. In the figure above, if radius *OA* is 8 and the
    area of right triangle *OAB* is 32, what is the area
    of the shaded region?

    ◯ 64π + 32
    ◯ 60π + 32
    ◯ 56π + 32
    ◯ 32π + 32
    ◯ 16π + 32

Advanced

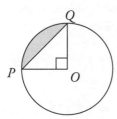

12. In circle O above, if $\triangle POQ$ is a right triangle and radius OP is 2, what is the area of the shaded region?

   ○ $4\pi - 2$
   ○ $4\pi - 4$
   ○ $2\pi - 2$
   ○ $2\pi - 4$
   ○ $\pi - 2$

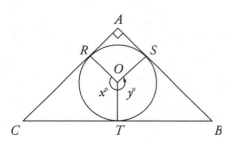

13. In the figure above, right triangle ABC is circumscribed about a circle O. If R, S, and T are the three points at which the triangle is tangent to the circle, then what is the value of $x + y$?

   ○ 180
   ○ 210
   ○ 240
   ○ 270
   ○ It cannot be determined from the information given.

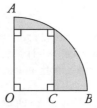

14. In the figure above, AB is an arc of a circle with center O. If the length of arc AB is 5π and the length of CB is 4, what is the sum of the areas of the shaded regions?

   ○ $25\pi - 60$
   ○ $25\pi - 48$
   ○ $25\pi - 36$
   ○ $100\pi - 48$
   ○ $100\pi - 36$

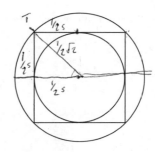

15. In the figure above, the smaller circle is inscribed in the square and the square is inscribed in the larger circle. If the length of each side of the square is s, what is the ratio of the area of the larger circle to the area of the smaller circle?

   ○ $2\sqrt{2} : 1$
   ○ $2 : 1$
   ○ $\sqrt{2} : 1$
   ○ $2s : 1$
   ○ $s\sqrt{2} : 1$

SOLIDS

A **solid** is a three-dimensional figure (a figure having length, width, and height), and is therefore rather difficult to represent accurately on a two-dimensional page. Figures are drawn "in perspective," giving them the appearance of depth. If a diagram represents a three-dimensional figure, it will be specified in the accompanying text.

Fortunately, there are only a few types of solids that appear with any frequency on the GRE: rectangular solids, including cubes; and cylinders.

Other types, such as spheres, may appear, but typically will only involve understanding the solid's properties and not any special formula. Here are the terms used to describe the common solids:

Vertex: The vertices of a solid are the points at its corners. For example, a cube has eight vertices.

Edge: The edges of a solid are the line segments which connect the vertices and form the sides of each face of the solid. A cube has twelve edges.

Face: The faces of a solid are the polygons that are the boundaries of the solid. A cube has six faces, all squares.

Volume: The volume of a solid is the amount of space enclosed by that solid. The volume of any uniform solid is equal to the area of its base times its height.

Surface Area: In general, the surface area of a solid is equal to the sum of the areas of the solid's faces.

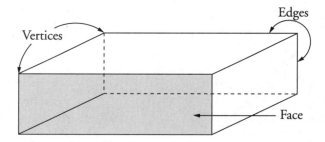

Rectangular Solid: A solid with six rectangular faces (all edges meet at right angles). Examples are cereal boxes, bricks, etc.

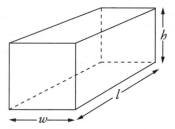

Volume = area of base × height = length × width × height = $\ell \times w \times h$.

Surface area = sum of areas of faces = $2\ell w + 2\ell h + 2wh$.

Cube: A special rectangular solid with all edges equal ($\ell = w = h$), such as a die or a sugar cube. All faces of a cube are squares.

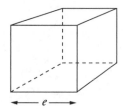

Volume = area of base × height = $\ell \times w \times h = e^3$.
Surface area = sum of areas of faces = $6e^2$.

Cylinder: A uniform solid whose horizontal cross section is a circle; for example, a soup can. We need two pieces of information for a cylinder: the radius of the base, and the height.

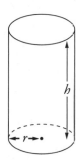

Volume = area of base × height = $\pi r^2 \times h$
Lateral surface area = circumference of base × height = $2\pi r \times h$
Total surface area = areas of bases + LSA = $2\pi r^2 + 2\pi rh$.

You can think of the surface area of a cylinder as having two parts: one part is the top and bottom (the circles), and the other part is the lateral surface. In a can, for example, the area of both the top and the bottom is just the area of the circle, or lid, which represents the top; hence, πr^2 for the top and πr^2 for the bottom, yielding a total of $2\pi r^2$. For the lateral surface, the area around the can, think of removing the can's label. When unrolled, it's actually in the shape of a rectangle. One side is the height of the can, and the other side is the distance around the circle, or circumference. Hence, its area is $h \times (2\pi r)$, or $2\pi rh$. And so, the total surface area is $2\pi r^2 + 2\pi rh$.

Sphere: A sphere is made up of all the points in space a certain distance from a center point; it's like a three-dimensional circle. The distance from the center to a point on the sphere is the radius of the sphere. A basketball is a good example of a sphere. A sphere is not a uniform solid; the cross sections are all circles, but are of different sizes. (In other words, a slice of a basketball from the middle is bigger than a slice from the top.)

It is not important to know how to find the volume or surface area of a sphere, but occasionally a question might require you to understand what a sphere is.

SOLIDS EXERCISE

Find the volume and surface area of each of the solids in #1–5. (Answers follow the exercise.)

1. A rectangular solid with dimensions 4, 6, and 8.

2. A rectangular solid with dimensions 3, 4, and 12.

3. A cube with edge 6.

4. A cube with edge $\sqrt{2}$.

5. A cylinder with height 12 and radius 6. (Find the total surface area.)

6. What is the area of a face of a cube with vol-ume 64?

ANSWER KEY—SOLIDS

1. 192, 208
2. 144, 192
3. 216, 216
4. $2\sqrt{2}$, 12
5. 432π, 216π
6. 16

SOLIDS TEST

1. What is the ratio of the volume of a cylinder with radius r and height h to the volume of a cylinder with radius h and height r?

   ○ $\dfrac{r}{h}$

   ○ $\dfrac{h}{r}$

   ○ $\dfrac{1}{1}$

   ○ $\dfrac{\pi r}{h}$

   ○ $\dfrac{h}{\pi r}$

2. A cube and a rectangular solid are equal in volume. If the lengths of the edges of the rectangular solid are 4, 8, and 16, what is the length of an edge of the cube?

   ○ 4

   ○ 8

   ○ 12

   ○ 16

   ○ 64

3. When 16 cubic meters of water are poured into an empty cubic container, it fills the container to 25 percent of its capacity. What is the length of one edge of the container, in meters?

   ○ $2\sqrt{2}$

   ○ 4

   ○ $4\sqrt{2}$

   ○ 8

   ○ 16

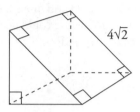

$4\sqrt{2}$

4. If the solid above is half of a cube, then the volume of the solid is

   ○ 16

   ○ 32

   ○ 42

   ○ 64

   ○ $64\sqrt{2}$

5. Milk is poured from a full rectangular container with dimensions 4 inches by 9 inches by 10 inches into a cylindrical container with a diameter of 6 inches. Assuming the milk does not overflow the container, how many inches high will the milk reach?

   ○ $\dfrac{60}{\pi}$

   ○ 24

   ○ $\dfrac{40}{\pi}$

   ○ 10

   ○ 3π

6. What is the radius of the largest sphere that can be placed inside a cube of volume 64?

   ○ $6\sqrt{2}$

   ○ 8

   ○ 4

   ○ $2\sqrt{2}$

   ○ 2

7. Each dimension of a certain rectangular solid is
an integer less than 10. If the volume of the
rectangular solid is 24 and one edge has length
4, which of the following could be the total
surface area of the solid?

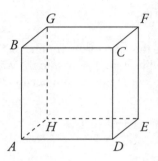

○ 48

○ 52

○ 56

○ 60

○ 96

8. Which of the following statements about the
cube above must be true?

   I. *FD* is parallel to *GA*.

   II. △*GCF* and △*AHD* have the same
   area.

   III. *AF* = *GD*

○ I only

○ I and II only

○ I and III only

○ II and III only

○ I, II, and III

LINES AND ANGLES TEST
ANSWERS AND EXPLANATIONS

1. 50

Since the three marked angles form a straight angle, the sum of their measures is 180°. So we can set up an equation to solve for x:

$$x + x + 80 = 180$$
$$2x + 80 = 180$$
$$2x = 100$$
$$x = 50$$

2. 145°

Notice that $\angle AOE$ and $\angle BOD$ are vertical angles, and therefore must have equal measures. $\angle BOD$ is made up of one angle with a measure of 105°, and a second angle with a measure of 40°; it must have a measure of 105° + 40°, or 145°. Therefore, $\angle AOE$ must also have a measure of 145°.

3. 300

In the diagram, the unmarked angle and the 30° angle are vertical angles; therefore, the unmarked angle must also have a measure of 30°. The sum of the measures of the angles around a point is 360°, so we can set up the following equation:

$$30 + x + w + 30 + z + y = 360$$

Rearranging the terms on the left side of the equation gives:

$$w + x + y + z + 60 = 360$$
$$w + x + y + z = 360 - 60 = 300$$

4. 90

There's no way to find either x or y alone, but their sum is a different story. Since AD is a straight line, the angle marked $x°$, the angle marked $y°$, and the right angle together make up a straight angle, which measures 180°.

So

$$x + y + 90 = 180$$
$$x + y = 180 - 90 = 90$$

5. 30

Together, the angle marked $x°$ and the angle marked $y°$ form a straight angle, so $x + y$ equals 180. We're also told that $y = 5x$.

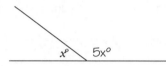

Substitute $5x$ for y:

$$x + y = 180$$
$$x + 5x = 180$$
$$6x = 180$$
$$x = 30$$

6. 50

$\angle AFD$ is a straight angle. The angle marked 40°, the right angle, and the angle marked $x°$ together form $\angle AFD$; therefore, they must sum to 180°.

$$x + 90 + 40 = 180$$
$$x + 130 = 180$$
$$x = 50$$

7. I and II only

From the diagram, we see that the angle marked $y°$ is supplementary to a right angle, which measures 90°. This means that y must be $180 - 90$, or 90. We are told that x equals y, so x must also be 90. This means that ℓ_2 and ℓ_3 are each perpendicular to ℓ_1; therefore, they must be parallel to each other. Thus, statements I and II are true. But statement III is not necessarily true. For instance, ℓ_3 intersects ℓ_1, but never meets ℓ_2.

8. 54

The sum $v + w + x + y$ must equal 180 since the angles with these measures together form a straight line. Since the question asks for the value of y, define all variables in terms of y. If $w = 2x$ and $x = \dfrac{y}{3}$, then $w = \dfrac{2y}{3}$. Similarly, $v = 2w$, so $v = 2\left(\dfrac{2y}{3}\right)$ or $\dfrac{4y}{3}$.

Substitute the angles in terms of y into the equation:

$$v + w + x + y = 180$$

$$\frac{4y}{3} + \frac{2y}{3} + \frac{y}{3} + y = 180$$

$$\frac{7y}{3} + y = 180$$

$$\frac{10y}{3} = 180$$

$$y = \frac{3}{10} \times 180 = 3 \times 18 = 54$$

9. II and III only

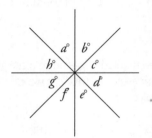

Check each expression to see which sets of angles sum to 180°.

I: $a + b + e + h$. Since angles h, a, b, and c together make up a straight angle, $h + a + b + c = 180$. Since we don't know whether $e = c$, we can't be sure that $a + b + e + h = 180$. So statement I is out. Eliminate choices one, three, and five.

This leaves the second choice, II only, and the fourth choice, II and III only. Therefore, statement II must be included in the correct answer. So we immediately skip to checking statement III.

III: $a + b + d + g$. Angles a, b, c and d sum to 180, and $g = c$ (vertical angles), so it's also true that $a + b + d + g = 180$. Therefore, statement III is OK, and the fourth choice is correct.

As a check, we can test the expression in statement II (although it's not necessary to do so during the actual exam):

II: $b + e + g + h$. Angles e, f, g, and h sum to 180°. Is b equal to f? Yes, since they are a pair of vertical angles. So, sure enough, statement II is OK.

10. It cannot be determined from the information given.

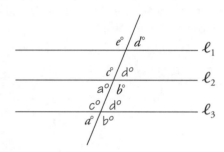

We're given that ℓ_1, ℓ_2, and ℓ_3 are all parallel to one another. Remember, when parallel lines are cut by a transversal, all acute angles formed by the transversal are equal, all obtuse angles are equal, and any acute angle is supplementary to any obtuse angle. We can get 2 pairs of supplementary angles from the 5 marked angles:

$$\underbrace{a+b}_{180}+\underbrace{c+d+e}_{180}$$

We're left with $360 + e$. Since we don't know the value of e, we cannot find the sum.

11. I and III only

We have three pairs of vertical angles around the point of intersection: a and d, b and e, and c and f. Therefore, $a = d$, $b = e$, and $c = f$. Let's look at the three statements one at a time.

I: $a + b = d + e$. Since $a = d$ and $b = e$, this is true. Eliminate the fourth choice.

II: $b + e = c + f$. We know that $b = e$ and $c = f$, but now how the pairs relate to each other. Statement II does not have to be true. Eliminate choices (2) and (5).

III: $a + c + e = b + d + f$. This is true, since $a = d$, $c = f$, and $b = e$. That is, we can match each angle on one side of the equation with a different angle on the other side. Statement III must be true.

Statements I and III must be true.

12. 1

Since AE is a line segment, all the lengths are additive, so $AE = AD + DE$. We're told that $AD = 6$ and $AE = 8$. So $DE = AE - AD = 8 - 6 = 2$. We're also told that $BE = 6$. So $BD = BE - DE = 6 - 2 = 4$. We have the length of BD, but still need the length of BC. Since $CD = 3(BC)$, the situation looks like this:

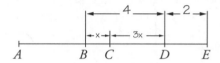

Here x stands for the length of BC. Since $BD = 4$, we can write:

$$x + 3x = 4$$
$$4x = 4$$
$$x = 1$$

13. II only

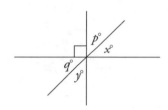

Before we look at the choices, let's see what information we can get from the diagram. We can see that angles p and x together are supplementary to the right angle, so p and x together must form a right angle. The same is true for the angles q and y. We also have these two pairs of vertical angles: $p = y$ and $x = q$. Now let's look at the three statements.

I: $p = x$ and $q = y$. This will be true only if $p = 45$. Since we have no way of knowing the exact measure of p, this can be true, but doesn't have to be. Eliminate choices (1), (4), and (5).

II: $x + y = 90$. This is true since $q + y = 90$ and $x = q$. Eliminate choice (3).

Since we've eliminated four answer choices, we can safely pick choice (2) without checking statement III. For practice, though, let's have a look anyway:

III: $x = y = 45$. There is no indication from the diagram that the angles x and y must have the same degree measure. Statement III does not have to be true.

Statement II only must be true.

14. 40

The angle marked $(2x - 20)°$ and the angle marked $3x°$ together form a straight angle. This means that the sum of their degree measures must be 180.

$$(2x - 20) + (3x) = 180$$
$$2x - 20 + 3x = 180$$
$$5x = 200$$
$$x = \frac{200}{5} = 40$$

TRIANGLES TEST
ANSWERS AND EXPLANATIONS

1. 80

Notice that each marked angle makes a pair of vertical angles with one of the interior angles of the triangle.

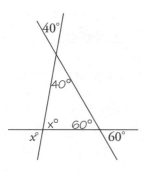

Since these marked angles have the same degree measure as the corresponding interior angles, the sum of their measures must equal 180.

$$x + 40 + 60 = 180$$
$$x = 180 - 100$$
$$x = 80$$

2. 60

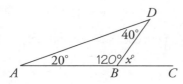

Notice that the angle marked $x°$ is supplementary to ∠ABD, and ∠ABD is an interior angle of △ABD. The sum of the measures of the 2 marked angles in △ABD is $20° + 40°$, or $60°$. Therefore, the third angle, ∠ABD, must have a measure of $180° - 60°$, or $120°$. So $x = 180 - 120$, or 60.

A quicker way to get this problem is to remember that the measure of an exterior angle is equal to the sum of the measures of the two remote interior angles. Angle x is an exterior angle, so $x = 20 + 40$, or 60.

3. 130

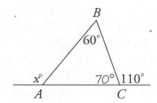

The angle with measure $x°$ is an exterior angle of the triangle; therefore it must equal the sum of the two remote interior angles: ∠ABC and ∠BCA. ∠ABC has a measure of $60°$. ∠BCA is supplementary to the angle marked $110°$; its measure must be $180° - 110°$, or $70°$. Therefore, $x = 60 + 70$, or 130.

4. 45

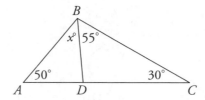

What are the three interior angles of △ABC? They are ∠ABC, with measure $50°$, ∠ACB, with measure $30°$, and ∠ABC, which is made up of the angle marked $x°$ and an angle with measure $55°$. All these angles combined sum to $180°$. Therefore,

$$50 + 30 + x + 55 = 180$$
$$135 + x = 180$$
$$x = 180 - 135$$
$$x = 45$$

5. **100°**

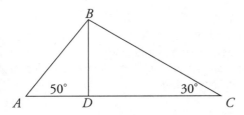

Notice that we're given the measure of two interior angles in △ABC: ∠BAC measures 50° and ∠BCA measures 30°. Therefore, ∠ABC, the third interior angle in △ABC, measures 180 − (50 + 30), or 180 − 80, or 100°. Since BD bisects ∠ABC, BD splits up ∠ABC into two smaller angles equal in measure, ∠ABD and ∠DBC. Therefore, the measure of ∠DBC is half the measure of ∠ABC, so ∠DBC measures $\frac{1}{2}$ (100), or 50°. Now we can use this information along with the fact that ∠BCA measures 30° to find ∠BDC. Since these three angles are interior angles of △BDC, their measures sum to 180°. So ∠BDC measures 180 − (50 + 30), or 100°.

6. **90°**

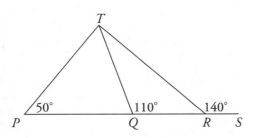

Identify the two interior angles of △PRT remote to the exterior angle marked 140°. ∠TPR with measure 50° is one of them and ∠PTR, whose measure we're trying to find, is the other. Since 50° plus the measure of ∠PTR must sum to 140°, the measure of ∠PTR = 140° − 50°, or 90°.

7. **36**

Since the angle marked $x°$ and the angle marked $y°$ together form a straight angle, their measures must sum to 180°.

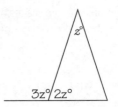

Substitute in $2z$ for x and $3z$ for y, and solve for z.

$$x + y = 180$$
$$2z + 3z = 180$$
$$5z = 180$$
$$z = \frac{1}{5} \cdot 180 = 36$$

8. **150 − y**

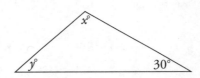

Once again, we are dealing with the sum of the interior angles in a triangle. We can write:

$$x + y + 30 = 180$$
$$x + y = 180 − 30$$
$$x + y = 150$$

Subtracting y from each side, we find that $y = 150 − y$.

9. 40

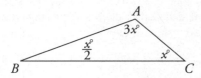

In △*ABC*, the measures of the three interior angles must sum to 180:

$$\frac{x}{2} + 3x + x = 180$$

$$\frac{9}{2}x = 180$$

$$x = 180 \cdot \frac{2}{9} = 40$$

10. 65

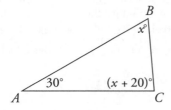

In △*ABC*, the sum of the degree measures of the interior angles is 180:

$$x + (x + 20) + 30 = 180$$

$$2x + 50 = 180$$

$$2x = 180 - 50$$

$$2x = 130$$

$$x = \frac{130}{2} = 65$$

11. 80

The measures of the three interior angles are in the ratio of 2:3:4, and they must add up to 180°. So the three angles must have degree measures that are 2*x*, 3*x*, and 4*x*, where *x* is a number to be found.

$$2x + 3x + 4x = 180$$

$$9x = 180$$

$$x = 20$$

The largest angle has measure 4*x*, or 4(20), which is 80.

12. 220

Since the 140° angle is an exterior angle, it is equal to the sum of the two remote interior angles. One of these is supplementary to angle *x*, and the other is supplementary to angle *y*. So these two interior angles have measures $180 - x$ and $180 - y$:

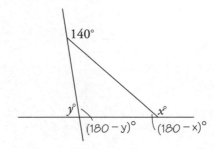

So $140 = (180 - x) + (180 - y)$

$$140 = 360 - x - y$$

$$140 = 360 - (x + y)$$

$$x + y + 140 = 360$$

$$x + y = 220$$

13. 70

Since *BC* is parallel to *AD*, ∠*GBF* must have the same degree measure as *x* (two parallel lines cut by transversal *AG*). Finding *x*, then, is the same as finding the measure of ∠*GBF*.

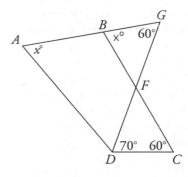

Let's look at triangles △*BFG* and △*DCF*. The two interior angles of these two triangles at point *F* must have the same degree measure, since they are a pair of vertical angles. In addition, each triangle has a 60° angle. Since we have two triangles with two pairs of equal angles, the third pair of angles must be equal, too, because the sum of all three angles in any triangle is 180°. The third angle in $\triangle DCF$ has measure 70°; therefore, $\angle GBF = x° = 70°$.

14. I and II only

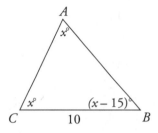

Statement I:

We could solve for the value of x here, but it's easier to ask "could x be 50?" If x were 50, then the triangle would have two 50° angles and a third angle with measure less than 50°. But this would make the total less than 180°. Therefore, x must be greater than 50, and Statement I is true. Eliminate the second choice.

Statement II:

The shortest side of a triangle will always be opposite the angle of smallest measure. Two of the angles have measure x; the third, $\angle CBA$, has a measure less than that: $x - 15$. Since $\angle CBA$ is the smallest angle, the side opposite it, side AC, must be the shortest side. Since CB has length 10, AC must be less than 10. Statement II is true. Eliminate the first and fourth choices.

Statement III:

$\angle ACB$ and $\angle BAC$ both have a measure of $x°$, so $\triangle ABC$ is isosceles. Therefore, AB has the same length as CB (they're opposite the equal angles). Since BC has a length of 10, AB must also have a length of 10. Statement III is not true.

Statements I and II only must be true.

15. $2\sqrt{10}$

First, solve for the length of BC, the shortest side. We can then find the length of AB and the length of AC using the Pythagorean theorem.

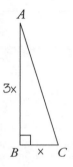

The area of any right triangle equals one-half the product of the legs. If BC has a length of x, then AB has a length of $3x$. (If BC is one-third the length of AB, then AB is three times the length of BC.) The area of the triangle is one-half their product, or $\frac{1}{2}(x)(3x)$. This equals 6.

$$\frac{1}{2}(x)(3x) = 6$$
$$3x^2 = 12$$
$$x^2 = 4$$
$$x = 2$$

BC has a length of 2. So AB, which is $3x$, is 6. Now use the Pythagorean theorem to find AC.

$$AC^2 = AB^2 + BC^2$$
$$AC^2 = (6)^2 + (2)^2$$
$$AC^2 = 36 + 4$$
$$AC = \sqrt{40} = \sqrt{4 \cdot 10} = (\sqrt{4})(\sqrt{10}) = 2\sqrt{10}$$

16. $8\sqrt{2}$

Draw yourself a diagram so that the picture is more clear:

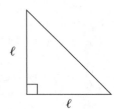

In an isosceles right triangle, both legs have the same length. So,

$$\text{area} = \frac{1}{2}\,\ell \times \ell = \frac{\ell^2}{2}$$

We're given that the area is 32, so we can set up an equation to solve for ℓ:

$$\frac{\ell^2}{2} = 32$$

$$\ell^2 = 64$$

$$\ell = 8$$

Remember, the ratio of the length of the legs to the length of the hypotenuse in any isosceles right triangle is $1 : \sqrt{2}$.

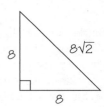

Since the legs have a length of 8, the hypotenuse is $\sqrt{2}$ times 8, or $8\sqrt{2}$.

An alternative is to use the Pythagorean theorem to find the hypotenuse:

$$\text{hyp}^2 = 8^2 + 8^2$$

$$\text{hyp}^2 = 64 + 64$$

$$\text{hyp}^2 = 128$$

$$\text{hyp} = \sqrt{128} = \sqrt{64 \cdot 2} = 8\sqrt{2}$$

17. 4

If $\angle DBA$ has a measure of 60°, $\angle CBD$, which is supplementary to it, must have a measure of $180 - 60$, or 120°. $\angle DCB$ has a measure of 30°; that leaves $180 - (120 + 30)$, or 30 degrees for the remaining interior angle: BDC.

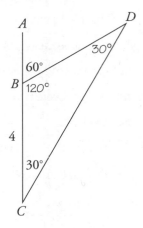

Since $\angle BCD$ has the same measure as $\angle BDC$, $\triangle BCD$ is an isosceles triangle, and the sides opposite the equal angles will have equal lengths. Therefore, BD must have the same length as BC, 4.

18. 2

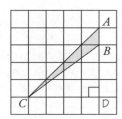

(Note that we've added point D for clarity).

The area of a triangle is $\frac{1}{2} \times$ base $\times$ height. If we treat AB as the base of $\triangle ABC$, then the triangle's height is CD.

Each square has side 1, so we can just count the squares. $AB = 1$, $CD = 4$, so the area is $\frac{1}{2} \times 1 \times 4 = 2$.

19. $\dfrac{d\sqrt{7}}{12}$

We know one of the sides we're given is the hypotenuse; since the hypotenuse is the longest side, it follows that it must be the larger value we're given. The side of length $\dfrac{d}{3}$ must be the hypotenuse, since d is positive (all lengths are positive), and $\dfrac{1}{3}$ of a positive value is always greater than $\dfrac{1}{4}$ of a positive value. Now we can use the Pythagorean theorem to solve for the unknown side, which we'll call x.

$$(\text{hypotenuse})^2 = (\text{leg})^2 + (\text{leg})^2$$

$$\left(\frac{d}{3}\right)^2 = \left(\frac{d}{4}\right)^2 + x^2$$

$$\frac{d^2}{9} = \frac{d^2}{16} + x^2$$

$$\frac{d^2}{9} - \frac{d^2}{16} = x^2$$

$$\frac{16d^2 - 9d^2}{144} = x^2$$

$$\frac{7d^2}{144} = x^2$$

$$x = \frac{d\sqrt{7}}{12}$$

Another way we can solve this, that avoids the tricky, complicated algebra is by picking a number for d. Let's pick a number divisible by both 3 and 4 to get rid of the fractions: 12 seems like a logical choice. Then the two sides have length $\dfrac{12}{3}$, or 4, and $\dfrac{12}{4}$, or 3. If one of these is the hypotenuse, that must be 4, and 3 must be a leg. Now use the Pythagorean Theorem to find the other leg:

$$(\text{leg})^2 + (\text{leg})^2 = (\text{hyp})^2$$

$$(\text{leg})^2 + (3)^2 = (4)^2$$

$$(\text{leg})^2 + 9 = 16$$

$$(\text{leg})^2 = 7$$

$$\text{leg} = \sqrt{7}$$

Now plug in 12 for d into each answer choice; the one which equals $\sqrt{7}$ is correct.

$$\frac{5 \times 12}{12} = 5 \quad \text{Discard.}$$

$$\frac{12}{\sqrt{7}} \neq \sqrt{7} \quad \text{Discard.}$$

$$\frac{12}{5} \neq \sqrt{7} \quad \text{Discard.}$$

$$\frac{12}{12} = 1 \quad \text{Discard.}$$

$$\frac{12\sqrt{7}}{12} = \sqrt{7} \quad \text{Correct.}$$

20. 30

Drawing a diagram makes visualizing the situation much easier. Picture a ladder leaning against a building:

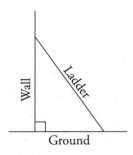

This forms a right triangle, since the side of the building is perpendicular to the ground. The length of the ladder, then, is the hypotenuse of the triangle; the distance from the foot of the building to the base of the ladder is one leg; the distance from the foot of the building to where the top of the ladder touches the wall is the other leg. We can write these dimensions into our diagram:

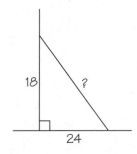

The one dimension we're missing (what we're asked to find) is the length of the ladder, or the hypotenuse. Well, we could use the Pythagorean Theorem to find that, but these numbers are fairly large, and calculating will be troublesome. When you see numbers this large in a right triangle, you should be a little suspicious; perhaps the sides are a multiple of a more familiar Pythagorean Triplet. One leg is 18 and another leg is 24; 18 is just 6×3, and 24 is just 6×4. So we have a multiple of the familiar 3-4-5 right triangle. That means that our hypotenuse, the length of the ladder, is 6×5, or 30.

21. 6

This problem involves as much algebra as geometry. The Pythagorean theorem states that the sum of the squares of the legs is equal to the square of the hypotenuse, or, in this case:

$$x^2 + (x + 2)^2 = (2x - 2)^2$$

and from here on in it's a matter of algebra:

$$x^2 + x^2 + 4x + 4 = 4x^2 - 8x + 4$$
$$12x = 2x^2$$
$$2x^2 - 12x = 0$$
$$2x(x - 6) = 0$$

When the product of two factors is 0, one of them must equal 0. So we find that

EITHER | **OR**
$2x = 0$ | $x - 6 = 0$
$x = 0$ | $x = 6$

According to the **equation,** the value of x could be either 0 or 6, but according to the **diagram,** x is the length of one side of a triangle, which must be a positive number. This means that x must equal 6 (which makes this a $6:8:10$ triangle).

Another way to do this problem is to try plugging each answer choice into the expression for x, and see which one gives side lengths which work in the Pythagorean Theorem. Choice (1) gives us 6, 8, and 10 (a Pythagorean Triplet) for the three sides of the triangle, so it must be the answer.

QUADRILATERALS TEST
ANSWERS AND EXPLANATIONS

1. 55

The fastest way to get the total area is to count the number of shaded small squares in each row (there's a pattern here: each row has one more shaded square than the row above it), and add. This gives a total of $1 + 2 + 3 + 4 + 5 + 6 + 7 + 8 + 9 + 10$, or 55 shaded squares.

2. 85

Keep in mind that the measures of the interior angles of a quadrilateral sum to 360°. Is this useful to us in this problem? Well, the angles marked 75° and 60° are both supplementary to the two unmarked interior angles in the diagram. There are 4 interior angles in the quadrilateral: the two unmarked angles, and the angle marked 50° and the one marked $x°$. The angle supplementary to the 75° angle must have a measure of $180 - 75$, or 105°. The angle supplementary to the 60° angle must have a measure of $180 - 60$, or 120°.

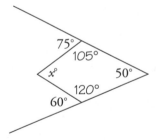

Now that we know the measures of three of the interior angles, we can set up an equation to solve for x:

$$x + 105 + 50 + 120 = 360$$
$$x + 275 = 360$$
$$x = 360 - 275 = 85$$

3. 115

What is the sum of the interior angles of a pentagon? Drawing two diagonals from a single vertex, we can divide a pentagon into three triangles.

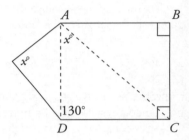

The sum of the interior angles must be three times the sum of each triangle: $3 \times 180 = 540°$. Therefore, the two angles with measure x, the two right angles, and the 130° angle must sum to 540°. So we can set up an equation to solve for x:

$$x + x + 90 + 90 + 130 = 540$$
$$2x + 310 = 540$$
$$2x = 230$$
$$x = 115$$

4. $\frac{1}{2}$

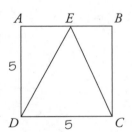

The height of $\triangle DEC$ is the perpendicular distance from point E to base DC, and that's the same as the length of side AD or side BC of the square. The base of $\triangle DEC$ is also a side of the square, so the area of $\triangle DEC$ must equal one half the length of a side of the square times the length of a side of the square. Or, calling the length of a side s, the area of $\triangle DEC$ is $\frac{1}{2}s^2$, while the area of the square is just s^2. Since the triangle has half the area of the square, the ratio is 1:2, or $\frac{1}{2}$.

5. $192.00

We can break the figure up into two rectangles, as shown in the diagram.

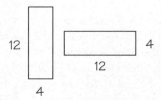

The area of a rectangle equals length × width, so each of these rectangles has an area of 4 × 12, or 48 square meters. Adding these areas together gives us 48 + 48, or 96 square meters. Each square meter of tile costs $2.00, so the total cost for 96 square meters is $2 × 96, or $192.

6. 24

Each of these squares must have an area equal to one-fifth of the area of the whole figure: $\frac{1}{5} \times 20 = 4$. For squares, area = side², or $\sqrt{area}$ = side. Since $\sqrt{4}$ = 2, the length of each side of the squares must be 2. How many of these sides make up the perimeter? The perimeter consists of 3 sides from each of four squares, for a total of 3 × 4, or 12 sides. Each side has a length of 2, for a total perimeter of 12 × 2, or 24.

7. $\frac{1}{4}$

Watch out for the trap: the ratio of areas is *not* the same as the ratio of lengths. We can pick numbers for the length and width of rectangle A. Let's pick 4 for the length and 2 for the width. The area of rectangle A is then 4 × 2, or 8. The length of rectangle B is twice the length of rectangle A: 2 × 4 = 8; the width of rectangle B is twice the width of rectangle A: 2 × 2 = 4. So the area of rectangle B is 8 × 4, or 32. Therefore, the ratio of the area of rectangle A to the area of rectangle B is $\frac{8}{32}$, or $\frac{1}{4}$.

As a general rule for similar polygons, the ratio of areas is equal to the square of the ratio of lengths.

8. 620

We're given the lengths of three of the four sides of $ABCD$; all we need to find is the length of side AD. If we drop a perpendicular line from point C to side AD and call the point where this perpendicular line meets side AD point E, we divide the figure into rectangle $ABCE$ and right triangle CDE.

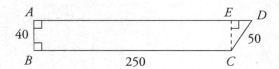

Since $ABCE$ is a rectangle, AE has the same length as BC, 250. Similarly, EC has the same length as AB, 40. We can now find the length of ED: it is a leg of a right triangle with hypotenuse 50 and other leg 40. This is just 10 times as big as a 3:4:5 right triangle; therefore, ED must have a length of 10 × 3, or 30. So AD, which is $AE + ED$, is 250 + 30, or 280. Now we can find the perimeter:

$$AB + BC + CD + AD = \text{perimeter}$$
$$40 + 250 + 50 + 280 = 620$$

9. $\dfrac{1}{2}$

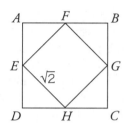

The key here is that *E*, *F*, *G*, and *H* are all midpoints of the sides of square *ABCD*. Therefore, the four triangles inside square *ABCD* are isosceles right triangles. We can pick a value for the length of each leg of the isosceles right triangles (all the legs have the same length). Let's pick 1 for the length of each leg. Then the length of each side of square *ABCD*, which is twice as long as each leg, is 2. So the area of square *ABCD* is 2 × 2, or 4. At the same time, the length of each hyptenuse is $1 \times \sqrt{2}$, or $\sqrt{2}$. This is the same as the length of each side of square *EFGH*, so the area of square *EFGH* is $\sqrt{2} \times \sqrt{2}$, or 2. Therefore, the ratio of the areaof *EFGH* to the area of *ABCD* is $\dfrac{2}{4}$, or $\dfrac{1}{2}$.

We can also attack this problem by using a more common sense approach. If we connect *EG* and *FH*, we'll have eight isosceles right triangles which are all the same size:

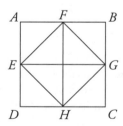

Square *EFGH* is composed of 4 of these triangles, and square *ABCD* is composed of 8 of these triangles. Since all of these triangles are the same size, square *EFGH* is half the size of square *ABCD*, and the ratio we're looking for is $\dfrac{1}{2}$.

10. 49

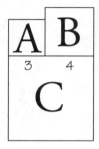

From the diagram we see the top side of square *C* is made up of a side of *A* and a side of *B*. So we can find the length of the sides of squares *A* and *B* to get the length of each side of square *C*. Since the area of square *A* is 9, each of its sides must have a length of $\sqrt{9}$, or 3. Similarly, since the area of square *B* is 16, each of its sides must have a length of $\sqrt{16}$, or 4. So, the length of each side of square *C* must be 4 + 3, or 7. The area of a square is the length of a side squared; therefore, square *C* has area 7^2, or 49.

11. 96

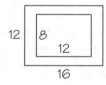

Sketch a diagram. We can see that adding a 2 inch frame to the picture extends both the length and the width by 2 inches in each direction, or by a total of 4 inches along each side. The outside dimensions of the frame are therefore 8 + 4, or 12, by 12 + 4, or 16. The area of the frame is the total area enclosed by both the frame and picture, minus the area of the picture, or

$$(12 \times 16) - (8 \times 12) = 12(16 - 8)$$
$$= 12 \times 8$$
$$= 96$$

12. 120

Since the sum of the interior angles of a quadrilateral is $360°$, $A + B + C + D = 360°$. At the same time, $A + B + C = 2D$. So we can make a substitution for $A + B + C$ in our first equation, to get:

$$2D + D = 360°$$
$$3D = 360°$$
$$D = 120°$$

13. It cannot be determined from the information given.

The area ($L \times W$) of a rectangle by itself tells us very little about its perimeter ($2L + 2W$). We can pick different values for the length and width to see what we get for the perimeter. For example, the length could be 4 and the width 3 ($4 \times 3 = 12$). In this case, the perimeter is $(2)(4) + (2)(3)$, or 14. On the other hand, the length could be 6 and the width 2 ($6 \times 2 = 12$). In this case the perimeter is $(2)(6) + (2)(2)$, or 16. Since more than one perimeter is possible based on the given information, the answer must be the fifth choice.

14. 5

The shaded area and the two small squares all combine to form the large square, *LMNO*. Therefore the area of square *LMNO* equals the sum of the shaded area and the area of the two small squares. We know the shaded area; we can find the areas of the two small squares since we're given side lengths for each square. The smallest square has a side of length 3; its area is 3^2, or 9. The other small square has a side of length 6; its area is 6^2, or 36. The area of square *LMNO*, then, is $9 + 36 + 76 = 121$. If square *LMNO* has an area of 121, then each side has a length of $\sqrt{121}$, or 11. Since we have an expression for the length of a side of the large square in terms of *x*, we can set up an equation and solve for *x*:

$$2x + 1 = 11$$
$$2x = 10$$
$$x = 5$$

15. 25

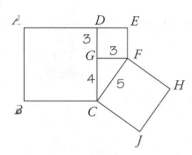

In order to determine the area of square *FCJH*, we can find the length of side *FC*, which is the hypotenuse of $\triangle FGC$. We can find the length of *FC* by finding the lengths of *FG* and *GC*.

Since *ABCD* has area 49, each side must have length $\sqrt{49}$, or 7. Therefore, *DC* has length 7. Since *DEFG* has area 9, side *FG* must have length $\sqrt{9}$, or 3. *DG* is also a side of the same square, so its length is also 3. The length of *GC* is the difference between the length of *DC* and the length of *DG*: $7 - 3 = 4$. Now we have the lengths of the legs of $\triangle FGC$: 3 and 4, so this must be a 3-4-5 right triangle. So *CF* has length 5. The area of square *FCJH* is the square of the length of *CF*: $5^2 = 25$.

16. 16

The bases of $\triangle AEB$ and $\triangle ACD$ both have the same length, since $AB = CD$. So we just need to find the relationship between their respective heights. *AC* and *BD* intersect at the center of the rectangle, which is point *E*. Therefore, the perpendicular distance from *E* to side *AB* is half the distance from side *CD* to side *AB*. This means that the height of $\triangle AEB$ is half the height of $\triangle ACD$. So the area of $\triangle ACD$ is twice the area of $\triangle AEB$: $2 \times 3 = 16$.

17. $\dfrac{5w^2}{4}$

The sum of all four sides of 6w. The two short sides add up to $\dfrac{w}{2} + \dfrac{w}{2}$, or w. This leaves $6w - w$, or 5w, for the **sum** of the other two sides. So **each** long side is $\dfrac{1}{2}(5w)$, or $\dfrac{5}{2}w$. So,

$$\text{Area} = \left(\dfrac{w}{2}\right)\left(\dfrac{5w}{2}\right) = \dfrac{5w^2}{4}$$

18. **80%**

The best way to solve this problem is to pick a value for the length of a side of square A. We want our numbers to be easy to work with, so let's pick 10 for the length of each side of square A. The length of each side of square B is 100 percent greater, or twice as great as a side of square A. So the length of a side of square B is 2×10, or 20. The length of each side of square C is 50 percent greater, or $1\dfrac{1}{2}$ times as great as a side of square B.

So the length of a side of square C is $1\dfrac{1}{2} \times 20$, or 30. The area of square A is 10^2, or 100. The area of square B is 20^2, or 400. The sum of the areas of squares A and B is $100 + 400$, or 500. The area of square C is 30^2, or 900. The area of square C is greater than the sum of the areas of squares A and B by $900 - 500$, or 400. The percent that the area of square C is greater than the sum of the areas of squares A and B is $\dfrac{400}{500} \times 100\%$, or 80%.

19. **360**

First of all, if a rectangle has perimeter 10, what could its dimensions be? Perimeter = $2L + 2W$, or $2(L + W)$. The perimeter is 10, so $2(L + W) = 10$, or $L + W = 5$. Since L and W must be integers, there are two possibilities: $L = 4$ and $W = 1$ $(4 + 1 = 5)$, or $L = 3$ and $W = 2$ $(3 + 2 = 5)$. Let's consider each case separately. If $L = 4$, then how many of these rectangles would fit along the length of the larger rectangle? The length of the larger rectangle is 60: $60 \div 4 = 15$, so 15 smaller rectangles would fit, if they were lined up with their longer sides against the longer side of the large rectangle. The width of the smaller rectangles is 1, and the width of the large rectangle is 24, $24 \div 1 = 24$, so 24 small rectangles can fit against the width of the large rectangle. The total number of small rectangles that fit inside the large rectangle is the number along the length times the number along the width: $15 \times 24 = 360$. In the second case, $L = 3$ and $W = 2$. $60 \div 3 = 20$, so 20 small rectangles fit along the length; $24 \div 2 = 12$, so 12 small rectangles fit along the width. So the total number of small rectangles is 20×12, or 240. We're asked for the greatest number, which we got from the first case: 360.

CIRCLES TEST
ANSWERS AND EXPLANATIONS

1. 16π

We need to find the radius in order to get the circumference. We're given that the area is 64π, so we can use the area formula to get the radius:

$$\text{Area} = \pi r^2 = 64\pi$$
$$r^2 = 64$$
$$r = 8$$

The circumference, which is $2\pi r$, is $2\pi(8)$, or 16π.

2. 18

Each side of $\triangle ABC$ connects the centers of two tangent circles, and each side passes through the point where the circumference of the circles touch. Therefore, each side is composed of the radii of two of the circles: AB is made up of a radius of A and a radius of B, BC is made up of a radius of B and a radius of C, and AC is made up of a radius of A and a radius of C:

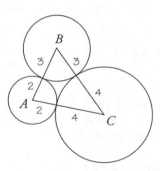

The sum of the lengths of these sides is the perimeter. Since we have two radii of each circle, the perimeter is twice the sum of the radii: $2(2 + 3 + 4) = 18$.

3. 45

We need to use the following ratio:

$$\frac{\text{length of arc}}{\text{circumference}} = \frac{\text{measure of arc's central angle}}{360°}$$

The measure of the arc's central angle is marked x degrees, and we're given that the length of the arc is $\frac{1}{8}$ of the circumference. So,

$$\frac{1}{8} = \frac{x}{360}$$
$$x = 45$$

4. $\dfrac{5}{9}$

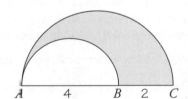

Method I:

The area of the shaded region equals the difference in areas of the two semicircles; to find the fraction of the larger semicircle the shaded region occupies, we first find the area of the shaded region, then divide this by the area of the larger semicircle. The area of a semicircle is $\frac{1}{2}$ the area of the whole circle, or $\frac{1}{2}\pi r^2$. Here, the larger semicircle has a diameter of 6. Its radius is $\frac{1}{2}$ the diameter, or 3, and its area equals $\frac{1}{2}\pi r^2 = \frac{1}{2}\pi(3)^2$, or $\frac{9}{2}\pi$. The smaller circle has a diameter of 4 and a radius of 2, for an area of $\frac{1}{2}\pi(2)^2$, or 2π. The area of the

shaded region equals

$$\frac{9\pi}{2} - 2\pi = \frac{9\pi}{2} - \frac{4\pi}{2}$$
$$= \frac{5\pi}{2}$$

The fraction of the larger semicircle the shaded region occupies is

$$\frac{\frac{5\pi}{2}}{\frac{9\pi}{2}} = \frac{5\pi}{2} \times \frac{2}{9\pi}$$
$$= \frac{5}{9}$$

Method II:

Avoid most of this work by exploring the ratios involved here. Any two semicircles are similar. The ratio of AB to AC is 4 to 6 or 2 to 3. The ratio of all linear measures of the two circles (circumference, radius) will also have this ratio. The area ratio will be the **square** of this, or 4 to 9. The small semicircle has $\frac{4}{9}$ the area of the large semicircle, leaving $\frac{5}{9}$ of the area of the large semicircle for the shaded region.

5. $2\sqrt{3}$

Sketch a diagram:

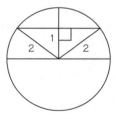

Since the radius of the circle is 2, the end-points of the line are both 2 inches from the center. The line can be seen as the legs of two right triangles, each of which has a hypotenuse of 2 and a leg of 1. Each of the legs that make up the line must have a length equal to

$\sqrt{2^2 - 1^2}$, or $\sqrt{3}$. The total length of the line is twice this, or $2\sqrt{3}$.

6. 42π

Since we're given the diameter of the semicircle around AB, we should begin with this semicircle. The radius of semicircle AB is $\frac{1}{2}(4)$, or 2. The area of a semicircle is half the area of the circle, or $\frac{1}{2}\pi r^2$. So the area of semicircle AB is $\frac{1}{2}\pi(2)^2$, or 2π. $BC = 2AB$, so $BC = 2(4)$, or 8.

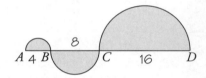

The radius of semicircle BC is 4, so the area of semicircle BC is $\frac{1}{2}\pi(4)^2$, or 8π. $CD = 2BC$, so $CD = 2(8)$, or 16.

The radius of semicircle CD is 8, so the area of semicircle CD is $\frac{1}{2}\pi(8)^2$, or 32π. Adding the three areas together gives us $2\pi + 8\pi + 32\pi$, or 42π.

7. 2

Since we know the area of circle O, we can find the radius of the circle. And if we find the length of OA, then AB is just the difference of OB and OA.

Since the area of the circle is 100π, the radius must be $\sqrt{100}$ or 10. Radius OC, line segment CA, and line segment OA together form a right triangle, so we can use the Pythagorean theorem to find the length of OA. But notice that 10 is twice 5 and 6 is twice 3, so right triangle ACO has sides whose lengths are in a $3:4:5$ ratio.

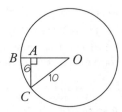

OA must have a length of twice 4, or 8. *AB* is the segment of radius *OB* that's not a part of *OA*; its length equals the length of *OB* minus the length of *OA*, or $10 - 8 = 2$.

8. 50π

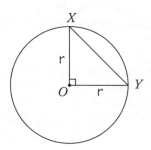

Each leg of right triangle *XOY* is also a radius of circle *O*. If we call the radius *r*, then the area of $\triangle XOY$ is $\frac{1}{2}(r)(r)$, or $\frac{r^2}{2}$. At the same time, the area of circle *O* is πr^2. So, we can use the area of $\triangle XOY$ to find r^2, and then multiply r^2 by π to get the area of the circle.

$$\text{Area of } \triangle XOY = \frac{r^2}{2} = 25$$
$$r^2 = 50$$
$$\text{Area of circle } O = \pi r^2 = \pi(50) = 50\pi$$

Note that it's unnecessary (and extra work) to find the actual value of *r*, since the value of r^2 is sufficient to find the area.

9. 125%

The fastest method is to pick a value for the diameter of the circle. Let's suppose that the diameter is 4. Then the radius is $\frac{4}{2}$, or 2, which means that the area is $\pi(2)^2$, or 4π. Increasing the diameter by 50% means adding on half of its original length: $4 + (50\%$ of $4) = 4 + 2 = 6$. So the new radius is $\frac{6}{2}$, or 3, which means that the area of the circle is now $\pi(3)^2$, or 9π. The percent increase is $\frac{9\pi - 4\pi}{4\pi} \times 100\% = \frac{5\pi}{4\pi} \times 100\%$, or 125%.

10. 20,000

Since the lighthouse can be seen in all directions, its region of visibility is a circle with the lighthouse at the center. Before the change, the light could be seen for 60 miles, so the area of visibility was a circle with radius 60 miles. Now it can be seen for 40 miles further, or for a total of $60 + 40$, or 100 miles. The area is now a circle with radius 100 miles:

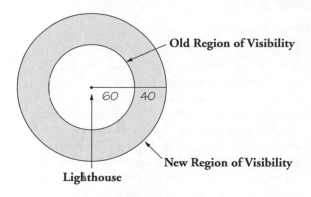

The increase is just the difference in these areas; that is, the shaded region on the above diagram.

$$\text{Increase} = \text{New area} - \text{old area}$$
$$= \pi(100)^2 - \pi(60)^2$$
$$= 10,000\pi - 3,600\pi$$
$$= 6,400\pi$$

The value of π is a bit more than 3, so $6{,}400\pi$ is a bit more than $3 \times 6{,}400$, or just over 19,200. The only choice close to this is 20,000.

11. $8\sqrt{2}$

Let's call the end-points of the arc A and B and the center of the circle C. Major arc AB represents $\frac{3}{4}$ of 360°, or 270°. Therefore, minor arc AB is $360° - 270°$, or 90°. Since AC and CB are both radii of the circle, $\triangle ABC$ must be an isosceles right triangle:

We can find the distance between A and B if we know the radius of the circle. Major arc AB, which takes up $\frac{3}{4}$ of the circumference, has a length of 12π, so the entire circumference is 16π. The circumference of any circle is 2π times the radius, so a circle with circumference 16π must have radius 8. The ratio of a leg to the hypotenuse in an isosceles right triangle is $1:\sqrt{2}$. The length of AB is $\sqrt{2}$ times the length of a leg, or $8\sqrt{2}$.

12. 4

We're looking for the length of CD. Note that OC is a radius of the circle, and if we knew the length of OC and OD, we could find CD, since $CD = OC - OD$. Well, we're given that OB has a length of 10, which means the circle has a radius of 10, and therefore OC is 10. All that remains is to find OD and subtract. The only other piece of information we have to work with is that AB has length 16. How can we use this to find OD? If we connect O and A, then we create two right triangles, $\triangle ADO$ and $\triangle BDO$:

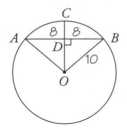

Since both of these right triangles have a radius as the hypotenuse, and both have a leg in common (OD), then they must be equal in size. Therefore, the other legs, AD and DB, must also be equal. That means that D is the midpoint of AB, and so DB is $\frac{1}{2}$ (16), or 8.

Considering right triangle BDO, we have a hypotenuse of 10 and a leg of 8; thus the other leg has length 6. (It's a 6-8-10 Pythagorean Triplet.) So OD has length 6, and $CD = 10 - 6 = 4$.

13. $6\sqrt{2} - 6$

Connect the centers of the circles O, P, and Q as shown. Each leg in this right triangle consists of two radii. The hypotenuse consists of two radii plus the diameter of the small circle.

We can find the radii of the large circles from the given information. Since the total area of the four large circles is 36π, each large circle has area 9π. Since the area of a circle is πr^2, we know that the radii of the large circles all have length 3.

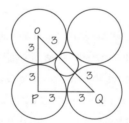

Therefore, each leg in the isosceles right triangle OPQ is 6. The hypotenuse then has length $6\sqrt{2}$. (The hypotenuse of an isosceles right triangle is always $\sqrt{2}$ times a leg.) The hypotenuse is equal to two radii plus the diameter of the small circle, so $6\sqrt{2} = 2(3) + \text{diameter}$, or $\text{diameter} = 6\sqrt{2} - 6$.

MULTIPLE FIGURES TEST
ANSWERS AND EXPLANATIONS

1. 5π

It may be helpful to draw your own diagram.

If a rectangle is inscribed in a circle, all four of its vertices are on the circumference of the circle and its diagonals pass through the center of the circle. This means that the diagonals of the rectangle are diameters of the circle. Here we are told that the diagonals have length 5, which means that the diameter of the circle is 5. The circumference of a circle is $2\pi r$, or πd, which in this case is 5π.

2. 24

Area = $b \times h$. We are given the base of this rectangle ($PO = 6$), but we need to find the height. Let's draw a perpendicular line from point Q to OP and label the point R as shown below:

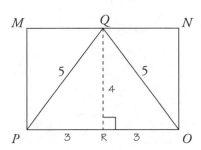

Now look at right triangle PQR. In an isosceles triangle, the altitude bisects the base, so QR bisects OP. Therefore, $PR = \dfrac{1}{2}$ (6), or 3.

Hypotenuse QP is 5. This is an example of the famous 3-4-5 right triangle. Therefore, segment QR must have length 4. This is equal to the height of rectangle $MNOP$, so the area of the rectangle is $b \times h = 6 \times 4$, or 24.

3. 16π

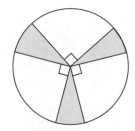

The three right angles define three sectors of the circle, each with a central angle of 90°. Together, the three sectors account for $\dfrac{270°}{360°}$, or $\dfrac{3}{4}$ of the are of the circle, leaving $\dfrac{1}{4}$ of the circle for the shaded regions. So the total area of the shaded regions = $\dfrac{1}{4} \times \pi(8)^2$, or 16π.

4. $\sqrt{\pi}$

The area of a square with side x is x^2. The area of a circle with radius r is πr^2. Since the two areas are equal, we can write

$$x^2 = \pi r^2$$

We need to solve for $\dfrac{x}{r}$:

$$\frac{x^2}{r^2} = \pi$$

$$\frac{x}{r} = \sqrt{\pi}$$

5. 18

Notice that both squares share a side with right triangle *CDE*. Since square *CEFG* has an area of 36, *CE* has a length of $\sqrt{36}$, or 6. Since right triangle *CDE* has a 45° angle, *CDE* must be an isosceles right triangle. Therefore, *CD* and *DE* are the same length. Let's call that length *x*:

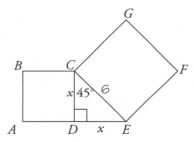

Remember, we're looking for the area of square *ABCD*, which will be x^2. Using the Pythagorean theorem on $\triangle CDE$, we get:

$$(\text{leg})^2 + (\text{leg})^2 = (\text{hypotenuse})^2$$
$$x^2 + x^2 = 6^2$$
$$2x^2 = 36$$
$$x^2 = 18$$

So the area is 18. (There's no need to find *x*.)

6. $\dfrac{5}{2}\pi$

We can easily find the area of the circle given its diameter. The diameter is 5, so the radius is $\dfrac{5}{2}$ and the area is $\pi\left(\dfrac{5}{2}\right)^2$ or $\dfrac{25}{4}\pi$. This is equal to the area of the triangle. We know the base of the triangle is 5, so we can solve for the height:

$$\frac{1}{2}(5)(h) = \frac{25}{4}\pi$$
$$5h = \frac{25}{2}\pi$$
$$h = \frac{5}{2}\pi$$

7. 34

The central rectangle shares a side with each of the four squares, and the four squares form the legs of the four right triangles. So we need to use the information that we're given about the rectangle. Two of its sides have a length of 4, so the two squares that share these sides must also have sides of length 4. The other two sides of the rectangle have a length of 3, so the other two squares, which share these sides, must also have sides of length 3. Each triangle shares a side with a small square and a side with a large square, so the legs of each triangle have lengths of 3 and 4, respectively.

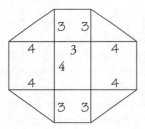

Since the legs are of length 3 and 4, the hypotenuse of each triangle must have a length of 5. To get the perimeter, we use the lengths of the hypotenuse and a side from each square:

$$\text{Perimeter} = 4(5) + 2(4) + 2(3)$$
$$= 20 + 8 + 6$$
$$= 34$$

8. 360°

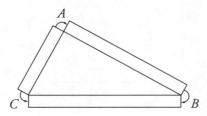

There are four angles at each of the three vertex points of the triangle, making a total of 12 angles. The sum of the angles around each vertex is equal to the measure of a full circle, 360°. The total measure of the 12 angles around all three points is 3(360°) = 1,080°. At each point there are two right angles and one angle of the triangle. For all three points there are six right angles for a total of 540°, and the three interior angles of the triangle for another 180°. Therefore,

$$540 + 180 + \angle A + \angle B + \angle C = 1{,}080$$

$$\angle A + \angle B + \angle C = 360$$

9. 21

Drop radii *AO* and *BP* to form rectangle *ABPO*. (We've added points *O* and *P* into the diagram for clarity.)

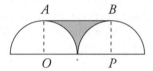

The shaded area is equal to the area of the rectangle minus the area of the two quarter-circles. The base of the rectangle is two radii, or 14, and the height is one radius, or 7. Therefore, the area of the rectangle = bh = $14 \times 7 = 98$. The area of two quarter circles is the same as the area of one semi-circle, or $\frac{1}{2}\pi r^2$. Since the radius is 7, the area is $\frac{1}{2}\pi(7)^2 = \frac{49}{2}\pi$. We only need to estimate the answer, and the answer choices are far enough apart for us to approximate. Since $\frac{49}{2}$ is almost 25 and π is close to 3, the area of the semicircle is about 75. Therefore, the shaded area is approximately 98 − 75, or 23. Choice (1), 21, is closest to this.

10. 16

Each side of square *EFGH* consists of 2 radii of the quarter-circles. So we need to find the radius of each

quarter-circle to get the length of the square's sides. If we put these four quarter-circles together we'd get a whole circle with a circumference of $4 \times \pi$, or 4π. We can use the circumference formula to solve for the radius of each quarter-circle:

$$\text{Circumference} = 2\pi r = 4\pi$$

$$r = 2$$

So each side of square *EFGH* has length 2 × 2, or 4. Therefore, the perimeter of the square is 4(4), or 16.

11. $56\pi + 32$

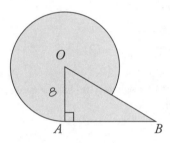

The total area of the shaded region equals the area of the circle plus the area of the right triangle minus the area of overlap. The area of circle *O* is $\pi(8)^2$, or 64π. We're told that the area of right triangle *OAB* is 32. So we just need to find the area of overlap, the area of right triangle *OAB* inside circle *O*, which forms a sector of the circle. Let's see what we can find out about $\angle AOB$, the central angle of the sector.

The area of right triangle *OAB* is 32, and the height is the radius. So $\frac{1}{2}(8)(AB) = 32$, or $AB = 8$. Since $AB = OA$, $\triangle OAB$ is an isosceles right triangle. Therefore, $\angle AOB$ has a measure of 45°. So the area of the sector is $\frac{45}{360}(64\pi)$, or 8π. Now we can get the total area of the shaded region:

$$64\pi + 32 - 8\pi = 56\pi + 32$$

12. $\pi - 2$

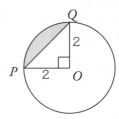

The area of the shaded region is the area of the quarter-circle (sector *OPQ*) minus the area of right triangle *OPQ*. The radius of circle *O* is 2, so the area of the quarter-circle is

$$\frac{1}{4}\pi r^2 = \frac{1}{4} \times \pi(2)^2 = \frac{1}{4} \times 4\pi = \pi$$

Each leg of the triangle is a radius of circle *O*, so the area of the triangle is

$$\frac{1}{2}bh = \frac{1}{2} \times 2 \times 2 = 2$$

Therefore, the area of the shaded region is $\pi - 2$.

13. 270

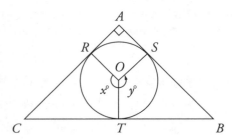

A line tangent to a circle is perpendicular to the radius of the circle at the point of tangency. Since *AC* is tangent to circle *O* at *R* and *AB* is tangent to circle *O* at *S*, $\angle ARO$ and $\angle ASO$ are 90° angles. Since three of the angles in quadrilateral *RASO* are right angles, the fourth, $\angle ROS$,

must also be a right angle. $\angle ROS$, *x*, and *y* sum to 360°, so we can set up an equation to solve for $x + y$.

$$x + y + 90 = 360$$
$$x + y = 360 - 90$$
$$x + y = 270$$

14. $25\pi - 48$

The total area of the shaded regions equals the area of the quarter-circle minus the area of the rectangle. Since the length of arc *AB* (a quarter of the circumference of circle *O*) is 5π, the whole circumference equals $4 \times 5\pi$, or 20π. Thus, the radius *OE* has length 10. (We've added point *E* in the diagram for clarity.) Since *OB* also equals 10, $OC = 10 - 4$, or 6. This tells us that $\triangle OEC$ is a 6-8-10 right triangle and $EC = 8$.

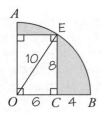

Now we know the dimensions of the rectangle, so we can find its area: area $= l \times w = 8 \times 6 = 48$. Finally, we can get the total area of the shaded regions:

$$\text{Area of shaded regions} = \frac{1}{4} \times \pi \times (10)^2 - 48$$

$$= 25\pi - 48$$

15. 2 : 1

The length of each side of the square is given as s. A side of the square has the same length as the diameter of the

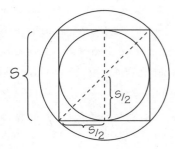

smaller circle. (You can see this more clearly if you draw the vertical diameter in the smaller circle. The diameter you draw will connect the upper and lower tangent points where the smaller circle and square intersect.) This means that the radius of the smaller circle is $\frac{s}{2}$, so its area is $\left(\frac{s}{2}\right)^2 \pi$, or $\frac{s^2}{4}\pi$. Now draw a diagonal of the square, and you'll see that it's the diameter of the larger circle. The diagonal breaks the square up into two isosceles right triangles, where each leg has length s as in the diagram above. So the diagonal must have length $s\sqrt{2}$. Therefore, the radius of the larger circle is $\frac{s\sqrt{2}}{2}$, so its area is $\left(\frac{s\sqrt{2}}{2}\right)^2 \pi$, or $\frac{2s^2}{4}\pi$, or $\frac{s^2}{2}\pi$. This is twice the area of the smaller circle.

SOLIDS TEST
ANSWERS AND EXPLANATIONS

1. $\dfrac{r}{h}$

Let's express the volume of a cylinder with radius r and height h first. (Call it cylinder A.)

$$\text{Volume} = \text{area of base} \times \text{height} = \pi r^2 h$$

For the cylinder with radius h and height r (cylinder B),

$$\text{Volume} = \pi h^2 r$$

Then the ratio of the volume of A to the volume of B is $\dfrac{\pi r^2 h}{\pi h^2 r}$. We can cancel the factor πrh from both numerator and denominator, leaving us with $\dfrac{r}{h}$.

2. 8

We can immediately determine the volume of the rectangular solid since we're given all its dimensions: 4, 8, and 16. The volume of a rectangular solid is equal to the product $\ell \times w \times h$. So the volume of this solid is $16 \times 8 \times 4$, and this must equal the volume of the cube as well. The volume of a cube is the length of an edge cubed, so we can set up an equation to solve for e:

$$e^3 = 16 \times 8 \times 4$$

To avoid the multiplication, let's break the 16 down into 2×8:

$$e^3 = 2 \times 8 \times 8 \times 4$$

We can now combine 2×4 to get another 8:

$$e^3 = 8 \times 8 \times 8$$
$$e = 8$$

The length of an edge of the cube is 8.

3. 4

Once we find the cube's volume, we can get the length of one edge. Since 16 cubic meters represents 25 percent, or $\dfrac{1}{4}$, of the volume of the whole cube, the cube has a volume of 4×16, or 64 cubic meters. The volume of a cube is the length of an edge cubed, so $e^3 = 64$. Therefore e, the length of an edge, is 4.

4. 32

This figure is an unfamiliar solid, so we shouldn't try to calculate the volume directly. We are told that the solid in question is half of a cube. We can imagine the other half lying on top of the solid forming a complete cube.

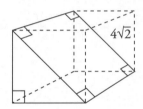

Notice that the diagonal with length $4\sqrt{2}$ forms an isosceles right triangle with two of the edges of the cube, which are the legs of the triangle. In an isosceles right triangle, the hypotenuse is $\sqrt{2}$ times each of the legs. Here the hypotenuse has length $4\sqrt{2}$, so the legs have length 4. So the volume of the whole cube is $4 \times 4 \times 4$, or 64. The volume of the solid in question is one-half of this, or 32.

5. $\dfrac{40}{\pi}$

From the situation that's described we can see that the volume of the milk in the cylinder is the same volume as the rectangular container. The volume of the rectangular container is $4 \times 9 \times 10$, or 360 cubic inches. The volume of a cylinder equals the area of its base times its height, or $\pi r^2 h$. Since the diameter is 6 inches, the radius, r, is 3 inches. Now we're ready to set up an equation to solve for h (which is the height of the milk):

$$\text{Volume of milk} = \text{Volume of rectangular container}$$

$$\pi(3)^2 h = 360$$

$$h = \frac{360}{9\pi} = 40\pi$$

6. 2

It may be helpful to draw a quick diagram, like this one:

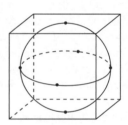

The sphere will touch the cube at six points. Each point will be an endpoint of a diameter and will be at the center of one of the cubic faces. (If this isn't clear, imagine putting a beach ball inside a cube-shaped box.) So, the diameter extends directly from one face of the cube to the other, and is perpendicular to both faces that it touches. This means that the diameter must have the same length as an edge of the cube. The cube's volume is 64, so each edge has length $\sqrt[3]{64}$, or 4. So the diameter of the sphere is 4, which means that the radius is 2.

7. 52

The given conditions narrow down the possibilities for the solid's dimensions. The volume of a rectangular solid is length $\times$ width $\times$ height. Since one of these dimensions is 4, and the volume is 24, the other two dimension must have a product of $\dfrac{24}{4}$, or 6. Since the dimensions are integers, there are two possibilities: 2 and 3 ($2 \times 3 = 6$), or 1 and 6 ($1 \times 6 = 6$). We can work with either possibility to determine the total surface area. If our result matches an answer choice, we can stop. If not, we can try the other possibility. Let's try 4, 2, and 3:

$$\begin{aligned}\text{Surface area} &= 2lw + 2lh + 2wh \\ &= 2(4)(2) + 2(4)(3) + 2(2)(3) \\ &= 16 + 24 + 12 = 52\end{aligned}$$

Since choice (2) is 52, we've found our answer.

8. I, II, and III

We need to go through the Roman numeral statements one at a time.

Statement I:

Intuitively or visually, you might be able to see that FD and GA are parallel. It's a little trickier to prove mathematically. Remember, two line segments are parallel if they're in the same plane and if they do not intersect each other. Imagine slicing the cube in half, diagonally (as in question 4) from FG to AD.

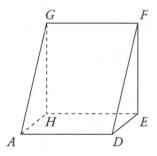

The diagonal face will be a flat surface, with sides AD, FD, FG, and GA. So FD and GA are in the same plane. They both have the same length, since each is a diagonal of a face of the cube. FG and DA also have the same length, since they're both edges of the cube. Since both pairs of opposite sides have the same length, ADFG must be a parallelogram. (In fact, it's a rectangle.) So FD and GA, which are opposite sides, are parallel. Eliminate choice (4).

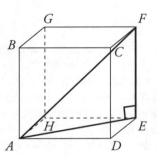

Statement II:

△GCF is half of square BCFG, and △AHD is half of square ADEH. Both squares have the same area, so both triangles must also have the same area. Eliminate choices (1) and (3).

Statement III:

Draw in diagonals AE and AF to get right triangle AEF. Also draw in diagonals HD and GD to get right triangle DGH.

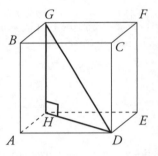

AE and HD are both diagonals of the same square, so AE = HD. FE and GH are both edges of the cube, so FE = GH. Since right triangle AEF and right triangle DGH have corresponding legs of the same length, they must also have hypotenuses of the same length. AF and GD are the respective hypotenuses, so AF = GD.

Therefore, statements I, II, and III are true.

PART THREE

Question Type Review

Chapter 5
Quantitative Comparisons

Half of the points available in the math sections of the GRE come from questions in the QC format. Quantitative Comparisons are designed to be answered more quickly than the other math problem types—practically twice as fast as problems of similar difficulty in other formats. However, to be able to attack QCs quickly and efficiently, you must be comfortable with the format. You must be prepared to use shortcuts to compare the columns, instead of grinding out calculations.

GET FAMILIAR WITH THE DIRECTIONS AND ANSWER CHOICES

QCs are the only questions type on the GRE with four instead of five answer choices. Here's what they look like:

- ○ The quantity in Column A is greater.
- ○ The quantity in Column B is greater.
- ○ The two quantities are equal.
- ○ The relationship cannot be determined from the information given.

> **Kaplan Exclusive**
>
> Memorizing the four answer choices for QCs in practice saves you a lot of time on Test Day.

Because the answer choices to QCs never change, from here on in we will omit the answer choices from the QC examples in this book. To score high on QCs, learn what the answer choices stand for, and know these cold.

The directions to QCs look something like this:

Directions: Compare the quantities in Column A and Column B. Then decide which of the following is true:

- ○ The quantity in Column A is greater.
- ○ The quantity in Column B is greater.
- ○ The two quantities are equal.
- ○ The relationship cannot be determined from the information given.

Common information: In a question, information concerning one or both of the quantities to be compared is centered above the two columns. A symbol that appears in both columns represents the same thing in Column A as it does in Column B.

THE 2 BASIC PRINCIPLES OF QUANTITATIVE COMPARISONS

The first three answer choices all represent definite relationships between the quantities in Column A and Column B. But the fourth represents a relationship that cannot be determined. Here are two things to remember about the fourth answer choice that will help you decide when to pick it:

Principle 1. Choice 4 Is Never Correct If Both Columns Contain Only Numbers

The relationship between numbers is unchanging, but choice 4 means more than one relationship is possible.

Principle 2. Choice 4 Is Always Correct If You Can Demonstrate Two Different Relationships Between the Columns

Here's what we mean. Suppose you ran across the following QC:

Column A	Column B
$2x$	$3x$

If x is a positive number, Column B is greater than Column A. If $x = 0$, the columns are equal. If x equals any negative number, Column B is less than Column A. Because more than one relationship is possible, the answer is choice 4. In fact, as soon as you find a second possibility, stop working and choose choice 4.

On this question we *picked numbers* to compare the two quantities. This is just one strategy that can be used to quickly find the correct answer to a QC.

KAPLAN'S 6-STEP METHOD FOR QUANTITATIVE COMPARISONS

Here are six Kaplan-exclusive strategies that will enable you to make quick comparisons.

Step 1. Compare, Don't Calculate

This strategy is especially effective when you can estimate the quantities in a QC.

Step 2. Compare Piece by Piece

This works on QCs that compare two sums or two products.

Step 3. Make One Column Look Like the Other

This is a great approach when the columns look so different that you can't compare them directly.

Step 4. Do the Same Thing to Both Columns

Change both columns by adding, subtracting, multiplying, or dividing by the same amount on both sides in order to make the comparison more apparent.

Step 5. Pick Numbers

Use this to get a handle on abstract algebra QCs.

Step 6. Redraw the Diagram

Redrawing a diagram can clarify the relationships between measurements.

Kaplan Exclusive

Picking numbers for Word Problems differs from doing so in QCs. In QCs, we use dramatically different numbers the second time around (negative values, very large numbers, etc.)—we want to emphasize the *difference* between the two quantities. When we pick numbers for Word Problems, we *always* use numbers that are easy to work with.

AVOID QC TRAPS

Stay alert for questions designed to fool you by leading you to the obvious, wrong answer.

Don't be tricked by misleading information. For example, if Column A states, "Joaquin is taller than Bob," and Column B states, "Joaquin's weight in pounds Bob's weight in pounds," you may think, "Joaquin is taller so he weighs more." But there's no guaranteed relationship between height and weight. You don't have enough information, so the answer is choice 4, not choice 1.

Don't assume. A common QC mistake, for example, is to assume that variables represent positive integers. Fractions or negative numbers often show another relationship between the columns. You must be absolutely sure about the information in Columns A and B.

Don't forget to consider other possibilities. This is especially true if an answer looks too obvious. For example, Column A may be "Three Multiples of 3<10," and Column B may be "18." While 3, 6, and 9 add up to 18, zero is also a multiple of 3. So Column A could also be 0, 3, and 9, or 0, 6, and 9, which give totals of 12 and 15, respectively. Since the colums could be equal or Column B could be greater, the correct answer is choice 4.

Don't fall for look-alikes. Just because two expressions look similar, they may be mathematically different. For example, if Column A is $\sqrt{5} + \sqrt{5}$ and Column B is $\sqrt{10}$, you might think the answer is choice 3. But in fact, the answer is choice 1.

For full examples of how these strategies work, pick up a copy of Kaplan's *GRE Exam Premier Program* or *GRE Exam Comprehensive Program*.

QUANTITATIVE COMPARISONS—PRACTICE TEST ONE

10 minutes—15 Questions

Compare the quantities in Column A and Column B, and select the appropriate answer choice from those at the bottom of the page. Darken the corresponding oval below the question.

	Column A	**Column B**
1.	0.04504	0.045134

    ①   ②   ③   ④

John is older than Karen.

	Column A	**Column B**
2.	John's weight, in pounds	Karen's weight, in pounds

    ①   ②   ③   ④

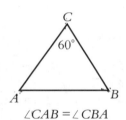

$\angle CAB = \angle CBA$

	Column A	**Column B**
3.	AB	AC

    ①   ②   ③   ④

$a + 7 = 10$
$b - 2 = 5$

	Column A	**Column B**
4.	$\dfrac{a + 7}{b - 2}$	$\dfrac{(a + 7)(b - 2)}{20}$

    ①   ②   ③   ④

	Column A	**Column B**
5.	$\dfrac{1}{8} + \dfrac{1}{9}$	$\dfrac{1}{5}$

    ①   ②   ③   ④

6.	$\sqrt{39{,}899}$	200

    ①   ②   ③   ④

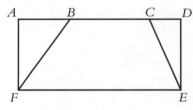

ADEF has a perimeter 32.
$\angle ADE \neq 90°$

7.	Perimeter of *FBCE*	32

    ①   ②   ③   ④

The finance plan for the purchase of a television requires 25 percent of the cost as an initial down payment and 12 monthly payments of $30.00 each.

8.	Total cost of the television	$480.00

    ①   ②   ③   ④

    ①   The quantity in Column A is greater.
    ②   The quantity in Column B is greater.
    ③   The two quantities are equal.
    ④   The relationship cannot be determined from the information given.

Column A	Column B

$$13 < a < 15$$

$$15 < b < 17$$

9. $a + b$ 30

    ①   ②   ③   ④

10. The perimeter of a   The circumference of
    triangle with area 8   a circle with area 8π

    ①   ②   ③   ④

11. $(0.3)^6$ $(0.2)^9$

    ①   ②   ③   ④

On a 50-question test, 1 point is given for each
question answered correctly and half of a point is
deducted for each question answered incorrectly.
No points are given for questions which remain
unanswered. A student who answered 48 questions received a total of 36 points.

12. Number of questions   9
    answered incorrectly

    ①   ②   ③   ④

Column A	Column B

O is the center of the circle with radius 6.

13. Area of the shaded   18
    region

    ①   ②   ③   ④

Small cubes with edges of length 2 and spheres
with radius 1 are being packed into a crate with
dimensions 2 by 8 by 12.

14. The number of   The number of spheres
    cubes that can fit   that can fit in the crate
    in the crate

    ①   ②   ③   ④

$$\frac{8x + 2}{10} - \frac{4x - 1}{5} = \frac{4x - 1}{10} - \frac{8x + 2}{5}$$

15. $8x + 2$ $4x - 1$

    ①   ②   ③   ④

①   The quantity in Column A is greater.
②   The quantity in Column B is greater.
③   The two quantities are equal.
④   The relationship cannot be determined from the information given.

KAPLAN

QUANTITATIVE COMPARISONS—PRACTICE TEST TWO

10 minutes—15 Questions

Compare the quantities in Column A and Column B, and select the appropriate answer choice from those at the bottom of the page. Darken the corresponding oval below the question.

Column A	Column B
1. $(50)(10)(8)$	$(10)(5)(90)$

   ①   ②   ③   ④

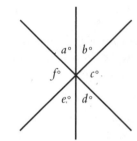

2. $a + c + e$ $b + d + f$

   ①   ②   ③   ④

3. The number of hours it   The number of hours
    takes a train to travel   it takes a car to travel
    700 miles   700 miles

   ①   ②   ③   ④

$$y < 0$$

4. $10(1 - y)$ $10(y - 1)$

   ①   ②   ③   ④

Column A	Column B
5. $\dfrac{0.09}{0.0003}$	30

   ①   ②   ③   ④

There are x dictionaries in a bookstore. After $\dfrac{1}{8}$ of them were purchased, 10 more dictionaries were shipped in bringing the total number of dictionaries to 52.

6. x 50

   ①   ②   ③   ④

7. $(41)^2 - (21)^2$ $(41 - 21)^2$

   ①   ②   ③   ④

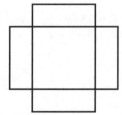

Two boards with dimensions 2 meters by 4 meters overlap to form the figure above. All the angles shown have measure 90°.

8. The perimeter of the 16
    figure, in meters

   ①   ②   ③   ④

    ①   The quantity in Column A is greater.
    ②   The quantity in Column B is greater.
    ③   The two quantities are equal.
    ④   The relationship cannot be determined from the information given.

Column A   **Column B**

9. $(\sqrt{5} + \sqrt{5})^2$ $5 + 5\sqrt{5}$

   ①   ②   ③   ④

10. The average (arithmetic mean) of 100, 101, and 103   The median of 100, 101, and 103

   ①   ②   ③   ④

11. The number of different prime factors of 18   3

   ①   ②   ③   ④

A and B are points of the circumference of the circle with center O. The length of chord AB is 15.

12. Circumference of circle O 12π

   ①   ②   ③   ④

Column A   **Column B**

$$x = \frac{4}{3}r^2h^2$$

$$x = 1$$

r and h are positive

13. h $\dfrac{\sqrt{3}}{2r}$

   ①   ②   ③   ④

$\triangle ABC$ lies in the xy-plane with C at $(0,0)$, B at $(6,0)$, and A at (x, y), where x and y are positive. The area of $\triangle ABC$ is 18.

14. y 6

   ①   ②   ③   ④

For $x \neq y$, $x \, \Phi \, y = \dfrac{x + y}{x - y}$

$$p > 0 > q$$

15. $p \, \Phi \, q$ $q \, \Phi \, p$

   ①   ②   ③   ④

①   The quantity in Column A is greater.
②   The quantity in Column B is greater.
③   The two quantities are equal.
④   The relationship cannot be determined from the information given.

KAPLAN

QUANTITATIVE COMPARISONS—PRACTICE TEST THREE

10 minutes—15 Questions

Compare the quantities in Column A and Column B, and select the appropriate answer choice from those at the bottom of the page. Darken the corresponding oval below the question.

Column A   **Column B**

1. $\dfrac{1}{3} + \dfrac{1}{3}$ $\dfrac{1}{3} \times \dfrac{1}{3}$

   ① ② ③ ④

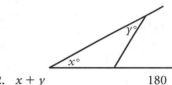

2. $x + y$ 180

   ① ② ③ ④

3. 16 percent of 30   15 percent of 31

   ① ② ③ ④

$$x^5 = -32$$

4. x^3 $2x^2$

   ① ② ③ ④

$$x < y < z$$
$$0 < z$$

5. x 0

   ① ② ③ ④

Column A   **Column B**

$$6(10)^n > 60{,}006$$

6. n 6

   ① ② ③ ④

In a three-digit number y, the hundreds' digit is 3 times the units' digit.

7. The units' digit of y 4

   ① ② ③ ④

8. The perimeter of a square with side 4   The circumference of a circle with diameter 5

   ① ② ③ ④

$$\ell_1 \parallel \ell_2$$

9. $2(x + y)$ $x + a + y + b$

   ① ② ③ ④

---

① The quantity in Column A is greater.
② The quantity in Column B is greater.
③ The two quantities are equal.
④ The relationship cannot be determined from the information given.

KAPLAN

Column A	Column B

$$\frac{2x}{3} = \frac{2y}{5} = \frac{2z}{7}$$

z is positive.

10. $x + y$ z

  ①   ②   ③   ④

The product of two integers is 10.

11. The average (arithmetic   3
mean) of the integers

  ①   ②   ③   ④

The remainder when n is divided by 3 is 1, and the remainder when $n + 1$ is divided by 2 is 1.

12. The remainder when   3
$n - 1$ is divided by 6

  ①   ②   ③   ④

Circle with center T.

13. RT RS

  ①   ②   ③   ④

Column A	Column B

After 5 adults leave a party, there are 3 times as many children as adults. After 25 children leave the party, there are twice as many adults as children.

14. The original number   14
of adults

  ①   ②   ③   ④

There are at least 200 apples in a grocery store. The ratio of the number of oranges to apples is 9 to 10.

15. The number of   200
oranges in the store

  ①   ②   ③   ④

①   The quantity in Column A is greater.
②   The quantity in Column B is greater.
③   The two quantities are equal.
④   The relationship cannot be determined from the information given.

KAPLAN

QUANTATATIVE COMPARISONS—PRACTICE TEST FOUR

10 minutes—15 Questions

Compare the quantities in Column A an Column B, and select the appropriate answer choice from those at the bottom of the page. Darken the corresponding oval below the question.

Column A **Column B** **Column A** **Column B**

1. $(-5)^3$ $(-5)^2$

    ①   ②   ③   ④

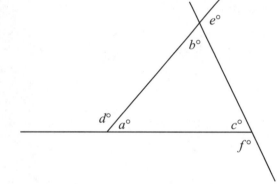

2. $2(a + b + c)$ $d + e + f$

    ①   ②   ③   ④

A jar contains 40 marbles,
15% of which are green.

3. Number of green   6
    marbles in the jar

    ①   ②   ③   ④

$$x^2 - 9 = 0$$

4. x 0

    ①   ②   ③   ④

5. $\dfrac{5}{32} + \dfrac{15}{16}$ $\dfrac{1}{16} + 1$

    ①   ②   ③   ④

6. $\dfrac{1}{5}$ $\dfrac{1}{\sqrt{24}}$

    ①   ②   ③   ④

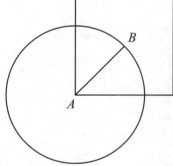

Point A is the center of the circle above.
Point B is the center of the square above.

7. Circumference   Perimeter
    of the circle   of the square

    ①   ②   ③   ④

   ①   The quantity in Column A is greater.
   ②   The quantity in Column B is greater.
   ③   The two quantities are equal.
   ④   The relationship cannot be determined from the information given.

Column A	Column B

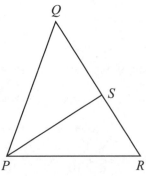

Area of ΔPSR is 15
$QS > SR$

8. Area of ΔPQR 30

   ①   ②   ③   ④

Sarah is n years old. In five years from now, she will be 4 times as old as Nick, who is now 6 years old.

9. 19 .... n

   ①   ②   ③   ④

$$\frac{a+b}{c} = 7$$

$$\frac{a-b}{c} = 5$$

10. b c

   ①   ②   ③   ④

11. The number of different 6
    factors of 24

   ①   ②   ③   ④

Column A	Column B

The ratio of the number of boys to the number of girls in the class was 4 to 3. After 2 new boys and 3 new girls joined the class, the ratio became 6 to 5.

12. The original number 18
    of boys in the class

   ①   ②   ③   ④

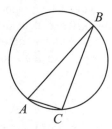

AB is a diameter of the circle above
$\angle ABC = 20°$

13. $\angle BAC$ .... 70°

   ①   ②   ③   ④

Isosceles ΔDEF lies in the xy-plane with D at $(-3,0)$ and F at $(3,0)$. The length of DE is 5.

14. y-coordinate of point E 4

   ①   ②   ③   ④

$$s = (t+r)^2$$

$$s = 4$$

15. $2 - r$ .... t

   ①   ②   ③   ④

  ①   The quantity in Column A is greater.
  ②   The quantity in Column B is greater.
  ③   The two quantities are equal.
  ④   The relationship cannot be determined from the information given.

KAPLAN

QUANTITATIVE COMPARISONS TEST ONE ANSWERS AND EXPLANATIONS

1.   Choice 2

To see which decimal is larger, we need to compare the digits after the decimal in each column. The first three digits after the decimal (0, 4, and 5) are the same in both columns. However, the fourth digit is different: 0 in column A and 1 in column B. Since 1 is greater than 0, the quantity of column B is larger.

2.   Choice 4

This question tells you that John is older than Karen. Does that mean John is heavier than Karen? Of course not. There is no way to determine someone's weight given only his or her age. Never make foolish assumptions. We need more information to solve this question.

3.   Choice 3

The sum of the measures of the three angles in any triangle equals 180 degrees. If $\angle ACB$ measures 60 degrees, then the sum of the other two angles, $\angle CAB$ and $\angle CBA$, is 120 degrees. Since $\angle CAB$ and $\angle CBA$ are equal in measure, $\angle CAB$ and $\angle CBA$ each measure $\frac{1}{2}$ of 120 or 60 degrees. Now, we have a triangle with three 60° angles; therefore, it is an equilateral triangle, and all the sides are equal. Line segment AB is equal to line segment AC and the columns are equal.

4.   Choice 2

We could solve for a and b but there's a quicker way. Plug in the values of $(a + 7)$ and $(b - 2)$ directly into the expressions. In column A we're left with $\frac{10}{5}$ or 2.

Column B becomes $\frac{(10)(5)}{20} = \frac{50}{20} = 2\frac{1}{2}$. Since $2\frac{1}{2}$ is greater than 2, column B is larger.

5.   Choice 1

Instead of finding a lowest common denominator to add the fractions, look for a shortcut. In column B, $\frac{1}{5}$ is the same as $\frac{1}{10} + \frac{1}{10}$. Now compare the columns, one piece at a time. Since $\frac{1}{8} > \frac{1}{10}$ and $\frac{1}{9} > \frac{1}{10}$, the sum $\frac{1}{8} + \frac{1}{9}$ is greater than the sum of $\frac{1}{10} + \frac{1}{10}$ or $\frac{1}{5}$. Column A is larger.

6.   Choice 2

To get rid of the radical sign, let's square both columns. $(\sqrt{39,899})^2$ becomes 39,899 and $(200)^2$ becomes 40,000. Since 40,000 is larger than 39,899, column B is larger.

7.   Choice 2

Since we know that $ADEF$ has perimeter 32, in effect we have to compare the perimeter of $FBCE$ to the perimeter of $ADEF$. They share line segment BC and side FE, so we have to compare the sum $AF + AB + CD + DE$ to the sum $FB + CE$. Start by comparing FB to the sum $AF + AB$. These are the sides of triangle ABF, and since the sum of any two sides of a triangle is greater than the third side, FB must be less than $AB + AF$. Similarly, in $\triangle CDE$, $CD + DE > CE$. The perimeter of $FBCE$ is less than the perimeter of $ADEF$.

①   The quantity in Column A is greater.
②   The quantity in Column B is greater.
③   The two quantities are equal.
④   The relationship cannot be determined from the information given.

8. Choice 3

Try to set the two columns equal. If the set cost $480, then the down payment was 25% of $480 or $\frac{1}{4} \times 480 = \$120$. This leaves $360, which exactly equals 12 monthly payments of $30 each. Therefore, the total cost of the television set must be $480, and the columns are equal.

9. Choice 4

Not all numbers are integers! If a were 14 and b were 16, then the columns would be equal. But a could just as easily equal 13.5 and b equal 15.5, in which case their sum would be 29, and column B would be larger. Or a could equal 14.5 and b equal 16.5, in which case column A would be larger. There is more than one possibility; the answer is choice 4.

10. Choice 4

Start by drawing some diagrams. The circle in column B is easy; we know what a circle looks like. The triangle in column A presents more of a problem, though: triangles come in all shapes and sizes. Some are long and flat, others tall and thin. Since the area of the circle is more than three times the area of the triangle, it is relatively easy to imagine a small triangle inside of a circle, in which case the circumference of the circle would be much larger than the perimeter of the triangle, and column B would be bigger. So let's try to make column A larger; can we do that? Certainly. A very long, very thin triangle would have a very large perimeter, without necessarily a large area. For instance, one with base 64 and height $\frac{1}{4}$ would have area 8, but would have a much larger perimeter than the circle. We need more information before we can compare the columns.

or

11. Choice 1

Both 0.3 and 0.2 are fractions between 0 and 1. What happens to these numbers when you square them, or raise them to a positive power? They get *smaller*. Therefore, the quantities in the two columns are going to be very small fractions. But which is smaller? Well, since the numbers keep getting smaller as we raise them to higher and higher powers, $(0.2)^9$ will be smaller than $(0.2)^6$. And since $0.2 < 0.3$, $(0.3)^6 > (0.2)^6$. Therefore, $(0.3)^6 > (0.2)^6 > (0.2)^9$ and column A is larger.

12. Choice 2

Again, assume the columns are equal. The student answered 48 questions. If 9 were incorrect, then the number of correct answers is $48 - 9$ or 39. Since $\frac{1}{2}$ point is deducted for each question answered incorrectly, then we have to deduct $\frac{1}{2} \times 9$ or 4.5 from 39, making his score 34.5. But the student's actual score was higher than that; it was 36. So he must have answered fewer than 9 wrong to get a score of 36. Therefore, column B must be larger than the number of questions answered incorrectly. (Of course, we don't care how many questions he actually got wrong; only that it was fewer than 9.)

13. Choice 2

The area of the right triangle inside the circle is equal to $\frac{1}{2}$ base $\times$ height. Since the legs of the triangle are both radii of the circle; and since the circle has radius 6, the area of the triangle must be $\frac{1}{2}(6) \times (6)$ or 18—the quantity in column B. So in effect the question is asking which is larger, the triangle or the shaded region? By eyeballing, you can probably tell that the area of the triangle is larger than the area of the shaded region. If you are suspicious, draw another triangle adjacent to the first that overlaps the shaded region. The two

① The quantity in Column A is greater.
② The quantity in Column B is greater.
③ The two quantities are equal.
④ The relationship cannot be determined from the information given.

triangles are equal in area because each one is half of the square. Since the shaded area is inside the triangle, the area of the triangle must be greater than the shaded area.

14. Choice 3

This is a difficult visualization problem. You may have thought you need to know the formula for the volume of a sphere to answer this, but you don't. What is a sphere with radius 1? It has a diameter of twice 1, or 2. So how does it compare to a cube with edge of length 2? The sphere is certainly smaller than the cube; in fact, it would fit exactly inside the cube. The dimensions of the crate are 2 by 8 by 12; let's let the 2 dimension be the height of the crate. So we have a relatively flat crate, with dimensions 12 by 8, and height 2. How many layers of cubes would fit into this crate? Since each cube also has height 2, we can fit exactly one layer of cubes in. Now how many layers of spheres can fit in? Again, exactly one layer of spheres. Each sphere has height 2, the same as the crate, so we can't fit another layer of spheres in. There's also no other space in the crate to fit more spheres in. We can pack the cubes into the crate efficiently, without any wasted space, but we can't do that with the spheres; there's always going to be some wasted space. Each sphere, although it is smaller than a cube, will still require as much space as a cube. It's the same thing as trying to fit two circles of diameter 2 into a rectangle with dimensions 2 by 4—you can only fit 2 in. The two columns are equal.

15. Choice 3

It may have occurred to you as you looked at the ugly equation that the sides look somewhat similar. Each side has a fraction with $8x + 2$ in the numerator and one with $4x - 1$ in the numerator. You may have said to yourself "There must be some reason for this." And in fact, there is. So it might occur to you to rename both of these expressions; to call them something else for the time being, and see whether you can simplify the rest of the equation. So let's let $(8x + 2) = a$ and $(4x - 1) = b$. We now have

$$\frac{a}{10} - \frac{b}{5} = \frac{b}{10} = \frac{a}{5}$$

To get rid of the fractions, multiply the whole equation by 10. That leaves us with

$$a - 2b = b - 2a, \text{ or}$$
$$3a = 3b$$
$$a = b$$

Or plugging back in what a and b represent, $8x + 2 = 4x - 1$. The two columns are equal.

①   The quantity in Column A is greater.
②   The quantity in Column B is greater.
③   The two quantities are equal.
④   The relationship cannot be determined from the information given.

QUANTITATIVE COMPARISONS TEST TWO ANSWERS AND EXPLANATIONS

1.   Choice 2

Divide both sides by 10 to get (50)(8) in column A and (5)(90) in column B. Divide again by 10 to get (5)(8) in column A and (5)(9) in column B. Divide once more by 5, and we're left with 8 in column A and 9 in column B.

2.   Choice 3

There are three sets of vertical angles in this diagram: (a, d), (b, e), and (f, c). In column A we can substitute b for e since they are vertical angles, and therefore equal: this leaves us with the sum $a + b + c$ in column A. Since these are the three angles on one side of a straight line, they sum to 180. Similarly, column B, $b + d + f$ is the same thing as $d + e + f$, or also 180. The two columns are equal.

3.   Choice 4

You may have read this and thought to yourself, "Well, a train moves much faster than a car. Therefore column B must be bigger." Well, trains may move faster than cars in the real world, but not on the GRE. That falls into the category of foolish assumptions. For all we know, the car is some new model that travels 350 miles per hour, while the train could be some broken down old locomotive that can't handle more than 15 miles per hour. We need more information.

4.   Choice 1

Dividing both columns by 10, we get $(1 - y)$ in column A and $(y - 1)$ in column B. Since y is less than 0, $(1 - y)$ is 1 minus a negative number, which will give us a positive result. So column A is positive. On the other hand, $(y - 1)$ is a negative number minus 1, which gives a negative result. So column B is negative. Since a positive number is always greater than a negative number, column A is larger.

5.   Choice 1

Change the decimal fraction in column A to something more manageable. Multiply both the numerator and denominator by 10,000—the same as moving each decimal point four digits to the right.

$$\frac{0.09}{0.0003} \times \frac{10{,}000}{10{,}000} = \frac{900}{3}$$
$$= 300$$

Column A is larger.

6.   Choice 2

Let's try to set the columns equal. If x is 50, then the bookstore started out with 50 dictionaries. Then $\frac{1}{8}$ of them were purchased. Well, we can see already that the columns can't be equal, since $\frac{1}{8}$ of 50 won't give us an integer. But let's go ahead, and see whether the answer is (1) or (2). Since $\frac{1}{8}$ of 50 is close to 6, after these dictionaries were purchased, the store would have been left with about 50 − 6 or 44 dictionaries. Then they received 10 more, giving a total of about 54 dictionaries. But this is more than the store actually ended up with; they only had 52. Therefore, they must have started with *fewer* than 50 dictionaries, and column B is bigger. (As always, the last thing we care about is how many dictionaries they really had.)

①   The quantity in Column A is greater.
②   The quantity in Column B is greater.
③   The two quantities are equal.
④   The relationship cannot be determined from the information given.

7. Choice 1

You should have decided immediately that there must be a shortcut here; that multiplying out the values of the columns would take too long. (It may also have occurred to you that the answer cannot be choice 4—since all you are dealing with here are numbers, there must be some way to compare the columns, even if you do have to calculate the values.) So you might have asked yourself whether the columns look like anything familiar. In fact, column A looks a lot like a difference of squares. It can be factored, then, into

$$(41)^2 - (21)^2 = (41 - 21)(41 + 21)$$
$$= (20)(62)$$

Now how does this compare to $(41 - 21)^2$ or $(20)^2$ in column B? Column A is larger: 20×62 is larger than 20×20.

8. Choice 3

You may have thought this was a choice (4); after all, we don't know exactly where the boards overlap, whether it is in the middle of each board, as pictured, or whether it is near the end of one of the boards. But that doesn't matter; all we need to know is that they overlap, and that all the angles are right angles. If the boards did not overlap it would be easy to find the perimeter: $2 + 2 + 4 + 4$ or 12 for each board, or 24 for both boards. Now, since the boards do overlap, the perimeter of the figure will be smaller than that, but how much smaller? It will be smaller by the amount of that "lost perimeter" in the middle; the perimeter of the square where the boards overlap. (We know it's a square, since we're told all the angles are right angles.) The length of a side of that square is the shorter dimension of each of the boards: 2. Therefore, the perimeter of the square is 4×2 or 8. The perimeter of the figure, then, is $24 - 8$ or 16. The two columns are equal.

9. Choice 1

Start by squaring the quantity in column A: $(\sqrt{5} + \sqrt{5})^2$ is the same as $(2\sqrt{5})^2$ which is $2^2 \times (\sqrt{5})^2$ or 4·5 or 20. Subtract 5 from both columns, and we're left with 15 in column A and $5\sqrt{5}$ in column B. Now divide both sides by 5, and we're left with 3 in column A and $\sqrt{5}$ in column B. If you did not know that $3 > \sqrt{5}$, you could square both sides—but you really should know that $\sqrt{5}$ is less than 3; after all, 3^2 is 9. Column A is larger.

10. Choice 1

This question requires no computation but only a general understanding of how averages work, and what the word "median" means. The median of a group of numbers is the "middle number"; it is the value above which half of the numbers in the group fall, and below which the other half fall. If you have an even number of values, the median is the average of the two "middle" numbers; if you have an odd number of values, the median is one of the values. Here, in column B, the median is 101. In column A, if the numbers were 100, 101, and 102, then the average would also be 101, but since the third number, 103, is larger than 102, then the average must be larger than 101. Column A is greater than 101, and column B equals 101; column A is larger.

11. Choice 2

First find all the factors 18: these are 1, 2, 3, 6, 9, and 18. The only prime factors are 2 and 3. (Remember that 1 is *not* a prime number.) Since there are only 2 prime factors (2 and 3) of 18, column B is larger.

① The quantity in Column A is greater.
② The quantity in Column B is greater.
③ The two quantities are equal.
④ The relationship cannot be determined from the information given.

12. Choice 1

Start with the information we are given. We know that the length of the chord is 15. What does that mean? Well, since we don't know exactly where A or B is, that doesn't mean too much, but it does tell us that the distance between two points on the circumference is 15. Fine. That tells us nothing much about the radius or diameter of the circle *except* that the diameter must be at least 15. If the diameter were less than 15, then you couldn't have a chord that was equal to 15. The diameter is always the longest chord in a circle. So the diameter of the circle is 15 or greater, so the circumference must be at least 15π. That means that column A must be larger than column B.

13. Choice 3

This is a complex equation. (No kidding, you say.) Since column A has only h in it, we want to solve the equation in terms of h, leaving us with h on one side of the equal sign and r on the other. First substitute the value for x into the equation, then solve for h in terms of r.

$x = \frac{4}{3}r^2h^2$ Substitute 1 for x.

$1 = \frac{4}{3}r^2h^2$ Divide both sides by $\frac{4}{3}$.

$\frac{3}{4} = r^2h^2$ Take the square root of both sides. (This is okay, since we know that r and h are positive.)

$\frac{\sqrt{3}}{2} = rh$ Cross-multiply to get h alone.

$h = \frac{\sqrt{3}}{2r}$ The two columns are equal.

14. Choice 3

A diagram can be very helpful for solving this problem. We know where points B and C are; they're on the x-axis. We don't know where A is however, which may

have made you think that the answer is choice 4. But we're given more information; we know that the triangle has area 18. The area of any triangle is one-half the product of the height and the base. Let's make side BC the base of the triangle; we know the coordinates of both points, so we can find their distance, and the length of that side. C is at the origin, the point (0,0); B is at the point (6,0). The distance between them is the distance from 0 to 6 along the x-axis, or just 6. So that's the base; what about the altitude? Well, since we know that the area is 18, we can plug what we know into the area formula.

$$\text{Area} = \frac{1}{2}\text{base} \times \text{height}$$

$$18 = \frac{1}{2} \times 6 \times \text{height}$$

$$\text{Height} = \frac{18}{3}$$

$$\text{Height} = 6$$

So that's the other dimension of our triangle. The height is the distance between the x-axis and the point A. Now we know that A must be somewhere in the first quadrant, since both the x- and y-coordinates are positive. Now we don't care about the x-coordinate of the point, since that's not what's being compared; we care only about the value of y. We know that the distance from the x-axis to the point is 6, since that's the height of the triangle; and we know that y must be positive. Therefore, the y-coordinate of the point must be 6; that's what the y-coordinate *is*: a measure of the point's vertical distance from the x-axis. (Note that if we hadn't been told that y was positive, there would be two possible values for y: 6 and −6. A point that's 6 units below the x-axis would also give us a triangle with height 6.) We still don't know the x-coordinate of the point, and in fact we can't figure that out, but we don't care. We know that y is 6; therefore, the two columns are equal.

①   The quantity in Column A is greater.
②   The quantity in Column B is greater.
③   The two quantities are equal.
④   The relationship cannot be determined from the information given.

KAPLAN

15. Choice 4

Again, picking numbers will help you solve this problem. With symbolism problems like this, it sometimes helps to put the definition of the symbol into words. For this symbol, we can say something like "$x \Phi y$ means that you take the sum of the two numbers, and divide that by the difference of the two numbers." One good way to do this problem is to pick some values. We know that p is positive and q is negative. So suppose p is 1 and q is −1. Let's figure out what $p \Phi q$ is first. We start by taking the sum of the numbers, or $1 + (-1) = 0$. That's the numerator of our fraction, and we don't really need to go any further than that. Whatever their difference is, since the numerator is 0, the whole fraction must equal 0. (We know that the difference can't be 0 also, since $p \neq q$.) So that's $p \Phi q$; now what about $q \Phi p$? Well, that's going to have the same numerator as $p \Phi q$: 0. The only thing that changes when you reverse the order of the numbers is the denominator of the fraction. So $q \Phi p$ has a numerator of 0, and that fraction must equal 0 as well.

So we've found a case where the columns are equal. Let's try another set of values, and see whether the columns are always equal. If $p = 1$ and $q = -2$, then the sum of the numbers is $1 + (-2)$ or -1. So that's the numerator of our fraction in each column. Now for the denominator of $p \Phi q$ we need $p - q$ or $1 - (-2) = 1 + 2 = 3$. Then the value of $p \Phi q$ is $\frac{-1}{3}$. The denominator of $q \Phi p$ is $q - p$ or $-2 - 1 = -3$. In that case, the value of $q \Phi p$ is $\frac{-1}{-3}$ or $\frac{1}{3}$. In this case, the columns are different; therefore, the answer is Choice 4.

① The quantity in Column A is greater.
② The quantity in Column B is greater.
③ The two quantities are equal.
④ The relationship cannot be determined from the information given.

QUANTITATIVE COMPARISONS TEST THREE
ANSWERS AND EXPLANATIONS

1. Choice 1

$\frac{1}{3} + \frac{1}{3}$ is $\frac{2}{3}$. $\frac{1}{3} \times \frac{1}{3} = \frac{1}{9}$. Since $\frac{2}{3} > \frac{1}{9}$, column A is larger.

2. Choice 2

The sum of the three interior angles of a triangle is 180°. Since x and y are only two of the angles, their sum must be less than 180 degrees. Column B is larger.

3. Choice 1

16 percent of 30 is $\frac{16}{100}(30)$ or $\frac{(16)(30)}{100}$. Similarly, 15 percent of 31 is $\frac{15}{100}(31)$ or $\frac{(15)(31)}{100}$. We can ignore the denominator of 100 in both columns, and just compare $(16)(30)$ in column A to $(15)(31)$ in column B. Divide both columns by 15; we're left with 31 in column B and $(16)(2)$ or 32 in column A. Since $32 > 31$, column A is larger.

4. Choice 2

Start by working with the sign of x, and hope that you won't have to go any further than that. If x^5 is negative, then what is the sign of x? It must be negative—if x were positive, then *any* power of x would also be positive. Since x is negative, then x^3 in column A must also be negative. But what about column B? Whatever x is, x^2 must be positive (or zero, but we know that x can't be zero); therefore, the quantity in column B must be positive. We have a positive number in column B, a negative number in column A: column B must be bigger.

5. Choice 4

We could pick numbers here, or else just use logic. We know that z is positive, and that x and y are less than z. But does that mean that x or y must be negative? Not at all—they could be, but they could also be positive. For instance, suppose $x = 1$, $y = 2$ and $z = 3$. Then column A would be larger. However, if $x = -1$, $y = 0$, and $z = 1$, then column B would be larger. We need more information to solve this question.

6. Choice 4

Divide both sides of the inequality by 6. We're left with $(10)^n > 10{,}001$. $10{,}001$ can also be written as $10^4 + 1$, so we know that $(10)^n > 10^4 + 1$. Therefore, n must be 5 or greater, and that's the quantity in column A. Column B is 6; since n could be less than, equal to, or greater than 6, we need more information.

7. Choice 2

Try to set the columns equal. Could the units' digit of y be 4? If it is, and the hundreds' digit is 3 times the units' digit, then the hundreds' digit must be . . . 12? That can't be right. A digit must be an integer between 0 and 9; 12 isn't a digit. Therefore, 4 is too big to be the units' digit of y. We don't know what the units' digit of y is (and we don't care either), but we know that it must be less than 4. Column B is larger than column A.

8. Choice 1

The perimeter of a square with side 4 is $4(4)$ or 16. The circumference of a circle is the product of π and the diameter, so the circumference in column B is 5π. Since π is approximately 3.14, $5(\pi)$ is approximately $5(3.14)$ or 15.70, which is less than 16. Column A is larger.

   ①   The quantity in Column A is greater.
   ②   The quantity in Column B is greater.
   ③   The two quantities are equal.
   ④   The relationship cannot be determined from the information given.

9. Choice 3

Column B is the sum of all the angles in the quadrilateral. The sum of the angles in any quadrilateral is 360 degrees. In column A, angle x and y are angles made when a transversal cuts a pair of parallel lines: in this case, ℓ_1 and ℓ_2. Such angles are either equal or supplementary. Angles x and y obviously aren't equal, so they must be supplementary, and their sum is 180. Then $2(x + y) = 2 \times 180$ or 360. The columns are equal.

10. Choice 1

One way to work here is to pick numbers. Just make sure that anything you pick satisfies the requirements of the problem. How about picking $x = 3$, $y = 5$, and $z = 7$, since in the equation these numbers would cancel with their denominators, thus leaving us with the equation $2 = 2 = 2$. Therefore, we know that these values satisfy the equation. In addition, if $z = 7$ then it is positive, so we have satisfied the other requirement as well. Then the sum of x and y, in column A, is $3 + 5$ or 8. This is larger than z, so in this case, column A is larger. That's just one example though: we should really try another one. In fact, any other example we pick that fits the initial information will have column A larger. To see why, we have to do a little messy work with the initial equations; on the test, you should just pick a couple of sample values, then go on to the next questions.

Start by dividing all of the equations through by 2, and multiply all of the terms through by $3 \times 5 \times 7$, to eliminate all the fractions. This leaves us with

$$35x = 21y = 15z$$

Now let's put everything in terms of x.

$$x = x \qquad y = \frac{35}{21}x = \frac{5}{3}x \qquad z = \frac{35}{15}x = \frac{7}{3}x$$

Then in column A, the sum of x and y is $x + \frac{5}{3}x = \frac{8}{3}x$. In column B, the value of z is $\frac{7}{3}x$. Now since z is positive, x and y must also be positive. (If one of them is negative, that would make all of them negative.)

Therefore x is positive, and $\frac{8}{3}x > \frac{7}{3}x$. Column A is larger.

The moral here is that proving that one column must be bigger can involve an awful lot of time on some GRE QC questions—more time than you can afford on the test. Try to come up with a good answer, but don't spend a lot of time proving it. Even if you end up showing that your original suspicion was wrong, it's not worth it if it took 5 minutes away from the rest of the problems.

11. Choice 4

The best place to start here is with some pairs of integers that have a product of 10, 5 and 2 have a product of 10, as do 10 and 1, and the average of each of these pairs is greater than 3, so you may have thought that A was the correct answer. If so, you should have stopped yourself, saying "That seems a little too easy for such a late QC question. They're usually trickier than that." In fact, this one was. There's nothing in the problem that limits the integers to *positive* numbers: they can just as easily be negative. -10 and -1 also have a product of 10, but their average is a *negative* number—in other words, *less* than column B. We need more information here; the answer is D.

① The quantity in Column A is greater.
② The quantity in Column B is greater.
③ The two quantities are equal.
④ The relationship cannot be determined from the information given.

12. Choice 3

The best way to do this question is to pick numbers. First we have to figure out what kind of number we want. Since $n + 1$ leaves a remainder of 1 when it's divided by 2, we know that $n + 1$ must be an *odd* number. Then n itself is an even number. We're told that n leaves a remainder of 1 when it's divided by 3. Therefore, n must be 1 more than a multiple of 3, or $n - 1$ is a multiple of 3. So what are we looking for? We've figured out that n should be an even number, that's one more than a multiple of 3. So let's pick a number now: how about 10? That's even, and it's one more than a multiple of 3. Then what's the remainder when we divide $n - 1$, or $10 - 1 = 9$, by 6? We're left with a remainder of 3: 6 divides into 9 one time, with 3 left over. In this case, the columns are equal.

Now since this a QC question, and there's always a possibility that we'll get a different result if we pick a different number, we should either pick another case, or else use logic to convince ourselves that the columns will always be equal. Let's do the latter here. Since n is even, $n - 1$ must be odd. We saw before that $n - 1$ is a multiple of 3, so we now know that it is an *odd* multiple of 3. Does this tell us anything about $n - 1$'s relation to 6? Yes, it does: any odd multiple of 3 cannot be a multiple of 6; since 6 is an even number, all its multiples must also be even. But any odd multiple of 3 will be exactly 3 *more* than a multiple of 6. Try it out, if you doubt me: 9 is an odd multiple of 3, and it's 3 more than 6; 27 is an odd multiple of 3, and it's 3 more than 24. So in fact, the columns will always be equal, regardless of the value of n.

13. Choice 3

There are lots of steps involved with this problem, but none of them is too complicated. The circle has its center at point T. To start with the triangle at the right, its vertices are at T and two points on the circumference of the circle. This makes two of its sides radii of the circle.

Since all radii must have equal length, this makes the triangle an *isosceles* triangle. In addition, we're told one of the base angles of this triangle has measure 60°. Then the other base angle must also have measure 60° (since the base angles in an isosceles triangle have equal measure). Then the sum of the two base angles is 120°, leaving $180 - 120$ or 60° for the other angle: the one at point T.

Now $\angle RTS$ is opposite this 60° angle; therefore, its measure must also be 60°. $\triangle RST$ is another isosceles triangle; since $\angle RTS$ has measure 60°, the other two angles in the triangle must also measure 60°. So what we have in the diagram is two equilateral triangles. RS and RT are two sides in one of these triangles; therefore they must be of equal length, and the two columns are equal.

14. Choice 1

Start by setting the columns equal. Suppose there were originally 14 adults at the party. Then after 5 of them leave, there are $14 - 5$ or 9 adults left. There are 3 times as many children as adults, so there are 3×9 or 27 children. Then 25 children leave the party, so there are $27 - 25$ or 2 children left. So 9 adults and 2 children remain at this party. Is that twice as many adults as children? No, it is more than 4 times as many. So this clearly indicates that the columns can't be equal—but does it mean that column A is bigger or column B is bigger? Probably the simplest way to decide is to pick another number for the original number of adults, and see whether the ratio gets better or worse. Suppose we started with 13 adults. After 5 adults leave, there are $13 - 5$ or 8 adults. Three times 8 gives you 24 children. Now if 25 children leave, we're left with $24 - 25$ or -1 children. But that's no good; how can you have a negative number of children? This means that we've gone the wrong way; our ratio has gotten worse instead of better. So 14 isn't right for the number of adults, and 13 is even worse, so the correct number must be something *more* than 14, and column A is larger.

①   The quantity in Column A is greater.
②   The quantity in Column B is greater.
③   The two quantities are equal.
④   The relationship cannot be determined from the information given.

15. Choice 4

We know that the ratio of oranges to apples is 9 to 10, and that there are "at least" 200 apples. Well, the ratio means that there are more apples than oranges. How does that help us? Good question. It helps us because it tells us that there could be fewer than 200 oranges in the store. Could there be more than 200? Sure: if there were a lot more than 200 apples, say 600 apples, then there would be a lot more than 200 oranges. So we've got one situation in which column A is larger, and another case in which column B is larger. We need more information to decide.

① The quantity in Column A is greater.
② The quantity in Column B is greater.
③ The two quantities are equal.
④ The relationship cannot be determined from the information given.

QUANTATATIVE COMPARISONS TEST FOUR
ANSWERS AND EXPLANATIONS

1.   Choice 2

The number in column A is a negative number in odd power, which is always negative: $(-5)^3 = -125$. The number in column B is a negative number in even power, which is always positive: $(-5)^2 = 25$. A positive number is always greater than a negative number, so the number in column B is greater.

2.   Choice 3

The sum of the measures of the three angles in any triangle equals 180°. Thus, the quantity in column A is $2(a + b + c) = 2(180) = 360$. We can calculate the quantity in column B by expressing the measures of angles $d°$, $e°$, and $f°$ in terms of the measures of angles $a°$, $b°$, and $c°$. Since angles $a°$ and $d°$ form a straight line, they are supplementary and their sum is 180°: $a + d = 180$. Then, $d = 180 - a$. Similarly, angles $b°$ and $e°$ are supplementary and angles $c°$ and $f°$ are supplementary, so $e = 180 - b$ and $f = 180 - c$. Now we can rewrite the sum of d, e, and f as

$$
\begin{aligned}
d + e + f &= (180 - a) + (180 - b) + (180 - c) \\
&= 180 + 180 + 180 - (a + b + c) \\
&= 3(180) - 180 \\
&= 2(180) \\
&= 360.
\end{aligned}
$$

The quantity in column B is the same as the quantity in column A.

3.   Choice 3

The number of green marbles in the jar is 15% of 40, or $\dfrac{15(40)}{100} = \dfrac{600}{100} = 6$. The columns are equal.

4.   Choice 4

The only thing we know about x is that $x^2 - 9 = 0$, or $x^2 = 9$. That means that x can be either positive or negative square root of 9: $x = 3$ or $x = -3$. Thus, x can be either greater or less than 0. The answer is Choice 4.

5.   Choice 1

Instead of calculating the sums of the fractions by finding the common denominator, we can try to make the columns look alike. We can rewrite $\dfrac{15}{16}$ as $1 - \dfrac{1}{16}$, or $1 - \dfrac{2}{32}$. Then, the quantity in column A equals $\dfrac{5}{32} + 1 - \dfrac{2}{32} = 1 + \dfrac{3}{32}$. The quantity in column B equals $\dfrac{1}{16} + 1$, or $1 + \dfrac{2}{32}$. Now it is clear that column A is larger.

6.   Choice 2

We can get rid of the radical sign by squaring both columns. $\dfrac{1}{5}$ becomes $\dfrac{1}{25}$ and $\dfrac{1}{\sqrt{24}}$ becomes $\dfrac{1}{24}$. 25 is greater than 24, so $\dfrac{1}{25}$ is less than $\dfrac{1}{24}$. The fraction in Column B is larger.

①   The quantity in Column A is greater.
②   The quantity in Column B is greater.
③   The two quantities are equal.
④   The relationship cannot be determined from the information given.

KAPLAN

7. Choice 1

We can try to answer this question by eyeballing. The radius of the circle is half of the diagonal of the square. If this circle were drawn with its center at the center of the square, the square would be inscribed inside of the circle.

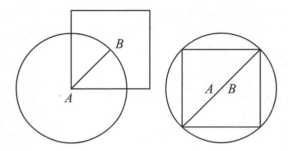

Thus, it appears that the circumference of the circle is greater than the perimeter of the square. To make sure, we can pick a number for the radius of the circle: $AB = 1$. Then the circumference of the circle is $2\pi (1) = 2\pi$, which approximately equals $2(3.14) = 6.28$. AB, half of the diagonal of the square, is 1, so the diagonal of the square is 2. Since two sides and a diagonal of a square form an isosceles right triangle, the ratio of a side of the square to a diagonal is 1 to $\sqrt{2}$. Thus, a side of the square with a diagonal of 2 is $2(\frac{1}{\sqrt{2}}) = \frac{(\sqrt{2})(\sqrt{2})}{\sqrt{2}} = \sqrt{2}$.

The perimeter of the square is then $4\sqrt{2}$, or approximately $4(1.4) = 5.6$. The circumference of the circle is greater than the perimeter of the square.

8. Choice 1

We need to compare the area of $\triangle PQR$ to 30. The area of $\triangle PQR$ is the sum of the areas of $\triangle PSR$ and $\triangle PQS$, and the area of $\triangle PSR$ is 15. Thus, we need to compare the area of $\triangle PQS$ to $30 - 15 = 15$, or to the area of $\triangle PSR$.

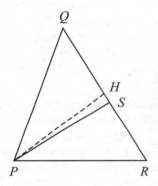

If PH is the height of $\triangle PQS$ dropped from point P to QS, then the area of $\triangle PQS$ is $\frac{1}{2}(PH)(QS)$. However, PH is also the height of $\triangle PSR$ dropped from point P to SR, so the area of $\triangle PSR$ is $\frac{1}{2}(PH)(SR)$. Since QS is greater than SR, the area of $\triangle PQS$ is greater than the area of $\triangle PSR$, 15. Therefore, the area of $\triangle PQR$ is greater than 30.

9. Choice 2

Let's set the columns equal. If Sarah is 19 years old, in 5 years from now she will be $19 + 5 = 24$ and 4 times older than Nick. Then, Nick's age in 5 years from now is $\frac{24}{4} = 6$. However, Nick is 6 years old now, so in 5 years he will be older than 6. Thus, Sarah's age has to be greater than 19. Column B is larger.

①　The quantity in Column A is greater.
②　The quantity in Column B is greater.
③　The two quantities are equal.
④　The relationship cannot be determined from the information given.

10. Choice 3

It might look like we would need more information to compare b and c, since we have three unknown variables and only two equations. However, sometimes systems of equations could be solved for a combination of variables. Let's see if we can determine the ratio of b and c. Consider the first equation.

$$\frac{a+b}{c} = 7$$

$$\frac{a}{c} + \frac{b}{c} = 7$$

$$\frac{b}{c} = 7 - \frac{a}{c}$$

Now solve the second equation for $\frac{b}{c}$.

$$\frac{a-b}{c} = 5$$

$$\frac{a}{c} - \frac{b}{c} = 5$$

$$\frac{a}{c} - 5 = \frac{b}{c}$$

$$\frac{b}{c} = \frac{a}{c} - 5$$

Add the two results together.

$$\frac{b}{c} + \frac{b}{c} = 7 - \frac{a}{c} + \left(\frac{a}{c} - 5\right)$$

$$2\frac{b}{c} = 7 - \frac{a}{c} + \frac{a}{c} - 5$$

$$2\frac{b}{c} = 2$$

$$\frac{b}{c} = 1$$

The ratio of b and c is 1 no matter what the value of a is. The columns are equal.

11. Choice 1

The factors of 24 are 1, 2, 3, 4, 6, 8, 12, and 24. Since there are 8 of them, column A is larger.

12. Choice 2

Let's start by setting the columns equal. If the original number of boys in the class is 18, then the ratio of 18 and the number of girls is 4 to 3. That means that the number of girls is $18 \div \frac{4}{3} = 18(\frac{3}{4}) = \frac{54}{4} = 13.5$. This cannot be correct, since the number of girls has to be an integer. Thus, the columns cannot be equal. The best way to proceed is to pick a variable for the original number of boys and set up and equation. If the original number of boys is x, then the original number of girls is $x \div \frac{4}{3} = x(\frac{3}{4}) = \frac{3x}{4}$. After 2 new boys and 3 new girls join the class, the ratio becomes $\frac{x+2}{\frac{3x}{4}+3}$, or $\frac{6}{5}$.

$$\frac{x+2}{\frac{3x}{4}+3} = \frac{6}{5}$$

$$5(x+2) = 6\left(\frac{3x}{4}+3\right)$$

$$5x + 10 = \frac{18x}{4} + 18$$

$$5x - \frac{9x}{2} = 18 - 10$$

$$\frac{10x}{2} - \frac{9x}{2} = 8$$

$$\frac{x}{2} = 8$$

$$x = 16$$

The original number of boys in the class is 16, which is less than 18. Column B is larger.

①   The quantity in Column A is greater.
②   The quantity in Column B is greater.
③   The two quantities are equal.
④   The relationship cannot be determined from the information given.

KAPLAN

13. Choice 3

It might look like there is not enough information to compare $\angle BAC$ and 70°, since we only know the measure of $\angle ABC$. However, we also know that AB is a diameter of the circle.

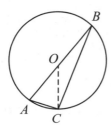

If point O is the center of the circle, then OC and OB are radii of the circle. Thus, $OC = OB$ and ΔBOC is isosceles. We can find the measure of $\angle BOC$. The angles opposite the equal sides of an isosceles triangle are equal, so $\angle OCB = \angle ABC = 20°$. $\angle BOC = 180° - \angle OCB - \angle ABC = 180° - 20° - 20° = 140°$. Since we know the measure of $\angle BOC$, we can also find the measure of its supplementary angle, $\angle AOC$: $\angle AOC = 180° - \angle BOC = 180° - 140° = 40°$. $\angle AOC$ is isosceles since $OA = OC$, so $\angle OCA = \angle BAC$.

$\angle OCA + \angle BAC + \angle AOC = 180°$

$2\angle BAC + 40° = 180°$

$2\angle BAC = 180° - 40°$

$2\angle BAC = 140°$

$\angle BAC = 70°$

The columns are equal.

14. Choice 4

Let's make a quick sketch of the xy-plane and ΔDEF. We place point D at $(-3, 0)$ and point F at $(3, 0)$. Since ΔDEF is isosceles, point E has to be somewhere on the y-axis.

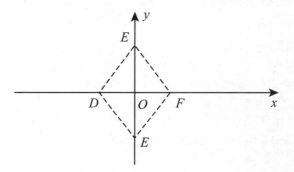

ΔDOE is a right triangle. The length of DE is 5 and the length of OD is 3. That means, ΔDOE is a 3-4-5 Pythagorean triplet and $OE = 4$. Thus, as can be seen from the picture, the y-coordinate of point E can be either 4 or -4. Therefore, we need more information in order to compare the columns.

15. Choice 4

Since we need to compare t and $2 - r$, let's use the first equation to express t in terms of r. We can plug the value of s into the first equation.

$$4 = (t + r)^2$$

Any quadratic equation can have two solutions, so $t + r$ is either positive or negative square root of 4, which is 2.

$$t + r = 2 \quad \text{or} \quad t + r = -2$$
$$t = 2 - r \quad \text{or} \quad t = -2 - r$$

We need more information in order to compare the columns.

① The quantity in Column A is greater.
② The quantity in Column B is greater.
③ The two quantities are equal.
④ The relationship cannot be determined from the information given.

Chapter 6
Word Problems

To truly do well on GRE math, you need to develop an approach that keeps you from getting bogged down on hard questions or from making careless errors.

THE 2 BASIC PRINCIPLES OF GRE QUESTION TYPES

The GRE math section has two defining characteristics, which we've translated into two basic principles.

Principle 1. The GRE is not a math test…

Traditional math tests require that you show all your work before you get credit—they test the *process* as well as the answer. But the GRE tests only the answer—*how* you get there isn't important. Since time is usually your biggest concern on the GRE, the best way to each solution is the quickest way, and that is often not by "doing the math."

Principle 2. …it's a critical reasoning test

GRE math questions are created to measure *critical reasoning,* your ability to recognize the core math concept in a problem and come up with the right answer. As a result, while the questions aren't necessarily mathematically difficult, they *are* tricky. That means that hard Word Problems will have traps in the answer choices. We'll show you how to avoid them. And we'll show you how to take advantage of question formats to give you more of what you need on test day—time.

KEEP THESE FOUR POINTS IN MIND AS YOU WORK THOUGH WORD PROBLEMS:

1. Read through the whole problem first to get a sense of the overall problem. Don't pause for details.
2. Name the variables in a way that makes it easy to remember what they stand for. For example, call the unknown quantity Bill's age B, and the unknown quantity Al's age A.
3. When you are asked to find numeral examples for unknown quantities, the Word Problem will give you enough information to set up a sufficient number of equations to solve for those quantities.
4. Be careful of the order in which you translate terms. For example, consider the following common mistranslation: 5 less than 4x equals 9. This translates as $4x - 5 = 9$, not $5 - 4x = 9$.

WORD PROBLEMS ON THE GRE

Word Problems account for a significant portion of the math problems on the GRE. The question is presented in ordinary language; indeed it often involves some ordinary situation such as the price of goods. To be able to solve the problem mathematically, however, we must be able to translate the problem into mathematical terms. Suppose the core of a problem involves working with the equation: $3J = S - 4$. In a word problem, this might be presented as follows:

If the number of macaroons John had tripled, he would have four macaroons less than Susan.

Your job will be to translate the problem from English to math. A phrase like "three times as many" can translate as "$3J$"; the phrase "four less than Susan" can become "$S - 4$."

The key to solving Word Problems is isolating the words and phrases that relate to a particular mathematical process. In this chapter you will find a Translation Table (on page 250), showing the most common key words and phrases and their mathematical translation. Once you have translated the problem, you will generally find that the concepts and processes involved are rather simple. The test makers figure that they have made the problem difficult enough by adding the extra step of translating from English to math. So, once you have passed this step you stand an excellent chance of being able to solve the problem.

WORD PROBLEMS LEVEL ONE

You've had experience with Word Problems in which only numbers are involved—some of these can be quite complicated.

These complications become even more challenging when variables are used instead of numbers. If you don't see immediately what operations to use, imagine that the variables are numbers and see whether that gives you a clue.

Basic Arithmetic and Algebraic Operations in Word Problems

In this section, we give examples of when to use each of the four basic operations: addition, subtraction, multiplication, and division.

Addition—You add when:

> You are given the amounts of individual quantities and you want to find the total.

> **Example:** If the sales tax on a $12.00 lunch check is $1.20, the total amount of the check is $12.00 + 1.20$ or 13.20.

You are given an original amount and the amount of increase.

Example: If the price of bus fare increased from 55 cents by 35 cents, the new fare is
55 + 35 = 90 cents.

Subtraction—You subtract when:

You are given the total and one part of the total. You want to find the other part (the rest).

Example: If there are 50 children and 32 of them are girls, then the number of boys is
50 − 32 = 18 boys.

You are given two numbers and you want to know how much **more** or how much **less** one number is than the other. The amount is called the **difference**.

Example: How much larger than 30 is 38?

$$38 \quad - \quad 30 \quad = \quad 8$$
$$\uparrow \qquad\qquad \uparrow$$
$$\text{larger} \qquad \text{smaller}$$
$$\downarrow \qquad\qquad \downarrow$$

Example: How much less is a than b? $b \quad - \quad a \quad = \quad b-a$

Note: In word problems, difference typically means **absolute** difference; that is larger − smaller.

Multiplication—You multiply when:

You are given the value for **one** item; you want to find the total value for **many** of these items.

Example: If 1 book costs $6.50, then 12 copies of the same book cost 12 × $6.50 = $78.

Division—You divide when:

You are given the amount for **many** items, and you want the amount for **one**. (Division is the inverse of multiplication.)

Example: If the price of 5 pounds of apples is $6.75, then the price of one pound of apples is
$6.75 ÷ 5 or $1.35.

You are given the amount of one group and the total amount for all groups, and you want to know how many of the small groups fit into the larger one.

Example: If 240 students are divided into groups of 30 students, then there are 240 ÷ 30 = 8
groups of 30 students.

Translating English Into Algebra

In some Word Problems, especially those involving variables, the best approach is to translate directly from an English sentence into an algebraic "sentence," i.e., into an equation. You can then deal with the equation by using the techniques we have discussed in the previous chapters.

The Translation Table below lists some common English words and phrases, and the corresponding algebraic symbols.

TRANSLATION TABLE

Equals, is, was, will, be, has, costs, adds up to, is the same as	=
Times, of, multiplied by, product of, twice, double, half, triple	• or ×
Divided by, per, out of, each, ratio of __ to __	÷
Plus, added to, sum, combined, and, more than, total	+
Minus, subtracted from, less than, decreased by, difference between	−
What, how much, how many, a number	x, n, etc.

Example: Beatrice   gets   3 dollars more than   twice Alan's wage

                        ↓   ↓

                        B   = $2A$ $+3$

Some Word Problems can be fairly complicated; nonetheless, the solution merely involves understanding the scenario presented, translating the given information, and taking things one step at a time.

Example: Steve is now five times as old as Craig was 5 years ago. If the sum of Craig's and Steve's ages is 35, in how many years will Steve be twice as old as Craig?

⚬ 2

⚬ 5

⚬ 10

⚬ 15

⚬ 25

Let c = Craig's current age
Let s = Steve's current age

Translate the first sentence to get the first equation:

$$s \qquad = \qquad 5(c - 5)$$

Steve's   is   Five times
current   Craig's age
age   5 years ago

Translate the first part of the second sentence to get the second equation:

$$c + s \qquad = \qquad 35$$

The sum of	is	35
Craig's and		
Steve's ages		

Now we are ready to solve for the two unknowns. Solve for c in terms of s in the second equation:

$$c + s = 35$$
$$c = 35 - s$$

Now plug this value for c into the first equation and solve for s:

$$s = 5(c - 5)$$
$$s = 5(35 - s - 5)$$
$$s = 5(30 - s)$$
$$s = 150 - 5s$$
$$6s = 150$$
$$s = 25$$

Plug this value for s into either equation to solve for c:

$$c = 35 - s$$
$$c = 35 - 25$$
$$c = 10$$

So Steve is currently 25 and Craig is currently 10. We still haven't answered the question asked, though; we need to set up an equation to find the number of years after which Steve will be twice as old as Craig.

Let x be the number of years from now in which Steve will be twice as old as Craig.

$$25 + x = 2(10 + x)$$

Solve this equation for x.

$$25 + x = 20 + 2x$$
$$x = 5$$

So Steve will be twice as old as Craig in 5 years. Answer choice 2.

BASIC WORD PROBLEMS LEVEL ONE EXERCISE

Translate the following directly into algebraic form. Do not reduce the expressions. (Answers are on the following page.)

1. z is x less than y.

2. The sum of 5, 6 and a.

3. If n is greater than m, the positive difference between twice n and m.

4. The ratio of $4q$ to $7p$ is 5 to 2.

5. The product of a decreased by b and twice the sum of a and b.

6. A quarter of the sum of a and b is 4 less than a.

7. Double the ratio of z to a plus the sum of z and a equals z minus a.

8. If \$500 were taken from F's salary, then the combined salaries of F and G will be double what F's salary would be if it were increased by a half of itself.

9. The sum of a, b and c is twice the sum of a minus b and a minus c.

10. The sum of y and 9 decreased by the sum of x and 7 is the same as dividing x decreased by z by 7 decreased by x.

ANSWER KEY—BASIC WORD PROBLEMS EXERCISE

1. $z = y - x$

2. $5 + 6 + a$

3. $2n - m$

4. $\dfrac{4q}{7p} = \dfrac{5}{2}$

5. $(a - b) \cdot 2(a + b)$

6. $\dfrac{a + b}{4} = a - 4$

7. $\dfrac{2z}{a} + z + a = z - a$

8. $F - 500 + G = 2\left(F + \dfrac{F}{2}\right)$

9. $a + b + c = 2[(a - b) + (a - c)]$

10. $(y + 9) - (x + 7) = \dfrac{x - z}{7 - x}$

BASIC WORD PROBLEMS LEVEL ONE TEST

Solve the following problems and choose the best answer. (Answers and explanations are at the end of the chapter.)

Basic

1. Before the market opens on Monday, a stock is priced at $25. If its price decreases $4 on Monday, increases $6 on Tuesday, and then decreases $2 on Wednesday, what is the final price of the stock on Wednesday?

    ○ $12

    ○ $21

    ○ $25

    ○ $29

    ○ $37

2. Between 1950 and 1960 the population of Country *A* increased by 3.5 million people. If the amount of increase between 1960 and 1970 was 1.75 million more than the increase from 1950 to 1960, what was the total amount of increase in population in Country *A* between 1950 and 1970?

    ○ 1.75 million

    ○ 3.5 million

    ○ 5.25 million

    ○ 7 million

    ○ 8.75 million

3. Greg's weekly salary is $70 less than Joan's, whose weekly salary is $50 more than Sue's. If Sue earns $280 per week, how much does Greg earn per week?

    ○ $160

    ○ $260

    ○ $280

    ○ $300

    ○ $400

4. During the 19th century a certain tribe collected 10 pieces of copper for every camel passing through Timbuktu in a caravan. If in 1880 an average of 8 caravans passed through Timbuktu every month, and there was an average of 100 camels in each caravan that year, how many pieces of copper did the tribe collect from the caravans over the year?

    ○ 800

    ○ 8,000

    ○ 9,600

    ○ 80,000

    ○ 96,000

5. A painter charges $12 an hour while his son charges $6 an hour. If father and son work the same amount of time together on a job, how many hours does each of them work if their combined charge for labor is $108?

    ○ 6

    ○ 8

    ○ 9

    ○ 12

    ○ 18

6. A certain book costs $12 more in hardcover than in softcover. If the softcover price is $\frac{2}{3}$ of the hardcover price, how much does the book cost in hardcover?

   ○ $8
   ○ $15
   ○ $18
   ○ $20
   ○ $36

7. During a certain week, a post office sold $280 worth of 14-cent stamps. How many of these stamps did they sell?

   ○ 20
   ○ 2,000
   ○ 3,900
   ○ 20,000
   ○ 39,200

8. Liza was 2*n* years old *n* years ago. What will be her age, in years, *n* years from now?

   ○ 4*n*
   ○ 3*n*
   ○ 2*n* + 2
   ○ 2*n*
   ○ 2*n* − 2

9. During a drought the amount of water in a pond was reduced by a third. If the amount of water in the pond was 48,000 gallons immediately after the drought, how many thousands of gallons of water were lost during the drought?

   ○ 16
   ○ 24
   ○ 36
   ○ 64
   ○ 72

10. A man has an estate worth $15 million that he will either divide equally among his 10 children or among his 10 children and 5 stepchildren. How much more will each of his children inherit if his 5 stepchildren are excluded?

   ○ $500,000
   ○ $1,000,000
   ○ $1,500,000
   ○ $2,500,000
   ○ $5,000,000

Intermediate

11. An office has 27 employees. If there are 7 more women than men in the office, how many employees are women?

    ◯ 8

    ◯ 10

    ◯ 14

    ◯ 17

    ◯ 20

12. If the product of 3 and x is equal to 2 less than y, which of the following must be true?

    ◯ $6x - y - 2 = 0$

    ◯ $6x - 6 = 0$

    ◯ $3x - y - 2 = 0$

    ◯ $3x + y - 2 = 0$

    ◯ $3x - y + 2 = 0$

13. Four partners invested $1,600 each to purchase 1,000 shares of a certain stock. If the total cost of the stock is $8,000 plus a 2 percent commission, each partner should additionally invest what equal amount to cover the purchase of the stock?

    ◯ $100

    ◯ $110

    ◯ $220

    ◯ $440

    ◯ $880

14. At garage A, it costs $8.75 to park a car for the first hour and $1.25 for each additional hour. At garage B, it costs $5.50 for the first hour and $2.50 for each additional hour. What is the difference between the cost of parking a car for 5 hours at garage A and garage B?

    ◯ $1.50

    ◯ $1.75

    ◯ $2.25

    ◯ $2.75

    ◯ $3.25

15. At a certain high school, $\frac{2}{3}$ of the students play on sports teams. Of the students who play sports, $\frac{1}{4}$ play on the football team. If there are a total of 240 students in the high school, how many students play on the football team?

    ◯ 180

    ◯ 160

    ◯ 80

    ◯ 60

    ◯ 40

16. Ed has 100 dollars more than Robert. After Ed spends twenty dollars on groceries, Ed has 5 times as much money as Robert. How much money does Robert have?

    ◯ $20

    ◯ $30

    ◯ $40

    ◯ $50

    ◯ $120

17. Diane find that $2\frac{1}{2}$ cans of paint are just enough to paint $\frac{1}{3}$ of her room. How many more cans of paint will she need to finish her room and paint a second room of the same size?

- ⬭ 5
- ⬭ $7\frac{1}{2}$
- ⬭ 10
- ⬭ $12\frac{1}{2}$
- ⬭ 15

18. In a typical month, $\frac{1}{2}$ of the UFO sightings in the state are attributable to airplanes and $\frac{1}{3}$ of the remaining sightings are attributable to weather balloons. If there were 108 UFO sightings during one typical month, how many would be attributable to weather balloons?

- ⬭ 18
- ⬭ 24
- ⬭ 36
- ⬭ 54
- ⬭ 72

19. At a certain photography store, it costs Pete $1.65 for the first print and $0.85 for each additional print. How many prints of a particular photograph can Pete get for $20.00?

- ⬭ 19
- ⬭ 20
- ⬭ 21
- ⬭ 22
- ⬭ 23

20. There are enough peanuts in a bag to give 12 peanuts to each of 20 children, with no peanuts left over. If 5 children do not want any peanuts, how many peanuts can be given to each of the others?

- ⬭ 12
- ⬭ 15
- ⬭ 16
- ⬭ 18
- ⬭ 20

Advanced

21. The total fare for 2 adults and 3 children on an excursion boat is $14.00. If each child's fare is one half of each adult's fare, what is the adult fare?

   - ○ $2.00
   - ○ $3.00
   - ○ $3.50
   - ○ $4.00
   - ○ $4.50

22. Doris spent $\frac{2}{3}$ of her savings on a used car, and she spent $\frac{1}{4}$ of her remaining savings on a new carpet. If the carpet cost her $250, how much were Doris' original savings?

   - ○ $1,000
   - ○ $1,200
   - ○ $1,500
   - ○ $2,000
   - ○ $3,000

23. Gheri is n years old. Carl is 6 years younger than Gheri and 2 years older than Jean. What is the sum of the ages of all three?

   - ○ $3n + 16$
   - ○ $3n + 4$
   - ○ $3n - 4$
   - ○ $3n - 8$
   - ○ $3n - 14$

24. A class of 40 students is to be divided into smaller groups. If each group is to contain 3, 4, or 5 people, what is the largest number of groups possible?

   - ○ 8
   - ○ 10
   - ○ 12
   - ○ 13
   - ○ 14

25. Philip has twice as many salamanders as Matt. If Philip gives Matt 10 of his salamanders, he will have half as many as Matt. How many salamanders do Philip and Matt have together?

   - ○ 10
   - ○ 20
   - ○ 30
   - ○ 40
   - ○ 60

26. In a group of 60 workers, the average salary is $80 a day per worker. If some of the workers earn $75 a day and all the rest earn $100 a day, how many workers earn $75 a day?

   - ○ 12
   - ○ 24
   - ○ 36
   - ○ 48
   - ○ 54

PERCENT, RATIO, AND RATES WORD PROBLEMS

Percent Problems

Very many Word Problems are percent problems; in fact, the majority of percent problems are presented in this form. We have already looked at percents in the arithmetic chapter; let's just look at a few examples using terms that you will often find in percent Word Problems.

Profit: The profit made on an item is the selling price minus the cost to the seller. (If the cost is more than the selling price, it is a loss.)

> **Example:** A store is selling a video monitor for $600. If the store makes a profit of 20 percent of its cost, what was the cost of the monitor to the store?
>
> If we let C represent the cost, then we set up an equation to find the cost:
>
> $$\text{Cost} + \text{Profit} = \text{Selling Price}$$
>
> $$C + (20\%)C = \$600$$
>
> $$C + \frac{1}{5}C = \$600$$
>
> $$\frac{6}{5}C = \$600$$
>
> $$C = \$600 \times \frac{5}{6} = \$500$$

> The cost of the monitor to the store was $500.

Gross and net: Gross is the total amount before any deductions are made, while **net** is the amount after deductions are made. For instance, gross pay is the total amount of money earned, while net pay is gross pay minus any deductions, such as tax.

Discount: The discount on an item is usually a percent of a previous price for the item.

> **Example:** If a dress usually selling for $120 is sold at a 40% discount, what is the sale price of the dress?
>
> The discount is 40% of $120, or $40\% \times \$120 = \frac{2}{5} \times \$120$
>
> $$= \$48$$
>
> So the sale price is $120 − $48 = $72.
>
> Notice that if the dress is sold at a 40% discount, the sale price is (100% − 40%) or 60% of the original price:
>
> $$60\% \times \$120 = \frac{3}{5} \times \$120$$
>
> $$= \$72$$

Ratios and Rates

Other common Word Problems are those involving ratios and rates. This is not really surprising, as many of the math topics that we commonly encounter in the real world (percent profits, rates of work, etc.) are often presented in plain English.

We have already looked at ratios and rates in the arithmetic chapter. Let's just have a look at how we can deal with them as Word Problems.

Example: There are 36 marbles in a bag containing only blue and red marbles. If there are three red marbles for every blue marble, how many blue marbles are there in the bag?

Translate from English into math. "three red marbles for every blue marble" means the ratio of red : blue = 3 : 1

Set up a proportion with a part to whole ratio to find the number of blue marbles. The ratio of the number of blue marbles to the total number of marbles is 1 : [1 + 3] or 1 : 4.

Using b for the number of blue marbles, we have the proportion:

$$\frac{1}{4} = \frac{b}{36}$$
$$4b = 36$$
$$b = 9$$

So there are 9 blue marbles in the bag.

Rates are even more commonly presented as Word Problems than ratios. A rate is simply a ratio that relates two different quantities that are measured in different units. Examples include speed, which can be measured in miles per hour, or cost, which is dollars per item, or work, which can be measured in pay per hour.

The two most common types of rates problem involve motion and work.

Motion: The basic formula for motion problems is

Distance = Rate × Time

Which can also be arranged as $\text{Rate} = \dfrac{\text{Distance}}{\text{Time}}$ or $\text{Time} = \dfrac{\text{Distance}}{\text{Rate}}$

This is a very important formula and you should remember it. It is perhaps easiest to remember if you consider the everyday situation of driving a car. The distance travelled (in miles) = the speed of the car (in miles per hour) × time driving at that speed (in hours). For instance, if you are driving at 50 miles per hour for two hours, how far do you travel? The distance travelled is 50 miles per hour × 2 hours = 100 miles. (Notice how the unit "hours" cancels out when you multiply).

Example: Bob travels 60 miles in $1\frac{1}{2}$ hours. If he travels at the same rate for another 3 hours, how many more miles will he travel?

First find the speed at which he is traveling.

$$\text{Distance} = \text{rate} \times \text{time}$$

$$60 \text{ miles} = \text{rate} \times 1\frac{1}{2} \text{ hours}$$

$$\frac{60 \text{ miles}}{1\frac{1}{2} \text{ hours}} = \text{rate}$$

$$40 \text{ miles per hour} = \text{Rate}$$

If he travels for 3 hours at 40 miles per hour he will travel

$$3 \text{ hours} \times 40 \frac{\text{miles}}{\text{hour}} = 120 \text{ miles.}$$

Notice how units divide and multiply just like numbers. When we say 40 miles per hour we mean

$$\frac{40 \text{ miles}}{1 \text{ hour}}$$

So then when we multiply 40 miles per hour by 3 hours we get

$$\frac{40 \text{ miles}}{1 \text{ hour}} \times 3 \text{ hours} = 120 \text{ miles}$$

It is often useful to have the units we want to end up with in mind when we do the problem, as in the following example:

Example: If David paints houses at the rate of h houses per day, how many houses does he paint in d days, in terms of h and d?

- ○ $\dfrac{h}{d}$
- ○ hd
- ○ $\dfrac{h+d}{2}$
- ○ $h-d$
- ○ $\dfrac{d}{h}$

First note that the answer should tell us a number of houses. Now look at the units of the given information. We have $h \dfrac{\text{houses}}{\text{days}}$ and d days.

Find a combination of the units $\dfrac{\text{"houses"}}{\text{days}}$ and "days" that will leave us with "houses." Notice that if we multiply the terms

$$h \dfrac{\text{houses}}{\text{days}} \times d \text{ days} = hd \text{ houses}$$

the "days" cancel out and we are left with "houses," the desired result. Thus, the answer is hd.

Units are important in many types of Word Problems. Units can measure time, length, weight, etc. We can multiply and divide units, and even raise them to higher powers. We must be especially careful when changing from one unit to another, such as minutes to hours, or feet to inches.

To change to smaller units: you need a greater number of smaller units, so multiply.

To change to larger units: you need a smaller number of larger units, so divide.

Don't worry about memorizing any obscure conversion factors, like feet to miles, or fluid ounces to gallons—if you need to convert units, the conversion factors will be given to you. An exception to this is that you are expected to know the divisions of time—days in a week, seconds in a minute, months in the year, etc.

Example: Change 10 hours to minutes.

There will be **more** minutes than hours, so we multiply by 60, the number of minutes in one hour.

$$10 \text{ hours} = 10 \text{ hours} \times \dfrac{60 \text{ minutes}}{1 \text{ hour}} = 600 \text{ minutes}$$

The Units Cancellation Method (UCM) is a useful way of keeping track of units. When multiplying or dividing by a conversion factor, the units cancel in the same way as numbers or variables; for instance, inches in a numerator cancels with inches in a denominator. If you are unsure whether to multiply or divide by a conversion factor, check to see which will leave you with only the desired units.

Example: Change 120 minutes to hours.

We want to cancel out the minutes, so we have to multiply 120 minutes by a fraction (equal to 1) with hours in the numerator and minutes in the denominator:

$$120 \text{ minutes} = 120 \text{ minutes} \times \dfrac{1 \text{ hour}}{60 \text{ minutes}} = 2 \text{ hours}$$

Example: Convert 10 inches per second to feet per minute. (1 foot = 12 inches)

Use the UCM successively to eliminate the unwanted units.

$$\frac{10 \text{ inches}}{\text{second}} = 10 \frac{\text{inches}}{\text{second}} \times \frac{1 \text{ foot}}{12 \text{ inches}} \times 60 \frac{\text{seconds}}{\text{minute}}$$

$$= \frac{10 \times 60}{12} \times \frac{\text{feet}}{\text{minute}}$$

$$= 50 \text{ feet per minute}$$

One other thing worth bearing in mind is that metric units are commonly used on the GRE. While it is not essential to know the conversions between these units, it helps to be somewhat familiar with what they measure.

Volume is measured in liters. A milliliter is $\dfrac{1}{1{,}000}$ of a liter.

Length is measured in meters. A centimeter is $\dfrac{1}{100}$ of a meter.

Weight is measured in grams. A kilogram is 1,000 grams.

Work: Work Problems tend to be harder than other rate problems. Happily, they appear irregularly on the test, and are usually among the hardest questions on the exam. It is useful to keep in mind that the greater the rate (the faster you work), the sooner you get the job done. If you can imagine how varying the parameters affects the time it takes to do the job, you can usually solve the problem by using logic.

Example: It takes 6 people 6 days to do a job. How many days would it take 2 people working at the same rate to do the job?

    ◯ 3

    ◯ 6

    ◯ 12

    ◯ 16

    ◯ 18

We have **fewer** people so it would take **more** time. (Discard the first two answer choices.) First find out how long it takes 1 person to do the job. If 6 people take 6 days, then 1 person will take 6 times as long, i.e., 6 × 6 days = 36 days. If 1 person takes 36 days, 2 people will take half as long, i.e., 36 days ÷ 2 = 18 days.

KAPLAN

Work problems often involve people working together.

Example: John can weed a garden in 3 hours. If Mary can weed the garden in 2 hours, how long will it take them to weed the garden at this rate, working together but independently?

Determine how much work John can do in a certain unit of time (one hour is convenient), and how much work Mary can do in the same hour, then add the results to find how much they can do together in an hour. From that, we can find how long it will take them to finish the job.

If John needs 3 hours to do the whole job, then in each hour, $\frac{1}{3}$ of the time, he will do $\frac{1}{3}$ of the job. Similarly, if Mary can do everything in 2 hours, each hour she will do $\frac{1}{2}$ of the job. Then in 1 hour, John and Mary together will do

$$\frac{1}{3} + \frac{1}{2} = \frac{2}{6} + \frac{3}{6} = \frac{5}{6} \text{ of the job.}$$

Now if they do $\frac{5}{6}$ of the job in 1 hour, how long will it take them to do the whole job?

It will take the inverse of $\frac{5}{6}$, or $\frac{6}{5}$ hours. (Try it with easier numbers: if you do $\frac{1}{2}$ of the job in 1 hour, you will do the whole job in the inverse of $\frac{1}{2}$, or 2, hours.)

There is a general formula that can be used to find out how long it takes a number of people working together to complete a task, the Work Formula. Let's say we had three people, the first takes t_1 units of time to complete the job, the second t_2 units of time to complete the job and the third t_3 units of time. If the time it takes all three working together to complete the job is T then

$$\frac{1}{t_1} + \frac{1}{t_2} + \frac{1}{t_3} = \frac{1}{T}$$

For instance, in the example above, we can call the amount of time it takes John to weed the garden t_1 and the amount of time it takes Mary t_2. That is, $t_1 = 3$ hours and $t_2 = 2$ hours. So, if T represents how much time it takes them working together (but independently), we get $\frac{1}{3} + \frac{1}{2} = \frac{1}{T}$. So, $\frac{5}{6} = \frac{1}{T}$, and $T = \frac{6}{5}$ hours.

In general, with work problems, you can assume that each person works at the same rate as he does even when working with another person—don't worry that John and Mary will spend so much time chatting they won't get any of that garden done. That's what the "working together but independently" meant in the question stem.

Since work problems appear only irregularly on the GRE, it's quite possible none will be present on the test you take. So if you're having trouble remembering or utilizing the Work Formula, don't worry about it too much. You're probably better off spending your time elsewhere.

Picking Numbers

Picking numbers is often an easier way to tackle ratio or percent Word Problems, and provides a useful backup strategy if you cannot solve the problem using more traditional techniques. Picking numbers is especially helpful in ratio and percent problems. But be careful—try to pick a number that's easy to work with. In a ratio problem pick a number that is divisible by all the numerators and denominators. In percent problems it is almost always best to pick 100, since calculating percents of 100 is extremely easy.

Example: At the Frosty Ice Cream store, the number of cones sold fell by 20 percent in November. If sales fell by a further 25 percent in December, what was the percent decrease in the number of cones sold in the whole two-month period?

　　○　10%

　　○　20%

　　○　35%

　　○　40%

　　○　45%

Let the original number of cones sold be 100. The number of cones sold in November is 20% less than this, 20% of 100 is 20, so the number of cones sold in November is $100 - 20 = 80$.

The number of cones sold in December is 25% less than this amount. 25% of $80 = \frac{1}{4}$ of $80 = 20$. So the number of cones sold in December is $80 - 20 = 60$.

The difference between the original number of cones sold and the number of cones sold in December is $100 - 60 = 40$ cones. If sales fell by 40 cones, the percent decrease in sales was $\frac{40}{100} \times 100\%$, or 40%.

Backsolving

Backsolving can be used on many Word Problems, especially if running answer choices through the question stem seems like it would be quicker than setting up equations and solving.

Example: An insurance company provides coverage according to the following rules: the policy pays 80 percent of the first $1,200 of cost and 50 percent of the cost above $1,200. If a patient had to pay $490 of the cost of a certain procedure himself, how much did the procedure cost?

　　○　$1,200

　　○　$1,300

　　○　$1,500

　　○　$1,700

　　○　$1,800

(continued on next page)

(continued from page 147)

Since each answer choice represents a possible amount of the procedure's cost, we can pick a choice, assume that this was the cost of the procedure, and apply the insurance company's rules on that choice. The answer choice that results in the patient paying $490 is correct.

Let's start with the middle choice. If it is correct, then the procedure cost $1,500. We know that the policy pays 80% of the first $1,200, so the patient pays 20% of the first $1,200 of the cost. We also know that the policy pays 50% of any cost above $1,200, so that means the patient must pay 50% of the cost above $1,200. Looking at the middle choice, $1,500: the patient pays 20% of the first $1,200, or $0.2 \times \$1,200 = \$240$. The part of the cost above $1,200 is $1,500 − $1,200, or $300. Since the patient pays 50% of that, the patient's share is one-half of $300, or $150. That's a total expense for the patient of $240 + $150 = $390.

So, if the procedure cost $1,500, then the patient would have paid $390. But we know from the question stem that the patient paid $490. So we know that choice is too small. In order for the patient to have spent $490, the procedure must have cost more than $1,500. So that means that the first two answer choices are also wrong, and we can eliminate them. Just by trying one smartly selected answer choice, we were able to narrow it down to two choices.

Looking at the fourth choice, $1,700, again the patient pays $240 of the first $1,200. Now the excess amount is $1,700 − $1,200 = $500. Since the patient pays 50% of the excess, this part of the charge is $0.5 \times \$500$, or $250. That's a total of $250 + $240 = $490. This is the same as the amount the patient pays in the question stem, so this choice is correct.

If the fourth choice had yielded too low an answer, the only option would be to choose the fifth choice, since it is the only answer choice greater than the fourth choice and thus the only one which could yield a greater result. Backsolving often allows you to find the correct answer by checking at most two possibilities. It's primarily useful on problems with numerical answer choices, and problems where you're able to determine whether the choice you tried was too high or too low.

PERCENT, RATIO, AND RATES WORD PROBLEMS

Solve the following problems and choose the best answer. (Answers and explanations are at the end of the chapter.)

Basic

1. What is the percent profit made on the sale of 1,000 shares of stock bought at $10 per share and sold at $12 per share?

   ○ 0.2%

   ○ 2%

   ○ $16\frac{2}{3}$%

   ○ 20%

   ○ 25%

2. A subway car passes an average of 3 stations every 10 minutes. At this rate, how many stations will it pass in one hour?

   ○ 2

   ○ 12

   ○ 15

   ○ 18

   ○ 30

3. What is the percent discount on a jacket marked down from $120 to $100?

   ○ $16\frac{2}{3}$%

   ○ 20%

   ○ 30%

   ○ $33\frac{1}{3}$%

   ○ 40%

4. If a car travels $\frac{1}{100}$ of a kilometer each second, how many kilometers does it travel per hour?

   ○ $\frac{3}{5}$

   ○ $3\frac{3}{5}$

   ○ 35

   ○ 72

   ○ 100

5. If John buys a stereo marked down 7 percent from its $650 original price while Sally buys the same stereo marked down only 5 percent, how much more does Sally pay for the stereo?

   ○ $2

   ○ $12

   ○ $13

   ○ $78

   ○ $618

6. If a train travels m miles in 5 hours, how many miles will it travel in 25 hours?

   ○ $\frac{m}{25}$

   ○ $\frac{m}{5}$

   ○ $5m$

   ○ $25m$

   ○ $\frac{5}{m}$

7. At a record store, a record is priced at 60 percent of the price of the compact disk of the same title. If a compact disk is priced at $15, how much less does the record cost?

   ○ $5

   ○ $6

   ○ $9

   ○ $10

   ○ $12

8. A certain mule travels at $\frac{2}{3}$ the speed of a certain horse. If it takes the horse 6 hours to travel 20 miles, how many hours will the trip take the mule?

   ○ 4

   ○ 8

   ○ 9

   ○ 10

   ○ 30

9. What is the percent profit an ice cream seller makes on vanilla ice cream if vanilla ice cream costs him 90 cents per scoop to make and he sells it at $1.20 per scoop?

   ○ 25%

   ○ 30%

   ○ $33\frac{1}{3}$%

   ○ 40%

   ○ 50%

10. Two cars travel away from each other in opposite directions at 24 miles per hour and 40 miles per hour respectively. If the first car travels for 20 minutes and the second car for 45 minutes, how many miles apart will they be at the end of their trips?

    ○ 22

    ○ 24

    ○ 30

    ○ 38

    ○ 42

11. An encyclopedia salesman makes a 10 percent commission on any sales. If he sells a set of encyclopedias at $700 instead of the original price of $800, how much less of a commission does he earn?

    ○ $7

    ○ $8

    ○ $10

    ○ $70

    ○ $80

12. A car travels 60 kilometers in one hour before a piston breaks, then travels at 30 kilometers per hour for the remaining 60 kilometers to its destination. What is its average speed in kilometers per hour for the entire trip?

    ○ 20

    ○ 40

    ○ 45

    ○ 50

    ○ 60

13. A survey finds that 80 percent of the apartments in City G have smoke alarms installed. Of these, 20 percent have smoke alarms that are not working. What percent of the apartments in City G were found to have working smoke alarms?

- ⬭ 60%
- ⬭ 64%
- ⬭ $66\frac{2}{3}$%
- ⬭ 70%
- ⬭ 72%

14. If a tree grew 5 feet in n years, how many inches did the tree grow per year on the average during those years? (1 foot = 12 inches.)

- ⬭ $60n$
- ⬭ $\dfrac{5}{n}$
- ⬭ $\dfrac{5}{12n}$
- ⬭ $\dfrac{12n}{5}$
- ⬭ $\dfrac{60}{n}$

15. A baseball team increased its home attendance 20 percent in each of two successive years. If home attendance was 1 million the year before the first increase, what was the attendance the year of the second increase?

- ⬭ 1,200,000
- ⬭ 1,400,000
- ⬭ 1,440,000
- ⬭ 1,500,000
- ⬭ 1,600,000

16. If Bill can mow $\dfrac{3}{4}$ of his lawn in one hour, how many minutes does it take Bill to mow his entire lawn?

- ⬭ 45
- ⬭ 75
- ⬭ 80
- ⬭ 90
- ⬭ 100

17. If a camera priced at $360 represents a potential profit of 20 percent to a store if sold, what was the original cost of the camera to the store?

- ⬭ $288
- ⬭ $300
- ⬭ $310
- ⬭ $320
- ⬭ $342

Intermediate

18. If an item costs $800 after a 20 percent discount, what was the amount of the discount?

    ○ $200

    ○ $160

    ○ $120

    ○ $80

    ○ $20

19. John buys R pounds of cheese to feed N people at a party. If $N + P$ people come to the party, how many more pounds of cheese must John buy in order to feed everyone at the original rate?

    ○ $\dfrac{NP}{R}$

    ○ $\dfrac{N}{RP}$

    ○ $\dfrac{N + P}{R}$

    ○ $\dfrac{P}{NR}$

    ○ $\dfrac{PR}{N}$

20. A store sells a watch for a profit of 25 percent of the cost. What percent of the selling price is the profit?

    ○ 5%

    ○ $16\dfrac{2}{3}\%$

    ○ 20%

    ○ $33\dfrac{1}{3}\%$

    ○ 45%

21. If it takes ten minutes to fill $\dfrac{5}{12}$ of a hole, how many minutes will it take to fill the rest of the hole at this rate?

    ○ 12

    ○ 14

    ○ 16

    ○ 18

    ○ 24

22. A builder purchases 25 windows at 25 percent off the total price of $1,200. If the builder receives an additional discount of $75 for the purchase, how much did each window cost her?

    ○ $48

    ○ $45

    ○ $36

    ○ $33

    ○ $25

23. If Carol can finish a job in 5 hours and Steve can finish the same job in 10 hours, how many **minutes** will it take both of them together to finish the job?

    ○ 160

    ○ 180

    ○ 200

    ○ 210

    ○ 220

24. One class in a school is 30 percent boys. If a second class that is half the size of the first is 40 percent boys, what percent of both classes are boys?

- ⬭ 20%
- ⬭ 25%
- ⬭ 28%
- ⬭ 30%
- ⬭ $33\frac{1}{3}\%$

25. If John can paint a room in 30 minutes and Tom can paint it in 1 hour, how many **minutes** will it take them to paint the room working together?

- ⬭ 10
- ⬭ 15
- ⬭ 18
- ⬭ 20
- ⬭ 24

26. If a driver travels m miles per hour for 4 hours and then travels $\frac{3}{4}m$ miles per hour every hour thereafter, how many miles will she drive in 10 hours?

- ⬭ $\frac{15}{2}m$
- ⬭ $8m$
- ⬭ $\frac{17}{2}m$
- ⬭ $10m$
- ⬭ $\frac{21}{2}m$

27. A motorist travels 90 miles at rate of 20 miles per hour. If he returns the same distance at a rate of 40 miles per hour, what is the average speed for the entire trip, in miles per hour?

- ⬭ 20
- ⬭ $\frac{65}{3}$
- ⬭ $\frac{80}{3}$
- ⬭ 30
- ⬭ $\frac{130}{3}$

28. Phil is making a 40-kilometer canoe trip. If he travels at 30 kilometers per hour for the first 10 kilometers, and then at 15 kilometers per hour for the rest of the trip, how many minutes longer will it take him than if he makes the entire trip at 20 kilometers per hour?

- ⬭ 15
- ⬭ 20
- ⬭ 35
- ⬭ 45
- ⬭ 50

29. In a certain school, 50 percent of all male students and 60 percent of all females students play a varsity sport. If 40 percent of the students at the school are male, what percent of the entire student body DO NOT play a varsity sport?

- ⬭ 44%
- ⬭ 50%
- ⬭ 55%
- ⬭ 56%
- ⬭ 60%

KAPLAN

30. John runs from his home to his school at an average speed of 6 miles per hour, and then walks home along the same route at an average speed of 3 miles per hour. If his whole journey took one hour, how many miles is his home from his school?

    ○ 9

    ○ 6

    ○ 4

    ○ 3

    ○ 2

31. The workforce of a company is 20 percent part-time workers, with the rest of the workers full-time. At the end of the year 30 percent of the full-time workers received bonuses. If 72 full-time workers received bonuses, how many workers does the company employ?

    ○ 132

    ○ 240

    ○ 280

    ○ 300

    ○ 360

Advanced

32. Pipe *A* can fill a tank in 3 hours. If pipe *B* can fill the same tank in 2 hours, how many minutes will it take both pipes to fill $\frac{2}{3}$ of the tank?

   ○ 30

   ○ 48

   ○ 54

   ○ 60

   ○ 72

33. A factory cut its labor force by 16 percent, but then increased it by 25 percent of the new amount. What was the net percent change in the size of the workforce?

   ○ a 5% decrease

   ○ no net change

   ○ a 5% increase

   ○ a 9% increase

   ○ a 10% increase

34. If snow falls at a rate of *x* centimeters per minute, how many **hours** would it take for *y* centimeters to fall?

   ○ $\dfrac{x}{60y}$

   ○ $\dfrac{y}{60x}$

   ○ $\dfrac{60x}{y}$

   ○ $\dfrac{60y}{x}$

   ○ $60xy$

35. If a dealer had sold a stereo for $600, he would have made a 20 percent profit. Instead, the dealer sold it for a 40 percent loss. At what price was the stereo sold?

   ○ $300

   ○ $315

   ○ $372

   ○ $400

   ○ $440

36. If four men working at the same rate can do $\frac{2}{3}$ of a job in 40 minutes, how many minutes would it take one man working at this rate to do $\frac{2}{5}$ of the job?

   ○ 80

   ○ 88

   ○ 92

   ○ 96

   ○ 112

37. Bob and Alice can finish a job together in 3 hours. If Bob can do the job by himself in 5 hours, what percent of the job does Alice do?

   ○ 20%

   ○ 30%

   ○ 40%

   ○ 50%

   ○ 60%

GENERAL WORD PROBLEMS TEST

Solve the following problems and choose the best answer. (Answers and explanations are at the end of the chapter.)

1988	$250
1989	$300
1990	$360

1. Robert's rent increased each year by the same percent, as shown in the chart above. At that rate, what was his rent in 1991?

   ○ $420

   ○ $430

   ○ $432

   ○ $438

   ○ $440

2. In a certain baseball league, each team plays 160 games. After playing half of their games, team A has won 60 games and team B has won 49 games. If team A wins half of its remaining games, how many more games must team B win to have the same record as team A at the end of the season?

   ○ 48

   ○ 49

   ○ 50

   ○ 51

   ○ 52

3. If a man earns $200 for his first 40 hours of work in a week and is then paid one-and-one-half times his regular hourly rate for any additional hours, how many hours must he work to make $230 in a week?

   ○ 4

   ○ 5

   ○ 6

   ○ 44

   ○ 45

4. If 10 millimeters equal 1 centimeter, how many square centimeters does 1 square millimeter equal?

   ○ 0.01

   ○ 0.1

   ○ 1

   ○ 10

   ○ 100

5. Team X and team Y have a tug of war. From their starting positions team X pulls team Y forward 3 meters, and are then pulled forward themselves 5 meters. Team Y then pulls team X forward 2 meters. If the first team to be pulled forward 10 meters loses, how many more meters must team Y pull team X forward to win?

   ○ 0

   ○ 4

   ○ 6

   ○ 8

   ○ 14

6. An hour-long test has 60 problems. If a student completes 30 problems in 20 minutes, how many seconds does he have on average for completing each of the remaining problems?

   ○ 60

   ○ 70

   ○ 80

   ○ 90

   ○ 100

7. The sum of the lengths of all the roads in county Z is 1,400 miles. If the sum of the lengths of unpaved roads is $\frac{3}{4}$ the sum of the lengths of paved roads, how many more miles of paved roads than unpaved are there in county Z?

   ○ 200

   ○ 400

   ○ 600

   ○ 800

   ○ 1,000

8. In a certain class, 3 out of 24 students are in student organizations. What is the ratio of students in student organizations to students not in student organizations?

   ○ $\frac{1}{8}$

   ○ $\frac{1}{7}$

   ○ $\frac{1}{6}$

   ○ $\frac{1}{5}$

   ○ $\frac{1}{4}$

9. On the face of a regular die, the dots are arranged in such a way that the total number of dots on any two opposite faces is 7. If the figure above shows a regular die, what is the total number of dots on the faces that are not shown?

   ○ 7

   ○ 9

   ○ 12

   ○ 13

   ○ 14

10. A student averages 72 on 5 tests. If the lowest score is dropped, the average rises to 84. What is the lowest score?

   ○ 18

   ○ 24

   ○ 32

   ○ 43

   ○ 48

11. Achmed finds that by wearing different combinations of the jackets, shirts and pairs of trousers that he owns, he can make up 90 different outfits. If he owns 5 jackets and 3 pairs of trousers, how many shirts does he own?

   ○ 3

   ○ 6

   ○ 12

   ○ 18

   ○ 30

KAPLAN

12. Jean is driving from Mayville to a county fair in Yorkville. After driving for two hours at an average speed of 70 kilometers per hour, she still has 80 kilometers left to travel. What is the distance between the two towns, in kilometers?

○ 220

○ 250

○ 260

○ 270

○ 280

13. A store offers a variety of discounts that range between 10 percent and 25 percent inclusive. If a book is discounted to a price of $2.40, what was its greatest possible price originally?

○ $2.64

○ $3.00

○ $3.20

○ $10.80

○ $24.00

14. A man earns N dollars a month and spends S dollars a month on rent. If he then spends $\frac{3}{8}$ of the remainder on food, how much, in dollars, is left over for other expenses, in terms of N and S?

○ $\frac{3}{8}(N - S)$

○ $\frac{3}{8}(N + S)$

○ $\frac{5}{8}(N - S)$

○ $\frac{5}{8}(N + S)$

○ $\frac{8}{3}(N - S)$

9	8	6	3

15. The figure above shows an example of a 4-digit customer identification code. If the digits in the code must appear in descending numerical order and no digit can be used more than once, what is the difference between largest and smallest possible codes?

○ 6,666

○ 5,555

○ 5,432

○ 4,444

○ 1,111

16. The kinetic energy K, in joules, provided by the mass of a particle m, in kilograms, with a velocity of v meters per seconds, is given by the equation $K = \frac{1}{2}mv^2$. If a particle had a velocity of 4 meters per second and a kinetic energy of 144 joules, then the mass, in kilograms, of this particle must be

○ 16

○ 18

○ 24

○ 44

○ 64

17. Bill purchases an item and receives no change. Before the purchase, he had only a five-dollar bill, two ten-dollar bills, and a twenty-dollar bill. How many distinct possibilities are there for the total amount of his purchase?

  ○ 3

  ○ 4

  ○ 6

  ○ 9

  ○ 10

Type of Pet	Number of Households	Average Number of Pets per Household
Dogs Only	16	1.5
Cats Only	24	1.25
Dogs & Cats	8	3.25

18. The table above gives the type and number of pets owned by a group of 48 households that own only cats and dogs. If the ratio of the total number of cats to the total number of dogs is 5 : 3, how many dogs are there?

  ○ 18

  ○ 24

  ○ 30

  ○ 36

  ○ 48

19. Jane knits 72 stitches to the line and uses $\frac{1}{4}$ inch of yarn in each of the stitches. How many lines can she knit with 10 yards of yarn? (1 yard = 3 feet; 1 foot = 12 inches)

  ○ 10

  ○ 20

  ○ 30

  ○ 40

  ○ 50

20. Robert purchased $2,000 worth of U.S. savings bonds. If bonds are sold in $50 or $100 denominations only, which of the following CANNOT be the number of U.S. savings bonds that Robert purchased?

  ○ 20

  ○ 27

  ○ 30

  ○ 40

  ○ 50

21. A supply of sugar lasts for 30 days. If its use is increased by 50 percent, how many days would the same amount of sugar last?

  ○ 15

  ○ 20

  ○ 25

  ○ 30

  ○ 45

22. Bucky leaves Amity for Truro, which is 8 miles away, at the same time that Robin leaves Truro for Amity. If neither of them stops along the way, and they meet along the road 2 miles from Amity, what is the ratio of Bucky's average speed to Robin's average speed?

  ○ $\frac{1}{4}$

  ○ $\frac{1}{3}$

  ○ $\frac{1}{1}$

  ○ $\frac{3}{1}$

  ○ $\frac{4}{1}$

23. On a scaled map, a distance of 10 centimeters represents 5 kilometers. If a street is 750 meters long, what is its length on the map, in centimeters? (1 kilometer = 1,000 meters)

    ○ 0.015

    ○ 0.15

    ○ 1.5

    ○ 15

    ○ 150

24. Oak trees line both sides of a street for a length of $\frac{3}{8}$ of a kilometer. If there is 16 meters of space between the trees, and each tree is 1 meter wide, how many trees are there along the street? (1 kilometer = 1,000 meters)

    ○ 36

    ○ 40

    ○ 42

    ○ 44

    ○ 46

25. A lighthouse blinks regularly 5 times a minute. A neighboring lighthouse blinks regularly 4 times a minute. If they blink simultaneously, after how many seconds will they blink together again?

    ○ 20

    ○ 24

    ○ 30

    ○ 60

    ○ 300

26. A vault holds only 8-ounce tablets of gold and 5-ounce tablets of silver. If there are 130 ounces of gold and silver total, what is the greatest amount of gold that can be in the vault, in ounces?

    ○ 40

    ○ 80

    ○ 120

    ○ 128

    ○ 130

27. At a parade, balloons are given out in the order blue, red, red, yellow, yellow, yellow, blue, red, red, yellow, yellow, yellow, etc. If this pattern continues, how many red balloons will have been given out when a total of 70 balloons have been distributed?

    ○ 18

    ○ 22

    ○ 24

    ○ 26

    ○ 35

28. If the cost of p plums priced at 25 cents each equals the cost of $p - 6$ nectarines priced at 28 cents each, then p equals

    ○ 26

    ○ 42

    ○ 52

    ○ 56

    ○ 66

29. In July the price of a stock increased by 10 percent. In August, it declined by 20 percent. If in September the price increased by 10 percent, by what percent of the original July price has the stock changed in price from the start of July to the end of September?

    ◯ 0%

    ◯ 3.2%

    ◯ 4.4%

    ◯ 20%

    ◯ 40%

30. If 1 tic equals 3 tacs and 2 tacs equal 5 tocs, what is the ratio of one tic to one toc?

    ◯ $\dfrac{15}{2}$

    ◯ $\dfrac{6}{5}$

    ◯ $\dfrac{5}{6}$

    ◯ $\dfrac{3}{10}$

    ◯ $\dfrac{1}{15}$

31. If John gives Allen 5 dollars and Allen gives Frank 2 dollars, the three boys will have the same amount of money. How much more money does John have than Allen?

    ◯ $3

    ◯ $5

    ◯ $6

    ◯ $7

    ◯ $8

32. If sheets of paper are 0.08 centimeters thick and 500 sheets cost $3.00 how much will a stack of paper 4 meters thick cost? (1 meter = 100 centimeters)

    ◯ $30

    ◯ $45

    ◯ $60

    ◯ $72

    ◯ $96

33. Ms. Smith drove a total of 700 miles on a business trip. If her car averaged 35 miles per gallon of gasoline and gasoline cost an average of $1.25 per gallon, how much did she spend on gasoline during the trip?

    ◯ $17.50

    ◯ $25.00

    ◯ $35.00

    ◯ $70.00

    ◯ $250.00

34. There are 7 people on committee *A* and 8 people on committee *B*. If three people serve on both committees, how many people serve on only one of the committees?

    ◯ 8

    ◯ 9

    ◯ 10

    ◯ 11

    ◯ 12

35. Anne owes Bob $4, Bob owes Carol $3, and Carol owes Anne $5. If Carol settles all the debts by giving money to both Anne and Bob, how much will she give Anne?

- ◯ $1
- ◯ $2
- ◯ $3
- ◯ $4
- ◯ $5

36. John can shovel a driveway in 50 minutes. If Mary can shovel the driveway in 20 minutes, how long will it take them, to the nearest minute, to shovel the driveway if they work together?

- ◯ 12
- ◯ 13
- ◯ 14
- ◯ 16
- ◯ 18

37. A butcher buys 240 kilograms of beef for $380. If 20 percent of the beef is unusable, at approximately what average price per kilogram must he sell the rest of the beef in order to make a profit of 25 percent?

- ◯ $2.30
- ◯ $2.40
- ◯ $2.45
- ◯ $2.47
- ◯ $2.55

38. A vending machine dispenses gumballs in a regularly repeating cycle of ten different colors. If a quarter buys 3 gumballs, what is the minimum amount of money that must be spent before three gumballs of the same color are dispensed?

- ◯ $1.00
- ◯ $1.75
- ◯ $2.00
- ◯ $2.25
- ◯ $2.50

39. During a season in a certain baseball league every team plays every other team in the league ten times. If there are ten teams in the league, how many games are played in the league in one season?

- ◯ 45
- ◯ 90
- ◯ 450
- ◯ 900
- ◯ 1,000

40. Henry and Eleanor are waiting in line for a movie. If Henry is fourth in line, and there are n people ahead of Eleanor, where $n > 4$, how many people are between Henry and Eleanor?

- ◯ $n - 5$
- ◯ $n - 4$
- ◯ $n - 3$
- ◯ $n + 3$
- ◯ $n + 4$

WORD PROBLEMS LEVEL ONE TEST ANSWERS AND EXPLANATIONS

1. $25

Translate directly into math. A price decrease makes the price smaller, so we subtract. A price increase makes the price greater so we add. So for the final price we get

$$\$25 - \$4 + \$6 - \$2 = \$25 + \$0 = \$25$$

So the final price is $25.

2. 8.75 million

In Country A, the amount of population increase between 1960 and 1970 was 1.75 million **more** than the amount of increase between 1950 and 1960, or 1.75 million **more** than 3.5 million. It must have been 1.75 + 3.5 million or 5.25 million. The total growth in population over the two decades equals 3.5 million, the amount of growth during the 50's, plus 5.25 million, the amount of growth during the 60's, for a total increase of 8.75 million.

3. $260

Sue makes $280. If Joan makes $50 **more** than this, then Joan must make $280+$50 or $330. Greg makes $70 **less** than this amount, or $330 − $70 or $260.

4. 96,000

Find out how many camels passed through Timbuktu over the course of the year, then multiply that by the number of pieces of copper collected for each camel. Each month an average of 8 caravans with an average of 100 camels per caravan passed through the town; therefore, an average of 8 × 100 or 800 camels a month passed through Timbuktu. Over a year there must have been 12 times this amount, or 12 × 800 or 9,600 camels. They collected 10 pieces of copper for each of these. Over the year they collected 10 × 9,600 or 96,000 pieces of copper.

5. 6

When the painter and his son work together, they'll charge the sum of their hourly rates, $12 + $6 or $18 per hour. Their bill equals the product of this combined rate and the number of hours they work. Therefore $108 must equal $18 per hour times the number of hours they work. We need to divide $108 by $18 per hour to find the number of hours. $108 ÷ $18 = 6. They must have worked 6 hours.

6. $36

The price of the softcover edition plus the difference in price between the hardcover and softcover editions equals the price of the hardcover edition. We're told that this difference is $12. We're also told that the softcover price is simply two-thirds of the hardcover price. Calling the hardcover price H (since that's what we're ultimately looking for), we can set up an equation:

$$\text{Softcover price} + 12 = \text{hardcover price}$$
$$\frac{2}{3}H + 12 = H$$
$$12 = H - \frac{2}{3}H$$
$$12 = \frac{1}{3}H$$
$$36 = H$$

The hardcover price is $36.

7. 2,000

To calculate the number of 14¢ stamps sold by the post office, divide the total amount of money spent on these stamps by the cost for each stamp. This means dividing $280 by 14¢. Since the units are not the same, we convert $280 to cents by multiplying by 100, to give 28,000¢, so that we are dividing cents by cents. We get

$$
\begin{array}{r}
2,000 \\
14 \overline{)28,000} \\
\underline{28} \\
0
\end{array}
$$

8. 4n

Lisa was 2n years old n years ago. Since it is now n years later, she must be 2n + n or 3n years old now. And in another n years? She will have aged n more years by then, so she will be 3n + n or 4n years old.

This type of problem is ideal for picking numbers. We can choose a value for n, determine the result we need, and then evaluate each answer choice using the same value to see which one gives the same result. Say n = 5. Then Lisa was 10 years old 5 years ago. So she is currently 15. In another 5 years, she'll be 20.

Which answer choice equals 20 when n is 5? The first choice, 4n = 20. This looks promising, but we still need to check the other choices. If you substitute 5 for n, you'll find none of the other choices equals 20.

9. 24

One third of the original volume of water in the pond was lost during the drought. The amount of water that remains must be two thirds of the original amount, that is twice as much as was lost. So the one third that was lost is equal to half of what was left. That is, the amount of water lost = 48,000 ÷ 2 = 24,000 gallons of water.

Or, set up an equation where W represents how much water was originally in the pond:

$$
W - \frac{1}{3}W = 48,000
$$

$$
\frac{2}{3}W = 48,000
$$

$$
W = 72,000
$$

The amount lost was $\frac{1}{3}$ of the original amount, or $\frac{1}{3}$

of W which is $\frac{1}{3}(72,000) = 24,000$.

10. $500,000

The amount each of the children stands to gain equals the difference between what he or she will make if the stepchildren are excluded and what he or she will make if they're included. If the stepchildren are excluded, the children will inherit $15 million divided by 10 (the number of children) or $1.5 million each. If the stepchildren are included, they'll inherit $15 million divided by 15 (the number of children and stepchildren combined) or $1 million each. The difference is $1.5 million − $1 million or $500,000.

11. 17

What two numbers seven apart add up to 27? With trial and error you should be able to find them soon; 10 and 17; there must be 17 women working at the office.

Alternatively, set up two equations each with two unknowns. There are 27 employees at the office total, all either men or women, so m (the number of men) + w (the number of women) = 27. There are 7 more women than men, so:

$$
m + 7 = w \text{ or } m = w - 7
$$

Substituting $w - 7$ for m into the first equation, we get:

$$(w - 7) + w = 27$$
$$2w - 7 = 27$$
$$2w = 34$$
$$w = 17$$

There are 17 women in the office. (In problem like this, it's a good idea to check at the end to make sure you answered the right question. It would have been easy here to misread the question and solve for the number of men.)

12. $3x - y + 2 = 0$

Translate into math, remembering "2 less than y" means $y - 2$, not $2 - y$.

The product of 3 and x is equal to 2 less than y.

$$3x = y - 2$$
$$3x = y - 2$$

We must determine which of the answer choices corresponds to this. Since all the choices are equations where the right side is equal to zero, move all the terms to the left side. We get

$$3x - y + 2 = 0$$

13. $440

The cost of stock = $8,000 + 2%$ of $8,000

$$= \$8,000 + \$160$$
$$= \$8,160$$

The 4 partners have already invested $1,600 each, that is 4 × $1,600 = $6,400. They need to invest $8,160 − $6,400 = $1,760 more in total, and $1,760 ÷ 4 = $440 more per partner.

Or, since each invests an equal amount, each will ultimately invest $8,160 ÷ 4 = $2,040. If each partner already invested $1,600, the amount each one still needs to invest is $2,040 − $1,600 = $440. (Notice how it's a little less arithmetic to divide the whole amount into quarters first and then subtract.)

14. $1.75

We need to compute the cost of 5 hours at each garage. Since the two garages have a split-rate system of charging, the cost for the first hour is different from the cost of each remaining hour. The remaining hours after the first one (in this case, there are 4 of them), are charged at an hourly rate.

The first hour at garage A costs $8.75.
The next 4 hours cost 4 × $1.25 = $5.00.
The total cost for parking at garage
$A = \$8.75 + 5.00$
$= \$13.75$

The first hour at garage B costs $5.50.
The next 4 hours cost 4 × $2.50 = $10.00.
The total cost for parking at garage
$B = \$5.50 + 10.00$
$= \$15.50$

The difference in cost = $15.50 − $13.75 = $1.75.

15.   40

Find the number of students who play on any sports team, then multiply by $\frac{1}{4}$ to find the number of students who play football. $\frac{2}{3}$ of the 240 students play some sport, or $\frac{2}{3} \times 240$ or 160 students. $\frac{1}{4}$ of these play football; that equals $\frac{1}{4} \times 160$ or 40 students.

Therefore, 40 students play football.

16. $20

We can translate to get two equations. Let E be the amount Ed has and R be the amount Robert has.

"Ed has $100 **more** than Robert" becomes $E = R + 100$.

"Ed **spends** $20" means he'll end up with $20 less, or $E - 20$. "5 **times as much as** Robert" becomes $5R$. So $E - 20 = 5R$.

Substitute $R + 100$ for E in the second equation and solve for R:

$$E - 20 = 5R$$
$$R + 100 - 20 = 5R$$
$$R + 80 = 5R$$
$$80 = 4R$$
$$20 = R$$

So Robert has $20.

17. $12\frac{1}{2}$

Diane has painted $\frac{1}{3}$ of a room with $2\frac{1}{2}$ cans of paint.

We know that the whole room will need 3 times as much paint as $\frac{1}{3}$ of the room, so the total paint needed to paint the room equals $3 \times 2\frac{1}{2}$ cans, or $7\frac{1}{2}$ cans. To paint 2 rooms, she would need $2 \times 7\frac{1}{2}$ cans, or 15 cans. But the question asks how many **more** cans of paint Diane needs; she has already used $2\frac{1}{2}$ cans. We subtract: 15 cans minus $2\frac{1}{2}$ cans leaves $12\frac{1}{2}$ cans to finish the first room and paint the second.

18. 18

We need to find a fraction of a fraction. The total number of UFO sightings is 108. Of these, $\frac{1}{2}$ turn out to be airplanes: $\frac{1}{2} \times 108 = 54$. If $\frac{1}{2}$ are airplanes, $\frac{1}{2}$ are not, so 54 sightings remain that are not airplanes. Of these 54, $\frac{1}{3}$ are weather balloons. We multiply $\frac{1}{3} \times 54$, which equals 18, to get the number of weather balloons.

19. 22

One thing we must do here before we start is pick a unit to work with: either dollars or cents. It doesn't matter which we choose; it's a personal preference. We'll work with dollars. The first print uses up $1.65 of the $20.00 Pete has available. This leaves him $20.00 − $1.65 or $18.35 for the rest of the prints, at a rate of 85¢ or $0.85 per print. We could divide here, but it's easier to work with it this way: 10 additional prints would cost 10 times as much or $8.50, so 20 additional prints must cost 2 × $8.50 or $17.00. Now we can add on individual prints at $0.85 each: 21 additional prints cost $17.00 + $0.85 or $17.85, 22 additional prints cost $17.85 + $0.85 or $18.70. But this is more than the $18.35 Pete has available. So Pete can only afford 21 additional prints, **plus** the $1.65 first print, for a total of 22 prints.

20. 16

Find the total number of peanuts in the bag, then divide by the new number of children who will be sharing them. There are enough peanuts to give 12 nuts to each of 20 children, so there are 12 × 20 peanuts or 240 peanuts total.

After 5 children drop out, there remain 20 − 5 or 15 children to share the 240 peanuts. Each will get $\frac{240}{15}$ or 16 peanuts.

21. $4.00

If each adult's fare is twice as much as each child's fare, then 2 adult fares costs as much as 4 child fares. So the 2 adult fares are as expensive as 4 children's fares. This, added to the 3 children's fares, gives us a total of $4 + 3$ or 7 children's fares. This equals the $14. If 7 children's fares cost $14, then the cost of each child's fare is $\frac{14}{7}$ or $2. Adult fares cost twice as much or $4.

22. $3,000

The $250 that Doris spent on the carpet is one quarter of the one-third of Doris's savings that's left over after she buys the car, or $\frac{1}{4} \times \frac{1}{3} = \frac{1}{12}$ of her original savings. Therefore, her original savings must have been $12 \times$ $250 or $3,000.

23. $3n - 14$

Gheri is n years old. Carl is 6 years younger than Gheri, or $n - 6$ years old. Jean is 2 years younger than Carl, or $n - 6 - 2 = n - 8$ years old. The sum of their ages is then $n + (n - 6) + (n - 8) = 3n - 14$ years.

24. 13

We will get the maximum number of groups by making each group as small as possible. Each group must have at least 3 people in it, so divide 40 by 3 to find the number of 3-person groups. $40 \div 3 = 13$ with a remainder of 1. So we have 13 groups with 1 person left over. Since each group must have at least 3 people, we must throw the extra lonely student in with one of the other groups. So we have 12 groups with 3 students each, and one group with 4 students, for a maximum total of 13 groups.

25. 30

Let p represent Philip's salamanders and m Matt's salamanders. If Philip has twice as many salamanders as Matt, we can write

$$p = 2m$$

If Philip gives Matt 10 salamanders, then he will have 10 fewer, or $p - 10$, and Matt will have 10 more or $m + 10$. In this case Philip would have half as many as Matt, so

$$p - 10 = \frac{1}{2}(m + 10)$$

We have two equations with two variables. (Note that although the number of salamanders each owns has changed, the variables p and m still have the same meaning: the original number of salamanders.) We can solve for p and m. Substitute our first expression for p, that is $p = 2m$, into the second equation and solve for m.

$$2m - 10 = \frac{1}{2}(m + 10)$$
$$4m - 20 = m + 10$$
$$3m = 30$$
$$m = 10$$

Since $p = 2m$, if $m = 10$, then $p = 20$. The total number of salamanders is $p + m = 20 + 10$ or 30.

26. 48

If the average salary of the 60 workers is $80, the total amount received by the workers is 60 × $80 or $4,800. This equals the total income from the $75 workers plus the total income from the $100 workers. Let x represent the number of $75 workers.

Since we know there are 60 workers altogether, and everyone earns either $75 or $100, then $60 - x$ must earn $100. We can set up an equation for the total amount received by the workers by multiplying the rate times the number of workers receiving that rate and adding:

$$75x + 100(60 - x) = 4,800$$

Solve this equation to find x, the number of workers earning $75.

$$75x + 6,000 - 100x = 4,800$$
$$-25x = -1,200$$
$$25x = 1,200$$
$$x = 48$$

There were 48 workers earning $75.

PERCENT, RATIO, AND RATES WORD PROBLEMS TEST ANSWERS AND EXPLANATIONS

1. 20%

The percent profit equals the amount of profit divided by the original price of the stock (expressed as a percent). On each share a profit of $12 − $10 or 2 dollars was made. Each share originally cost 10 dollars. The percent profit equals

$\frac{2}{10}$ or 20%.

2. 18

The subway will pass $\frac{60}{10}$ or 6 times as many stations in one hour as it passes in 10 minutes. In 10 minutes it passes 3 stations; in 60 minutes it must pass 6 × 3 or 18 stations.

We could also use the U.C.M. The train passes 3 stations every 10 minutes, or $\frac{3\ \text{stations}}{10\ \text{minutes}}$.

To convert this to hours, multiply by $\frac{60\ \text{minutes}}{1\ \text{hour}}$:

$$\frac{3\ \text{stations}}{10\ \text{minutes}} \times \frac{60\ \text{minutes}}{1\ \text{hour}} = \frac{18\ \text{stations}}{1\ \text{hour}}$$

If the train passes 18 stations per 1 hour, it passes 18 stations in one hour.

3. $16\frac{2}{3}$%

The percent discount equals the amount of discount divided by the **original** price. The amount of discount is $120 − $100 or 20 dollars. The original price was $120. The percent discount equals

$$\frac{20}{120} = \frac{1}{6} \text{ or } 16\frac{2}{3}\%$$

4. 36

Find the number of seconds in an hour, then multiply this by the distance the car is traveling each second. There are 60 seconds in a minute and 60 minutes in one hour; therefore, there are 60 × 60 or 3,600 seconds in an hour. In one second the car travels $\frac{1}{100}$ kilometers; in one hour the car will travel $3,600 \times \frac{1}{100}$ or 36 kilometers.

5. $13

This problem is not as hard as calculating how much each of them paid and then subtracting John's amount from Sally's—there's a shortcut we can use, since their discounts are percents of the same whole. If John buys the stereo at 7% discount and Sally buys it at a 5% discount, the difference in the amount of the discount they get is 7% − 5%, or 2% of the original price of $650. The difference is 2% of $650 or $\frac{1}{50}$ of 650 dollars.

$$\frac{1}{50} \times 650 = \frac{650}{50} = \frac{65}{5} = 13$$

Sally pays $13 more.

6.   5*m*

How many 5-hour periods are in a 25-hour trip? $25 \div 5$ or 5 periods. So the train will travel 5 times as far in 25 hours than it does in 5 hours. Since it goes *m* miles in 5 hours, the train must go 5 times as far in 25 hours, or 5*m* miles.

Or, just use the formula Distance = Rate × Time. Here the rate is *m* miles in 5 hours, and the amount of time traveled is 25 hours. Therefore:

$$\text{Distance} = \frac{m \text{ miles}}{5 \text{ hours}} \times 25 \text{ hours}$$
$$= 5m \text{ miles}$$

So the train travels 5*m* miles.

7. $6

The difference we need is the price of the compact disk minus the price of the record, or the price of the compact disk minus 60% of the price of the compact disk, which is just 40% of the compact disk price. We need only find 40% of 15 dollars. The fractional equivalent of 40% is $\frac{2}{5}$, so difference is $\frac{2}{5} \times 15$ dollars or 6 dollars.

8.   9

Since it travels at $\frac{2}{3}$ the speed of the horse, the mule covers $\frac{2}{3}$ of the distance the horse does in any given amount of time, leaving $\frac{1}{3}$ of the distance left to travel.

So in the time the horse has travelled the entire distance, the mule has only gone $\frac{2}{3}$ of the distance. So if the horse goes the whole distance in 6 hours, the mule goes $\frac{2}{3}$ of the distance in 6 hours. The mule has $\frac{1}{3}$ of the distance to go. It takes him 6 hours to get $\frac{2}{3}$ of the way, so it will take him half this, or 3 hours to get

the remaining $\frac{1}{3}$ of the way. Therefore the whole journey takes the mule $6 + 3 = 9$ hours.

Alternatively, consider finding the mule's rate by taking two-thirds of the horse's rate. The horse travels 20 miles in 6 hours; therefore, the horse's speed is $\frac{20 \text{ miles}}{6 \text{ hours}}$. The mule travels at $\frac{2}{3}$ this speed:

$$\frac{2}{3} \times \frac{20 \text{ miles}}{6 \text{ hours}} = \frac{20 \text{ miles}}{9 \text{ hours}}.$$

Now we can use this rate to determine how long it takes the mule to make the trip. The mule needs 9 hours to travel 20 miles.

9. $33\frac{1}{3}\%$

The first thing we must do is find a single unit to work with. Convert $1.20 to cents. (We could work with dollars, but by working with the smaller unit we'll avoid decimals.) There are 100 cents in a dollar, so $1.20 = 120 cents. The ice cream costs him only 90 cents per scoop. The ice cream seller makes $120 - 90$ or 30 cents of profit on every scoop of ice cream he sells.

His percent profit is the amount of profit divided by the cost to him, or $\frac{30}{90} = \frac{1}{3}$ or $33\frac{1}{3}\%$.

10.   38

Since the cars are traveling in opposite directions, the distance between the two cars equals the sum of the distances each car travels. The first car travels 20 minutes or a third of an hour, so it goes only $\frac{1}{3}$ the distance it would travel in an hour, or $\frac{1}{3}$ of 24 miles or 8 miles.

The second car travels 45 minutes or $\frac{3}{4}$ of an hour. It goes $\frac{3}{4}$ of the distance it would go in an hour, or $\frac{3}{4}$ of 40 or 30 miles. The two cars are then 8 + 30 or 38 miles apart.

11. $10

The salesman has lost out on 10% of the $100 difference between the original price of the encyclopedia and the reduced selling price. 10% of $100, or $\frac{1}{10}$ of $100, is $10.

12. 40

The average speed equals the total distance the car travels divided by the total time. We're told the car goes 60 kilometers in an hour before its piston breaks, and then travels another 60 kilometers at 30 kilometers an hour. The second part of the trip must have taken 2 hours (if you go 30 miles in one hour, then you'll go twice as far, 60 miles, in twice as much time, 2 hours). So the car travels a total of 60 + 60 or 120 miles, and covers this distance in 1 + 2 or 3 hours. Its average speed equals 120 miles divided by 3 hours, or 40 miles per hour.

Notice that the average speed over the entire trip is **not** simply the average of the two speeds traveled over the trip. (That would be the average of 60 and 30, which is 45.) This is because the car spent different amounts of time travelling at these two different rates. Be wary of problems that ask for an average rate over a trip that encompassed different rates.

13. 64%

If 20% of the apartments with smoke alarms were found to have smoke alarms that are not working, then the remaining 80% of the apartments with smoke alarms have smoke alarms that **are** working. Since 80% of all apartments in the city have smoke alarms, and 80% of these have working smoke alarms, 80% of 80% of all the apartments in the city have working smoke alarms. 80% of 80% equals (converting to fractions) $\frac{8}{10} \times \frac{8}{10}$ of all the apartments in the city or $\frac{64}{100}$ of all apartments. $\frac{64}{100}$ is 64%.

Alternatively, since we are working with percents only, try picking numbers. Let the number of apartments in City G be 100. If 80% of these have smoke alarms, then 80% of 100 or 80 apartments have smoke alarms.

If 20% of these do not work, then 80% do work. 80% of 80 is $\frac{8}{10} \times 80 = 64$ apartments. If 64 of the 100 apartments in City G have working smoke alarms, then $\frac{64}{100}$, or 64%, have working smoke alarms.

14. $\dfrac{60}{n}$

This is simply a motion problem; it's just one in which the speeds are very slow. First find the speed at which the tree grew, in feet per year. It grew 5 feet in n years, so it grew at an average rate of $\dfrac{5 \text{ feet}}{n \text{ years}}$. Now we want the average distance it grew in 1 year.

$$\text{Distance} = \text{Rate} \times \text{Time}$$
$$= \frac{5 \text{ feet}}{n \text{ years}} \times 1 \text{ year}$$
$$= \frac{5}{n} \text{ feet}$$

But we were asked for the average amount grew in inches per year, so we must convert. As we're told, there are 12 inches in a foot, so

$$\frac{5}{n} \text{ feet} \times \frac{12 \text{ inches}}{1 \text{ foot}} = \frac{60}{n} \text{ inches.}$$

This is the average amount the tree grew in 1 year.

15. 1,440,000

During the year of the first increase, attendance climbed to 1 million plus 20% or $\frac{1}{5}$ of 1 million. $\frac{1}{5}$ of 1 million is 200,000, so attendance rose to 1,200,000, or 1.2 million. During the year of the second increase, attendance climbed to 1.2 million plus 20% or $\frac{1}{5}$ of 1.2 million. $\frac{1}{5}$ of 1.2 million is 240,000. The attendance the year of the second increase must have been 1,200,000 + 240,000 or 1,440,000.

16. 80

If Bill mows $\frac{3}{4}$ of his lawn in one hour, then one hour must represent $\frac{3}{4}$ of the time he needs to mow the entire lawn. Therefore, 60 minutes must equal $\frac{3}{4}$ of the time he needs to mow the entire lawn.

$$60 = \frac{3}{4} \times \text{(Total time)}.$$

Now solve for the total time.

$$\text{Total time} = 60 \times \frac{4}{3}$$
$$= 80$$

He will need 80 minutes to mow the whole lawn.

17. $300

A potential profit of 20% means the store will sell the camera for 20% more than they paid for it themselves.

The $360 price of the camera represents the cost of the camera to the store plus 20% of the cost of the camera to the store. Then

$$\text{Selling price} = 120\% \text{ of cost}$$
$$\$360 = \frac{120}{100} \times \text{cost}$$
$$\$360 \times \frac{100}{120} = \text{cost}$$
$$\$300 = \text{cost}$$

18. $200

The amount of the discount will *not* be 20% of $800; it will equal 20% of the original price of the item. Therefore you need to find this original price. You know the original price minus 20% of the original price equals $800. That is, 80% of the original price equals $800. Calling the original price x we have:

$$\$800 = 80\% \text{ of } x$$
$$\$800 = \frac{8}{10} \times x$$
$$\$800 \times \frac{10}{8} = x$$
$$\$1,000 = x$$

The original price was $1,000. The new price is $800. The amount of the discount was 20% of $1,000 or $200. (Or just subtract: $1,000 − $800 = $200.)

19. $\dfrac{PR}{N}$

If John buys R pounds for N people, he is planning on feeding his guests cheese at a rate of

$$\frac{R \text{ pounds}}{N \text{ people}} = \frac{R}{N} \text{ pounds per person.}$$

We need to know how much additional cheese John must buy for the extra P people. If John is buying $\frac{R}{N}$ pounds of cheese for each person, then he will need $P \times \frac{R}{N}$ or $\frac{PR}{N}$ pounds for the extra P people. We can check our answer by seeing if the units cancel out:

$$P \text{ people} \times \frac{R \text{ pounds}}{N \text{ people}} = \frac{PR}{N} \text{ pounds}$$

The other approach here is to get rid of all those annoying variables by picking numbers. Say John buys 10 pounds of cheese for 5 people (that is, $R = 10$ and $N = 5$). Then everyone gets 2 pounds of cheese. Also, say 7 people come, 2 more than expected (that is, $P = 2$). Then he needs 14 pounds to have enough for everybody to consume 2 pounds of cheese. Since he already bought 10 pounds, he must buy an additional 4 pounds. Therefore, the answer choice which equals 4 when we substitute 10 for R, 5 for N, and 2 for P is possibly correct:

$$\frac{(5)(2)}{10} \neq 4. \qquad \text{Discard}$$

$$\frac{5}{(10)(2)} \neq 4. \qquad \text{Discard}$$

$$\frac{5 + 2}{10} \neq 4. \qquad \text{Discard}$$

$$\frac{2}{(5)(10)} \neq 4. \qquad \text{Discard}$$

$$\frac{(2)(10)}{5} = 4. \qquad \text{Correct}$$

Since only the fifth choice gives 4, that must be the correct choice.

20. 20%

The easiest approach here is to pick a sample value for the cost of the watch, and from that work out the profit and selling price. As so often with percent problems, it will be simplest to pick 100. If the watch cost the store $100, then the profit will be 25% of $100 or $25. The selling price equals the cost to the store plus the profit: $100 + $25 or $125. The profit represents $\frac{25}{125}$ or $\frac{1}{5}$ of the selling price. The percent equivalent of $\frac{1}{5}$ is 20%.

21. 14

If $\frac{5}{12}$ of the hole is filled up, how much remains to be filled? $1 - \frac{5}{12}$, or $\frac{7}{12}$ of the hole. If $\frac{5}{12}$ of the hole is filled up in 10 minutes, how long does it take to fill up $\frac{1}{12}$ of the hole (the easiest fraction to work with here)? $\frac{5}{12}$ is 5 times bigger than $\frac{1}{12}$, so $\frac{1}{12}$ of the hole will take $\frac{1}{5}$ the time for $\frac{5}{12}$ of the whole, which is $\frac{1}{5}$ of 10 minutes, or 2 minutes. We want to know how long it will take to fill the rest of the hole: the missing $\frac{7}{12}$. That will be 7 times as long as $\frac{1}{12}$ of the hole; therefore, it takes 7×2 or 14 minutes to fill the rest of the hole.

22. $33

First find how much she paid for all the windows. She received a discount of 25%; that is, she paid 75% of the total price.

$$\text{Cost to builder} = 75\% \text{ of } \$1,200$$
$$= \frac{3}{4} \times \$1,200$$
$$= \$900$$

She received an extra $75 discount. That is, she paid $900 − $75 = $825. She bought 25 windows, so each cost her $\frac{\$825}{25} = \$33$.

23. 200

As with most work problems, the key here is to find what portion of the job is completed in some unit of time. Here one hour is a convenient unit. If Carol can do a whole job in 5 hours, that means she completes $\frac{1}{5}$ of the job in one hour. Steve can do the job in 10 hours; he completes $\frac{1}{10}$ of the job in one hour. Together in an hour they'll complete $\frac{1}{5} + \frac{1}{10}$ of the job, or $\frac{3}{10}$ of the job. They will do $\frac{1}{10}$ of the job in $\frac{1}{3}$ this time, that is in $\frac{1}{3}$ of an hour. They will do the whole job, or $\frac{10}{10}$ of the job, in $10 \times \frac{1}{3}$ hours $= \frac{10}{3}$ hours. One hour = 60 minutes, so

$$\frac{10}{3} \text{ hours} = \frac{10}{3} \times 60 \text{ minutes}$$
$$= \frac{600}{3} \text{ minutes}$$
$$= 200 \text{ minutes}$$

24. $33\frac{1}{3}$%

Pick a sample value for the size of one of the classes. The first class might have 100 students. That means there are 30% of 100 = 30 boys in the class. The second class is half the size of the first, so it has 50 students, of which 40% of 50 = 20 are boys. This gives us 100 + 50 = 150 students total, of whom 30 + 20 = 50 are boys.

So $\frac{50}{150} = \frac{1}{3}$ of both classes are boys. $\frac{1}{3}$ equals $33\frac{1}{3}$%.

25. 20

See what fractions of the room John and Tom paint in a minute working independently, then add these rates to see what fraction of the room they paint in a minute working together. If John can paint a room in 30 minutes, he paints $\frac{1}{30}$ of the room in 1 minute. If Tom can paint it in 1 hour, or 60 minutes, he paints $\frac{1}{60}$ of the room in 1 minute. Working together they will paint $\frac{1}{30} + \frac{1}{60}$ or $\frac{1}{20}$ of the room in 1 minute; therefore, they'll need 20 minutes to paint $\frac{20}{20}$, which is the entire room.

Or simply use the work formula. John takes 30 minutes to do the job, and Tom takes 1 hour, or 60 minutes, to do the job. If T = number of minutes needed to do the job working together, then

$$\frac{1}{30} + \frac{1}{60} = \frac{1}{T}$$
$$\frac{3}{60} = \frac{1}{T}$$
$$\frac{60}{3} = T$$
$$20 = T$$

So the time taken to do the job together is 20 minutes.

26. $\dfrac{17}{2}m$

Just apply the distance formula, Distance = Rate × Time, to the two segments of the trip. In the first 4 hours she drives 4m miles. In the next 6 hours she drives $6 \times \dfrac{3}{4}m = \dfrac{9}{2}m$ miles. The total number of miles she drives then is $\left(4m + \dfrac{9}{2}m\right)$ miles, or $\dfrac{17}{2}m$ miles.

27. $\dfrac{80}{3}$

Average miles per hour = $\dfrac{\text{Total miles}}{\text{Total hours}}$

The total miles is easy: he travels 90 miles there and 90 miles back, for a total of 180 miles. We can calculate the time for each part of the trip, and then add them for the total time.

Going there: he travels 90 miles at 20 miles per hour.

Since distance = rate × time, time = $\dfrac{\text{distance}}{\text{rate}}$.

So it takes him $\dfrac{90 \text{ miles}}{20 \text{ miles / hour}} = \dfrac{9}{2}$ hours to travel there.

Coming back: he travels 90 miles at 40 miles per hour, so it takes him $\dfrac{90}{40} = \dfrac{9}{4}$ hours to return home.

The total time = $\dfrac{9}{2} + \dfrac{9}{4} = \dfrac{18}{4} + \dfrac{9}{4} = \dfrac{27}{4}$ hours.

Therefore the average speed is
$\dfrac{\text{Total miles}}{\text{Total hours}} = 180 \div \dfrac{27}{4} = 180 \cdot \dfrac{4}{27} = \dfrac{80}{3}$.

(Note that the average speed is NOT just the average of the two speeds; since he spends more time going there than coming back, the average is closer to the speed going there. You could eliminate all but the second and third choices with this logic.)

28. 20

First find how long the trip takes him at the two different rates, using the formula:

$$\text{time} = \dfrac{\text{distance}}{\text{rate}}$$

He travels the first 10 km at 30 km per hour, so he takes $\dfrac{10}{30} = \dfrac{1}{3}$ hour for this portion of the journey.

He travels the remaining 30 km at 15 km per hour, so he takes $\dfrac{30}{15} = 2$ hours for this portion of the journey. So the whole journey takes him $2 + \dfrac{1}{3} = 2\dfrac{1}{3}$ hours.

Now we need to compare this to the amount of time it would take to make the same trip at a constant rate of 20 km per hour. If he travelled the whole 40 km at 20 km per hour, it would take $\dfrac{40}{20} = 2$ hours.

This is $\dfrac{1}{3}$ hour, or 20 minutes, shorter.

29. 44%

First find what percent of the entire population do play a varsity sport. We can do this by finding out what percent of all students are male students who play a varsity sport, and what percent of all students are female students who play a varsity sport, and then summing these values. 40% of the students are male, so 60% of the students are female.

First, what percent of all students are males who play a varsity sport? 50% of the males play a varsity sport, that is 50% of 40% = 20% of all the students.

Now for the women. 60% of the females play a varsity sport, that is 60% of 60% = 36% of all the students.

Sum the percents of males and females who play a varsity sport: 20% + 36% = 56% of the total student population.

The percent of all students who DO NOT play a varsity sport is 100% − 56% = 44%.

30. 2

If we can find how long either leg of the journey took, we can find the distance, since we know the speed at which he travels. The faster you go, the less time it takes. John goes to school twice as fast as he comes back from school; therefore, his trip to school will take only half as long as his trip back. If he spends x minutes going to school, his trip back will take $2x$ minutes. His total traveling time is $3x$ minutes, so $\frac{2x}{3x}$, or $\frac{2}{3}$, of his traveling time is spent coming back. Since his total traveling time is one hour, it takes him $\frac{2}{3}$ as long, or $\frac{2}{3}$ hour to come home, at a rate of 3 miles per hour.

Distance = rate × time, so the distance between his home and school is

$$3\,\frac{\text{miles}}{\text{hour}} \times \frac{2}{3}\ \text{hours} = 2\ \text{miles}.$$

31. 300

We are only given one figure for any group of workers: 72 for the number of full-time workers who received bonuses. We can find the total number of workers if we knew what percent of the total number of workers these 72 represent. 20% of the workers are part-time, so 80% of the workers are full-time.

30% of the full-time workers received bonuses, and this amounted to 72 workers.

If E is the number of workers employed by the company then 80% of E = the number of full-time workers, so

$$30\% \text{ of } 80\% \text{ of } E = 72$$
$$\frac{3}{10} \times \frac{8}{10} \times E = 72$$
$$\frac{24}{100} \times E = 72$$
$$E = 72 \times \frac{100}{24}$$
$$= 300$$

The company employs 300 workers.

32. 48

Find how many hours it takes both pipes to fill the entire tank, multiply by $\frac{2}{3}$, then convert to minutes. If pipe A fills the tank in 3 hours, it fills $\frac{1}{3}$ of the tank in one hour. Pipe B fills the tank in 2 hours; it must fill $\frac{1}{2}$ of the tank in one hour. So in one hour the two pipes fill $\frac{1}{2} + \frac{1}{3}$, or $\frac{5}{6}$ of the tank. If in one hour they fill $\frac{5}{6}$ of the tank, they need the inverse of $\frac{5}{6}$ or $\frac{6}{5}$ hours to fill the entire tank. It will take them $\frac{2}{3}$ of this amount of time to fill $\frac{2}{3}$ of the tank, or $\frac{2}{3} \times \frac{6}{5} = \frac{4}{5}$ of an hour.

Now convert to minutes. How many minutes is $\frac{1}{5}$ of

an hour? 5 goes into 60 twelve times so $\frac{1}{5}$ of an hour

is 12 minutes, and $\frac{4}{5}$ of an hour is 4×12 or 48

minutes. (Or one can convert directly by multiplying 60

minutes by $\frac{4}{5}$ and get $\frac{4}{5} \times 60 = 48$ minute.)

33. a 5% increase

Choose a sample value easy to work with; see what
happens with 100 jobs. If the factory cuts its labor force
by 16%, it eliminates 16% of 100 jobs or 16 jobs,
leaving a work force of $100 - 16$ or 84 people. It then

increases this work force by 25%. 25% of 84 is $\frac{1}{4}$ of

84 or 21. The factory adds 21 jobs to the 84 it had, for

a total of 105 jobs. Since the factory started with 100

jobs and finished with 105, it gained 5 jobs overall. This

represents $\frac{5}{100}$ or 5% of the total we started with.

There was a 5% increase.

34. $\frac{y}{60x}$

Method I:

First figure out how many minutes it would take for y
centimeters of snow to fall. The snow is falling at a
constant rate of x centimeters per minute; set up a
proportion to find how long it takes for y centimeters.
The ratio of minutes passed to centimeters fallen is a
constant.

$$\frac{1 \text{ minute}}{x \text{ centimeters}} = \frac{m \text{ minutes}}{y \text{ centimeters}}$$

Solve for m.

$$m \text{ minutes} = y \text{ centimeters} \cdot \frac{1 \text{ minute}}{x \text{ centimeters}}$$

$$m \text{ minutes} = \frac{y}{x} \text{ minutes}$$

Now we must convert from $\frac{y}{x}$ minutes to hours. Since
hours are larger, we must divide the minutes by 60.

$$\frac{y}{x} \text{ minutes} \times \frac{1 \text{ hour}}{60 \text{ minutes}} = \frac{y}{60x} \text{ hours.}$$

Always be sure to keep track of your units: as long as
they are in the right places, you can be sure you are
using the correct operation.

Method II:

First find out how long it takes for 1 centimeter of snow
to fall. We will eventually have to convert from minutes
to hours, so we might as well do it now. If x centimeters
of snow fall every minute, then 60 times as much will
fall in an hour, or $60x$ centimeters of snow. Then one
centimeter of snow will fall in the reciprocal of $60x$, or

$\frac{1}{60x}$ hours. We're almost at the end: 1 centimeter falls

in $\frac{1}{60x}$ hours, so y centimeters will fall in y times as

many hours, or $\frac{y}{60x}$ hours.

35. $300

Method I:

Find the cost of the stereo to the dealer, then subtract 40% of this to find the price it was sold for. The selling price equals the dealer's cost plus the profit. The dealer would have made a 20% profit if he had sold the stereo for $600; therefore, letting x represent the cost to the dealer,

$$600 = x + 20\% \text{ of } x$$
$$600 = 120\% \text{ of } x$$
$$600 = \frac{6}{5}x$$
$$x = \frac{5}{6} \cdot 600 = 500$$

Instead the dealer sold the stereo at a loss of 40%. Since 40% or $\frac{2}{5}$ of 500 is 200, he sold the stereo for $500 − $200 = $300.

Method II:

Let x represent the dealer's cost. Then we're told that $600 represents $x + 20\%$ of x or 120% of x. We want the value of $x − (40\% \text{ of } x)$ or 60% of x. Since 60% of x is one-half of 120% of x, the sale price must have been one-half of $600, or $300.

36. 96

First find how long it takes 4 men to complete the entire job, then from that we can find the time for 1 man, and then we can find how long it takes 1 man to do $\frac{2}{5}$ of the job.

If 4 men can do $\frac{2}{3}$ of a job in 40 minutes, they still have $\frac{1}{3}$ of the job to do. Since they have $\frac{1}{2}$ as much work left

as they have already done, it will take them $\frac{1}{2}$ as much time as they've already spent, or another 20 minutes. This makes a total of 60 minutes for the 4 men to finish the job. One man will take 4 times as long, or 240 minutes. He'll do $\frac{2}{5}$ of the job in $\frac{2}{5}$ as much time, or $\frac{2}{5} \times 240 = 96$ minutes.

Or, first determine how long it takes one man to do the job, and from this find how long it would take him to do $\frac{2}{5}$ of it. If 4 men do $\frac{2}{3}$ of the job in 40 minutes, 1 man does $\frac{1}{4}$ of this work or $\frac{1}{4} \times \frac{2}{3} = \frac{1}{6}$ of the job in 40 minutes. Therefore, it takes him 6 times as long to do the whole job, or $6 \times 40 = 240$ minutes. Again, he'll do $\frac{2}{5}$ of the job in $\frac{2}{5} \times 240 = 96$ minutes.

37. 40%

Here, work with the portion of the job Bob completes in one hour when he and Alice work together. Bob can do the job in 5 hours; he completes $\frac{1}{5}$ of the job in 1 hour. So in the 3 hours they both work, Bob does $3 \times \frac{1}{5}$, or $\frac{3}{5}$ of the job. Alice does the rest, or $1 − \frac{3}{5} = \frac{2}{5}$ of the job. The percent equivalent of $\frac{2}{5}$ is 40%. Alice does 40% of the job.

GENERAL WORD PROBLEMS TEST
ANSWERS AND EXPLANATIONS

1.   **$432**

We are told that Robert's rent increases at a constant percent; use the chart to determine the rate. His rent goes up to $300 in 1989 from $250 in 1988, or it increases $50. In fractional terms, this is $\frac{50}{250}$ or $\frac{1}{5}$. (Remember: always divide the amount of increase by the **original** whole.) It isn't necessary to convert $\frac{1}{5}$ to a percent; all we care about is the rate of increase, not whether we express it as a percent or as a fraction. At this rate, his 1991 rent was $\frac{1}{5}$ more than his 1990 rent, or

$$\$360 + \frac{1}{5}(\$360) = \$360 + \$72 = \$432$$

2.   **51**

Since the season is half over, there are 80 games left in the season. If team A wins half of the remaining games, that's another 40 games, for a total of $60 + 40$ or 100 games. Team B has won 49 games so far, so in order to tie team A, it must win another $100 - 49$ or 51 games.

3.   **44**

We need to learn the man's overtime rate of pay, but to do this we have to figure out his regular rate of pay. Divide the amount of money made, $200, by the time it took to make it, 40 hours. $200 ÷ 40 hours = $5 per hour. That is his normal rate. We're told that the man is paid time-and-a-half for overtime, so when working more than 40 hours he makes $\frac{3}{2} \times \$5$ per hour = $7.50 pe hour. Now we can figure out how long it takes the man to make $230. It takes him 40 hours to make the first

$200. The last $30 are made at the overtime rate. Since it takes the man one hour to make $7.50 at this rate, we can figure out the number of extra hours by dividing $30 by $7.50 per hour. $30 ÷ $7.50 per hour = 4 hours. The total time needed is 40 hours plus 4 hours or 44 hours.

4.   **0.01**

If 1 centimeter = 10 millimeters, then

$$(1 \text{ centimeter})^2 = (10 \text{ millimeters})^2$$
$$= 100 \text{ square millimeters.}$$

Therefore, 1 square millimeter = $\frac{1}{100}$ square centimeters = 0.01 square centimeters.

5.   **6**

Find out how far team X has moved thus far. They pulled team Y forward 3 meters, so X moved backward 3 meters. Then they were pulled forward 5 meters and then a further 2 meters. In total then they have moved forward $(-3) + 5 + 2 = 4$ meters. They must be pulled a further 6 meters to be pulled 10 meters forward.

6. 80

The student has done 30 of the 60 problems, and has used up 20 of his 60 minutes. Therefore, he has $60 - 30$ or 30 problems left, to be done in $60 - 20$ or 40 minutes. We find his average time per problem by dividing the time by the number of problems.

$$\text{Time per problem} = \frac{40 \text{ minutes}}{30 \text{ problems}} = \frac{4}{3} \text{ minutes}$$

Each minute has 60 seconds. There are more seconds than minutes, so we multiply by 60 to find the number of seconds.

$$\frac{4}{3} \text{ minutes} \times 60 \frac{\text{seconds}}{\text{minute}} = 80 \text{ seconds}$$

7. 200

We need to find the respective lengths of paved and unpaved roads, so that we can find the difference between the two. Call unpaved roads u and paved roads p. Then the sum of the lengths of the unpaved roads and paved roads is the sum of the lengths of all the roads in the county. So

$$u + p = 1,400$$

The sum of unpaved roads is $\frac{3}{4}$ the sum of paved roads. So

$$u = \frac{3}{4}p$$

We have two equations with two unknowns so we can solve for u and p. Substitute the value of u from the second equation into the first:

$$\frac{3}{4}p + p = 1,400$$

$$3p + 4p = 1,400 \times 4$$

$$7p = 5,600$$

$$p = 800$$

Since $u = \frac{3}{4}p$, $u = \frac{3}{4} \cdot 800 = 600$.

So there are 800 miles of paved roads and 600 miles of unpaved roads.

There are $800 - 600 = 200$ miles more of paved roads.

8. $\dfrac{1}{7}$

Since 3 out of 24 students are in student organizations, the remaining $24 - 3$ or 21 students are not in student organizations. Therefore, the ratio of students in organizations to students not in organizations is

$$\frac{\text{\# in organizations}}{\text{\# not in organizations}} = \frac{3}{21} = \frac{1}{7}.$$

9. 14

A die has six faces, where the number of dots on opposite faces sum to 7. Since we can see the faces corresponding to 1, 2, and 4 dots in the picture, the ones we cannot see must contain 6, 5, and 3 dots respectively. Since $6 + 5 + 3 = 14$, there are 14 dots hidden from view.

10. 24

We cannot find any individual score from the average, but we can find the sum of the scores. The difference between the sum of all the scores and the sum of the 4 highest scores will be the lowest score.

The average of all 5 tests is 72, so the sum of all the scores is $5 \times 72 = 360$.

The average of the 4 highest scores is 84, so the sum of the 4 highest scores is $4 \times 84 = 336$.

The difference between the sum of all the scores and the sum of the 4 highest scores will be the lowest score; that is, $360 - 336 = 24$.

11. 6

He owns 3 pairs of trousers and 5 jackets. For every pair of trousers, he can wear 5 different jackets, giving 5 different combinations for each pair of trousers, or $3 \times 5 = 15$ different combinations of trousers and jackets. With each of these combinations he can wear any of his different shirts. The different combinations of shirts, jackets and trousers is (number of shirts) $\times$ 15. We are told this equals 90, so

$$\text{number of shirts} = 90 \div 15$$
$$= 6$$

12. 220

Jean drives at an average rate of 70 kilometers per hour. That means that each hour, on average, she travels 70 kilometers. Therefore, in two hours she travels 2×70 or 140 kilometers. After driving for two hours, she still has another 80 kilometers to travel. Therefore, the total distance between the two towns is $140 + 80$ or 220 kilometers.

13. $3.20

We want to find the greatest possible original price of the item. Since we are given the price after the discount, the greatest original price will correspond to the greatest discount. (If we had been told the **amount** of discount, the greatest original price would have corresponded to the **smallest** percent discount; for instance, 10 is 25 percent of 40, but is only 10 percent of 100.)

So to have the greatest original price $2.40 must be the cost after a 25 percent discount. Then $2.40 is 100% − 25% = 75% of the original price, or $\dfrac{3}{4}$ of the original price. If the original price is p, then

$$\$2.40 = \frac{3}{4}p$$
$$\frac{4}{3}(2.40) = \frac{4}{3} \cdot \frac{3}{4}p$$
$$p = \$3.20$$

14. $\dfrac{5}{8}(N - S)$

The man earns $N a month and spends $S on rent; this leaves $N-S$ dollars for things other than rent. He spends $\dfrac{3}{8}$ of this amount on food, so the remainder is $1 - \dfrac{3}{8}$ or $\dfrac{5}{8}$ of the amount after rent. The amount left is $\dfrac{5}{8}(N - S)$.

15. 6,666

We need the difference between the largest and smallest possible codes. A digit cannot be repeated, and the digits must appear in descending numerical order. The largest such number will have the largest digit, 9, in the thousands' place, followed by the next largest digits, 8, 7, and 6, in the next three places, so 9,876 is the largest possible number. For the smallest, start with the smallest digit, 0, and put it in the ones' place. Work up from there—we end up with 3,210 as the smallest possible code. The difference between the largest and smallest codes is $9,876 - 3,210 = 6,666$.

16. 18

You don't need to know anything about physics to answer this one. We need to find the mass, so rearrange our equation to get m on one side.

$$K = \frac{1}{2}mv^2$$
$$2K = mv^2$$
$$\frac{2K}{v^2} = m$$

Now substitute in our values for K and v:

$$m = \frac{2 \cdot 144}{(4)^2}$$
$$= \frac{288}{16}$$
$$= 18$$

The mass is 18 kilograms.

17. 9

Bill had a five, two tens, and a twenty, for a total of $45. Since he didn't receive any change after purchasing an item, he must have paid **exactly** the amount of the purchase. He didn't have to spend all his money, though, so the cost wasn't necessarily $45. What we do know about the purchase price is that since all of Bill's bills are in amounts that are divisible by five, the purchase price must also be divisible by five. The smallest denomination that Bill has is a five-dollar bill. So we can start with $5, and then count up all the possible distinct combinations of these bills. There are $5 ($5 bill), $10 ($10 bill), $15 ($5 + $10 bills), $20 ($20 bill), $25 ($5 + $20 bills), $30 ($10 + $20 bills), $35 ($5 + $10 + $20 bills), $40 ($10 + $10 + $20 bills), and $45 (all 4 bills). So, in fact, all prices that are multiples of $5 between $5 and $45 are possible; there are 9 of them in all.

18. 30

We need the total number of dogs. We are given a ratio between all the cats and all the dogs, that is 5:3. So for every five cats we have three dogs. Therefore, out of every 8 animals, 3 will be dogs. This means the total number of dogs will be three-eighths times the total number of animals. So we need to find the total number of animals. The total number of animals is the sum of all the dogs living in Dog Only households, all the cats living in Cat Only households and all the animals living in Dog and Cat households. Now for any of these categories, we can say

$$\left(\begin{array}{c}\text{the average number of} \\ \text{pets per household}\end{array}\right) = \frac{\text{(the number of pets)}}{\text{(number of households)}}$$

Rearranging this we get that the number of pets in that category = the average number of pets × the number of households.

For Dogs Only, the number of dogs = 1.5 × 16 = 24 dogs.

For Cats Only, the number of cats = 1.25 × 24 = 30 cats.

For Cat and Dogs, the number of animals = 3.25 × 8 = 26 animals.

So the total number of animals is 24 + 30 + 26 = 80.

Finally, the total number of dogs is $\frac{3}{8} \times 80 = 30$.

19. 20

If Jane knits 72 stitches to the line and uses $\frac{1}{4}$ inch of yarn per stitch, that means she uses

$$72 \, \frac{\text{stitches}}{\text{line}} \times \frac{1 \text{ inch}}{4 \text{ stitch}} = 18 \text{ inches of yarn per line.}$$

But we need to find out how many lines she can knit with 10 **yards** of yarn. Since there are three feet in a yard and twelve inches in a foot, there must be

$$3 \, \frac{\text{feet}}{\text{yard}} \times 12 \, \frac{\text{inches}}{\text{feet}} = 36 \text{ inches in a yard. So 18}$$

inches is $\frac{18}{36}$ or $\frac{1}{2}$ yard. Each line requires $\frac{1}{2}$ yard of yarn to knit; each yard of yarn is enough for 2 lines. Therefore, 10 yards of yarn is enough for 10 × 2 or 20 lines.

20. 50

This is best solved intuitively. The maximum number of bonds that can be bought is when all the bonds are in $50 denominations. Since Robert bought $2,000 worth of bonds the maximum number of bonds he could buy is $\frac{\$2,000}{\$50} = 40$ bonds. If he bought 50 $50 bonds he would spend 50 × $50 = $2,500. This is too much. If he bought any $100 bonds he would spend even more money. So it is impossible to buy $2,000 worth of bonds by purchasing 50 $100 or $50 bonds.

21. 20

The **more** sugar you use, the **less** time it will last. So discard answer choices (4) and (5) straight away. We have increased the use by 50% or $\frac{1}{2}$, so we are using the sugar at a rate $1\frac{1}{2}$ times or $\frac{3}{2}$ of what it was. We will go through it in the inverse of $\frac{3}{2}$, or $\frac{2}{3}$ of the time, since the usage and the time are in an inverse relationship. The sugar will last $\frac{2}{3} \cdot 30 = 20$ days.

Or try picking numbers. Say we have 300 ounces of sugar, and we use it at a rate of 10 ounces per day. (The supply will last for 30 days. So we've satisfied the requirements of our question.) Now increase the rate by 50 percent; that means we would use $10 + 50\%(10)$, or 15 ounces per day. How long would our supply of 300 ounces last if we use 15 ounces per day? $\frac{300}{15} = 20$. So it's 20 days.

22. $\frac{1}{3}$

The **faster** we travel, the **more** distance we cover in a given amount of time. Drawing a diagram will help you calculate the distances. Bucky and Robin meet 2 miles from Amity; since Amity is 8 miles from Truro, they must be $8 - 2$ or 6 miles from Truro.

Since they left at the same time, Bucky traveled 2 miles in the same time it took Robin to travel 6 miles. Since they traveled for the same length of time, the ratio of their average speeds will be the same as the ratio of their distances.

So $\dfrac{\text{Bucky's average speed}}{\text{Robin's average speed}} = \dfrac{\text{Bucky's distance}}{\text{Robin's distance}}$

$$= \frac{2}{6}$$

$$= \frac{1}{3}$$

23. 1.5

Start by converting kilometers to meters. Since a meter is smaller than a kilometer, we must multiply. We are told that a length of 10 centimeters on the map represents 5 kilometers or 5,000 meters; therefore, 1 centimeter must represent $\frac{1}{10}$ as much, or 500 meters.

We want to know how many centimeters would represent 750 meters. We could set up a proportion here, but it's quicker to use common sense. We have a distance $\frac{3}{2}$ as great as 500 meters $(750 = \frac{3}{2} \times 500)$, so we need a map distance $\frac{3}{2}$ as great as 1 centimeter, or $\frac{3}{2} = 1.5$ centimeters.

24. 46

Each tree is 1 meter in width, and we need 16 meters between every two trees. Starting at the first tree, we have 1 meter for the tree, plus 16 meters space before the next tree, for a total of 17 meters. The second tree then takes up 1 meter, plus 16 meters space between that tree and the third tree, or 17 more meters. So we need 17 meters for each tree and the space before the next tree.

The street is $\frac{3}{8}$ kilometer long. We change this to meters (since we've been dealing with meters so far) by multiplying $\frac{3}{8}$ by 1,000—the number of meters in a kilometer. This gives us 375 meters to work with. Each tree and space takes up 17 meters, so we divide 17 into 375 to find the number of trees and spaces we can fit in. $\frac{375}{17}$ gives us 22 with 1 left over. So is 22 the number of trees we can fit on each side of the street?

No—this is the number of trees followed by a space. But we don't need a space after the last tree—we only need a space between a pair of trees; since there's no tree after the last one, there's no need to have a space there. So we use up 374 meters with 22 trees and spaces, and can then add one more tree in the last meter of space, for a total of 23 trees on each side. Since there are trees on both sides of the street, we can fit 46 trees in all.

25. 60

This is a cycles problem. To understand what's going on here, let's say that the first lighthouse blinks every 10 seconds. That means it blinks, then blinks again after 10 seconds, then again after 20 seconds from the first blink, then after 30 seconds, etc. Suppose a second one blinks every 15 seconds; then it blinks after 15 seconds, 30 seconds, 45 seconds, etc. They will blink together at each common multiple of 10 and 15, and the first time they will blink together again is at the least common multiple of 10 and 15, or after 30 seconds.

Now back to the problem. Start by converting everything to seconds. There are 60 seconds in a minute, so 5 times a minute is once every $\frac{60}{5}$ or 12 seconds. 4 times a minute works out to once every $\frac{60}{4}$ or 15 seconds. So we need to find the least common multiple of 12 and 15. You could work this out by finding the prime factors, but probably the easiest method is to go through the multiples of the larger number, 15, until you find one that is also a multiple of 12.

$$1 \times 15 = 15$$
$$2 \times 15 = 30$$
$$3 \times 15 = 45$$
$$4 \times 15 = 60 \quad \text{This is a multiple of 12:}$$
$$5 \times 12 = 60$$

The two lighthouses will blink together after 60 seconds.

26. 120

The vault has 130 ounces total of gold and silver. Each tablet of gold weight 8 ounces, each tablet of silver 5 ounces. Not all of the 130 ounces can be gold, since 130 is not a multiple of 8. There must be some silver in there as well. The largest multiple of 8 less than 130 is 16 × 8 or 128, but this can't be the amount of gold either, since this leaves only 130 − 128 or 2 leftover ounces for the silver, and each silver tablet weighs 5 ounces. So let's look at the multiples of 8 less than 128 until we find one that leaves a multiple of 5 when subtracted from 130. Well, in fact, the next smallest multiple of 8—15 × 8 or 120—leaves us with 130 − 120 or 10 ounces of silver, and since 2 × 5 = 10, this amount works. We have 15 tablets of gold for a total of 120 ounces, and 2 tablets of silver, for a total of 10 ounces. So 120 ounces is the greatest possible amount of gold.

27. 24

This balloon distribution is an unending series of cycles (at least unending until we run out of balloons). Each cycle is 1 blue, 2 red, and 3 yellow, so each cycle runs for 6 balloons, and has 2 red balloons. How many cycles will we go through over a period of 70 balloons? The largest multiple of 6 that is less than 70 is 66, so we will go through 11 complete cycles, and then go through the first 4 balloons in the next cycle. Since each cycle has 2 red balloons, we will have distributed 2 × 11 or 22 red balloons by the 66th. After the 66th balloon, we go through the beginning of a new cycle, so the 67th balloon is blue, the 68th and 69th red, and the 70th yellow. This adds 2 more red balloons to our earlier 22, for a total of 24 in the first 70.

28. 56

Translate what we are given into equations, and then solve for the number of plums. p plums at 25 cents each = 25p. ($p − 6$) nectarines at 28 cents each = 28($p − 6$).

These two quantities are equal, so

$$25p = 28(p - 6)$$

Solve for *p*.

$$25p = 28p - 168$$
$$168 = 28p - 25p$$
$$168 = 3p$$
$$\frac{168}{3} = p$$
$$56 = p$$

29. 3.2%

We need to realize that each time the stock changes its price by a percentage of **different** wholes. For instance, in July the original price increases by 10%. When it declines in August, it declines by 20% of the new price. So the net change after August will not be 10%−20% or −10%; it's not that easy. The best way to work with percent change is to pick a number. Usually 100 is the easiest number to start with for percents—it's real easy to take a percent of 100.

So say the original July price is $100. It increases by 10% or $10, up to $110. In August it declines by 20% of $110, or $\frac{1}{5} \times \$110 = \$22$. So now it's down to $110−$22 or $88. Then it goes up by 10% of $88 or $\frac{1}{10} \times \$88 = \$8.80$; this brings the price back up to $96.80, only $3.20 less than it started. The percent change equals the amount of change divided by the original whole (100 in this case), or $\frac{3.20}{100} \times 100\% = 3.2\%$

30. $\frac{15}{2}$

Method I:

Get both tics and tocs in terms of the same number of tacs. Since we are given the value of tics in terms of 3 tacs, and tocs in terms of 2 tacs, let's use the LCM of 2 and 3, or 6. If 1 tic equals 3 tacs, then 2 tics equal 6 tacs. If 2 tacs equal 5 tocs, then 6 tacs equal 3 × 5 or 15 tocs. Therefore, 2 tics = 6 tacs = 15 tocs. We don't care about tacs anymore; just tics and tocs. Divide to get

the ratio of units on one side, and the numbers on the other side.

$$2 \text{ tics} = 15 \text{ tocs}$$
$$\frac{1 \text{ tic}}{1 \text{ toc}} = \frac{15}{2}$$

Method II:

Use the units cancellation method. We are given tics in terms of tacs, and tacs in terms of tocs. Since we are only interested in the ratio of a tic to a toc, we must somehow eliminate the tacs from consideration. Write down the two ratios we are given.

1 tic = 3 tacs	2 tacs = 5 tocs
or	or
$\frac{1 \text{ tic}}{1 \text{ tac}} = \frac{3}{1}$	$\frac{1 \text{ tac}}{1 \text{ toc}} = \frac{5}{2}$

We have two ratios: in one, tacs are in the denominator, and in the other, they are in the numerator. If we multiply the two equations, the tac terms will cancel out, leaving us with the desired ratio:

$$\frac{1 \text{ tic}}{1 \text{ toc}} = \left(\frac{1 \text{ tic}}{1 \text{ tac}} \right)\left(\frac{1 \text{ tac}}{1 \text{ toc}} \right)$$
$$= \left(\frac{3}{1} \right)\left(\frac{5}{2} \right)$$
$$= \frac{15}{2}$$

31. $8

Let John's money = *J* and Allen's money = *A*. John gives $5 to Allen so now he has *J* − 5 and Allen has *A* + 5. Allen gives $2 to Frank so now he has $2 less, or *A* + 5 − 2 = *A* + 3. They all have the same amount of money now, so

$$A + 3 = J - 5$$

or

$$A + 8 = J$$

Since Allen needs $8 to have the same as John, John has $8 more.

32. $30

First we have to find the number of sheets of paper in the pile, and then calculate the cost from that. If you have trouble working with very small numbers (or very large numbers) and can't quite figure out how to calculate the number of sheets, you may want to try it with some easier numbers, just to see which operation we need. Suppose we've got sheets of paper one meter thick, and need to stack enough for four meters. To calculate the number of sheets we divide one into four: dividing the thickness for each sheet into the total thickness, and we end up with the number of sheets: 4.

$$\frac{\text{Total thickness}}{\text{Thickness per sheet}} = \text{Number of sheets}$$

Here, of course, we use the same technique. We divide the thickness per sheet into the total thickness. First, we must change the meters to centimeters (we could change the thickness per sheet into meters, but we've got enough zeros as it is). There are 100 centimeters in a meter, so in 4 meters there are 4×100 or 400 centimeters. Now we can divide.

$$\frac{400}{0.08} = \frac{40,000}{8} = 5,000$$

So we have 5,000 sheets. If 500 sheets cost $3, then 5,000 sheets will cost ten times as much, or $30.

33. $25.00

Take this one step at a time. If Ms. Smith's car averages 35 miles per gallon, then she can go 35 miles on 1 gallon. To go 700 miles, she will need $\frac{700}{35}$ or 20 gallons of gasoline. The average price of gasoline was $1.25 per gallon, so she spent $20 \times \$1.25$ or $25 for the 20 gallons on her trip.

34. 9

Of the 7 people on committee *A*, 3 of them are also on committee *B*, leaving $7 - 3$ or 4 people who are only on committee *A*. Similarly, there are 8 people on committee *B*; 3 of them are on both committees, leaving $8 - 3$ or 5 people only on committee *B*. There are 4 people only on *A*, and 5 people only on *B*, making $4 + 5$ or 9 people on only one committee.

35. $1

The important part of the money exchange is a person's **net** loss or gain. Carol is owed $3 by Bob, and she owes $5 to Anne. She needs a cash **loss** of $2 in order to settle all debts. Anne, on the other hand, is owed $5 by Carol and owes $4 to Bob. She must have a **gain** of $1. Since Carol settles all the debts, this $1 must come from Carol, and this is the answer. To finish the transactions, Carol has already given one of the two dollars in her net loss to Anne; she must give the other dollar to Bob. Since Bob is owed $4 and owes $3 for a net gain of $1, the $1 he gets from Carol makes all three of them solvent and happy.

36. 14 Minutes

John can shovel the whole driveway in 50 minutes, so each minute he does $\frac{1}{50}$ of the driveway. Mary can shovel the whole driveway in 20 minutes; in each minute she does $\frac{1}{20}$ of the driveway. In one minute the two of them do

$$\frac{1}{50} + \frac{1}{20} = \frac{2}{100} + \frac{5}{100}$$
$$= \frac{7}{100}$$

If they do $\dfrac{7}{100}$ of the driveway in one minute, they do

the entire driveway in $\dfrac{100}{7}$ minutes. (If you do $\dfrac{1}{2}$ of a

job in 1 minute, you do the whole job in the reciprocal of

$\dfrac{1}{2}$ or 2 minutes.) So all that remains is to round $\dfrac{100}{7}$ off

to the nearest integer. Since $\dfrac{100}{7} = 14\dfrac{2}{7}$, $\dfrac{100}{7}$ is

approximately 14. It takes about 14 minutes for both of

them to shovel the driveway.

Or use the work formula. T = number of minutes taken
when working together.

$$\frac{1}{20 \text{ minutes}} + \frac{1}{50 \text{ minutes}} = \frac{1}{T}$$

$$\frac{5}{100 \text{ minutes}} + \frac{2}{100 \text{ minutes}} = \frac{1}{T}$$

$$\frac{7}{100 \text{ minutes}} = \frac{1}{T}$$

$$\frac{100 \text{ minutes}}{7} = T$$

$$14 \text{ minutes} \approx T$$

37. $2.47

Calculate separately the amount of usable beef, and the
price at which he must sell all the beef to make a 25%
profit, then divide the total price by the number of
kilograms of usable beef.

Usable beef: he buys 240 kilograms, but 20% of this is
unusable. This means the remainder, 80% of the beef,
is usable. $80\% = \dfrac{4}{5}$, so $\dfrac{4}{5} \times 240 = 4 \times 48$, or 192. So
he can sell 192 kilograms.

Total price: he wants a 25% profit. Since he paid $380
for the beef, he must sell it for 25% more than $380, or

125% of $380. $125\% = \dfrac{5}{4}$, so he has to sell it for

$\dfrac{5}{4} \times \$380 = \$475$.

Price per kilogram: divide the total price ($475) by the
number of kilograms (192):

$$
\begin{array}{r}
2.47 \\
192 \overline{)\ 475.00} \\
384 \\
910 \\
768 \\
1420 \\
1344 \\
76
\end{array}
$$

The approximate price is $2.47 per pound.

38. $1.75

Since the vending machine dispenses gumballs in a
regular cycle of ten colors, there are exactly nine other
gumballs dispensed between each pair of gumballs of
the same color. For example, gumballs one and eleven
must be the same color, as must gumballs two and
twelve, forty-two and fifty-two, etc. To get three
gumballs all of the same color, we get one of the
chosen color, then nine of another color before another
of the chosen color, then nine of another color before
the third of the chosen color. That's a total of $1 + 9 +
1 + 9 + 1 = 21$ gumballs to get three matching ones.
Since each quarter buys three gumballs, and we need
twenty-one gumballs in all, we have to spend
$21 \div 3 = 7$ quarters to get three matching gumballs,
$7 \times 25¢ = \$1.75$.

39. 450

In our ten team league, each team plays the other nine teams ten times each. $9 \times 10 = 90$, so each team plays 90 games. Since there are 10 different teams, and $10 \times 90 = 900$, a total of 900 games are played by the 10 teams. But this counts each game twice, since it counts when team A plays team B as one game and when team B plays team A as another game. But they're the same game! So, we must halve the total to take into account the fact that two teams play each game. $\frac{900}{2} = 450$. So 450 games are played in total.

40. $n - 4$

There are n people ahead of Eleanor in line. One of them is Henry. Three more of them are in front of Henry (since Henry is fourth in line). So that makes 4 people who are **not** behind Henry. All the rest, or $n - 4$, are behind Henry and in front of Eleanor, so $n - 4$ is our answer.

Chapter 7
Data Interpretations

Five to seven questions in the quantitative section are in the Data Interpretation format. These questions require you, logically enough, to interpret the data supplied in a set of graphs or tables. The good news about these questions is that no new topics are tested on these sections; as on the QC section, the same topics are tested in a different way. They test your ability to work with percents, ratios, and averages in a different context; but the ideas and principles are the same.

THE 2 BASIC PRINCIPLES OF DATA INTERPRETATION QUESTIONS

The data you get for this question type often include a lot of useless information. They're like a reading passage in that way; not all the details are important, only the ones that they question you about. In fact, the test maker is interested in seeing whether you can distill what's *important* from the mess they give you. Keep these principles in mind.

Principle 1. Slow Down

There's always a lot going on in Data Interpretation problems—both in the data and in the questions themselves. Rushing through this information can necessitate a re-read or result in careless mistakes. Two reads usually take longer (and result in retaining less information) than one unhurried read.

Principle 2. A Question Is a Question Is a Question

Although Data Interpretation questions tend to be more time-consuming than Word Problems or QCs they aren't necessarily more difficult. Tables, bar graphs, and line graphs generally ask for values such as median and mode. Pie charts tend to focus on percentages and converting percentages to numbers.

KAPLAN'S 3-STEP METHOD FOR DATA INTERPRETATION QUESTIONS

Data Interpretation questions require a strong understanding of fractions and percents, and good attention to detail. Follow this method, and you won't have any trouble breezing through these questions

Step 1. Familiarize Yourself with the Tables and Graphs

Tables, graphs, and charts often come in complementary pairs (a manufacturer's total revenue and his revenue by product line, for example). Familiarize yourself with the information and with their complementary nature *before* you try to tackle the questions. Pay particular attention to these components:

- **Title.** This may sound obvious, but it's important. Read the chart title to ensure you get your information from the right source.

- **Scale.** Check the scales to see how the information is measured. A common mistake is giving the right quantity but the wrong units (e.g., minutes instead of seconds).
- **Notes.** Read any accompanying notes—they're often the key to answering the questions.
- **Key.** If there are multiple bars or lines on a graph, make sure to refer to and understand the key—another common trap is giving the correct quantity for the wrong item.

Step 2. Answer the Questions That Follow

Data Interpretation questions come in sets, with one or two pieces of data followed by either two or four questions. Questions later in a set tend to be trickier than earlier ones. For instance, if a question set contains two graphs, the first question likely refers to just one graph, and a later question may ask you to combine data from both graphs. If you didn't use both graphs for this later question, the chances are good you'd get it wrong.

Step 3. Approximate Wherever Possible

As we saw with Word Problems, estimation can be one of the fastest ways to solve math problems. Data Interpretation questions benefit from this strategy, as they tend to be the most time-consuming questions to answer. No matter how hard graph questions appear at first glance, you can take advantage of their answer-choice format: by approximating, you can sometimes quickly identify the right one.

TYPES OF DATA

There are several different kinds of charts and graphs that can show up on the test. The most common kinds are tables, bar graphs, line graphs, and pie charts.

Tables

Tables share many of the characteristics of graphs, except for the visual advantages—you can estimate values from a graph, but not from a table. Tables can be enormous and complicated, but the basic structure is always the same: columns and rows. Here's an example of a very simple one (much simpler than those that appear on the GRE):

JOHN'S INCOME: 1974–1978

YEAR	INCOME
1974	$20,000
1975	$22,000
1976	$18,000
1977	$15,000
1978	$28,000

An easy question on this table might ask for John's income in a particular year, or for the difference in income between two years. In this case, you would simply look up the amount for both years and subtract. A harder question might ask for John's average income per year over the five given years; then you would have to add up the five incomes, and divide to find the average.

Bar Graphs

These can be used to show visually the information that would otherwise appear in a table. On a bar graph, the *height* of each column shows its value. Here's the information from the table above presented as a bar graph:

JOHN'S INCOME, 1974–1978

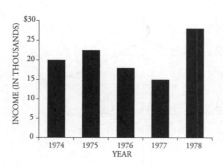

What's handy about a bar graph is that you can see the relative values by looking at their heights. By glancing at the graph above, for example, it's easy to see that John's income in 1978 was almost double his income in 1977. But we can see this only because the scale starts at zero; the scale could just as easily start somewhere *other* than zero.

JOHN'S INCOME, 1974–1978

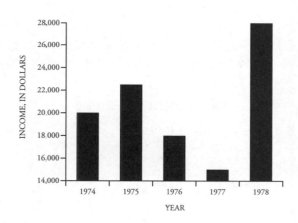

This graph presents the same information, but now we cannot estimate as recklessly as we did before. We can still tell at a glance that his 1978 income exceeded 1977, but we cannot quickly estimate the ratio.

In order to find some numerical value from a bar graph, find the correct bar (such as 1978 income), and move horizontally across from the top of the bar to the value on the scale on the left. Don't worry about getting too precise a value; usually, you will just have to get a rough idea. For example, John's 1978 income was approximately $28,000. Notice that this is different from a table, which we are given John's *exact* income.

Line Graphs

Line graphs follow the same principle as bar graphs, except the values are presented as points, rather than bars.

JOHN'S INCOME, 1974–1978

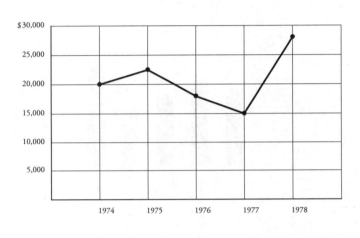

YEAR

As with bar graphs, the value of a particular year is the vertical distance from the bottom of the graph to the line. And also as with bar graphs, you can see the relative value of the described amounts by looking at their heights—with the caveat we mentioned before, that the base must be zero in order to estimate ratios.

Pie Charts

A pie chart shows how things are distributed; the fraction of a circle occupied by each piece of the "pie" indicates what fraction of the whole it represents. Usually, the pie chart will identify what percent of the whole each piece represents.

JOHN'S EXPENDITURES, 1974

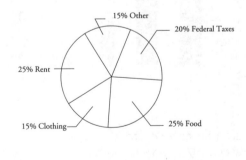

100% = $20,000

The total size of the whole pie is usually given under the graph; either as "TOTAL = $3,547" or "100% = $5.9 billion" or whatever. If we were asked to find the approximate amount of a particular piece of the pie, we would multiply the appropriate percent by the whole. For instance, to find the amount paid in federal taxes, find the slice labeled "Federal

Taxes," and we see that federal taxes represented 20 percent of his expenditures. Since the whole was $20,000, we find that John's federal taxes for 1974 were 20 percent of $20,000 or $\frac{1}{5} \times \$20,000 = \$4,000$.

Pie charts often travel in pairs. If so, be sure that you do not attempt to compare slices from one chart with slices from another. For instance, suppose we were given another pie chart for John's expenditures; one covering 1978.

JOHN'S EXPENDITURES, 1978

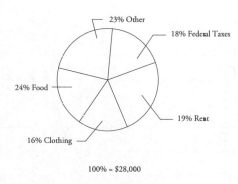

100% = $28,000

A careless glance might suggest that he paid less in federal taxes in 1978 than in 1974. Not true! His 1974 taxes were a greater percentage of his income than were his 1978 taxes, but his 1978 income was much greater than his 1974 income. In fact, he paid about $1,000 *more* in taxes in 1978 than in 1974. Since the totals for the two charts are different, the pieces of the pie are not directly comparable.

Double Graphs

Very often the GRE will present two graphs for the same set of questions, or one graph and a table. The two charts or graphs will be related in some way.

STUCK ELEVATORS IN COUNTRY X

Year	Stuck Elevators
1986	432
1987	459
1988	621
1989	645

Stuck elevators by Month, 1989

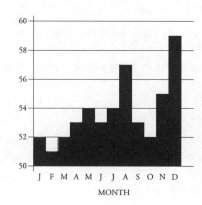

Here, the table covers stuck elevators, while the accompanying bar graph breaks the information down (so to speak) by month for 1989.

What can be more confusing is when they give you two graphs (either two line graphs or two bar graphs) occupying the same space. Sometimes both graphs will refer to the same vertical scale; other times, one graph will refer to a scale on the left, the other graph to a scale on the right.

JOHN'S INCOME AND FEDERAL TAXES, 1974–1978

Here we see the same graph of John's income, but with new information added. We now see at a glance not only John's income for a given year, but also the amount of federal taxes for that year. The income refers to the left-hand scale; the taxes to the right-hand scale. At this point, obviously, the number of potential questions has risen dramatically.

Double graphs are not really any more difficult than single graphs as long as you don't mix up the scales. Learn to double-check that you're using the correct scale when working with double graphs. If you find yourself getting confused, slow down and give yourself a chance to sort things out.

SKILLS TESTED BY DATA INTERPRETATION QUESTION

Percents and Ratios

At some point, virtually every set of Data Interpretation questions will involve percents in some way: keeping track of parts and wholes, percent increase, and percent decrease, etc. Many of the questions involve the difference between a percent and an amount, as in the earlier example involving the pie charts. If you're not good with percents, review the basics.

Estimation

You can often estimate on Data Interpretation, but first check to see how close the answer choices are—that will tell you how accurate you need to be. But before you estimate, check your units: are they in hundreds? thousands?

Make sure the scales start at zero.

In general, try to find precise values only as a last resort: remember, they're not interested in whether you can tell if a value is 3.17 or 3.18—they want to see whether you understand the basic concepts behind data.

Inference Questions

Most of the questions will involve percents, ratios, or just plain reading from the data. The only kind of question that is a little unusual is the inference question, in which you have to determine whether a statement can be "inferred" from the graph. This usually comes down to understanding the scope of the data. For instance, look at this inference question based on the two pie charts for John's income and taxes on pages 310 and 311.

Which of the following statements can be inferred from the charts?

   I. John paid more in federal taxes in 1978 than in 1974.

  II. John paid a higher percentage of his income in total taxes in 1974 than in 1978.

 III. John's medical expenditures were greater in 1978 than in 1974.

  ◯ I only

  ◯ II only

  ◯ I and II only

  ◯ I and III only

  ◯ I, II, and III

The first step in answering an inference question is to know what "infer" means. For the test makers it means you understand the scope of the graph, and the difference between what MUST be true and what MIGHT be true. In the question above, the first statement can be inferred from the information, as we saw before: The percentage paid in federal taxes decreased, but the actual amount of federal taxes paid increased. Statement II cannot be inferred for a simple reason: it refers to *total* taxes, while the pie charts only concern *federal* taxes. A subtle distinction, you might think, but you have to learn to look for these in inference questions. If the questions all say "federal taxes" and then one suddenly says "total taxes," there must be a reason; they must be trying to trip you up. Finally, statement III is not inferable either; medical expenditures must fall into the "other" category, and although the total "other" category increased between the two years, there's no reason to assume that *every* expenditure within that category also increased. For all we know, he had *no* medical expenditures in 1978. Only the first statement can legitimately be inferred, and the answer is (1).

Because inference questions are usually in the I, II, III format, you can always use the answer choices to your benefit. For instance, in the question above, if you realize that statement II is not inferable, you don't even have to look at statement I: every answer choice except for (2) includes it. You know that statement I *must* be true. So you can save time, and concentrate on statement III. This will often happen on such questions; as you decide the truth of the statements, eliminate answer choices.

In general, remember, there is nothing conceptually difficult about graphs, tables, and charts; they're just different ways of presenting information. If you are having trouble with these questions, try to determine whether the problem is with the format, or with the concepts involved.

DATA INTERPRETATION TEST

Questions 1–4 refer to the following chart.

FOREST LAND BY REGION IN THE CONTINENTAL UNITED STATES

Region	Land Area (1,000 acres)	Area Forested (1,000 acres)	Percent Forested
New England	40,119	32,460	81
Mid Atlantic	87,813	50,686	58
Lake States	207,952	53,011	25
Central	241,425	42,871	18
South	474,906	185,514	39
Pacific Coast	570,253	214,274	38
Rocky Mountain	546,959	136,378	25
Total U.S.	2,169,427	715,194	33

1. Which of the regions listed has the least amount of forested land?

   ◯ New England
   ◯ Lake States
   ◯ Central
   ◯ Pacific Coast
   ◯ Rocky Mountain

2. What is the approximate ratio of the amount of forested land in the South to the amount of forested land in New England?

   ◯ 1 : 2
   ◯ 2 : 1
   ◯ 1 : 6
   ◯ 6 : 1
   ◯ 12 : 1

3. Approximately what percent of all the forested land in the contiguous United States lies in either New England or the Mid-Atlantic Region?

   ◯ 8%
   ◯ 10%
   ◯ 12%
   ◯ 15%
   ◯ 20%

4. If 250,000 acres in the Lake States are urban and the land that is neither urban nor forested is farmland, then approximately what percent of the land area of the Lake States is farmland?

   ◯ 25%
   ◯ 49%
   ◯ 51%
   ◯ 62%
   ◯ 74%

Questions 5–9 refer to the following graphs.

NEW YORK AND WISCONSIN: POPULATION BY OFFICIAL CENSUS
1920–1980

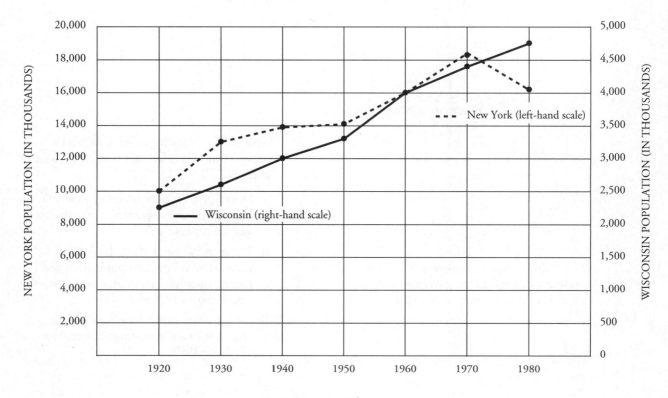

Note: Drawn to scale.

DENSITY OF POPULATION BY STATE
(Per square mile, land area only)

State	1920	1960	1970	1980
Arkansas	33.4	34.2	37.0	43.9
Illinois	115.7	180.4	199.4	205.3
New York	217.9	350.6	381.3	370.6
Texas	17.8	36.4	42.7	54.3
Wisconsin	47.6	72.6	81.1	86.5

5. What was the least densely populated of the listed states in 1960?

   ○ Arkansas
   ○ Illinois
   ○ New York
   ○ Texas
   ○ Wisconsin

6. In 1920, approximately how many more people were living in New York than in Wisconsin, in millions?

   ○ 0.5
   ○ 1
   ○ 3
   ○ 7.8
   ○ 10

7. In 1930, what was the approximate ratio of the number of people living in Wisconsin to the number of people living in New York?

   ○ 1 : 6
   ○ 1 : 5
   ○ 5 : 6
   ○ 6 : 5
   ○ 4 : 1

8. If in 1830 the density of New York was 44 people per square mile, and the area of New York has stayed constant since then, approximately what was the population of New York in 1830, in millions?

   ○ 1.2
   ○ 2.0
   ○ 3.5
   ○ 4.0
   ○ 4.8

9. Which of the following statements can be inferred from the information in the graph and table?

   I. Since 1920, the population of New York has always been more than twice the population of Wisconsin.

   II. Between 1960 and 1970, the percent increase in Wisconsin's population was greater than its percent increase in population between 1920 and 1930.

   III. Of the states listed, New York had the largest increase in population between 1920 and 1980.

   ○ I only
   ○ II only
   ○ III only
   ○ I and II only
   ○ I and III only

Questions 10–13 refer to the following information.

AFRICAN LANGUAGES OF KENYA BY LINGUISTIC FAMILY

NUMBER OF MOTHER-TONGUE SPEAKERS[1]

I. Major Bantoid Languages		II. Major Nilotic Languages		III. Major Kushitic Languages	
1. Kikuyu	4,602,000	A. Western Nilotic		1. Somali	225,000
2. Luhya	3,045,000	1. Luo	2,810,000		
3. Kamba	2,479,000	B. Eastern Nilotic			
4. Gusii	1,356,000	1. Kalenjin	2,374,000		
5. Meru	1,207,000	2. Masai	346,000		
6. Nyika	1,053,000	3. Turkana	297,000		
7. Embu	260,000	4. Sambur	106,000		————
TOTAL	14,002,000	TOTAL	5,933,000	TOTAL	225,000

Mother-Tongue Speakers of Unlisted African Languages	1,309,000
Population of Kenya	22,020,000[2]

[1]All Kenyans are assumed to have exactly one mother tongue.
[2]Includes speakers of non-African languages as mother tongue.

10. Other than mother-tongue speakers of an unlisted language, how many Kenyans have an Eastern Nilotic language as their mother tongue?

- ⬭ 106,000
- ⬭ 2,374,000
- ⬭ 2,810,000
- ⬭ 3,123,000
- ⬭ 5,933,000

11. Approximately what percent of the Kenyan population has as their mother tongue one of the seven listed Bantoid languages?

- ⬭ 47%
- ⬭ 52%
- ⬭ 64%
- ⬭ 67%
- ⬭ 70%

12. What is the approximate ratio of mother-tongue Masai speakers to mother tongue Turkana and mother tongue Sambur speakers combined in Kenya?

- ⬭ 3 : 1
- ⬭ 7 : 6
- ⬭ 1 : 1
- ⬭ 3 : 4
- ⬭ 7 : 8

13. According to the table, approximately what percent of the population of Kenya has a non-African mother tongue?

- ⬭ 0.25%
- ⬭ 1.3%
- ⬭ 2.5%
- ⬭ 5.0%
- ⬭ It cannot be determined from the information given

Questions 14–19 refer to the following graphs.

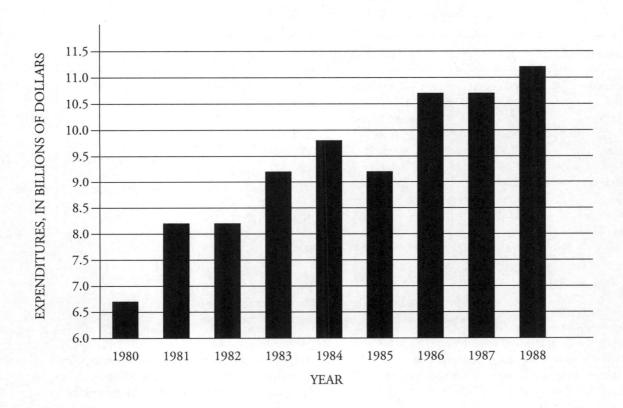

ADVERTISING EXPENDITURES, 1980–1988

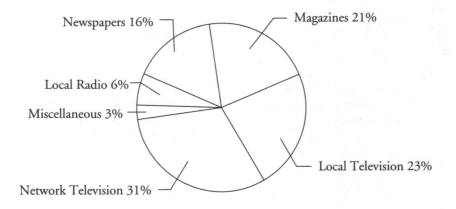

ADVERTISING EXPENDITURES, 1984

14. In which of the following years was the least amount spent on advertising?

   ○ 1984

   ○ 1985

   ○ 1986

   ○ 1987

   ○ 1988

15. Approximately how much was spent on magazine advertisements in 1984, in billions of dollars?

   ○ 1.05

   ○ 2.1

   ○ 2.6

   ○ 3.7

   ○ 4.2

16. In 1984, what was the ratio of the amount spent on newspaper advertising to the amount spent on local radio advertising?

   ○ 3 : 2

   ○ 8 : 3

   ○ 5 : 2

   ○ 2 : 1

   ○ 3 : 2

17. Approximately how much more was spent in 1984 for advertising in magazines than on advertising in newspapers?

   ○ S24 million

   ○ $49 million

   ○ $150 million

   ○ $350 million

   ○ $490 million

18. If in 1984 billboards accounted for 25 percent of the miscellaneous advertising expenditures, approximately what were the advertising expenditures on billboards in millions of dollars?

   ○ 50

   ○ 62

   ○ 74

   ○ 79

   ○ 89

19. If the amount spent for advertising on network television doubled from 1980 to 1984, approximately what percent of the advertising dollar was spent on network television in 1980?

   ○ 15.5%

   ○ 23%

   ○ 31%

   ○ 33%

   ○ 39%

Questions 20–24 refer to the following graphs.

SHIP INSPECTIONS AT PORT *P*
(in thousands of ships)

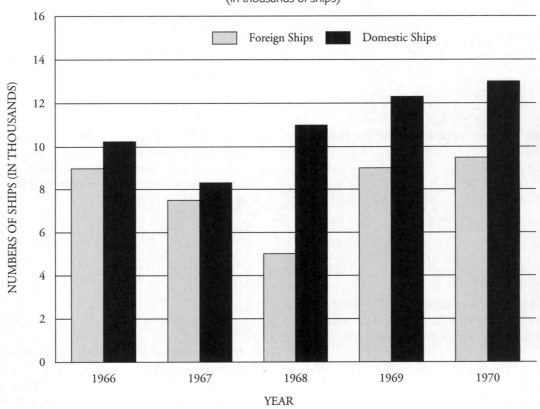

YEAR

Note: Drawn to scale.

DOMESTIC-SHIP INSPECTIONS AT PORT *P* BY TYPE, 1970

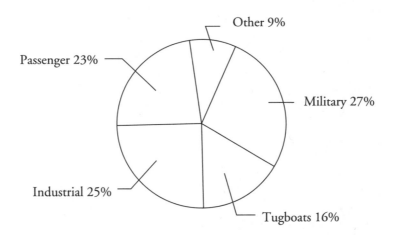

Note: Drawn to scale.

20. In 1969, the ratio of domestic ships inspected to foreign ships inspected was approximately

   ○ $\frac{9}{4}$

   ○ $\frac{2}{1}$

   ○ $\frac{5}{3}$

   ○ $\frac{8}{5}$

   ○ $\frac{4}{3}$

21. If in 1967, 12 percent of the foreign ships inspected were French, approximately how many French ships were inspected?

   ○ 700

   ○ 800

   ○ 900

   ○ 1,200

   ○ 1,900

22. If the average ship carries 500 tons of cargo, which of the following is closest to the number of tons of cargo inspected at Port *P* in 1968?

   ○ 1.0 million

   ○ 2.0 million

   ○ 4.0 million

   ○ 8.0 million

   ○ 16.0 million

23. In each of the years 1971 and 1972, the number of domestic industrial ships inspected increased over the previous year by 30 percent. Approximately how many domestic industrial ships were inspected in 1972?

   ○ 5,320

   ○ 5,490

   ○ 5,600

   ○ 5,720

   ○ 5,890

24. In 1970, approximately how many more domestic passenger ships were inspected than domestic tugboats at port *P* ?

   ○ 820

   ○ 855

   ○ 890

   ○ 910

   ○ 955

Questions 25–29 refer to the following graph.

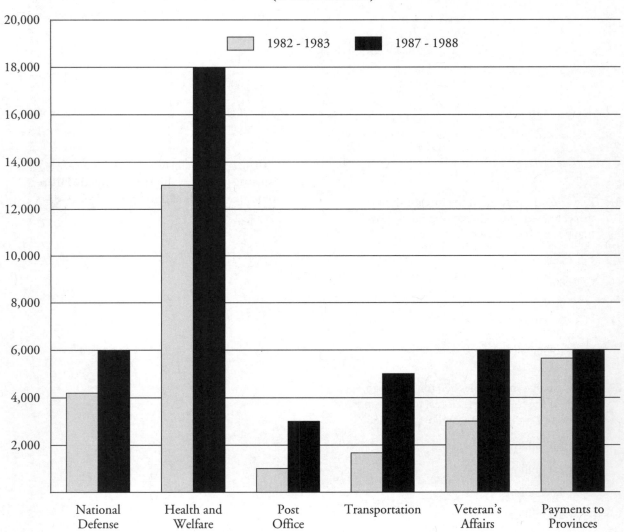

GOVERNMENT BUDGET, COUNTRY *X*
(in million of dollars)

Note: Drawn to scale

25. In Country *X*, approximately how much more was spent on national defense in fiscal year 1987–88 than in fiscal year 1982–83?

    ⬭ $1.5 billion

    ⬭ $1.8 billion

    ⬭ $2.0 billion

    ⬭ $2.5 billion

    ⬭ $2.9 billion

26. What was the approximate ratio of spending on national defense to spending on health and welfare in fiscal year 1987–88?

    ⬭ 1 : 4

    ⬭ 1 : 3

    ⬭ 2 : 5

    ⬭ 3 : 1

    ⬭ 4 : 1

27. Which of the following departments experienced the greatest percent increase in spending between fiscal years 1982–83 and 1987–88?

    ⬭ National Defense

    ⬭ Health and Welfare

    ⬭ Post Office

    ⬭ Transportation

    ⬭ Payments to Provinces

28. If the percent increase in national defense spending over the next five-year period exactly matches the percent increase between the two given fiscal years, what must be the approximate level of defense spending during fiscal year 1992–93?

    ⬭ $6.0 billion

    ⬭ $8.5 billion

    ⬭ $9.0 billion

    ⬭ $9.7 billion

    ⬭ $10.2 billion

29. How many of the given categories did NOT see an increase of at least 25 percent in 1987–88 over 1982–83?

    ⬭ 0

    ⬭ 1

    ⬭ 2

    ⬭ 3

    ⬭ 6

Questions 30–34 refer to the following information.

DISTRIBUTION OF AGES OF AMERICANS 55 YEARS OF AGE AND OLDER

1960

AGES 65-74
34%

AGES 55-64
48%

AGES
75-84
14.4%

85 AND OVER

3.6%

1980

AGES 65-74
32%

AGES 55-64
45%

AGES
75-84
16.3%

85 AND OVER

6.7%

| 1960 Population of U.S.: | 179,323,000 |
| Total Number 55 or older: | 32,134,000 |

| 1980 Population of U.S.: | 226,505,000 |
| Total Number 55 or older: | 47,247,000 |

30. In 1960, how many Americans were there between the ages of 55 and 64 inclusive?

⃝ 15.4 million

⃝ 16.2 million

⃝ 21.6 million

⃝ 86.0 million

⃝ 92.0 million

31. How many of the given categories saw an increase in their number in 1980 over 1960?

⃝ 0

⃝ 1

⃝ 2

⃝ 3

⃝ 4

32. In 1960, approximately how many more Americans were there between the ages of 65 and 74 inclusive than between 75 and 84 inclusive?

    ◯ 4.8 million

    ◯ 5.2 million

    ◯ 6.3 million

    ◯ 7.2 million

    ◯ 8.3 million

33. In 1980, approximately what percent of the total population of the United States was between the ages of 65 and 74 inclusive?

    ◯ 4%

    ◯ 7%

    ◯ 9%

    ◯ 16%

    ◯ 32%

34. Approximately how many of the Americans who were between the ages of 55 and 64 inclusive in 1960 were still alive in 1980?

    ◯ 6 million

    ◯ 8 million

    ◯ 10 million

    ◯ 12 million

    ◯ It cannot be determined from the information given

DATA INTERPRETATION
ANSWERS AND EXPLANATIONS

Forest Land in United States

This is a pretty straightforward table; the only thing to remember is that all the entries are in thousands of acres.

1.   New England

Scan the "Area Forested" column for the smallest value. New England has the smallest entry: 32,460 thousand acres; therefore, it is the answer.

2.   6 : 1

Look up the area forested for the two regions, then look at the answer choices to see which matches their ratio. Since the answer choices are pretty widely spread, we can estimate freely. The South has 185,514 thousand acres of forested land; New England 32,460 thousand acres. The ratio is about 180,000 to 30,000, which reduces to 6 : 1.

3.   12%

This is more difficult since our answer choices are all bunched between 8 and 20 percent; we have to be fairly exact in our estimation. Reading the first two figures in the "Area Forested" column, we see that there are 32,460 thousand forested acres in New England and 50,686 thousand in the South, for a total of about 83,000 thousand acres. We want to know what percent this represents of *all* the forested land in the contiguous United States. (Contiguous means touching, so it means all the states that touch each other: everything except Hawaii and Alaska.) We're told the total area of forested land at the bottom of the table—715,194 thousand acres. Clearly 83,000 thousand is a little more than one tenth of 715,000; therefore, choice 3 (12%) and choice 4 (15%) are the only two that might be correct. Fifteen percent looks easier to work with than 12 percent, so let's see whether that can be right. Ten percent of 700,000 would be 70,000, and 5 percent would be half of that, or 35,000. Therefore, 15 percent would be about 70,000 + 35,000 or 105,000. Well this is far too much, so 12%, must be right.

4.   74%

Watch your units here: the number of acres of urban land mentioned in the problem is given in acres, while all the figures in the table are in *thousands* of acres. Since 250,000 acres is just 250 thousand acres, let's be consistant with the chart, and just use 250 for the area of the urban land. The total area of forested and urban land in the Lake States is 53,011 + 250 or 53,261 acres. Now we can really use our answer choices here. We know that 53,011 is 25 percent of 207,952, since we're told that the percent forested in the Lake States is 25%. Now is 53,261 going to be a substantially different percent? Of course not—it's really very close. So the amount that's forested *plus* the amount that's urban will be just slightly more than 25 percent. Then what about the percent that is farmland? This is the land that is neither urban nor forested, so it is everything *except* that urban and forested land. Since a little more than 25 percent was urban and forested, a little less than 100%—25%, or a little less than 75% must be farmland. The only choice that is close to that is 74%.

New York and Wisconsin Population

There's a great deal of information given to us in one graph and one table. The graph concerns only Wisconsin and New York; the table concerns the densities of five different states. In the graph, the solid line refers to Wisconsin and the right-hand scale; the dotted line refers to New York and the left-hand scale. Keep in mind that everything is given in thousands on the graph.

5.   Arkansas

We need only use the table for this question; that gives us information on population density. Look down the column for 1960, and find the state with the smallest density. It's Arkansas, with 34.2 people per square mile.

6.   7.8

Now we refer only to the graph; we don't need the table. Find the vertical line for 1920; it's the first one in from the left. Now move up until you find the lines. The solid line is Wisconsin, and reading the *right-hand* scale we see that Wisconsin's population was approximately 2250 thousand, or 2.25 million. New York's dotted line is a little above Wisconsin's solid line; reading to the *left-hand* scale, we find that New York's 1920 population was approximately 10,000 thousand, or 10 million. The difference is 10 million—2.25 million, or approximately 7.75 million.

7.   1 : 5

We need the ratio of the number in Wisconsin in 1930 to the number in New York in 1930. Because of the different scales, we can't estimate the ratios by comparing the respective heights of the two graphs; we need to find the actual figures. The New York population in 1930 was approximately 13,000 thousand, or 13 million. In Wisconsin, it was about 2600 thousand, or about 2.6 million. The ratio of Wisconsin to New York, then, is approximately 2.6 : 13, or about 1 : 5.

8.   2.0

You have to reason with proportions here while also using the given table. Our table tells us New York's density for various years. The question gives us the density for 1830. The density of the state is the ratio of the population to the amount of land; if the amount of land stays constant, then the density will increase at the same rate as the population. Now we could work with any of the density figures given in the chart, but it's probably easiest to work with 1920s: New York's population in 1920 was approximately 10 million people, a very nice round number to work with. In addition, the 1830 density was 44 people per square mile: very close to one-fifth of the 1920 density, 217.9 people per square mile. That means the 1830 population must have been about one-fifth of the 1920 population. The 1920 population was about 10 million, so the 1830 population must have been approximately $\frac{1}{5}$ of 10 million or 2 million people.

9.   I only

Evaluate the three statements. Statement I is true, since the *smallest* population for New York over the period was about 10 million, while the *largest* population for Wisconsin was less than half of that—about 4.6 million. Statement I must be a part of the answer; choices 2 and 3 can be eliminated.

Statement II is a little harder. The percent increase is the ratio of the amount of increase to the original whole. So there are two things we're interested in. Looking at the solid line for the two periods, we see that the amount of change between 1960 and 1970 was about the same as the amount of change between 1920 and 1930. What does that tell us about the percent increase? Well, the population in 1960 was much greater than the population in 1920, so the *original whole* in 1960 was greater than the *original whole* in 1920. So we have the same approximate amount of increase for the two periods, but since we started at a smaller number in 1920 than in 1960, the percent increase for the earlier period must be greater than the percent increase for the later period. In other words, statement II is not true. At this point, we can eliminate everything except choices 1 and 5.

Evaluating statement III depends on understanding what the density figures mean. If we look at the change in the density figures, we can determine the largest increase in population *per square mile* for the period discussed. But does that translate to the largest population growth? Not necessarily. We need information about the areas of the states in order to answer the question. Texas, for instance, is a much larger state than New York, so it's possible that the smaller amount of increase per square mile in Texas would translate to a larger overall increase, because there are more square miles to be considered. So statement III is not inferable based on the information given. Statement I was the only acceptable inference.

African Languages

This was a difficult graph. The information is broken down and presented in a couple of different places, plus there are notes at the bottom. There are at least three different linguistic families of Kenyan languages: Bantoid, Nilotic, and Kushitic, and we're given a breakdown of the major languages within each of those families. It's important to realize that all those numbers are mother-tongued speakers, and the note at the bottom tells us that each Kenyan is assumed to have exactly one mother tongue. Below this chart we get the number of mother-tongue speakers of unlisted African languages. Note that some of these unlisted African languages could fall into one of the families outlined above; the lists above are only of the major languages. So a Kenyan with an African mother tongue could be listed in a couple of different places: either someplace on the chart, or else with the other unlisted African language speakers. Does this take care of everyone who lives in Kenya, then? No, so far we have only dealt with those who have African mother tongues. Some could have a non-African mother tongue: English, for instance. And we see confirmation of this: the note that goes with the total population of Kenya, tells us that the popula-tion includes speakers of non-African languages.

10. 3,123,000

At the bottom of the Nilotic (Nilo-Saharan) column we see there are 5,933,000 speakers of Nilotic languages total. Of these 2,810,000 speak Luo, a Western Nilotic language, while the rest are the Eastern Nilotic speakers we're interested in. Subtract the Luo speakers from the total to find the number of Eastern Nilotic speakers, but do it roughly to save time. (The answer choices aren't that close together.) The difference is a little more than 3 million; 3,123,000 must be our answer.

11. 64%

The percent will be the total number of speakers for the seven listed Bantoid languages divided by the total population of Kenya. At the bottom of the first column, the total number of Bantoid speakers is about 14 million, while the total population of the country is about 22 million. So the percent we want is around $\frac{14}{22}$. This fraction must be a little LESS than $\frac{2}{3}$ or $66\frac{2}{3}\%$, since $\frac{14}{21} = \frac{2}{3}$. The best choice is 64%.

12. 7 : 8

The answer choices aren't real close together here, so we can estimate again. We want the ratio of Masai speakers to Turkana and Sambur combined. These are all Eastern Nilotic languages, so it's the Nilotic column we're interested in. This tells us that there are 346,000 mother tongue Masai speakers in Kenya, or about 350,000. The number of Turkana and Samburu mother tongue speakers is 297,000 + 106,000 or about 400,000. The ratio we want is about $\frac{350,000}{400,000}$ or $\frac{35}{40} = \frac{7}{8}$ or 7 : 8.

13. 2.5%

To find what percent of the total population has a non-African mother tongue, we need two pieces of information: the total population of Kenya, and the number of non-African mother tongue speakers. The first piece we can find pretty easily; we're told that there are 22,020,000 people in Kenya. It's a bit harder to find the number of non-African mother tongue speakers. The information in the table gives us the speakers of the major Bantoid, major Nilotic, and major Kushitic languages. These are all African languages, since the title of the chart tells us that they're African. In addition, the information below the chart tells us that there are 1,309,000 mother-tongue speakers of unlisted African languages. Then all the African mother tongue speakers must be listed in one of these places, and if we add up the totals, we'll get the total having an African mother tongue. Subtracting that from the total population of Kenya will leave us with the number of *non-African* mother-tongue speakers: just what we want.

Adding up the numbers in the chart, we find that for the three language groups listed, the total of the major languages is 14,002,000 + 5,933,000 + 225,000 or approximately 20,225,000. Adding the speakers of unlisted African languages, we get 20,225,000 + 1,309,000 or approximately 21,500,000. Subtracting this from the total population of Kenya, we find that there are approximately 500,000 mother-tongue speakers of non-African languages.

All that's left now is to divide this into the total population. We get $\frac{500,000}{22,020,000}$ or approximately $\frac{5}{220}$ or $\frac{1}{44}$. Since this is slightly larger than $\frac{1}{50}$ or 2%, the best answer choice must be 2.5%.

Advertising Expenditures

Again, a pretty straightforward set of graphs; nothing too tricky. It's important to note two things about the bar graph at the top: the expenditures are in billions of dollars, and the graph does not begin at zero; six billion is the lowest point. This indicates that we can't estimate ratios directly from the bar graph. The pie chart refers only to the 1984 expenditures; we are given no information about the breakdown of expenditures for other years.

14. 1985

Straightforward graph reading. Don't bother with exact amounts here; just find the shortest bar for the year listed. Of the years listed, 1985 is the shortest.

15. 2.1

Find the total amount spent on advertising in 1984 from the bar graph, then multiply this by the percent spent on magazines, which is found in the pie chart. You can estimate here also because the answer choices are widely spaced. The bar graph shows just under 10 billion dollars was spent on advertising in 1984. The pie chart shows 21% or just more than a fifth of this amount went to magazines. $\frac{1}{5} \times 10$ billion is 2 billion; the amount spent was close to $2 billion.

16. 8 : 3

Don't find the actual amounts. From the pie chart we can see that 16% was spent on newspapers and 6% was spent on local radio. The ratio is just the ratio of these two percents, because they're percents of the same amount, the total amount spent on advertising.

$$\frac{16\%}{6\%} = \frac{16}{6} = \frac{8}{3}$$

17. 490 million

We know from the pie chart that 21 percent of the 1984 expenditures went to magazines and 16 percent went to newspapers. Since these are percents of the same whole, the difference in the amounts will be 21 − 16 or 5 percent of the whole, or 5 percent of the

1984 expenditures. To see this, if we let E represent the expenditures, then the difference is

$$21\%(E) - 16\%(E) = (21\% - 16\%)E = 5\%(E)$$

From the bar graph we see all expenditures totaled just under 10 billion dollars in 1984. The fractional form of 5% is $\frac{1}{20}$, so the difference is just under $\frac{1}{20}$ of 10 billion or 500 million.

18. 74

We first find the miscellaneous expenditures for 1984, and then find the billboard expenditures from that. The pie chart tells us the miscellaneous expenditures were 3 percent; since the total expenditures were just less than 10 billion, the miscellaneous expenditures were a little less than 3% × 10 billion or a little less than 300 million.

The billboard expenditures were 25 percent or $\frac{1}{4}$ of this, for a total of about 75 million.

19. 23%

We're told that the *amount* spent on network television doubled from 1980 to 1984, not the percent. First we need to find what was spent on network television in 1984, then we take half of that to get the 1980 expenditures, and finally we can estimate what percent of the total 1980 expenditures that represents. The pie chart shows 31 percent of all 1984 expenditures went to network television. Expenditures were just less than $10 billion, so network television expenditures in 1984 were just less than 31% of $10 billion, or about $3 billion. In 1980 they were half this or about $1.5 billion. Now we need to find what percent of the total expenditures for 1980 this $1.5 billion represented. The total expenditures in 1980 were about $6.6 billion. Then the percent was about

$$\frac{1.5 \text{ billion}}{6.6 \text{ billion}} = \frac{1.5}{6.6} = \frac{5}{22}$$

$\frac{5}{22}$ is a bit less than $\frac{1}{4}$ or a bit less than 25%. Only choice 2, 23%, is close.

Ship Inspections

This is a double bar graph, along with a pie chart. We can tell quickly that the domestic-ship inspections are always greater than the foreign-ship inspections (at least over the five-year period shown on the graph). The bar graph starts at zero (and is drawn to scale), so if necessary, we can estimate ratios from the bars directly. The pie chart, of course, refers only to the inspections in 1970, and only for domestic ships. In addition, we know nothing about how many ships actually travelled through the port (although this didn't come up in a question). Probably the most annoying thing about this graph set was that some of the questions had answer choices that were pretty close together; requiring caution when estimating.

20. $\frac{4}{3}$

As we said, since the bar graph is drawn to scale, and since the bars start at zero, we can do some quick estimation to narrow down our choices. In 1969, more domestic ships were inspected than foreign ships (not too surprising, since that's true for every year on the graph). So the ratio must be more than one. The solid bar is considerably less than twice the length of the shaded bar, so we can see that the answer can't be choice (1) or (2). Reading from the top of the 1969 solid bar over to the left, we see that a little more than 12 thousand domestic ships were inspected. Reading from the shaded bar to the left, we see that around 9 thousand foreign ships were inspected. So the answer is a little more than the ratio of 12 to 9, or a little less than $\frac{12}{9}$. Since, $\frac{12}{9}$ can be reduced to $\frac{4}{3}$, choice 5 is best.

21. 900

Find the number of foreign ships that were inspected in 1967, then take 12 percent of that amount. Foreign ships are represented by the shaded bars; the 1967 shaded bar is somewhere between 7 and 8 thousand. Let's say a little less than 8 thousand, and see where that gets us. The answer choices aren't widely spread, but they're not too close together either. Approximately what is 12 percent of 8 thousand?

$$\frac{12}{100} \times 8000 = 12 \times 80 = 960$$

So the answer must be a bit less than 960. Choice 3 is the only possibility here.

You may have approximated even more here, saying that 12 percent of 8 thousand is a little more than 10 percent of 8 thousand, or a little more than 800. The only problem with that is that 8 thousand was a little too high initially; the actual value is a little less than 8 thousand. So what you would be looking for is something a little more than 10 percent of something a little less than 8 thousand. It's getting pretty confusing at this point already; plus, if you figure that the little more and the little less cancel each other out, you could end up with 800 as your answer. In which case you would be wrong. The problem here is that the choices are spread far enough apart for us to do *some* rounding and estimation, but they're too close together for us to do *a lot* of estimation.

22. 8.0 million

Add the number of domestic ships inspected in 1968 to the number of foreign, then multiply the total number of ships inspected by 500 tons to get the total tonnage. Approximately 11,000 domestic ships were inspected in 1968, and approximately 5,000 foreign ships, for a total of about 16,000 ships. The tonnage per ship was 500 tons, so the total tonnage was 16,000 × 500. Since 500 is one-half of 1,000, we can simplify our arithmetic by doubling 500, and multiplying 16,000 by $\frac{1}{2}$. This gives us a total of 1,000 × 8,000 = 8,000,000 or 8 million tons.

23. 5,490

Here we need both the graph and the pie chart. We can find the number of domestic industrial ship inspections in 1970 by the combination of the two, then we can use the information in the question stem to extrapolate to the number for 1972. The answer choices are pretty close together again, so we should be careful with our estimations. In 1970, 25 percent or $\frac{1}{4}$ of the domestic-ship inspections were industrial ships. We learn that from the pie chart. In 1970, the total number of domestic-ship inspections was about 13 thousand. We know that from the bar graph. Putting the two pieces of information together, we see that approximately $\frac{1}{4}$ of 13 thousand or about 3,250 domestic industrial ships were inspected in 1970. Then in 1971, 30 percent more domestic industrial ships were inspected than in 1970. 30 percent of 3,250 is the same as 3×325 or 975. So the increase from 1970 to 1971 was 975 ships. This makes the 1971 total $3,250 + 975$ or 4,225 ships. Then in 1972 it increased by 30 percent. Now what's 30 percent of 4,225? Well, 30% of 4,000 is $\frac{3}{10}$ of 4,000 or 1,200. 30% of 225 is a little more than 30% of 200 which is 60. So 30% of 4,225 is a little more than $1,200 + 60$ or 1,260. So in 1972, a little more than $4,225 + 1,260$ or 5,485 ships were inspected.

24. 910

Again, we need both the graph and the pie chart. The simplest approach here is this: we are taking percents of the same whole; therefore, the difference in the two amounts is the same as the difference in the percents, multiplied by the whole. The whole here is the number of 1970 domestic-ship inspections, or 13 thousand ships. The percents are 23 percent for domestic passenger ships and 16 percent for domestic tugboats; giving us a difference of $23 - 16$ or 7 percent. Therefore, we want 7 percent of 13 thousand. Again, the choices are fairly close together, so let's just multiply the numbers rather than estimate.

$$7\% \times 13,000 = \frac{7}{100} \times 13,000 = 7 \times 130 = 910$$

Government Budget

25. 1.8 billion

We don't really need to get the actual figures for either fiscal year; all we want is the difference, and we can estimate that from the graph directly. The difference in the height of the two bars for defense spending is a bit less than one space; the solid bar goes up to one line, and the shaded bar goes a bit higher than the line immediately below that. So the difference must be a bit less than 2,000 million dollars or 2 billion, since that's how much each of those spaces represents.

26. 1 : 3

All we need to do is count the height of each bar. The National Defense solid bar goes up 3 spaces; the Health and Welfare solid bar goes up 9 spaces. We want the ratio of defense to health and welfare, so the ratio is 3 to 9 or 1 : 3. Naturally, we get the same answer if we actually determine the values. Reading the 1987–1988 national defense bar, it's clear that the amount of spending for that year was about 6 billion dollars. Spending in health and welfare was a lot more, or reading its towering bar, about 18 billion. The ratio is 6 billion to 18 billion, which is the same as 1 : 3.

27. Post Office

Here we have to be careful we know what we're looking for. We want the greatest *percent* increase; this is very different from the greatest *amount* of increase. We're not looking for the greatest difference in the heights of the two bars; we're looking for the largest ratio. For instance, Health and Welfare had a very large absolute difference, but its percent increase was not that great, since it started so high. Its percent increase certainly wasn't as high as Transportation's, for instance, which more than doubled between the two years. So what is the answer? It's best to estimate first, and narrow down the choices. If a couple of departments look close, we can figure out the real numbers then. Health and Welfare, as we said, was out, because its percent increase was smaller than Transportation's. Does any other department look like it more than doubled? The Post Office does, so that's a possibility, but National Defense definitely didn't, and neither did the Payments to Provinces. Veteran's Affairs looks like it may have doubled exactly, but we don't need to worry about it since it's not an answer choice. So it's down to Post Office and Transportation. The Post Office started at around 1,000 (since we only care about the ratio of the bars, we don't need to include the millions) and went up to around 3,000. The amount of increase was 3,000–1,000 or 2,000, and the original whole was 1000, for a percent increase of $\frac{2000}{1000}$ or 200%. Transportation started at around 1,700 or 1,800, and went up to around 5,000. The amount of increase was 3,200 or 3,300. Now we don't care what the actual percent increase was, only whether it was greater than 200%. And it wasn't; a 200% increase from 1,700 would be 3,400: more than the increase we had here.

28. 8.5 billion

Find the percent increase between the two periods shown, and then apply this percent increase to the 1987–88 level to figure out the 1992–93 level. One thing we should keep in mind is that we don't really have to work with percents unless we want to; we can keep the numbers as fractions. In 1982–83, the level of spending was a little more than $4 billion (say 4.25 billion); it increases to about $6 billion. Then the 1987–88 budget was about $\frac{6}{4.25}$ or $\frac{600}{425}$ times the 1982–83 budget. Now we don't need to figure out what the percent increase is; we can leave the number the way it is. If the percent increase stays constant, then so does the ratio between any two consecutive budgets. Then in 1992–93, the defense budget will again be $\frac{600}{425}$ times the previous defense budget, or (in billions of dollars),

$$\frac{600}{425} \times 6 = \frac{3600}{425} = \frac{144}{17}$$

At this point, we should just look at the answer choices. This fraction must be less than 10, since 144 is less than 10 × 17. Let's try 8.5: it's in the middle of the three choices that are less than 10, so even if we find that it's not right, we'll still know which choice is right. 8.5 × 17 = 144.5.

29. 1

What we're looking for, in effect, is which categories show an increase of less than 25%. We can estimate to make our work easier. National defense grew from a little more than 4 billion to about 6 billion. Well, if it had increased exactly 25%, then that would mean an increase of about 1 billion. Since it increased significantly more than that, we know it must have increased more than 25 percent. Health and Welfare grew from about 13 billion to 18 billion, an increase of about 5 billion. Since 5 billion is more than 25 percent of 13 billion, Health and Welfare isn't what we want, either. We can dismiss the next three categories, Post

Office, Transportation, and Veterans' Affairs, very quickly; just by looking at the graph, you should see that each department saw an increase of more than 25 percent. That leaves us with Payments to Provinces, and that too, we can evaluate very quickly, because there the increase was so slight it was obviously less than a 25 percent increase. That last category was the only one that did *not* see an increase in of 25% spending; therefore, the answer is 1: choice (2).

Americans and their Ages

The information in the graphs is not too tricky; we have two pie charts, and we are given the amounts of each whole under each pie chart. It's important to realize that the whole in each case is *not* the entire population of the country, it's only those who are 55 or over. The questions are pretty straightforward too, with the exception of the last, which may strike some as tricky, and others as just plain cruel.

30. 15.4 million

Under the 1960 pie chart we're told there were 32,134,000 Americans fifty-five or older during that year; the pie chart shows that of these, 48 percent were between the ages of 55–64 inclusive. That must be just a little less than one-half of the total figure; 15.4 million is the only answer less than one-half of 32 million.

31. 4

In 1980 there were about 47 million Americans 55 or older, while in 1960 there were only about 32 million; these figures are from under the charts. The proportions of some of the categories decreased from 1960 to 1980 (for example, the 55–64 group decreases from 48% to 45%), but given that the whole is so much bigger in 1980 than in 1960, it's pretty clear that the number of people must increase in each category, too. This is the kind of question where you should not do any calculations; since the whole is almost 50 percent more in 1980, we would need a much more dramatic decrease in any one category to get a decrease in number. All four categories increase; the answer is choice 5, which is 4.

32. 6.3 million

The answer choices are close enough that we have to be fairly exact in our estimations. The pie chart shows that 34% of all Americans 55 or over fell into the 65 to 74 age group in 1960, and 14.4% fell into the 75 to 84 age group. That means the difference in their number will be 34 percent − 14.4 percent or just under 20 percent of the total number. Just under 20 percent of 32 million means just under $\frac{1}{5}$ of 32 million or a little more than 6 million.

33. 7%

Find approximately how many Americans were between 65 and 74 (inclusive), then find what percent this is of the entire population. We know from the pie chart that 32 percent or just under a third of all Americans 55 or older fell into the 65 to 74 age group. The information beneath the graph tells us that 47,247,000 Americans were 55 or over; a third of this will be a bit less than 16 million. The total population of the United States at this time is given as around 226

million. What percent of 226 is 16? Well, obviously, it's less than 10%, which would be 22.6 million; and it's also greater than 5%, which would be 11.3 million. So it's either 7%, or 9%. At this point, it's simplest to multiply: 7% of 226 is 0.07 × 226 = 15.82. This is as close to 16 as we're going to get; choice 2 is the correct answer.

34. It cannot be determined from the information given

On the one hand, someone who was 55 in 1960 would be 75 in 1980; and someone who was 64 in 1960 would be 84 in 1980, so you might think that we can just compare the numbers. The problem is that we don't know whether the 75-year-old Americans in 1980 were the same ones who were here in 1960. There's the possibility that some people who were here in 1960 moved to another country, and that those who were here in 1980 came from another country. We need some information about that before we can answer the question.

A Note for International Students

About 250,000 international students pursue advanced academic degrees at the master's or Ph.D. level at U.S. universities each year. This trend of pursuing higher education in the United States, particularly at the graduate level, is expected to continue. Business, management, engineering, and the physical and life sciences are popular areas of study for students coming to the United States from other countries. If you are an international student planning on applying to a graduate program in the United States, you will want to consider the following.

- If English is not your first language, you will probably need to take the Test of English as a Foreign Language (TOEFL®) or show some other evidence that you're proficient in English prior to gaining admission to a graduate program. Graduate programs will vary on what is an acceptable TOEFL score. For degrees in business, journalism, management, or the humanities, a minimum TOEFL score of 600 (250 on the computer-based TOEFL) or better is expected. For the hard sciences and computer technology, a TOEFL score of 550 (213 on the computer-based TOEFL) is a common minimum requirement.

- You may also need to take the Graduate Record Exam (GRE®) or the Graduate Management Admission Test (GMAT®) as part of the admission process.

- Since admission to many graduate programs and business schools is quite competitive, you may want to select three or four programs you would like to attend and complete applications for each program.

- Selecting the correct graduate school is very different from selecting a suitable undergraduate institution. You should research the qualifications and interests of faculty members teaching and doing research in your chosen field. Look for professors who share your specialty. Also, select a program that meets your current or future employment needs, rather than simply a program with a big name.

- You need to begin the application process at least a year in advance. Be aware that many programs offer only August or September start dates. Find out application deadlines and plan accordingly.

- Finally, you will need to obtain an 1-20 Certificate of Eligibility in order to obtain an F-1 Student Visa to study in the United States.

KAPLAN ENGLISH PROGRAMS*

If you need more help with the complex process of graduate school admissions, or assistance preparing for the TOEFL, GRE, or GMAT, you may be interested in Kaplan's programs for international students. Kaplan English Programs were designed to help students and professionals from outside the United States meet their educational and career goals. At locations throughout the United States, international students take advantage of Kaplan's programs to help them improve their academic and conversational English skills, raise their scores on the TOEFL, GRE, GMAT, and other standardized exams, and gain admission to top programs. Our staff and instructors give international students the individualized instruction they need to succeed. What follows is a brief description of some of Kaplan's programs for international students.

General Intensive English

Kaplan's General Intensive English classes are designed to help you improve your skills in all areas of English and to increase your fluency in spoken and written English. Classes are available for beginning to advanced students, and the average class size is 12 students.

TOEFL and Academic English

This course provides you with the skills you need to improve your TOEFL score and succeed in an American university or graduate program. It includes advanced reading, writing, listening, grammar, and conversational English. You will also receive training for the TOEFL using Kaplan's exclusive computer-based practice materials.

GRE for International Students

The Graduate Record Exam (GRE) is required for admission to many graduate programs in the United States. Nearly one-half million people take the GRE each year. A high score can help you stand out from other test takers. This course, designed especially for non-native English speakers, includes the skills you need to succeed on each section of the GRE, as well as access to Kaplan's exclusive computer-based practice materials and extra verbal practice.

GMAT for International Students

The Graduate Management Admissions Test (GMAT) is required for admission to many graduate programs in business in the United States. Hundreds of thousands of American students have taken this course to prepare for the GMAT. This course, designed especially for non-native English speakers, includes the skills you need to succeed on each section of the GMAT, as well as access to Kaplan's exclusive computer-based practice materials and extra verbal practice.

OTHER KAPLAN PROGRAMS

Since 1938, more than 3 million students have come to Kaplan to advance their studies, prepare for entry to American universities, and further their careers. In addition to the above programs, Kaplan offers courses to prepare for the SAT®, LSAT®, MCAT®, DAT®, USMLE®, NCLEX®, and other standardized exams at locations throughout the United States.

Applying to Kaplan English Programs
To get more information or to apply to any of Kaplan's programs, contact us at:

Kaplan English Programs
700 South Flower, Suite 2900
Los Angeles, CA 90017 USA
Phone (if calling from within the United States): (800) 818-9128
Phone (if calling from outside the United States): (213) 452-5800
Fax: (213) 892-1364
Website: www.kaplanenglish.com
Email: world@kaplan.com

*Kaplan is authorized under federal law to enroll nonimmigrant alien students.
Kaplan is accredited by ACCET (Accrediting Council for Continuing Education and Training).

Notes

Notes

Notes

Notes

Notes

Notes

Notes

Notes

Notes

Notes

Notes

Notes

Notes

Notes

Notes